The Reading and Preaching
of the Scriptures
in the
Worship of the Christian Church

Volume 1

THE BIBLICAL PERIOD

The Reading and Preaching
of the Scriptures
in the
Worship of the Christian Church

Volume 1

THE BIBLICAL PERIOD

Hughes Oliphant Old

WILLIAM B. EERDMANS PUBLISHING COMPANY
GRAND RAPIDS, MICHIGAN / CAMBRIDGE, U.K.

© 1998 Wm. B. Eerdmans Publishing Co.
255 Jefferson Ave. S.E., Grand Rapids, Michigan 49503 /
P.O. Box 163, Cambridge CB3 9PU U.K.

Printed in the United States of America

03 02 01 00 99 98   7 6 5 4 3 2 1

Library of Congress Cataloging-in-Publication Data

Old, Hughes Oliphant.
The reading and preaching of the Scriptures in the worship of the Christian church /
Hughes Oliphant Old.
p.   cm.
Includes bibliographical references and index.
Contents: v. 1. The biblical period.
ISBN 0-8028-4356-5 (alk. paper)
1. Preaching — History. 2. Public worship — History.
3. Bible — Homiletical use. 4. Bible — Liturgical use.
I. Title.
BV4207.O43 1998
264'.34 — dc21   97-30624
                                         CIP

To His Beatitude
TEOCTIST
Patriarch of Romania

God's faithfulness to your Church
gives me hope for my own

Contents

CHAPTER I

The Roots of the Christian Ministry
of the Word in the Worship of Israel   19

CHAPTER II
The Preaching of Christ and the Apostles   111

CHAPTER III
The Second and Third Centuries   251

Introduction

Presiding over the mantelpiece of our old New Jersey farmhouse just outside the city of Trenton is a portrait of one of my ancestors, Robert Chambers, wearing a white lace collar and holding in his hands a book with the title *Walker's Sermons.* For years I had wondered about that book of sermons which had obviously been so important to my double great-grandfather. I wondered who this preacher might have been and why those sermons were so treasured by him. Then one day when I was up in Princeton looking through the seminary library for something else I suddenly saw the same book, bound exactly the same way, with exactly the same title. I looked at the title page and discovered that Robert Walker had been the preacher at the High Kirk of St. Giles in the middle of the eighteenth century and that this particular edition of his sermons had been published in Trenton, the home of Robert Chambers, in 1820, five years before the portrait was painted. I began to realize that the portrait told me much about my spiritual heritage. The Chambers family had been sent to the prison colony of New Jersey during the reign of Charles II along with a whole shipload of Scotch Presbyterians who refused to conform to the king's religion. That shipload of devout Calvinists made quite an impact on the religious history of America. What the portrait suggests is that these New Jersey Presbyterians maintained a strong link with a very old tradition of preaching.

Right from the beginning American Protestantism has had outstanding preaching. John Cotton, Thomas Shepard, and Nathaniel Ward brought the traditions of English Puritan preaching to New England. With the Great

Awakening we began to develop our own school of preaching. And then there came what I have called the Great American School of preaching. It was truly a great school of preaching, yet, manifestly, in our own day we have seen it come to its end. Schools of preaching have a way of doing that, as the following pages will show. We don't need to be terribly discouraged about this. A new school will undoubtedly take its place. That has been the pattern for a couple of thousand years now. It is something about which we should rejoice rather than lament, and yet it is something about which we must be realistic. The formulas of Charles Finney, Phillips Brooks, and Harry Emerson Fosdick just don't work the way they used to.

So here I am, an American Protestant preacher, heir to a great tradition of preaching that goes back through the whole of American history. In fact, one could even say that America is a nation that was created by preaching. Yet I find myself looking around at a country filled with empty churches. There are plenty of pulpits but few preachers who are up to filling them. There are plenty of ministers but few who seem able to hold a congregation. Like so many other preachers of my generation, I find myself asking what has happened to preaching.

My thirteen years as pastor of a college town church in Indiana were drawing to a close when I got an invitation to come to the Center of Theological Inquiry in Princeton. I was very glad to get that call because it meant going home, home to New Jersey. But even more than that, it meant a chance to begin my next work on the history of Christian worship. This time I would address myself to the subject of preaching as worship.

Rather early in the development of this project I found myself explaining to Horton Davies, my colleague at the Center, that I intended to write several volumes on the history of preaching. Even for those of us who know him and are very fond of him, Professor Davies is a most august personage who is acclaimed for his six-volume history, *Worship and Theology in England.* Very politely he asked me what period I intended to cover. I told him that I wanted to begin with Moses and come up to the present. With genuine Oxford hauteur he responded, "Oh, dear, how audacious!" I smile every time I remember that response. It has served to warn me of the human limitations of such an attempt. Perhaps it is audacious. So many good sermons over so many centuries have been preached by so many worthy preachers, and so many of them have been recorded and have been preserved down to our own day! I really have to confess that writing the definitive history of preaching is quite beyond me, and in fact I have never had that in mind.

What I really started out to do was to write a book on preaching as worship. And it was on that basis that James McCord invited me to the Center of Theological Inquiry. Never having held an appointment to teach at a seminary or university and having spent my entire professional career in the pastorate, I was not particularly interested in producing a purely academic history of preaching. I was interested in learning about preaching in order to get some indication of how we American Protestant preachers might recover what seems in our day to have become a lost art. It was as a pastor that I wanted to write something for fellow pastors.

It was back in the seventies and eighties, if I remember correctly, that many of us began wondering what had happened to American preaching. It had obviously fallen on hard times. Some blamed this on competition with the mass media, and so they scrambled to adapt their preaching to the new techniques of mass media. Perhaps other forms of communication should be tried. There were those who decried the quality of preaching and those who decried preaching itself. Some figured that preaching had outlived its usefulness and needed to be de-emphasized. The liturgical movement was all too eager to replace preaching with "liturgy," as though the two were in some kind of opposition to each other. The more I thought about it, and the more I thought about the worship of my own congregation, the more concerned I was to understand preaching as worship. I wanted to discover how other pastors in other ages and other lands understood the relation of their preaching to the worship of God. I wanted to go back to the classics and see what they had to say.

If one is concerned with preaching as worship, there are a number of other questions that follow quite logically. There is the question of how preaching relates to the public reading of Scripture. The whole matter of the way one understands the authority of Scripture becomes much clearer once one sees its function in worship. When we see how central the reading of Scripture is to worship, then we recognize its very real authority. There is the question of the order of these readings. In fact, questions of lectionary have been vigorously discussed in the last thirty or forty years both in Europe and in America. Then there is the matter of how the reading and preaching of Scripture fit into the order of the service, how they relate to prayer and to the sacraments. It is with considerable conviction, therefore, that I've entitled this work *The Reading and Preaching of the Scriptures in the Worship of the Christian Church.*

It was only after I was well into the subject that it became more and more clear to me that what I really needed to do was to think out these

3

questions on an historical schema, even if I was not prepared to write a full-scale history of Christian preaching. Then, too, it was becoming increasingly clear that it had been a long time since anyone had tried writing a history of preaching. It was at this point that James McCord encouraged me to give it a try and to see just how much I could do.

Since I am writing on the reading and preaching of Scripture in the worship of the Christian Church and approaching it on an historical schema, there are several things I will have to leave a bit to the side even if they will have to be discussed to a certain extent. As tempting as it is to give much attention to the history of biblical exegesis or even to biblical hermeneutics, they are really quite different matters. We cannot try to provide a history of Christian rhetoric or to trace the story of homiletical theory. In the same way we cannot devote our primary attention to the theology of revelation. We will want to touch on all these subjects, especially when they are important for understanding the preaching of a given preacher or school of preaching. One can hardly discuss Origen without considering his principles of allegorical exegesis or John Chrysostom without looking at the Antiochene approach to grammatical-historical interpretation. Again, one can hardly appreciate the preachers of the Cappadocian School without understanding their use of rhetoric. When it comes to Augustine, it is his hermeneutics that is most of interest. He was a pacesetter in so many matters. His approach to rhetoric, so different from his Greek contemporaries, has been fairly consistently followed all down through the history of Western preaching. We will find this to be true throughout our study. Attention to one or more of these subjects will be demanded by some schools and not by others.

One of the most difficult problems in this study has been the matter of selection. When one considers the sheer mass of recorded sermons that Christian preachers have left behind, one realizes that they cannot all be read, let alone studied. Not all preachers can be studied; not even all schools of preaching can be studied. Some schools demand more attention, while others demand less. As the great historian of the Italian Renaissance Jakob Burckhardt used to put it, the art of history is selection. My aim has been to give a balanced picture of the whole of Christian preaching, yet I have recognized the need to look very carefully at those schools which have been formative of American Protestant preaching. In this there have been some surprises. I never expected that so much of the homiletical method I was taught in seminary had its origin in medieval times. The preaching orders, most especially the Franciscans and the Dominicans, were very creative in developing new preaching techniques. It was these medieval homileticians, not the Protestant Reformers, whom most of the members of the Great American School followed in shaping their sermons, and it was this method which I was taught in seminary. Strangely enough the so-called Great American School seemed oblivious to classical Protestantism. On the other hand, one would expect that the English Puritans, the Scottish Presbyterians, and the nineteenth-century evangelicals would have significant ideas on preaching, and indeed they do. Their whole culture was shaped by preaching. Besides that they have had a great influence on American preaching and American ideas about preaching. If I have given special attention to the preachers of Lutheran orthodoxy it is because their ideas are so solid and because they were so much more dynamic than they are ordinarily perceived to be. It is for a very different reason, however, that I have given attention to Byzantine preaching and the preachers of the Eastern Orthodox churches in Romania and Russia. It has been more difficult to get this information, but it helps balance out the picture. We have ignored the treasures of the Eastern churches too long! Usually the impression has been given that while Eastern Orthodoxy produced the first masters of the art, Basil of Caesarea, Gregory of Nazianzus, and John Chrysostom, these superb preachers never had any significant followers.

The problem of selection has been most difficult when dealing with the preachers of our own time. The natural selection that history makes has hardly begun. We are too close to our contemporaries to see them in perspective. My own personal taste would lead me to study a number of preachers whom I find especially gifted. On the other hand, there are some who seem to have claimed the ears of our contemporaries in a rather surprising way, and who seem to be doing a good and conscientious job, and therefore I have felt obligated to give them priority. A number of my colleagues have urged me to study certain of our contemporaries, but I have felt that I had to limit myself to twelve contemporary Americans, and that being the case I am going to have to limit myself to no more than two or three of any given denomination. I found this particularly difficult in regard to my own denomination, where I certainly have my favorites. There are at least a half-dozen Presbyterians I would have liked to single out.

One important factor that has guided my selection is the availability of actual sermons. A number of preachers I would have liked to have studied unhappily left behind few actual sermons. We have only a single recorded sermon of John Knox. Richard Baxter, for all the volumes he published, left us very little in the way of actual sermons. Neither Francis of Assisi nor Dominic got their sermons down on paper; we have a few scattered reports of their preaching, but no reliable texts. Some of their disciples, however, left us important collections of sermons, and so we have studied these to get an idea of what the Franciscan and the Dominican schools were like. Much of the preaching of the Middle Ages awaits publication.

Publication has been a problem. The libraries of Europe have countless sermons in manuscript that have yet to be edited. Quite a bit of work is being done to uncover these treasures right now, but it will be a while before all this can be studied. For the Eastern churches much the same is true except that the material is appearing even more slowly. Theophylact of Ochrid, the eleventh-century metropolitan of Bulgaria, had a reputation as a great preacher, but his sermons have never been published. How much I am tempted to search out these manuscripts and study them! I have been told that they can be studied in an ancient monastery hidden away in the mountains of the Balkans beside a beautiful lake, but I am afraid I will have to leave that scholarly adventure to others. Sometimes I have had the delight of studying manuscript sermons, but most often I decide that if I am not to lose sight of my purposes I have to confine myself to published sermons.

Another problem is that some schools of preaching have already received very good scholarly attention. The great nineteenth-century preachers have often been thoroughly studied. There are countless studies on the pulpit work of the Reformers, and patristic studies have produced a wide literature. There are scholarly editions of the sermons themselves and monographs on the various schools as well as studies and evaluations of individual preachers. When this is the case my work is relatively easy, but often a school of preaching or an individual preacher has received little scholarly attention. When this is the case my work has to be very tentative. In fact, no matter how good the material before me, I must always realize that I have to be humble about my attempts to understand it. But the attempt has to be made nonetheless. If one is going to speak to one's own time, one has to get to the end of the story or it will not mean anything to anyone.

There are, to be sure, many other problems in trying to tell the story of Christian preaching, especially if one really wants to tell the whole story. If one takes the problems too seriously one will never be able to put the story together. That is the difficulty with trying to give a definitive version of the story. It is a pretty big story. It would indeed be audacious of me to try to write a definitive history of preaching from Moses to the end of the twentieth century. And so I am not trying to give a definitive version of the story so much as to give a helpful version, that is, a version that will be helpful to people like myself, to American Protestant pastors who have been called to preach to our own time, the threshold of the third Christian millennium.

I. The Focus of Our Study

So, then, the purpose of this work is to come to an understanding of how preaching is worship, the service of God's glory. We want to see how preaching in one age after another has been done as a sacred service. It is upon the doxological function of preaching, then, that we wish to focus, even though surely other dimensions of preaching will unavoidably come into view. Although we will elaborate our discussion with a great number of different answers from a great variety of times and places, our basic question will always remain very simple: How is preaching worship? At the center of our discussion is, inevitably enough, Jesus.

Jesus came preaching. The picture is drawn so clearly in the Gospel of Luke. It was in the synagogue of Nazareth that Jesus opened up the book of the prophet Isaiah and, reading from the passage that spoke of how the long-promised Messiah would preach the gospel, announced that the promise had been kept. At the center of Jesus' ministry was this reading and interpreting of the Scriptures, this proclamation that they had been fulfilled. He gave himself to us in his preaching as well as in the agony of his prayer, his baptism of fire, his drinking the bitter cup, the suffering of his cross, and the victory of his resurrection. Jesus came preaching because he had been sent for this purpose by the Father. Similarly, Jesus sent his disciples out to preach: " 'As the Father has sent me, even so I send you' " (John 20:21). The earliest Church understood preaching to be at the heart of its mission. The Great Commission had made it clear: " 'Make disciples of all nations, baptizing them . . . teaching them to observe all that I have commanded you' " (Matt. 28:18-20). We find the same thing in the long ending to the Gospel of Mark: " 'Go into all the world and preach the gospel to the whole creation' " (Mark 16:15). And still again Luke makes this same point: " 'Repentance and the forgiveness of sins should be preached in his name to all nations' "

(Luke 24:47). It is hardly surprising that preaching has occupied a primary place in the worship of the Church. It was simply a matter of following both the example and the command of Christ. As we shall see, again and again Christian preachers have found in Jesus the inspiration for their preaching, whether Francis in medieval Assisi or George Truett in twentieth-century Dallas.

If we are truly to understand Christian preaching, we must see Jesus Christ as its center. First we must see Jesus as the fulfillment of generations of preaching and teaching that went before him, and second we must see Jesus as the type, or perhaps prototype, of generations of preaching that have followed him. He is both the pattern of preaching and the gospel to be preached. We preachers make sense only when we are understood as continuing the ministry of our Master. We have done our job only when we have borne witness to Christ, when we have taught all things that he has commanded us. It is the gospel of salvation in Christ that the preacher is commissioned to preach. Nothing the preacher does can be understood except in relation to this. "'Go into all the world and preach the gospel . . .'" (Mark 16:15). That is the touchstone of the preacher's ministry. The study before us will in the end have to do with how the Church has carried out the ministry of the Word that Jesus called the apostles to carry out. This is the service that has been asked of us. This is the worship we have been called to perform.

II. The Scope of Our Study

Not all preaching is worship in the same way. As this study has progressed, several genres of preaching have appeared, and these different genres suggest still different approaches to our basic question. These genres are analogous to the psalm genres developed by Old Testament scholars and are defined by the different aspects of the worship experience. Five of these genres have appeared and reappeared throughout the whole history of preaching. These five major genres are as follows:

1. Expository Preaching
2. Evangelistic Preaching
3. Catechetical Preaching
4. Festal Preaching
5. Prophetic Preaching

A number of minor genres could also be mentioned. For instance, funeral sermons, saint's-day sermons, and biographical sermons could form one genre; alms preaching or fund-raising sermons could form another; and penitential preaching and missionary preaching could form still others. In this study, however, these have been treated as different aspects of evangelistic preaching. One could divide catechetical preaching into doctrinal preaching and moral preaching, but in this study I have preferred to think in terms of three types of catechetical preaching, namely, doctrinal, moral, and liturgical. Again, monastic preaching could be treated as a separate genre, but I have thought it better to refer to it as spiritual catechism and see it as a very advanced form of catechetical preaching. In Reformed churches from the seventeenth to the nineteenth centuries, preparatory sermons and communion sermons were a distinct genre, just as Lenten and Advent sermons were a distinct genre at a certain period in the Catholic Church. The five major genres given above are somewhat arbitrary, but as the study has progressed, the list has proved its helpfulness. Perhaps at this point a brief elaboration of these genres will be helpful.

1. The expository sermon is the systematic explanation of Scripture done on a week-by-week, or even day-by-day, basis at the regular meeting of the congregation. This practice goes back to the worship of the synagogue long before the time of Jesus, when the Law was read through Sabbath by Sabbath, beginning each time where one had left off the Sabbath before. The idea was that the whole of the Law would be regularly read through in the course of worship. Two passages of the Old Testament illuminate this genre of preaching with particular clarity. First there was the solemn reading of the Law before the covenant assembly at the foot of Mount Sinai. The book of the covenant was read, the people vowed to keep it, they were sprinkled with the blood of the covenant, and then they shared a covenant meal. Reading through the Law was pivotal to this prototype of biblical worship. It was the same way with the worship of reconstituted Israel, which Ezra gathered at the water gate. Over the course of a few days the Law was read to the people in a worship assembly. It was read from beginning to end, and as it was read it was explained passage by passage. According to rabbinical tradition it was Ezra who was supposed to have organized the regular reading of the Scriptures, and apparently what was meant by this was that this marathon reading of the whole Law was simply unfolded at the regular Sabbath assembly of the congregation so that a portion was read each week. We will have considerably more to say about these two accounts of reading Scripture in worship as we begin

to unfold our study. With the establishment of the Church, the Law and the prophets were still read in Christian worship just as they had been in Jewish worship. When the apostle Paul exhorted Timothy to see to the public reading of the Scriptures, it is this sort of systematic reading through of the Law that was understood.

This was the basic principle, but in the course of time a number of other principles and variations developed. At a very early date, surely well before the time of Jesus, a second lesson came to be used. This lesson was chosen by the preacher as the key to interpreting the primary lesson. The primary lesson was taken from the Law, while the secondary lesson was taken from the prophets. The principle behind this is one of the basic principles of expository preaching: Scripture is best understood in terms of Scripture.

As we will show, Jesus was himself an expository preacher, as the Gospels make clear at several points. To be sure, we get only a few brief glimpses of the preaching of Jesus in the Gospels, but those brief glimpses show him explaining the text of Scripture as the classic expositors have done both before and after him. With Origen, a classic example of an expository preacher, we begin to get a more complete picture of Christian preaching. The patristic era provided many great expositors, but none reached the brilliance of John Chrysostom; his verse-by-verse interpretation of the Pauline Epistles is one of the pinnacles of the art of preaching. The Middle Ages produced several outstanding examples of expository preaching, such as Bernard of Clairvaux's marvelous series of sermons on the ninety-first psalm, Bonaventure's superb interpretation of the Gospel of John, and Robert Holcott's interpretation of Proverbs. The Reformation put renewed emphasis on expository preaching. Luther's postils pounded expository preaching into the Protestant pulpit. Zwingli, taking John Chrysostom as his example, began his ministry in Zurich by preaching through the Gospel of Matthew day by day, verse by verse, as the whole town gathered around his pulpit. One Reformer after another followed his example. The erudition of Calvin's pulpit commentary was remarkable. Ever since, Protestantism has never lacked preachers who followed in the tradition of Luther, Zwingli, and Calvin.

In its purest form, expository preaching follows the *lectio continua*, but there have been exceptions. Much fine expository preaching, particularly in German Lutheran pulpits, has followed the *lectio selecta*, that is, the lectionary. In addition, there is the remarkable ministry of Charles Haddon Spurgeon, who never planned out a systematic preaching schedule but relied on the guidance of the Holy Spirit to present him with the right text for each sermon, often a matter of only a few hours before entering the pulpit. In spite of this lack of system, Spurgeon must be ranked with the most outstanding expository preachers. In our own day there have been several great expository preachers. One thinks above all of Karl Barth's pupil, Walter Lüthi. Earl Palmer, who until recently was at First Presbyterian Church in Berkeley, is a fine contemporary example.

2. Evangelistic preaching is quite another genre. At its center is the proclamation of the Christian gospel. It is really only with Jesus that we come to understand the essence of evangelistic preaching. The call to repentance and the promise of the coming Messiah of John the Baptist and the Old Testament prophets before him prefigured the preaching of the gospel by Christ and the apostles, but evangelistic preaching in its more proper sense announces that the time is fulfilled; the time has come. Much of the preaching of the prophets was the preaching of repentance. When taken by itself this is something quite different from evangelistic preaching; but when the preaching of repentance is preparation for the announcement of the gospel, then it is part of evangelistic preaching. Evangelistic preaching responds most directly to the Great Commission of Jesus to go into all the world and preach the gospel, making disciples of all nations, baptizing them and teaching them all that Christ has commanded. Evangelistic preaching is closely related to baptism, as is quite clear from the classic text at the close of the Gospel of Matthew. While expository preaching and festal preaching are directed at the regular congregation, that is, at the covenant people, evangelistic preaching is directed at those outside the Church, or even those who have wandered away from the Church. In this respect evangelistic preaching is closely related to catechetical preaching, but we shall speak of that in a moment. Here I want to make the point that, just as baptism is the sacrament of gathering people into the Church, so evangelistic preaching is the preaching that is part of baptism. It is worship in the sense that baptism is worship.

Again it is Jesus who models for us evangelistic preaching just as he models expository preaching. When Jesus preaches in the synagogue of Nazareth, reads from the prophet Isaiah, and tells the congregation that what the prophet had promised is now fulfilled, he is giving us a perfect example of evangelistic preaching. The apostle Paul, too, was doing evangelistic preaching when he preached on the Areopagus in Athens or when he preached before the court of Festus; but whereas Jesus was presenting the gospel to the people of the Old Covenant, Paul was preaching to

11

pagans. Paul was modeling evangelistic preaching of a slightly different sort, but it was evangelistic preaching just the same.

Origen was one of the greatest evangelistic preachers. His evangelistic preaching was quite expository, to be sure. Day after day he preached through one book of the Old Testament after another, showing how it all spoke of Christ. He was constantly trying to show the Jews that Jesus was the fulfillment of the Law and the prophets and trying to show Greek philosophers that Christ was the end of their quest for truth. In fact, one can hardly understand Origen until one sees him as an evangelist who understood his mission very well. Origen was a successful evangelist, in fact, and there were many Christian preachers in the earliest days who saw evangelistic preaching much the same way Origen did.

In the fifth, sixth, and seventh centuries the missionary monks who took the Christian gospel to the barbarian tribes did a considerable amount of evangelistic preaching. They left few records behind of their considerable preaching activity, but the records they did leave show a solid understanding of the evangelistic mission and the place of evangelistic preaching. The presentation of the Christian faith that Columbanus made to Theodoric and the Visigothic court is one of the most interesting documents to come out of that whole epoch of Christian history. Pirmin of Reichenau left us a manual of missionary preaching that helps us understand a very distinctive approach to the work of evangelism.

All the way through the Middle Ages great evangelists appeared. Certainly Dominic and Francis need to be seen as evangelists. The evangelistic journeys of the Franciscan Berthold of Regensburg were typical of his day and seem to have done much to nourish Christian faith and life in South Germany, Switzerland, Austria, Bohemia, and Silesia. Surely Bernardino of Siena should be ranked among the greatest of Christian evangelists. He, too, was a Franciscan. Having a strong sense of the inroads of Renaissance culture on the Christian faith, he developed Lenten evangelistic campaigns that had a profound effect upon one Italian city after another. Florence, Siena, and Padua all fell under his spell. Anyone who has ever spent any time looking at Italian Renaissance painting knows what a tremendous impression Bernardino made on his age. He was greatly beloved by his age, being recognized as a saint before his death.

The great evangelists of the eighteenth century — the Wesleys, George Whitefield, Jonathan Edwards, Gilbert Tennent, and Samuel Davies — developed still another approach to evangelism. This approach is much more familiar to American Protestants. For the Wesleys, Whitefield, and, to some extent, Tennent and Davies, evangelistic preaching meant itinerant evangelistic preaching. This encouraged the development of the sermon barrel, which contained the essential message of salvation. There were always several sermons on repentance, a sermon on justification by faith, a sermon on the atoning sacrifice of Christ and the victory of the resurrection, a sermon on sanctification and growth in the Christian life, and a sermon on Christian hope. The series could be expanded or compacted depending on how long the evangelist planned to carry on his ministry in a particular place. Different evangelists had their particular emphases. Wesley, for instance, always underlined the call to holiness. For these eighteenth-century evangelists, evangelism implied a particular series of sermons that presented the Christian gospel, and these sermons were presented with an invitation to accept or reaffirm this gospel.

There probably has never been an evangelist who had a higher sense of evangelism as worship than Virginia's Samuel Davies. It was Davies who brought the Great Awakening to the South a generation before the American Revolution. The American pulpit has never known a greater orator. For Davies, evangelism was an invitation to the Lord's Table.

3. Catechetical preaching, like evangelistic preaching, relates to baptism, but it differs in that it assumes that those to whom the preaching is addressed have made the basic commitment to follow Christ and the Christian way of life. Catechetical preaching therefore outlines basic Christian teaching, often by explaining the Apostles' Creed, the Ten Commandments, the Lord's Prayer, and the sacraments. Catechetical preaching is by its very nature systematic. As we will show further on, it was the practice of the rabbis, long before the time of Jesus, to teach the interpretation of the Law in a systematic manner day by day in the courts of the Temple or in the synagogue school. This teaching was codified first in the Mishnah and then in the Talmud. There was nothing introductory about this systematic interpretation of the Law. In fact, it reached a high level of scholarly achievement as it was developed in the schools of Jerusalem and Babylon. Jesus and his disciples engaged in the same kind of learned discussion, as we can gather from the Sermon on the Mount. Many of the New Testament Epistles contain a considerable amount of moral catechism in their final chapters. The "Haustafeln," or household rules, found in I Peter, Ephesians, and the Pastoral Epistles reflects the same kind of moral instruction that the Jewish rabbis and their students discussed in the schools. These passages make it clear that even the earliest Christians considered it important to teach the Christian way of life to those who had accepted the gospel.

In the teaching of the patristic age we find a great amount of catechetical preaching. The *Catechetical Orations* of Gregory of Nazianzus give us an example of doctrinal preaching as he explains the doctrine of the Trinity. Cyril of Jerusalem and Ambrose of Milan provide examples of liturgical catechism. In Augustine's exposition of the First Epistle of John to the newly baptized we find a fine series of sermons on living the Christian life.

The Reformation gave a renewed emphasis to catechetical preaching. Early in the Reformation, Luther, Zwingli, Oecolampadius, Capito, and Bucer conducted series of catechetical sermons for the children of their churches. These were soon reduced to printed formularies, which presented the elementary doctrinal, moral, and liturgical teachings of the Christian faith in a series of questions and answers between the teacher and student. Before long Sunday afternoon catechetical preaching became a standard feature of Protestant worship. More and more it came to be directed not to beginners but to adults. During the age of Protestant Orthodoxy a number of preachers produced magnificent series of sermons on one or another of the standard catechisms. Jean Daillé and Jean Mestrezat produced a series on the *Huguenot Catechism,* and the series of Thomas Watson on the *Westminster Catechism* was regarded with particular favor. Watson was one of those learned Puritan divines who was ejected from his pulpit because he would not conform to the Anglican Settlement of 1662. His every word was cherished, and finally the devout of London provided him with a guild hall in which to lecture. Among the first generation of New Englanders, Thomas Shepard is known to have preached a series on Calvin's catechism. Even in the wilderness of Massachusetts, sound doctrine was cultivated, and people flocked to hear the systematic theology of a man of recognized piety.

In the middle of the last century the Catholic restoration in France produced significant doctrinal preaching. The sermons of Lacordaire, while not formally based on a catechism, were in fact a series of sermons directed toward reacquainting French intellectuals with the basic teachings they had deserted during the age of the French Revolution. Lacordaire filled the Cathedral of Notre Dame as he rejuvenated the Dominican tradition of the theologian-preacher. The Order of Preachers, suppressed in France at the time of the Revolution, was reconstituted, and a whole school of neo-Thomist doctrinal preachers was raised up.

4. Festal preaching explains the theme of the feast or holy day that is celebrated. One might trace the origins of festal preaching to the Passover

14

Haggadah, in which the child asks the father, "Why is this night different from any other?" and the father answers by reciting the sacred history of the deliverance from slavery in Egypt and the entry into the Promised Land. Although this was a recital of history, it was not an exposition of Scripture. Peter's sermon at Pentecost might well be considered a festal sermon because it tries to explain to the people of Jerusalem the unusual occurrences that had taken place that day by recounting the sacred history of Christ's death and resurrection. In festal preaching quite a bit of Scripture is quoted and explained, but the Scripture is quoted in order to explain the feast. The purpose of the sermon is not primarily the exposition of Scripture.

One of the oldest Christian sermons that has come down to us is the Easter sermon Melito of Sardis preached in the middle of the second century. This is obviously a festal sermon. Already certain texts were thought of as being traditional for the Christian celebration of Passover. Once again the account of the institution of Passover was read from Exodus, and the preacher interpreted the passage in a Christian sense. One expected to hear this every year at the Christian celebration of Passover. It belonged to what everyone knew was part of the feast. As the Christian calendar developed, traditions arose as to the appropriate Scripture lessons for the different holy days, the preparation for those holy days, and the days following. At the end of the fourth century, Augustine tells us about some of these traditions, which at that time were first beginning to appear. In the East, the Christian orators who had been trained in the classical schools of rhetoric saw in the festal sermon an opportunity to employ the art form of the panegyric. Gregory of Nazianzus produced magnificent Christian panegyrics for the feast of the Epiphany, for Easter, and for Pentecost. In the West, Leo the Great left us a sizeable collection of festal sermons. Apparently he did not preach on normal Sundays, but, as would have been appropriate for a high Roman official, Leo delivered panegyrics for the principal festivities of the year.

As time went on, the number of feasts requiring festal sermons increased, so that by the eighth century the Venerable Bede produced a cycle of festal sermons that covered about half the year. When Charlemagne began to set the liturgical foundations of his Holy Roman Empire, he wanted to ensure that every parish church in western Europe had a sermon for every Sunday and every feast day of the year. It was not only a most commendable goal but also an ambitious undertaking in the year 800. The responsibility of trying to realize Charlemagne's prophetic vision fell to Alcuin. On the basis of the lectionary for the Roman festal calendar, Alcuin put together a lectionary that had appointed readings not only for all the feast days and fast days of the year but for all the Sundays as well. All of these occasions demanded festal sermons. Much of the preaching of the Western Church from this point on was based on the festal calendar. Many of the sermons of Bernard of Clairvaux were festal sermons, as were the sermons of Anthony of Padua. The production of a complete cycle of sermons for the Gospels and Epistles of the year became something of an art form.

With the Reformation, Lutherans generally retained the medieval lectionary, at least for Sunday sermons. Luther, however, preached a *lectio continua* on weekdays, and a number of Lutherans such as Johann Brenz of Württemberg and Valerius Herberger of Silesia produced distinguished series of *lectio continua* sermons on various books of the Bible. In Reformed churches the lectionary based on the Christian year was completely abandoned and replaced by the *lectio continua*. With the Lutherans, at least until the age of Pietism, even festal preaching was apt to be expository preaching. The mighty baroque preachers of seventeenth-century Germany produced magnificent series of sermons for the Sunday Gospels and Epistles.

5. Prophetic preaching is another distinct genre of preaching. The genius of prophetic preaching is that God often has a particular word for a particular time and a particular place. Prophetic preaching by its very nature cannot be regularized, institutionalized, or made part of the religious establishment. The word that God gives to the prophet is often a message from outside the established religious or political order that calls for the reform of existing practice. Even in the Temple there were prophetic dimensions of traditional worship. Jeremiah and perhaps Isaiah were Temple prophets, but Elijah, Amos, and Micah were clearly outside the establishment. Amos in particular was no professional prophet, yet his ministry provides for us the epitome of the prophetic.

The preaching of the prophets of Israel was unique. Surely there were prophetic aspects of the preaching ministry of Jesus, but Jesus was not the prototype of the prophet the way he was the prototype of the evangelist. One might like to say that with the coming of the gospel the ministry of the prophet was no longer needed. Yet time and time again God has clearly had a special word for a special time and place. John Chrysostom's sermons on the statues in Antioch and his sermons directed against the luxury of the imperial court at Constantinople were great examples of prophetic preaching.

Prophetic preaching may or may not fit into some sort of liturgical setting. It may be preached completely outside the service of worship. On the other hand, it may come completely within a liturgical occasion, as did Jeremiah's Temple sermon reported in the seventh chapter of Jeremiah. The sermons of Jean Gerson preached at the Council of Constance might be called sermons preached by the establishment for the establishment, and yet they are examples of prophetic preaching at its best. On the other hand, the abolition and temperance sermons so important to what we have called the Great American School of preaching hardly claim to be liturgical and yet are an important part of the worship of the American church.

Genuine prophetic preaching has a way of showing up where one least expects it. One hardly expects prophetic preaching of the Middle Ages, and yet God obviously raised up great prophets in those days. Jean Gerson was only one of many. Joachim of Fiore is today regarded as somewhat eccentric because of his millenarianism, but his ministry had the effect of tightening up the spiritual intensity of his age. He helped the whole society find some very sound spiritual purposes. The pope was quite right in supporting him. A number of the Franciscans were as prophetic as they were evangelistic; again we must mention that superb preacher Bernardino of Siena. In Bohemia Jan Hus launched a prophetic ministry that inspires Christian piety even today. The witness he made was sealed with his own blood, as was the witness of the Florentine Dominican Savonarola. Today the greatness of Savonarola is only beginning to be appreciated. Catholics as well as Protestants are beginning to realize that his vision of a Christian republic is as significant today as it was in Renaissance Florence.

Among nineteenth-century evangelicals Scotland's two social reformers exercised a most prophetic ministry. Thomas Chalmers won a reputation as Scotland's Abraham Lincoln. No less significant, and no less a master of the pulpit, was Thomas Guthrie of Greyfriars in Edinburgh. The two of them struck one sound blow after another for the poor; their causes included child labor laws, temperance in the use of alcoholic beverages, the cleaning up of the slums, and universal education. One can understand how such preaching might not be recognized as worship. It was over against this kind of preaching that the Oxford Movement proposed to teach the English-speaking world to worship. Yet, as we shall see, Thomas Chalmers, Thomas Guthrie, and many another evangelical had a profound sense that their preaching was worship, and we will listen very carefully to what they have to say.

This brief delineation of the genres of preaching is perhaps the best introduction that can be made to the volumes which lie ahead. What has been attempted might be described as a history of preaching; but, as we have insisted, that does not really get to the heart of the matter. One might more correctly say that this book aims at being a study of Christian worship that is devoted to one particular aspect of the service of worship, namely, the reading and preaching of the Scriptures. The genres that are presented are liturgical genres, and the reason for this is simple: The questions we are asking are liturgical questions. We want to speak about one particular dimension of serving God's glory. We are confident that man's chief end, as the *Westminster Catechism* put it, is to glorify God and enjoy him forever. What we want to discuss here is how we are to do this in the reading and preaching of Scripture.

CHAPTER I

The Roots of the Christian Ministry of the Word in the Worship of Israel

More and more it is recognized that there is a strong continuity between the worship of Israel and the worship of the earliest Christians. Jesus himself preached in the way many Jewish rabbis of his time preached. He preached in the synagogues, as the Gospels themselves tell us. He even preached in the courts of the Temple, which had been the most prestigious of pulpits for a thousand years. In doing all this he followed the example of those who had gone before him. Even when Jesus preached on the hillsides or beside the Sea of Galilee he had plenty of examples to follow. The Gospel of Matthew saw Jesus' Sermon on the Mount as the fulfillment of the preaching of Moses begun on Mount Sinai. Jesus may or may not have had formal training in homiletics, but, more importantly, he had living examples to follow. The preaching of Jesus fit into a well-established tradition. The same was true of the preaching of the apostles. To understand the origins of Christian preaching we have to look at the magnificent tradition of preaching from which Christian preaching comes. In the worship of Israel, preaching had been cultivated for centuries.[1] Israel's worship was characterized by its focus on the

---

1. On the reading and preaching of the Old Testament Scripture in Judaism, see the following: Ismar Elbogen, *Der jüdische Gottesdienst in seiner geschichtlichen Entwicklung*

19

reading and preaching of Scripture. In the synagogue the liturgy revolved around the Holy Scriptures and their exposition. Even in the courts of the Temple the Law of Moses was constantly taught. The prophets had brought the Word of God to bear on every conceivable subject and in every possible place.

It is with the Torah, the sacred book of the Law of Moses, that we must begin if we are to discover the roots of the reading and preaching of the Word of God in Christian worship. We will, of course, need to go on to speak of the preaching of the prophets and the teaching of the wise. The Jewish Scriptures are traditionally made up of the books of the Law, the books of the prophets, and the books of Wisdom. Each type of sacred writing implied a different approach to preaching, and we will take each in turn. Nevertheless, there is something primary about the Law, and so it is there that we take up our study.

I. The Reading and Preaching of the Law

We know that in the time of Jesus the Torah, the Law of Moses, was regularly read and preached in worship. This was a cardinal characteristic of Jewish worship. The Acts of the Apostles tells us that Moses was read every Sabbath in the synagogue (15:21). We also know that daily, both in the courts of the Temple and in the rabbinical schools, the Torah was meticulously and systematically studied and discussed. In all four Gospels we read of Jesus teaching in the Temple. He was not the only rabbi who did this. We also read of Jesus as a boy entering into the discussion of the Law that was customarily held in the Temple. Many rabbis regularly taught in the Temple; indeed, the rabbis did much of their teaching there. What we want to turn our attention to here is how this practice got started. The rabbis in the time of Jesus assumed that the Scriptures were to be read and preached in worship, but how did this practice get started? Why was

---

(Hildesheim: Georg Olms, 1962), pp. 155-205; A. Z. Idelsohn, *Jewish Liturgy and Its Development* (New York: Schocken Books, 1975), pp. 137-49; Jacob Mann and Isaiah Sonne, *The Bible as Read and Preached in the Old Synagogue*, 2 vols. (New York: KTAV Publishing House, 1971; Cincinnati: Hebrew Union College, 1966); George Foot Moore, *Judaism in the First Centuries of the Christian Era*, 2 vols. (Cambridge: Harvard University Press, 1927-30); Leopold Zunz, *Die gottesdienstlichen Vorträge der Juden, historisch entwickelt* (Berlin: A. Asher, 1832).

this first thought of as an appropriate thing to do? What made it so important in the religious experience of God's people?

Did the practice of reading and preaching the Scriptures in worship go back to the time when the Scriptures first appeared? Were the Scriptures always read as sacred Scripture? Were they written to be read as Scripture, or were they produced for other purposes and only later when they began to be honored gradually given a place in the worship of the community? Ever since the Enlightenment many have assumed that the writings which eventually found their way into our Bible were produced like any other kind of literature and that it was only after a long time that they came to be regarded as Holy Scripture and found a place in public worship. Is this indeed the case? Could it be that the Scriptures, or at least some parts of them like the Law of Moses, were always regarded as the Word of God and were therefore read in the sacred assemblies of God's people as the Word of God? It is from the sacred writings themselves that we will have to try to find an answer to this crucial question.

A. Exodus

Recently there has been a new appreciation of the theological centrality of the book of Exodus in the Hebrew Scriptures. The saving act of grace that delivered Israel from Egypt and the gracious gift of the Law at Mount Sinai are presented to us in Exodus in terms of a covenantal theology.[2] This covenantal theology shows that there was far more to the Law than the legalistic interpretations that have all too often been given to these mighty acts of God. The covenant theology found in Exodus is a very profound understanding of the relationship of grace, law, and our communion with God. It is in the Sinai narrative, Exodus 19:1–24:11, at the very center of this profoundly theological work, that we find a description of a service of worship in which this covenantal relationship is experienced.

2. See Ronald E. Clements, *Exodus,* Cambridge Commentaries (Cambridge: Cambridge University Press, 1972); Walther Eichrodt, *Theology of the Old Testament,* trans. J. A. Baker, 2 vols. (Philadelphia: Westminster Press, 1961-67); M. G. Kline, *Treaty of the Great King* (Grand Rapids: Wm. B. Eerdmans Publishing Co., 1963); Dennis J. McCarthy, *Old Testament Covenant* (Richmond: John Knox Press, 1972); George E. Mendenhall, *Law and Covenant in Israel and the Ancient Near East* (Pittsburgh: Biblical Colloquium, 1955); and Mendenhall's article "Covenant" in *The Interpreter's Dictionary of the Bible,* 4 vols. and supp. vol. (Nashville: Abingdon Press, 1982), 1:714-23.

God's deliverance of Israel from slavery in Egypt, the revelation of the Law, and Israel's entering into covenantal fellowship with God in worship became the theological foundation of the faith of Israel. Throughout the rest of the Bible these central themes are interpreted and reinterpreted.[3] The Christian interpretation of these themes in the ministry of Jesus became central to the faith of the Church as well. Christians understood Christ's death and resurrection as a new Exodus and a new entry into the Promised Land. They understood the Gospels and the writings of the apostles as the Scriptures of the New Covenant and therefore read and preached the Scriptures of the New Covenant as the basis of their covenantal fellowship with God. Not surprisingly, there is a strong continuity between the faith of the Church and the faith of Israel. The worship of Israel at the foot of Mount Sinai became the prototype of the worship of God's people down through the centuries. This is especially true in regard to the ministry of the Word. In the synagogue even today the Scriptures are kept in the ark and are ceremonially taken out of the ark and read and then returned to the ark. The sermon is thought of as being delivered from the seat of Moses.

According to the oldest traditions, the reading of Scripture goes back as far as the worshiping assembly of Israel at the foot of Mount Sinai.[4] The Law had no more been given than it was read to Israel by Moses. In Exodus 24 we read of how Moses wrote all the words of the LORD, built an altar at the foot of the mountain, sent young men to make sacrifices, took half the blood of the sacrifice and threw it against the altar, then took the book of the covenant and read it in the hearing of the people.[5] After the people made a solemn covenant vow, "All that the LORD has spoken we will do," Moses threw the other half of the blood on the people, saying, "Behold the blood of the covenant which the LORD has made with you in accordance with all these words." It was then that Moses, Aaron and his two sons, and the seventy elders of Israel went up on Mount Sinai and

3. On the history of this interpretation, see Brevard S. Childs, *The Book of Exodus: A Critical, Theological Commentary,* The Old Testament Library (Philadelphia: Westminster Press, 1974).

4. W. Beyerlin, *Origins and History of the Oldest Semitic Traditions* (Oxford: B. Blackwell, 1965).

5. Martin Noth points to the fact that joining the reading and explaining of the Law to the covenant sacrifice is the significant point of the report and there is no compelling reason for separating them. Martin Noth, *Exodus: A Commentary,* The Old Testament Library (Philadelphia: Westminster Press, 1962), pp. 197ff.

ate and drank and beheld God.[6] How could one make more clear that the reading of God's Word was an essential constituent of the worship of Israel from its very beginning?

One school of biblical scholarship suggests that we have in Exodus 24:1-11 several strands of tradition.[7] In the first verse Moses is called by the LORD to come up the mountain with Aaron, Nadab and Abihu, and seventy of the elders of Israel. In the second verse Moses alone is called to come near to the LORD. In verses 3-8 the covenant is sealed by the sprinkling of blood, but in verses 9-11 it is sealed by a covenant meal. In verse 3 we learn that Moses told the people all the words of the LORD, but in verse 7 we discover that he read the book of the covenant to the people.[8] Are we to understand this as two events or as two traditions of the same event? As Brevard Childs has pointed out, there is very little agreement among Old Testament scholars as to how one should divide up the passage between the various traditions.[9] A simple division between Yahwist and Elohist traditions is not sufficient to explain the difficulties. Professor Childs goes on to point out that the final arrangement of the chapter is what should claim our attention, and indeed for our purposes we would do well to heed his advice.

When we study the full text of Exodus 24:1-11 as it has come down to us, a number of things become clear about the reading and preaching of the Word in the worship of ancient Israel. The worshiping assembly is called together at the foot of Mount Sinai to hear the Word of God. It is the ministry of Moses to bring this Word to the people. The Word is simply read to the people, if we take the story at face value. As we will see, there are reasons for thinking that this reading was accompanied by preaching, but if we stick to the tradition as it is recorded in Exodus

6. For a thorough study of Exodus 24, see Tse-Gun Song, *Sinai Covenant and Moab Covenant: An Exegetical Study of the Covenants in Exodus 19:1–24:11 and Deuteronomy 4:45–28:69* (Cheltenham and Gloucester: College of Higher Education, 1992), pp. 109-87.

7. For a discussion of the source criticism of this passage, see Childs, *Exodus,* pp. 499-502; and John I. Durham, *Exodus,* Word Biblical Commentary, vol. 3 (Waco, Tex.: Word Books, 1987), pp. 340ff.

8. For a short discussion of these problems, see Noth, *Exodus,* pp. 194-99.

9. If one uses the divine names as the key to dividing up the passage, then verses 1-8 would belong to J and verses 9-11 would belong to E; but consultation of the leading scholars shows the matter to be much more complicated than this. See Childs, *Exodus,* pp. 499-502.

24:1-11 it is the reading of Scripture with which we have to do. Moses reads the book of the covenant before the assembly of the people of Israel as an act of solemn worship. The covenant vow is made and then sealed by the sprinkling of the blood of the covenant and the sharing of a covenant meal. The reading of God's Word in the book of the covenant and the vow to live by that Word are the basis of the covenant fellowship sealed in the sprinkling of blood and experienced in the covenant meal. Obviously the reading of the Law in the worship of Israel is understood as essential to establishing and maintaining the covenant relationship.

Nothing is expressly said in Exodus 24:1-11 about preaching. It is the reading of the Law that figures in this story. We can perhaps draw from this that the reading of Scripture is primary in worship and that the place of the sermon is therefore to make that reading meaningful. The modern biblical scholar, however, will want to point out that the book of the covenant found in Exodus 21–23 is in fact an interpretation of the Law, so that for those who read Exodus at that level the passage at least suggests both reading the Law and interpreting the Law. Indeed, even in these earliest records one finds that the reading of the Scriptures entails their preaching. It is not for magical reasons, it is not even for legalistic reasons, that the Scriptures must be read in worship; it is rather because they must be understood and must guide the lives of the covenant people. The establishing of the covenant at this sacred assembly in the wilderness set the pattern for a whole series of covenant renewal services that followed.[10]

As we read further into the book of Exodus the relationship of worship to covenant becomes still clearer. When Israel committed apostasy by worshiping the golden calf, Moses interceded for Israel and the covenant was renewed.[11] Moses again went up the mountain and was told, " 'Write these words; in accordance with these words I have made a covenant with you and with Israel' " (Exod. 34:27). Moses came down the mountain and gave all the people of Israel "in commandment all that the LORD had spoken with him" (v. 32). Nothing is specifically said about reading the

10. On the service of covenant renewal, see Gerhard von Rad, *Old Testament Theology,* trans. David M. G. Stalker, 2 vols. (Edinburgh: Oliver & Boyd, 1973), 1:17ff. et passim.

11. Whether Exodus 34 reports a covenant renewal service or a different tradition of the giving of the covenant is not really germane to our discussion. Regardless of how one decides that question, it is still clear that Exodus 34 regards the recounting of the covenant stipulations as essential to covenant fellowship. Cf. Childs, *Exodus,* pp. 604-10.

book of the covenant or about preaching a sermon, but a previously unreported series of interpretations of liturgical legislation, sometimes called the ritual decalogue, is reported in detail (vv. 11-26).[12] These sources really do not allow us to distinguish between a reading of the written word and an interpretation or application of it. Perhaps the text intends us to understand both. What is most interesting here is that in this account of the renewal of the covenant after Israel's fall into idolatry it is explicitly stated that it is "in accordance with these words" that the covenant is made. The function of the reading and the preaching of the Word in worship is stated quite clearly and distinctly in Exodus 34 in a way that it was not in the earlier chapter. The ministry of the Word is the means of opening up and maintaining communion with God. For Moses himself on the top of Mount Sinai, it was not the sight of God that was the means of experiencing God's presence, but rather hearing his Word.

> And the LORD descended in the cloud and stood with him there, and proclaimed the name of the LORD. The LORD passed before him, and proclaimed, "The LORD, the LORD, a God merciful and gracious, slow to anger, and abounding in steadfast love and faithfulness, keeping steadfast love for thousands, forgiving iniquity and transgression and sin, but who will by no means clear the guilty, visiting the iniquity of the fathers upon the children and the children's children, to the third and the fourth generation." And Moses made haste to bow his head toward the earth, and worshiped. (vv. 5-8)

This is one of the central themes of the Law of Moses. This is why the worship of God by means of idols is unacceptable. What was true for Moses was true for the congregation of God's people. In hearing the Word we experience God's saving presence.

It is for this reason, of course, that worship is a means of grace. By entering into God's presence through word, prayer, and sacrament we are made holy as God is holy. God is a sacred fire, and to come near to him is to catch fire and glow with the same holy radiance. This begins to happen to us when we hear God's Word. We are transformed after the image of Christ. It is through entering into that covenant that we enjoy his presence and through abiding in his presence that we are made holy. Surely this is the meaning of the glow on the face of Moses (34:29-35). The whole purpose of reading and preaching Scripture in worship is that

12. Childs, *Exodus*, pp. 604-10.

by means of it we experience God's presence. Already in the Sinai traditions as they are recorded in Exodus we find this basic teaching of covenant theology. We will discover it again and again through the whole history of Christian worship.

Another point needs to be made. In Exodus 19 we read of what Martin Buber has called the eagles' wings sermon.[13] The very brief summary we have of this sermon shows us that it had some powerful ideas. It is here that Israel is called to be a kingdom of priests and a holy nation.

> And Moses went up to God, and the LORD called to him out of the mountain, saying, "Thus you shall say to the house of Jacob, and tell the people of Israel: You have seen what I did to the Egyptians, and how I bore you on eagles' wings and brought you to myself. Now therefore, if you will obey my voice and keep my covenant, you shall be my own possession among all peoples; for all the earth is mine, and you shall be to me a kingdom of priests and a holy nation. These are the words which you shall speak to the children of Israel."
>
> So Moses came and called the elders of the people, and set before them all these words which the LORD had commanded him. And all the people answered together and said, "All that the LORD has spoken we will do." And Moses reported the words of the people to the LORD. (vv. 3-8)

The first reading of Exodus 19 suggests that what we have here is a sermon that God sent Moses to preach to Israel immediately before the giving of the Law in Exodus 20. When one looks more closely, however, it becomes evident that what we have here is one of those brief summaries often used in Hebrew literature to introduce a longer narrative. These five verses are a summary of Exodus 19–24. If this is indeed the case then it would appear that this service of worship in which God united Israel to himself in the covenant did involve a sermon.[14]

A brief analysis of this sermon shows several things. The sermon starts out by remembering. Moses recounts the sacred history of how God delivered Israel from Egypt. "You have seen what I did to the Egyptians, and how I bore you on eagles' wings and brought you to myself." Then follows an admonition: "Now therefore, if you will obey my voice and

---

13. Martin Buber, *Moses: The Revelation and the Covenant* (New York: Harper Torch Books, 1958), pp. 101-9.
14. Childs, *Exodus*, pp. 360-61.

keep my covenant. . . ." It is because of what God has done in delivering Israel that Israel is therefore obligated to obedience. Finally, the sermon ends in a promise that God will be their God and they will be his people: "You will be my own possession." Even in this brief synopsis one notices the beautiful metaphors — "How I bore you on eagles' wings and brought you to myself" — and then that wonderful figure, so often developed throughout the history of God's people: "and you shall be to me a kingdom of priests and a holy nation." Surely the sermon included an exposition of exactly what the stipulations of that covenant were. One might even suggest that in the course of the momentous events of Sinai there were numerous sermons interpreting these mighty acts of God in which God revealed himself to Israel. As any experienced pastor knows, the secret of leading a congregation is interpreting to the people where one is going and what one is doing and why it is necessary and important to do it. To lead a congregation through what Moses had to lead Israel required a lot of interpretation. Just one sermon was not going to do it. This service of worship at Sinai must have gone on for several days — not the sixty-minute services of today's mainline Protestants, but much more like the camp meeting of our frontier days. It is this service of worship that is the prototype of Christian worship.

Finally, I would like to point to the fact that the Decalogue itself, very specifically the fourth commandment, suggests that preaching may well have been thought of as the central act of regular Sabbath worship. This is not explicitly stated, but there is good reason to think that it was implied. "Remember the Sabbath day" is the core of the commandment. The Hebrew word זכר, to remember, is a key term for the biblical understanding of worship.[15] The noun זכרון as we find it in Exodus 12:14 means very specifically a day of religious memorial. The commandment no doubt intends to teach us to observe a religious service at which God's mighty acts of creation and redemption are celebrated. Both the version in Exodus and the version in Deuteronomy make the point that the Sabbath is a day for remembering the works of creation and redemption

---

15. See Brevard S. Childs, *Memory and Tradition in Israel* (London: SCM Press, 1962); H. Eising, *"zākhar,"* and R. E. Clements, *"zākhār,"* in *Theological Dictionary of the Old Testament,* ed. G. Johannes Botterweck and Helmer Ringgren, trans. David E. Green, vol. 4 (Grand Rapids: Wm. B. Eerdmans Publishing Co., 1980), pp. 64-82, 82-87; and W. Schottroff, *"Gedenken" im alten Orient und in Alten Testament* (Neukirchen: Neukirchener Verlag, 1967).

(Exod. 20:8; Deut. 5:15). Exodus speaks of creation, Deuteronomy of redemption. To be sure, the observance of the day itself is the memorial, but would not a day of memorial include a time for recounting the traditions that were to be remembered? Would there not have been a time for reading the Law of Moses and expounding it? The observance of a memorial day would surely include recalling what one was celebrating, although it would also be more than a simple retelling of the sacred history.

One thing should certainly be very clear from the Sinai traditions found in Exodus. The Word of God was read and preached to the worshiping assembly of Israel immediately upon its revelation. The texts themselves make it clear that they were to be read and preached to the assembly of God's people. The Law was written to be read as Scripture in worship.

B. Deuteronomy

The book of Deuteronomy widens our appreciation of the Old Testament understanding of the ministry of the Word quite considerably. In literary form Deuteronomy is a long sermon or series of sermons preached by Moses at a service of covenant renewal just before entering the Promised Land.[16] If one takes this at face value, in Deuteronomy we have the first series of sermons that has come down to us from the biblical tradition. We have already spoken of the eagles' wings sermon, but that was not much more than an outline. The sermons of Deuteronomy are much more thoroughly worked out. The sermonic material in Deuteronomy portrays Moses as the first great preacher and the founder of the long tradition of biblical preaching.

A number of Old Testament scholars in the last few decades have interpreted Deuteronomy in this straightforward fashion and have come up with some important insights. Peter Craigie, for example, in his 1976 commentary, explains Deuteronomy as being indeed "the words that Moses spoke," as claimed in the title of the book as found in the Hebrew

---

16. Modern scholarship usually divides the book up into three sermons. Driver divides up the three sermons as follows: First Discourse, 1:6–4:40; Second Discourse, chapters 5–26 and 28; Third Discourse, chapters 29–30. Samuel Driver, *A Critical and Exegetical Commentary of Deuteronomy,* 3rd ed. (Edinburgh: T. & T. Clark, 1901), pp. i-ii. G. Ernest Wright, "Deuteronomy: Introduction and Exegesis," *Interpreter's Bible,* 2:329ff., follows essentially the same divisions.

Scriptures.[17] Craigie has studied the suzerainty treaties of the ancient Near East and has come to the conclusion that Deuteronomy fits very well into the intellectual environment of the age in which Moses is supposed to have lived. He finds no compelling reason for insisting that Deuteronomy could only have been written in the declining years of the Davidic monarchy. This is significant for the history of preaching, not so much because it means we have in Deuteronomy a rather extensive record of the preaching of Moses, but far more importantly because it shows us how the reading and preaching of Scripture fits into the covenant relationship. With George E. Mendenhall's discovery of the Hittite suzerainty treaties and his suggestion that they throw light on the biblical concept of covenant, biblical scholarship has carefully looked over a wide variety of treaty documents from the ancient Near East and has found that it is characteristic of these documents that they provide first for the writing out of the treaty and second for a ceremonial reading of this treaty at a solemn assembly. Similarly, central to ceremonial renewal is the reading and expounding of the stipulations of the covenant. If Craigie is right, then we have in the covenant theology of the Pentateuch the rationale for the reading and preaching of Scripture in worship — namely, that it is demanded by a covenantal understanding of our relationship to God and to each other.

Particularly striking in Craigie's analysis of the ancient Near Eastern treaty documents is how they foreshadow the tradition of expository preaching in both the synagogue and the Church. These documents normally begin by recounting the story of how the sovereign established his relationship with his subjects. The history of this relationship is recounted, followed by an outline of the general principles the relationship is to have. These principles are codified as certain general stipulations or commandments, but then these general stipulations are followed by a more lengthy working out of these general stipulations in terms of specific stipulations or laws. Next there is a promise of blessings to those who keep these commandments and curses to those who break them. Finally, a list of witnesses is given.[18] Of the very essence of these treaties or covenants is that they are written down and regularly read and taught to the people in a public assembly. They are established and renewed

17. Peter Craigie, *The Book of Deuteronomy,* The New International Commentary on the Old Testament (Grand Rapids: Wm. B. Eerdmans Publishing Co., 1976), p. 17.
18. Craigie, *Deuteronomy,* pp. 22-24.

by a cultic celebration.[19] As Craigie presents it, Deuteronomy is a record of a covenant renewal ceremony held on the plains of Moab just before Israel entered into the Promised Land. It records the words of Moses in which he promulgated and expounded the covenant with the intention that these words were to be the Scriptures of the covenant community.

Looking at Deuteronomy from the standpoint of the more traditional sort of modern biblical criticism, one comes to much the same conclusions. As Gerhard von Rad explains it, the finished literary form consists of the giving of the commandments, an appeal to be faithful to the commandments, the renewing of the covenant vow, and the proclamation of the covenant blessings. In terms of the actual composition, however, it is "an artistic mosaic made up of many sermons on a great variety of subjects."[20] It is the product of intensive preaching activity on the part of the Levites.[21]

If we take von Rad's understanding of Deuteronomy and study the book as a compendium of the preaching of a whole school of preachers, then we notice several things about the nature of preaching as it was understood at the time. First we carefully note that this preaching activity was the work of the Levitical priesthood. All too often one assumes that the taproot of Christian preaching goes back to the ministry of the prophets; preaching is thought of as the religious concern of the prophets, over against the liturgical concerns of the priesthood. There may have been circles in which this was true, but those who gave us the book of Deuteronomy saw teaching and preaching as a cardinal function of the priesthood. Deuteronomy assumes that priests have a ministry of the Word. When Moses blessed the tribe of Levi he said:

"They shall teach Jacob thy ordinances,
    and Israel thy law;
they shall put incense before thee,
    and whole burnt offering upon thy altar."

(Deut. 33:10)

19. Craigie, *Deuteronomy,* pp. 28ff.

20. Von Rad, *Old Testament Theology,* 1:221.

21. On von Rad's view of preaching in Deuteronomy, see his monograph, *Studies in Deuteronomy,* trans. David M. G. Stalker (Chicago: H. Regnery, 1953). See also his commentary on Deuteronomy, *Das fünfte Buch Mose: Deuteronomium* (Göttingen: Vandenhoeck & Ruprecht, 1968).

It was the responsibility of the priestly tribe of Levi to be ministers of the Word every bit as much as to be ministers of the altar.

It may well be that the Deuteronomist was struggling to resist the influence of a Canaanite ideology in regard to cult, priesthood, and sacrifice that was having an increasingly strong influence on Israel. This Canaanite influence condoned the use of idols, an elaborate sacrificial system that went even to the extreme of the sacrifice of children, and other forms of cultic magic. On the other hand, those influenced by this Canaanite theology of worship tended to neglect the teaching of the Law and the recounting of the Sinai traditions, which had been a primary responsibility of the Levitical priesthood.

One discovers this same assumption throughout the Old Testament. In that eloquent prophetic oracle given to us by both Isaiah and Micah, we are told that in the last day all nations will go up to Jerusalem because of the teaching of the Word of the LORD:

"Come, let us go up to the mountain of the LORD,
    to the house of the God of Jacob;
that he may teach us his ways
    and we may walk in his paths."
For out of Zion shall go forth the law,
    and the word of the LORD from Jerusalem.

(Mic. 4:2)

Micah's denunciation of the priesthood of his day includes the charge that they "teach for hire" (3:11). Micah obviously assumes that teaching is a basic priestly function.

Jeremiah is the most obvious example of a priest who took very seriously the ministry of the Word. Jeremiah charges the priests with incompetence.

"The priests did not say, 'Where is the LORD?'
    Those who handle the law did not know me."

(Jer. 2:8)

The priests were supposed to interpret the Law to the people, but they could not interpret it truly because they did not know the God from whom it came.

An interesting passage in Chronicles claims that the decline of true religion in Judah was to be blamed on a priesthood that had ceased to

31

teach the people: "For a long time Israel was without the true God, and without a teaching priest, and without law" (II Chron. 15:3). One might imagine that the understanding of the priesthood as having a teaching and preaching ministry was something that was perhaps characteristic of a more primitive, preexilic concept of priesthood. One might further imagine that this concept eventually gave way to the idea that priests saw to the cultic responsibilities of the Temple and left teaching and preaching to others. But this is obviously not the case, for the Chronicler wrote rather late. Throughout the Old Testament we find the same assumption that is expressed in Deuteronomy. The ministry of the Word is essential to true priesthood. It had been a cardinal function of the priesthood ever since Moses established the Levitical priesthood and entrusted to it the tablets of the Law.

A second thing we must notice in Deuteronomy has a great deal to do with preaching — namely, its strong covenantal theology.[22] If God and his people are bound to each other in a covenantal relationship, then it is essential that the stipulations of this covenant be read and preached. In Deuteronomy we find the reading and preaching of Scripture to have the same liturgical significance we found in Exodus. In regard to Exodus we saw that it is in accordance with the Word, codified in the book of the covenant, that the covenant vow is made. The covenant vow is a vow of obedience to the Word of God. It is on the basis of this covenant that Israel enters into fellowship with God, and it is on the basis of this fellowship that the covenant blessings are bestowed. This is as true of the Moab covenant as it is of the Sinai covenant.

> These are the words of the covenant which the LORD commanded Moses to make with the people of Israel in the land of Moab, besides the covenant which he had made with them at Horeb. . . . Therefore be careful to do the words of this covenant. (Deut. 29:1, 9)

In Deuteronomy, just as in Exodus, it is on the basis of the covenant that Israel is able to worship and is received into the presence of God and enjoys communion with him. This is very clear in the introduction to the Decalogue as we find it in Deuteronomy (5:2-3). The proclamation of the

---

22. Among those who have brought the importance of covenant theology to the attention of modern scholarship is Ronald E. Clements, *God's Chosen People: A Theological Interpretation of the Book of Deuteronomy* (Valley Forge, Pa.: Judson Press, 1969); and Eichrodt, *Theology of the Old Testament.*

covenant was essential both when it was first established and when it was renewed with succeeding generations. Moses' action once again in Deuteronomy of *reading* and *expounding* the Law on the plains of Moab (1:5) was inherent in the whole nature of the covenant and a covenantal relationship.[23]

A great portion of the Law, as we find it in Exodus and Deuteronomy as well as in the remainder of the Pentateuch, has to do with worship. Not only do the first four commandments have to do with worship, but there is also a great amount of ceremonial legislation concerning feast days, the arrangement of the worship service, the conduct of the sacrifices, and even the construction of the Tabernacle. The Law is the basis of the worship; quite naturally, then, it is read at worship.

Father Norbert Lohfink has claimed that the literary style of Deuteronomy suggests that the book was written with the intention of its being read as Scripture in a service of worship. In a very careful analysis of the style of Deuteronomy he has come to the conclusion that its author very purposely gave it a hierarchical or liturgical tone, suitable to a ceremonial reading. It has a sort of prose rhythm to it. Certain symbolic phrases are constantly repeated. It is rich in stylized formulas, some of which were connected with the typical court etiquette of the ancient New East, which gave the public reading of the text a very solemn and official sound. Lohfink, in short, makes the point that Deuteronomy was supposed to be read liturgically.[24] This would be only natural for a religious community that had a covenantal understanding of its relationship to God.

Lohfink's findings have been developed even further by Duane Christensen, who suggests that the basic core of Deuteronomy is indeed the sermons of Moses and that it was Moses himself who composed the text to be chanted in public worship from then on.[25] Christensen's commentary is too recent to have been evaluated by Old Testament scholars, but if his theory does justice to the text we have an even stronger indication that the reading and preaching of Scripture were from the very beginning essential to the worship demanded by the covenant. That Scripture can

---

23. On the significance of the Hebrew root דבר particularly its meaning in the opening verses of Deuteronomy, see Duane L. Christensen, *Deuteronomy 1–11*, Word Biblical Commentary, vol. 6A (Dallas: Word Books, 1991), pp. 6-7.

24. Norbert Lohfink, S.J., *Das Haupt gebot. Eine Untersuchung literarischer Einleitungsfragen zu Dtn 5–11* (Rome: Pontificio Instituto Biblico, 1963).

25. Christensen, *Deuteronomy 1–11,* p. lxii.

be sung and that preaching should be hymnic is something we will find throughout the whole history of preaching, from Ephraem of Nisibis to Charles Wesley.

A third point we need to notice is the way the concept of the Word of God appears. The Hebrew term דבר, or word, refers to a spoken utterance. Deuteronomy makes it especially clear that God revealed himself to Israel not as a visible form but through the sound of words that were heard and written down (Deut. 4:10-13). These words were the command-ments — that is, the statutes and ordinances of the Law (4:1-3). One could speak of the Decalogue as the צשׂת הדכדים, quite literally, the ten words. At the very beginning of Deuteronomy we discover that the preaching contained in Deuteronomy consists of "the words that Moses spoke to all Israel" (1:1). These sermons are an explanation of the Law (1:5). דבר refers to the Word of God revealed to Moses as well as to the word preached by Moses to all Israel.

A fourth point to note is that it is in Deuteronomy that we find the first attempts to establish the regular reading of Scripture in worship. The most obvious attempt to do so is a passage in chapter 31, in which Moses is making his final preparations to leave Israel in the care of his successor, Joshua. We are told how Moses finished writing the Torah and gave it "to the priests the sons of Levi, who carried the ark of the covenant of the LORD, and to all the elders of Israel" (31:9-13). Then Moses commanded that every seven years, at the feast of booths, when all Israel came to appear before the LORD, the Law was to be read in the hearing of the people.[26]

Another attempt to establish the place of the Word in worship, less obvious, perhaps, but nevertheless important, is found in Deuteronomy 6, which has been traditionally understood as having to do with the daily reciting of the summary of the Law morning and evening by every faithful Jew. Here we are not dealing directly with a commandment as we were in Deuteronomy 31. Instead, we are dealing with the traditional interpreta-tion of the commandment. The text simply reads:

> "Hear, O Israel: The LORD our God is one LORD; and you shall love
> the LORD your God with all your heart, and with all your soul, and

26. Cf. G. Ernest Wright in his commentary on Deuteronomy in the *Interpreter's Bible*. The reading of the book of the covenant was a regular feature at the feast of tabernacles in several of the sanctuaries of Israel, such as Shiloh, Bethel, and Shechem, but it is not certain whether this was the case in Jerusalem. "Deuteronomy: Introduction and Exegesis," *Interpreter's Bible*, 2:512-16.

with all your might. And these words which I command you this day
shall be upon your heart; and you shall teach them diligently to your
children, and shall talk of them when you sit in your house, and when
you walk by the way, and when you lie down, and when you rise."
(6:4-7)

These words, as most will recognize, are part of the Shema recited in the
Jewish liturgy of morning and evening prayer. It belongs to the basic core
of the Jewish liturgy. Most often it is explained as the Jewish creed, but
more correctly it is understood as the summary of the Law. Jewish scholars
assure us that originally it was recited together with the Ten Commandments and two other passages of the Pentateuch as a sort of compendium
of Holy Scripture. In a day when written manuscripts of the Law were
very expensive, the only way to have the Law upon one's heart was to
memorize it. Memorizing the text of the Law was the foundation of a
Jewish education, and those who advanced far in the education of the
synagogue would eventually memorize the whole Torah, but most faithful
Jews were expected to memorize only the compendium or summary of
the Law, the Shema. By long Jewish tradition the Shema was recited every
morning and evening, "when you lie down and when you rise."

Both in the Ten Commandments as they are found in Deuteronomy 5 and in the summary of the Law in Deuteronomy 6 there is
this basic concern that the Law be taught and discussed. "You shall
teach them diligently to your children and you shall talk of them. . . ."
Fundamental to the covenant relationship is that every faithful child of
Israel have a thorough knowledge of the covenant Scriptures. The reading and preaching of Scripture is of the essence of the worship of the
covenant community.

Moses commanded the people of Israel to read the Law every seven
years at the feast of tabernacles. But what about the other, more frequent
worship assemblies? Especially we wonder about the Sabbath day assemblies, which obviously were so important in the worship of ancient Israel.
If the fourth commandment makes such an important point of weekly
worship on the Sabbath, then surely from a very early date the weekly
reading and preaching of Scripture had to be an essential element in the
worship of ancient Israel.

One would like to know so much more than Deuteronomy tells us. If
the Levites who preserved the Deuteronomic traditions carried on an intensive preaching mission, where and when did they do it? Was this preaching

done in the Temple? Was it related to any kind of worship service or set in some kind of liturgy? If the whole Law was read every seven years at the feast of tabernacles, and if the summary of the Law was recited every morning and evening, must there not have been some weekly reading of the Law at Sabbath worship? If the Sabbath was a day set aside for rest and worship, what was done in the way of worship? If the Sabbath was a day of remembering, would not some time have been set aside for recounting the stories that needed to be remembered? The fourth commandment of the Decalogue as it is found in Deuteronomy says that we are to *observe* the Sabbath day, rather than *remember* the Sabbath day. But even so Deuteronomy makes very clear the importance of remembering holy history as part of worship. The Deuteronomic version of the fourth commandment goes on to say, "'"You shall *remember* that you were a servant in the land of Egypt, and the LORD your God brought you out thence. . . . *Therefore* the LORD your God commanded you to keep the sabbath day"'" (5:15, emphasis added).[27] If weekly Sabbath worship was as fundamental to Jewish religious life as the Decalogue implies, would it not be quite natural for a good portion of that weekly worship to have been devoted to teaching the Law and remembering sacred history? If the priests were supposed to teach the Law to the people, how did they do it? Did the earliest Israelite sanctuaries observe the Sabbath by remembering the sacred history? If the summary of the Law was recited every day and the whole of the Law was read every Sabbath year, was there from earliest times a reading of a portion of the Law each Sabbath day? We know that in the time of Jesus this was a well-established tradition. How far back did this tradition go?

As much as we would like to know the answers to these questions, we simply have to admit that we do not know. We will have more to say about this later, but from the Pentateuch at least all we have is these few hints. The Levitical priesthood was supposed to have a ministry of the Word, and the weekly Sabbath was the central service of worship. This Sabbath worship gave special attention to remembering the works of creation and redemption. The conclusions we can draw from this should be fairly obvious, but the Pentateuch does not tell us that the reading and preaching of Scripture took place Sabbath by Sabbath.

The fifth thing to note about Deuteronomic preaching is what it

---

27. G. Ernest Wright comments, "The Sabbath is to be kept in remembrance of the deliverance from Egypt." "Deuteronomy: Introduction and Exegesis," *Interpreter's Bible,* 2:367.

tells us about the components of preaching. Gerhard von Rad has pointed out that the sermonic material found in Deuteronomy indicates a very distinct approach to the nature of preaching, consisting of three components.[28] The first component is remembrance;[29] we find that Deuteronomic preaching puts strong emphasis on recounting God's saving acts. The second component is interpretation; preaching involves elaboration and application of the Law to the concrete situations of the day. The third component is exhortation; Deuteronomic preaching is characterized by its hortatory style, its constant urging that Israel be obedient to the Law: God has loved us, preserved us, and been gracious to us; therefore let us live according to his commandments. Let us look at each of these in turn.

1. Much of Deuteronomy is devoted to the retelling of sacred history. God's gracious election of Israel and his mighty acts of salvation are the basis of the preacher's appeal for faithfulness. We hear of the victory over Sihon, king of Heshbon, and Og, king of Bashan. Inspiring his congregation with these stories of God's faithfulness, Moses exhorts the children of Israel to go in and take the Promised Land. " 'And now, O Israel, give heed to the statutes and the ordinances which I teach you, and do them; that you may live, and go in and take possession of the land which the LORD, the God of your fathers, gives you'" (Deut. 4:1). As von Rad understands it, the Deuteronomist recounts this sermon of Moses as the prototype of his own preaching. He continues reciting the words of Moses, which are no doubt the guidelines of the Deuteronomist's own preaching ministry:

> "Only take heed, and keep your soul diligently, lest you forget the things which your eyes have seen, and lest they depart from your heart all the days of your life; make them known to your children and your children's children — how on the day that you stood before the LORD your God at Horeb . . . the LORD spoke to you out of the midst of the fire; you heard the sound of words, but saw no form; there was only a voice. And he declared to you his covenant, which he commanded you to perform, that is, the ten commandments; and he wrote them upon two tables of stone. And the LORD commanded me at that time to teach you statutes and ordinances, that you might do them in the land which you are going over to possess." (4:9-14)

28. For the components of Deuteronomic preaching, see von Rad, *Studies in Deuteronomy,* pp. 11-24.

29. On the significance of remembrance in worship see Childs, *Memory and Tradition in Israel,* pp. 74-80.

The stories of God's faithfulness are repeated again and again. God can be expected to be faithful again and again. The Levitical preachers in their day maintained the ministry of Moses, repeating to each new generation the sacred stories of God's faithfulness. They saw Moses as the great teacher of the mighty acts of God, and they followed his example in their own ministry.

In chapter 6 we find a very good summary of Deuteronomic preaching:

> "When your son asks you in time to come, 'What is the meaning of the testimonies and the statutes and the ordinances which the LORD our God has commanded you?' then you shall say to your son, 'We were Pharaoh's slaves in Egypt; and the LORD brought us out of Egypt with a mighty hand; . . . And the LORD commanded us to do all these statutes, . . . for our good always, that he might preserve us alive, as at this day.' " (vv. 20-24)

The story of the deliverance from Egypt is retold at some length, along with the gift of the Law, which is "for our good always, that he might preserve us." The gift of the Law is every bit as much an act of grace as the deliverance from Pharaoh. The faithful Levitical preacher, like the father, recounts the faithfulness of God in delivering his people as well as his faithfulness in giving the Law, that Israel might return to faithfulness.

Telling the story of God's faithfulness is essential to Deuteronomic preaching. It is on the basis of God's faithfulness that Moses would stir up the courage of Israel to enter the Promised Land. Israel need not be afraid of the Canaanites: " 'Remember what the LORD your God did to Pharaoh and to all Egypt' " (Deut. 7:18). Remembering is of the essence of worship, and especially in preaching the congregation worships by remembering the mighty acts of God. This is especially clear in Deuteronomy 8. Here Israel is admonished, " 'And you shall remember all the way which the LORD your God has led you' " (8:2). Then the preacher recounts at length the story of God's providential care during the years of the wilderness and his gift of a rich land, " 'a land of brooks of water, of fountains and springs, flowing forth in valleys and hills, a land of wheat and barley, of vines and fig trees and pomegranates, a land of olive trees and honey. . . . And you shall eat and be full, and you shall bless the LORD your God for the good land he has given you' " (8:7-10). Remembering leads to thanksgiving, and thanksgiving to faithfulness.

2. Another component of preaching as we find it in Deuteronomy

is the interpretation of the Law. This is clear from the introduction to the book of Deuteronomy, where we read, "Beyond the Jordan, in the land of Moab, Moses undertook to explain this law" (Deut. 1:5). Samuel Driver, one of the great Old Testament scholars of the last century, tells us that the phrase "undertook to explain" suggests that the purpose of Deuteronomic preaching is to expound the Law of Moses.[30] As we find in Deuteronomy, the Law is interpreted and applied to the situation at hand. The interpretation is not a matter of historical reconstruction but rather of contemporary application. In other words, Deuteronomy has a keen sense of hermeneutics.

In chapter 4, for example, we find a significant interpretation of the second commandment, the commandment against the worship of images. On the day when God revealed himself on Mount Sinai, chapter 4 tells us, no form was seen, only a voice was heard (4:12). God reveals himself not visually but audibly. God reveals himself by his Word. Therefore Israel is to worship God by hearing his Word and obeying it. Here we have a homiletical explanation of why Israel is not to worship God by means of idols. God has not revealed himself to our sight but rather to our hearing; he has revealed not his form but his will. The second commandment is homiletically elaborated in such a way that it is made particularly relevant to the Canaanite fertility religions. God is not to be represented by any male or female forms. The second commandment is then applied against those who worshiped solar, lunar, and astral divinities. They are not to be worshiped because the sun, the moon, and the stars are known to all people. The true God is the God who has revealed himself to Israel alone. Revelation is not a matter of nature but of grace. Finally, our preacher makes the point that idols are the works of human hands. Why should we worship the work of our hands, when the creations of our hands are so vastly inferior to the work of God's hands? With reasons such as these, the preacher exhorts his congregation to keep the commandment against idolatry.

In chapter 16 we find a series of regulations for the keeping of the three annual pilgrimage feasts — Passover; Pentecost, or the feast of weeks; and the feast of booths. The observance of the feasts is probably to be understood as an interpretation of the fourth commandment, the commandment to keep the Sabbath. Notice how each of these feasts is worked out in a sabbatical manner. Both Passover and the feast of booths are kept for seven days, while the feast of weeks is to be held seven weeks after

30. Driver, *Deuteronomy*, pp. 8-9.

Passover. In chapters 19 to 21 there is a long interpretation of the commandment against killing. This is followed by a long elaboration of the commandment against adultery.

Obviously not all the laws found in Deuteronomy fit neatly under one or another of the Ten Commandments, but, as is patent from the text itself, the legal material in Deuteronomy is essentially a homiletical interpretation of the Mosaic Law. It was the job of the priests to interpret the Law, not just as a matter of jurisprudence in court, but homiletically in the teaching of the people in order that the Law might guide their lives. In ancient Israel the Law was not merely a basis for judging the wicked. Much more, it was the basis of guiding the righteous. Already — yes, even in the Old Testament — we discover that Law was given not to condemn the world, but that the world might have life, and have it more abundantly.[31] It was to this end that the Levitical priesthood, as we find it in Deuteronomy, carried out its ministry of preaching.

3. Finally, we need to point to the fact that the preaching we find in Deuteronomy gives strong emphasis to exhortation.[32] Again and again in Deuteronomy we hear words of exhortation: "'And now, O Israel, give heed to the statutes and ordinances which I teach you, and do them'" (Deut. 4:1); "'Only take heed, and keep your soul diligently, lest you forget the things which your eyes have seen, and lest they depart from your heart'" (4:9). Again in chapter 6 the hortatory style comes to the fore: "'Hear, O Israel: The LORD our God is one LORD; and you shall love the LORD your God with all your heart, and with all your soul, and with all your might. And these words which I command you this day shall be upon your heart'" (6:4-6). In fact, this hortatory style dominates the book of Deuteronomy in a remarkable and overpowering way. Surely one of the most beautiful of these exhortations is found in chapter 30: "'This commandment which I command you this day is not too hard for you, neither is it far off. . . . But the word is very near you; it is in your mouth and in your heart, so that you can do it'" (30:11, 14). These imperatives are phrased in so many artful ways that indeed one gets the sense of why von Rad calls Deuteronomy a patchwork quilt or colorful collage of bits and pieces of a great variety of sermons. This hortatory style flavors Deuteronomy with its own special spice.

31. Cf. Wright, "Deuteronomy: Introduction and Exegesis," *Interpreter's Bible*, 2:378.
32. Von Rad, *Studies in Deuteronomy*, pp. 14ff., speaks at some length of the importance of parenesis in Deuteronomy.

The Levitical preachers whose work we come to know in Deuteronomy understood the need for exhortation. They knew that human minds forget and human hearts can harden. They understood well that again and again the faithful must be exhorted to faith and the saints must be inspired to holiness. All the way through the Pentateuch we hear how God's people lost sight of the vision and how their faith turned into rebellion. As much as they exalted in God's faithfulness after they had crossed the Red Sea, they did not get very far out into the wilderness before they began to murmur. The same old temptations presented themselves, and it was the job of the preacher to stir up the faithfulness of the people in the face of these temptations. Sometimes these same old temptations presented themselves in different forms, and it was the job of the preacher to recognize the same old dangers in their new forms and warn the people. At other times there were unique temptations in unique situations, and then the preacher had to apply the Law to the new situation and appeal to the congregation to recognize the danger. As one studies the book of Deuteronomy one recognizes that it is the work of a very conscientious priesthood, a priesthood ministering to God's people in days of apostasy. We gather from prophets of the same period such as Micah and Jeremiah that this apostasy was all too often to be found in the priesthood as well as in the palace, but Deuteronomy is witness to the conscientious ministry of a significant element of the priesthood even in the darkest days of Israel.

II. The Ministry of the Word among the Prophets

Roland de Vaux, in his monumental work on the institutions of ancient Israel, sums up the difference between the ministry of the Word as it was exercised by the priests and the ministry of the Word as it was exercised by the prophets. He tells us that the priests were concerned with the interpretation and application of the Word of God as it was revealed in the Law of Moses, while the prophets were concerned with proclaiming the Word of God as God revealed that Word directly to the prophet. The prophet was a man who was "directly inspired by God to give a particular message in definite circumstances."[33]

33. Roland de Vaux, *Ancient Israel*, 2 vols. (New York and Toronto: McGraw-Hill Book Co., 1965), 2:354.

41

The striking thing about the preaching ministry of the prophets is that the prophets understood themselves to be proclaiming the Word of God. The prophets did not claim to be men of profound wisdom and insight, wide knowledge of the ways of history, and great sensitivity to the human situation. It was not that they were so convinced of the truth of their interpretation of current events and so impassioned by the moral imperatives of what they thought ought to be done that they were willing to call their view the word of God in order to get people to listen. As they understood it, God had given them his Word. It was not their word; it was God's Word. They maintained that what made the difference between them and the false prophets was that God had spoken to them but had not spoken to the false prophets.[34]

When the prophets claimed to pronounce the Word of God, they had something quite dynamic in mind. They understood that Word to be a powerful force, an authoritative word by which God ruled his kingdom, a creative word by which the heavens and earth came into existence, a word of judgment that made the crooked straight and the rough places smooth, a redemptive word by which God's ultimate purposes were brought to fulfillment. For the prophets, God's Word was not so much a phonetic reality as an ultimate reality, not so much communication of ideas as turning on a light in a dark room, a light that fills the void of human existence with purpose, or turning on the headlights of a car, making clear the road ahead.

Having made these introductory remarks, let us look at the ministry of a number of different prophets to get a broader picture of how that ministry was carried out. We will begin with the story of Samuel because it gives us several pictures of the ministry of the prophets in its earliest form.[35]

---

34. This is shown with great clarity by John A. Bright, *Jeremiah: A New Translation with Introduction and Commentary*, The Anchor Bible, vol. 21 (Garden City, N.Y.: Doubleday & Co., 1965).

35. On the origins of prophecy in Israel, see J. Bergrich, "Das priesterliche Heilsorakel," in *Zeitschrift für die alttestamentliche Wissenschaft* 52 (1934): 81ff.; Hans-Joachim Kraus, *Gottesdienst in Israel* (Munich: Chr. Kaiser Verlag, 1962), pp. 122-33; Johannes Pedersen, *Israel: Its Life and Culture*, 4 vols. (London: Geoffrey Cumberlege; Copenhagen: Banner og Korch, 1959), 3:107-40; von Rad's chapter, "Prophecy before the Classical Period," in *Old Testament Theology*, 2:6-32; R. Rendtorff, "προφήτης." *Theological Dictionary of the Old Testament*, ed. G. Kittel and G. Friedrich, trans. G. Bromiley, 10 vols. (Grand Rapids: Wm. B. Eerdmans Publishing Co., 1964-76), 6:796-812, especially pp. 796-804; and H. H. Rowley, *Worship in Ancient Israel: Its Forms and Meaning* (London: SPCK, 1981), pp. 144-75.

A. Samuel and Elijah

First, let us look at the story of the ministry of Eli to Hannah, the woman who was to become the mother of Samuel. This well-loved story tells how Hannah accompanied her husband year after year to the sanctuary at Shiloh to worship. Hannah was barren, and this particular year she wept bitterly before the LORD. Eli the priest saw her weeping and gave her his benediction: "'Go in peace, and the God of Israel grant your petition'" (I Sam. 1:17). In time Hannah bore a son, who was named Samuel. This story gives us a good idea of day-to-day pastoral care as it was doubtless practiced in the various sanctuaries of Israel about a thousand years before Christ. In this encounter, Eli exercised the ministry of both priest and prophet. It must have been the function of priests not only to conduct the sacrifices but also to instruct the people in how to pray and to assure them that their prayer would be heard. A number of psalms show that it was a regular thing during the course of a sacrifice for a prophetic oracle to be given to the effect that God had heard the prayer of those offering the sacrifice.[36]

The traditions that have come down to us about the ministry of Eli give us only hints of the full extent of his ministry. He was priest at the sanctuary of Shiloh, where the ark of the covenant was enshrined. The priests of Shiloh must have been thought of as the guardians of the Sinai tradition. They must have taken special pride in their knowledge of the tablets of the Law, one of the treasures within the ark of the covenant. Surely if anyone was well versed in the precepts of the book of the covenant it would have been these priests. Whatever written manuscripts existed or whatever oral traditions there were that recorded God's revelation at Sinai must have been well known by the priests at Shiloh. Surely one of the reasons one would make a pilgrimage to Shiloh would be to hear the priests recount these traditions.

This is, of course, speculation, but if we may be allowed to read between the lines surely we can imagine that the priests of Shiloh would regularly, each Sabbath, spend some time recounting the traditions of which they were the special guardians.[37] At the very heart of those tradi-

---

36. On the function of prophetic oracles in the worship of Israel, cf. Sigmund Mowinckel's chapter, "The Prophetic Word in the Psalms," in *The Psalms in Israel's Worship*, trans. D. R. Ap-Thomas, 2 vols. (New York: Abingdon Press, 1962), 2:53-73.

37. On the close connection between the Law, the worship of the sanctuary, and the giving of oracles, cf. Pedersen, *Israel*, 3:160.

tions was setting aside the Sabbath as a day for remembering those traditions, as the text of the Decalogue makes so clear: " 'Remember the sabbath day, to keep it holy' " (Exod. 20:8); and in the Deuteronomic version: " ' "You shall remember that you were a servant in the land of Egypt, and the LORD your God brought you out thence with a mighty hand and an outstretched arm; therefore the LORD your God commanded you to keep the sabbath day" ' " (Deut. 5:15). The recounting of this sacred history and the study of these sacred laws must have been a major part of the Sabbath day observances at Shiloh and at any other Israelite sanctuary. The boy Samuel must have often heard the sacred texts read and explained. This teaching would have been the special attraction of Shiloh, its drawing card; even the venal sons of Eli would have recognized that. As a boy brought up in the Temple, Samuel would have been taught to read the sacred texts and recite the oral traditions.

As a child I used to wonder what the boy Samuel did in the Temple with all those priests. Now that I have learned something about the way Jewish education works, and has worked for millennia, I have a pretty good idea. Samuel and a number of other boys were being taught the sacred traditions, both the written and the oral ones. Every sanctuary had its school, because it was of the essence of a covenantal religion to remember the sacred history and to learn the sacred ways. This was all made quite clear in the Shema as we find it in Deuteronomy 6: " 'And these words which I command you this day shall be upon your heart; and you shall teach them diligently to your children' " (6:6-7). Samuel was not the only boy who was taken to the Temple and entrusted to the priests to learn the traditions of Sinai. Samuel was well versed in these traditions, and it was because of this that he was a prophet.

Samuel himself combined a number of prophetic and priestly functions.[38] It was while he was presiding at a sacrifice at a high place that Saul sought him out to inquire of the LORD where he might find his father's asses. God had already spoken to Samuel about Saul, and with a prophetic sign Samuel consecrated Saul as king over Israel. One sees Samuel as a priest presiding at the sacrifice, but when God revealed to him that Saul was the man whom he had chosen to be the first king of Israel we see Samuel in the role of the prophet. Obviously the text presents

---

38. Von Rad points out several different ways in which Samuel was regarded in the different strands of the tradition. Interestingly enough, he sums up by saying that Samuel is best regarded as a preacher of the Law. *Old Testament Theology,* 2:7 n. 2.

this revelation of God's will concerning Saul's future in the most straight-forward manner. When Samuel anointed Saul, he was clearly doing it with full divine authority based on a direct revelation of God to the prophet.

Another example is the story of Saul's return from his victory over the Amorites. Samuel had blessed Saul before his departure and given him an oracle that he was to bring back no spoil. Saul disobeyed the oracle and returned with spoil, claiming that the best of it would be given to God in sacrifice. Samuel met the king and rebuked him with the famous line, "'To obey is better than sacrifice'" (I Sam. 15:22). In the ensuing conflict between the two men, Samuel uttered another prophetic oracle promising that God would tear the kingdom from Saul's hand.

While a number of points here speak of the way the ministry of the Word was carried out at that time, two are particularly interesting. The first is the prophetic oracle that Samuel delivered to Saul on his going out to battle. It must have been a normal thing for kings to consult Temple prophets or diviners as to whether or not it was propitious to go out on a certain military mission. Even more interesting is the second point, Samuel's instruction of Saul when he comes to offer his spoil as a sacrifice. Here we have the most basic kind of prophetic concern for true worship. As both priest and prophet, Samuel tells Saul that the sacrifice Saul intends to offer is not pleasing to God; it is a disobedient sacrifice, a ceremonial transgression that is in no way to be regarded as a merely ritualistic concern. Here we see that the ministry of the prophet as we find it in I Samuel is thoroughly integrated with the priestly ministry. Samuel receives direct revelations from God, and he interprets the ancient traditions. While nothing is mentioned about Samuel interpreting Scripture or preaching sermons, we do find several instances where Samuel makes a vivid inter-pretation of the tradition.

Turning to the book of Kings, we see the prophetic ministry develop-ing in a different direction. Elijah is the central figure. In the story of the contest on the top of Mount Carmel, Elijah is called a נביא, a prophet. In fact, he is called the prophet of the LORD, נביא ליהוה (I Kings 18:22). The uniqueness of this Hebrew word has often been stressed. Originally it probably referred to the ecstatic visionaries or diviners found in the fertility religions of the ancient Near East. Elijah is very different from these. He is contrasted with the prophets of Baal, נביאי הבצל. From the story it is evident that Elijah does not share the ecstatic practices of the Canaanite prophets. For Elijah, to be a נביא is something much more profound.[39] As time went on, Elijah became the prototype of the prophetic movement. Communities of prophets began to develop, communities that were not particularly connected to the Temple but were the champions of the oldest traditions of the religion of Israel. They resisted Canaanite tendencies that were evidently most influential both at court and in the religious sanctuaries supported by the court. Elijah was passionately devoted to monotheism and forthrightly opposed to idolatry. His polemic against the idolatry of the prophets of Baal is bald mockery. He was a staunch supporter of ancient family rights as opposed to the growing demands of a centralized government, as we see in the story of Naboth's vineyard. His flight to Mount Sinai shows his devotion to the Law of Moses, yet there is no talk here of Holy Scripture or the interpretation of Scripture.

Again we are tempted to read between the lines. If Elijah was so devoted to the Sinai traditions that he took refuge at Sinai, would this not imply that he knew the Sinai traditions by heart? In those days religious leaders would certainly have committed both the written and the oral traditions to memory. The written text was unpointed, so one had to know it by heart. As for the oral tradition, there was no other way to learn it, to meditate on it, or to interpret it. If the Sinai traditions were not at the heart of Elijah's religious life and the life of his religious community, why then would he flee to Sinai? It seems highly probable that the prophetic communities had the covenant Scriptures at the center of their common life.

Elijah's visit to Mount Sinai has important implications for the nature of the prophetic ministry. The Elijah stories have always spoken to us about the most profound experiences of prayer and therefore remind us of the intimate connection between the life of prayer and the revelation of God's prophetic Word. These stories tell of several dramatic confrontations, such as the contest on Mount Carmel, but from the stories that have come down to us it is hard to construe these confrontations as sermons. Elijah's words when he confronts King Ahab in Naboth's vineyard and delivers to him the Word of the Lord almost constitute a sermon. But having said all this, it is clear that the stories about Elijah reveal a prophet to whom God spoke in the clearest and most direct way.

When we turn to the literary prophets we find many of the same patterns. Here, however, the prophetic oracles have been preserved with

---

39. Rendtorff, "προφήτης κτλ," *Theological Dictionary of the New Testament*, 6:796-812; B. D. Napier, "Prophet," *Interpreter's Dictionary of the Bible*, 3:896-919.

considerably more care. Oracles, however, are not sermons. Perhaps oracles could have been delivered in the course of a sermon; they could also have been delivered in the course of prayers at the Temple, as in the case of the passages from the psalms we mentioned above. It seems to have been more usual, however, that prophetic oracles were delivered during a confrontation, often with an appropriate prophetic sign. Isaiah's confrontation with King Ahaz at the conduit of the Upper Pool is a good example. On the other hand, the oracles Amos pronounced against the nations come much closer to what we might call a sermon. Not only is this oracle or series of oracles of a length that would be more consistent with what we would call a sermon, but it has a sort of oratorical or homiletical development. It is this sort of development that distinguishes the prophetic oracle from the prophetic sermon. Let us look at several oracles that, for one reason or another, might also be called sermons.

B. Amos

Amos is usually considered the first of the literary prophets, which means that Amos is the first prophet whose words were recorded and preserved in literary form.[40] There is more to the distinctiveness of Amos than that, however. Amos was a prophet in the sense that his life was defined by his call to bear a particular word of God at a particular time in the history of God's people.[41] He was not a prophet by virtue of serving an institution or belonging to an order or profession. He was unique because God sent him to proclaim a word of judgment against the apostate kingdom of Israel, yet this word of judgment for a particular time and place was to be sacred Scripture for the whole of God's people from age to age. For our purposes it is important to recognize that the sermons of Amos as they have come down to us, like the sermons of Moses, are more than sermons. Somehow, by the grace of God, they are the Word of God.

40. On how Amos came to be put down in literary form, see James Luther Mays, *Amos: A Commentary*, The Old Testament Library (Philadelphia: Westminster Press, 1976), pp. 12ff.; and Hans Walter Wolff, *Dodekapropheton 2, Joel und Amos*, 2nd ed., Biblischer Kommentar altes Testament, vol. XIV/2 (Neukirchen-Vluyn: Neukirchener Verlag, 1975), pp. 129ff.

41. On the life and mission of Amos, see Francis I. Andersen and David Noel Freedman, *Amos: A New Translation with Introduction and Commentary*, The Anchor Bible, vol. 24A (New York: Doubleday, 1989), pp. 83ff.

The concept of the Word of God is clearly discernible in Amos. Quite objectively God speaks. It is not just a matter of a subjective intuition on the part of the prophet. God has a message for his people. It is the prophet's job to proclaim it.

> "Surely the Lord GOD does nothing,
>   without revealing his secret
>   to his servants the prophets.
> The lion has roared;
>   who will not fear?"

(Amos 3:7-8)

The Hebrew words אמר and אמרה have more to do with the outward act of speaking, while the word דבר has to do with the message or inner meaning of what is spoken.[42] With the prophets, the phrase דבר יהוה, the Word of the LORD, had come to mean the revealed Word of God. The book of Amos may be identified as the words of Amos דברי עמוס, but there is no question that the whole book was regarded as דבר יהוה, the Word of the LORD.[43] This can be seen by a comparison of the first three verses of Amos 1. The book is introduced as the "words of Amos," but then we are told, "the LORD roars from Zion, and utters his voice from Jerusalem." Following this, several oracles are introduced with the phrase "Thus says the LORD," כה אמר יהוה. A similar phrase is used to introduce the book of Hosea: "The Word of the LORD that came to Hosea," דבה יהוה אשר היה אל הושע. For the prophets, the word that they preached was as much the Word of God as the word that Moses preached.

Amos was not a prophet by profession, as were Elijah and Elisha and their followers.[44] As the text itself tells us, he was neither a prophet nor the son of a prophet (Amos 7:14). Somewhat romantically he has usually been thought of as a humble loner, a shepherd, a dresser of sycamore trees. More recent scholarship, however, has suggested that he was more likely a sheep breeder who was also involved in other lines of agricultural commerce, somewhat like the ranchers of our own Southwest. The language

---

42. O. Procksch, "λέγω," *Theological Dictionary of the New Testament,* 4:91-92.

43. Procksch, "λέγω," *Theological Dictionary of the New Testament,* 4:96-98.

44. See the objection of Douglas Stuart to the usual understanding of this statement. What made a prophet a prophet was that God gave him his Word to preach, not what profession he followed. *Hosea-Jonah,* Word Biblical Commentary, vol. 31 (Waco, Tex.: Word Books, 1984), p. 284.

of Amos alone is an indication that he was a man of culture and sophistication. Clearly he had experience in public speaking. One cannot marshal such brilliant oratory without practice! Back in Tekoa, he must have been at least one of the elders of the gate. It might have been there that he gained experience not only in public speaking but also in applying the Law. If the elders of the gate were responsible for maintaining justice and righteousness in the local community, they would have to have been able to expound the Law. The sanctuary would not have been the only place where the traditions of Sinai were recounted and interpreted. We have little information about Amos apart from the fingerprints of his language, but they do, in fact, tell us quite a bit. Amos was no pickup truck–driving "bubba." He was a man of wisdom and experience who had the gift of expressing himself with both clarity and power. Let us look at three of the sermons he has left behind.[45]

1. We turn first to Amos 1 and 2,[46] where we find an easily recognizable sermon. The sermon comes to us, no doubt, in an abbreviated form, but all the essential elements seem to be there.[47] It is divided into eight paragraphs, each of which begins with the words "Thus says the LORD." Most of these paragraphs also end with the refrain "says the LORD." We notice here what we have said already about the prophetic understanding of the ministry of the Word. There is a strong sense that this is indeed the Word of God, not just the wisdom of the ancients, the word of tradition, or even the keen insight of the prophet, but the revealed Word of God.

Even though these prophetic oracles are clearly understood as the Word of God, however, they are directed to the human mind and will so as to get the attention and obedience of the people to whom they are addressed. The Law, the Decalogue, was understood as the Word of God in the most direct sense, too, but the Law, or at least the Decalogue, was apodictic. It applied to any place or time; regular pronouncement of it was sufficient. The prophetic oracle generally was understood to be the Word of God in every bit as direct a way, but it was sharpened and pointed to be shot like an arrow into a particular situation.

In the sermon found in Amos 1 and 2, the series of oracles has been lined up and the point of the sermon sharpened by an artful use of rhetoric

45. On the literary style of Amos, see Stuart, *Hosea-Jonah*, pp. 285ff.
46. On the literary composition of this passage, see Andersen and Freedman, *Amos*, pp. 206-18. On its rhetorical unity, see Mays, *Amos*, pp. 22-28.
47. On this sermon as a series of oracles, see Stuart, *Hosea-Jonah*, p. 308.

so as to move the hearts and wills of eighth-century Israelites. In this sermon there is a very clever homiletical line of attack — a sermon outline, if you will. Amos goes after the approval of his hearers by calling down the judgment of God on one after another of Israel's enemies. He pronounces God's judgment first on Damascus, then on the Philistines, next on Tyre and Edom. As the hellfire mounts higher and higher, the congregation becomes increasingly delighted; the listeners are shocked at the sins of their neighbors, convinced that their enemies are indeed worthy of the most devastating judgment.

It is here that the homiletical strategy comes into play. Having excited the congregation to recognize the need to punish other nations for their sins, Amos now turns to the sins of Israel.

> Thus says the LORD:
> "For three transgressions of Israel,
>   and for four, I will not revoke the punishment;
> because they sell the righteous for silver,
>   and the needy for a pair of shoes —
> they that trample the head of the poor into the dust of the earth,
>   and turn aside the way of the afflicted;
> a man and his father go in to the same maiden,
>   so that my holy name is profaned;
> they lay themselves down beside every altar
>   upon garments taken in pledge;
> and in the house of their God they drink
>   the wine of those who have been fined."
>
> (2:6-8)

How can the Israelites avoid being shocked at the sins of Israel just as they had at the sins of the Syrians and the Philistines? What makes these two chapters of Amos a sermon rather than simply an oracle or a series of oracles is this rhetorical sharpening, this hermeneutical directing of the material.

Again there are so many questions we would like to ask for which the text gives too little material for full answers. Are we, for example, to imagine that this homiletical sharpening is the outward form provided by the preacher for the inner meaning that is the Word of God? That is, are we to understand the rhetorical and the hermeneutical as merely the outward shell or husk of the inner kernel that is the Word of God? When the prophets preached, as Amos preached here, did they take a divinely

50

given oracle and spin around it a sermon, as though the oracle were the text and the rest artistic development or homiletical elaboration? Again, we would like to ask how the literary form of this sermon as we find it in the book of Amos might have differed from the way it was actually preached. So much biblical literature appears to have been preserved for us in concentrated form. Did Amos actually preach in poetic form, or is the poetic form an indication that the material has been reduced to essentials so that it could more easily be memorized and passed on to posterity?

Despite the risks involved in deciding on some of these questions, I would like at least to propose some answers. This sermon as we have it today claims in the most straightforward way that as a whole it is the Word of God. What else can we make of the constantly repeated introduction, "Thus says the LORD," or the constantly repeated refrain, "says the LORD"? Amos 1:2 is apparently an introduction or exordium to the whole sermon:[48]

> "The LORD roars from Zion,
>   and utters his voice from Jerusalem;
> the pastures of the shepherds mourn,
>   and the top of Carmel withers."

Through the use of a metaphor Amos claims that his sermon has its origins in the source of all true teaching, the sanctuary of Jerusalem. He may be uttering this word in Bethel, but it is nevertheless the Word of the Lion of Judah. Obviously Amos thought of the sermon as a whole being the Word of God. He would no doubt have looked at any attempt to distinguish between the sermon being the Word of God and the sermon containing the Word of God as an attempt of sinners to evade the full force of the message. In the same way Amos would surely have resisted any attempt by an editor to find out precisely which words should be printed in red as the veritable words of God that the prophet heard from the mouth of God himself. From what has come down to us we get the impression that Amos himself would have regarded the whole word preached as the Word of God. Not only the prophetic oracles themselves are the Word of God but also the way in which they have been homileti-

---

48. Scholarly opinion is divided on the connection between Amos 1:2 and the verses that follow it. Compare Andersen and Freedman, *Amos*, pp. 218-22; Mays, *Amos*, pp. 20-22; and Stuart, *Hosea-Jonah*, pp. 299-302.

cally arranged and made more effective by rhetoric. One approaches the hearing of the Word of God not as one approaches the eating of nuts — cracking the shell, eating the meat of the nut, and throwing the shell away. Rather, one approaches the Word of God as one eats grapes — eating the whole thing, skin, pulp, and seeds.

While Amos no doubt considered the whole sermon as he preached it, with all its rhetorical devices and homiletical forms, as the Word of God, we as members of the Church have only the canonical form of the book as it has come down to us. For us it is the sermon in its canonical form as we find it in the first two chapters of Amos that is the Word of God. And yet, we must point out, in order not to lose the prophetic sense of the dynamics of God's Word, even today in the Christian Church, when a preacher preaches this text, that sermon is the Word of God. As we shall see in volume 3, the fifteenth-century Italian preacher Girolamo Savonarola preached through the prophecies of Amos with such insight that many of his contemporaries recognized that he had exercised the prophetic ministry among them. The Protestant Reformers were also willing to call the preached word the Word of God, while recognizing a distinction between the Scriptures and a sermon on the Scriptures. This Sunday's sermon as we hear it in our own experience may not be the Word of God in a canonical sense, but there is indeed a sense in which it is the Word of God. God speaks to us today in a way that is very real.

2. Another sermon that shows us something of the preaching ability of Amos is his sermon against the "cows of Bashan" in chapter 4.[49] If what we have here is indeed a capsulized sermon that Amos preached in the capital of the Northern Kingdom, it must have drawn a crowd by virtue of its shocking introduction: "Hear this word, you cows of Bashan!" What a daring metaphor![50] Almost three thousand years later the words of Amos bring before our eyes the hefty matrons of Samaria enjoying the costly luxuries of the day, sitting on their ivory couches, preening their elaborate coiffures, and anointing themselves with perfumed cosmetics. The luxury of these pampered women was bought at the expense of the misery of the

49. Whatever may be the sources of Amos 4, we will look at the chapter in its canonical form as a single sermon beginning with the provocative introduction, "Hear this word, you cows of Bashan . . . ," and ending with the doxology, "For lo, he who forms the mountains, and creates the wind . . . the LORD, the God of Hosts, is his name." As it now stands, this chapter contains a coherent form and message, which, we believe, reflect the prophetic school of preaching.

50. On how this metaphor was understood at the time, see Mays, *Amos,* p. 72.

poor. They and their men had used the art of politics to monopolize the good things of life. The story of Jezebel and Naboth's vineyard must have been repeated a thousand times.

The power of the metaphor is that the picture immediately suggests to us plenty of contemporary parallels. We hardly need to be told that Bashan was renowned as a rich pastureland, famous for its cattle — not unlike Texas, perhaps. Even if we have not the foggiest notion where Bashan might be, we know where that kind of cow lolls around today. We get the picture. If Samaria was bad, Hollywood is worse! We hardly need to be told that women like this are still in operation all these centuries later, insisting that their men provide them luxury upon luxury. They act like divas on their divans. They think they are goddesses of fertility. They fancy themselves madonnas. Women like that offend us. We are hardly surprised that they offend God.

After this shocking metaphor Amos fires a bitter stanza of irony at his congregation.

"Come to Bethel, and transgress;
    to Gilgal, and multiply transgression;
bring your sacrifices every morning,
    your tithes every three days;
offer a sacrifice of thanksgiving of that which is leavened,
    and proclaim freewill offerings, publish them;
    for so you love to do, O people of Israel!" says the Lord GOD.
                                     (4:4-5)

The worship in the sanctuaries of Israel had increasingly taken on Canaanite ways. In spite of the express stipulations of the Law of Moses that sacrifices were not to be made with leavened bread, the priests of Bethel and Gilgal and doubtless Samaria and other sanctuaries as well had decided that it would be more ecumenical to use leavened bread.[51] They knowingly violated the prescriptions of Scripture in order to make worship more inclusive, more pluralistic. The sumptuous liturgical forms of the old Canaanite religion were becoming popular once again. These lavish sacrifices turned solemn worship into a carnival, and God was offended by this kind of worship.

51. It is uncertain here whether Amos is criticizing the sacrifices as being contrary to the Law of Moses or merely the ambiguity of sinful people reveling in worship and completely ignoring the moral obligations of their religion. Here I am inclined to agree with Stuart, *Hosea-Jonah,* p. 338, rather than Andersen and Freedman, *Amos,* p. 433.

The rhetoric of the sermon is so powerful because it is so transparent! It speaks to the situation today as much as it spoke to eighth-century Israel. By seeing today through such a transparent history, today becomes clearer than ever.

The body of the sermon is made up of five stanzas, all recounting to Israel how God had issued warnings by sending seasons of drought; various disasters of war, fire, and plague; and visitations of blight, mildew, and locust.

> "I overthrew some of you,
>   as when God overthrew Sodom and Gomorrah,
>   and you were as a brand plucked out of the burning;
> yet you did not return to me," says the LORD.
>
> (4:11)

The point of each of the five stanzas is the same, as is made clear by the refrain: "'Yet you did not return to me,' says the LORD." Finally the pronouncement of judgment falls.

> "Therefore thus I will do to you, O Israel;
>   because I will do this to you,
>   prepare to meet your God, O Israel!"
>
> (4:12)

The sermon as we now have it concludes with a hymnic stanza. Sometimes it has to be in God's judgment that we finally discover his majesty. God is gracious and we pay no attention; God warns us and we will not listen. What else is God to do but let his judgment fall? If we will not reflect his glory by living a godly life, then we can expect nothing else than judgment. Whether in irony or in dreadful solemnity, the hymnic verse proclaims God's majesty:

> For lo, he who forms the mountains, and creates the wind,
>   and declares to man what is his thought;
> who makes the morning darkness,
>   and treads on the heights of the earth —
> the LORD, the God of Hosts, is his name!
>
> (4:13)

However this brief hymn came to conclude this sermon as it now stands, one thing is clear — it is as impressive a conclusion as any sermon ever had.[52] It makes abundantly clear that even a prophecy of doom can serve God's glory, revealing in awful terms the irreproachable holiness of God.

3. The funeral sermon found in Amos 5 and 6 is another example of Amos's oratorical skill.[53] The introduction to this sermon is striking. The sermon is a funeral dirge, a dirge for the entire Northern Kingdom.[54] The Qinah meter, the meter of lament, makes the funereal nature plain.

> "Fallen, no more to rise,
>   is the virgin Israel;
> forsaken on her land,
>   with none to raise her up."
>
> (5:2)

What gives a funeral dirge such a pathetic sound is its constant repetition. When this sermon was preached, these four lines must have been chanted over and over again. Only occasionally would the other stanzas of this sermon be inserted. But those stanzas would have been more than shocking. They would have been taken as blatantly seditious. It was a funeral dirge for the whole nation, and what was so bewildering was that the nation seemed to be prospering.

The body of the sermon is a series of oracles directed against dishonesty in government and superficiality in worship. Modern archaeology has shown that during the time of Amos Israel began to develop the sort of monarchy that employed a large civil service.[55] Big government led to

---

52. These hymnic phrases that appear throughout the book of Amos have been the subject of quite a bit of study. See Mays, *Amos*, pp. 83ff. Of particular interest are the articles of F. Horst, "Die Doxologien im Amosbuch," *Zeitschrift für die alttestamentliche Wissenschaft* 47 (1929): 45-54, and J. D. W. Watts, "An Old Hymn Preserved in the Book of Amos," *Journal of Near Eastern Studies* 15 (1956): 33-39. More recently on this subject, see W. Berg, *Die sogenannten Hymnenfragmente in Amosbuch* (Bern: Lang, 1974), and P. Carney, "Doxologies: A Scientific Myth," *Hebrew Studies* 18 (1977): 149-59.

53. What should be included in this sermon, even in its present form, is not as clear as in the two we have just discussed. Somewhat arbitrarily we have decided to treat the two chapters as one whole sermon. Wolff, on the other hand, makes a good case for regarding 5:1-17 as a single sermon (*Amos*, pp. 267-97). On the integrity of 5:1–6:14, see Andersen and Freedman, *Amos*, pp. 461-71.

54. See the comments of Douglas Stuart on these verses as funerary lament, *Hosea-Jonah*, p. 344.

55. On the contribution of archaeology to the understanding of the prophecies of Amos, see Andersen and Freedmen, *Amos*, passim.

the growth of a privileged class of officeholders who used taxation and confiscation as a means of filling their own pockets. The bureaucracy and the military ran up exorbitant expenses that had to be paid by the craftsman and the farmer. It was much the same with the religious sanctuaries. Again and again Amos fulminates about the liturgical excesses of Bethel and Gilgal. Luxury in both church and state had become a heavy burden on the poor.

> They hate him who reproves in the gate,
>   and they abhor him who speaks the truth.
> Therefore because you trample upon the poor
>   and take from him exactions of wheat,
> you have built houses of hewn stone,
>   but you shall not dwell in them;
> you have planted pleasant vineyards,
>   but you shall not drink their wine.
> For I know how many are your transgressions,
>   and how great are your sins —
> you who afflict the righteous, who take a bribe,
>   and turn aside the needy in the gate.
>
> (5:10-12)

The excessive taxation of the political bureaucracy, dishonesty in the courts, and the cheating of simple people in the markets have provoked the anger of God and killed the true Israel, the covenant people of God. It is because of this that Israel has come to an end and the funeral dirge is to be sung. Once more in verses 16 and 17 we come to the funeral dirge.

> Therefore thus says the LORD, the God of hosts, the Lord:
> "In all the squares there shall be wailing;
>   and in all the streets they shall say, 'Alas! alas!'
> They shall call the farmers to mourning
>   and to wailing those who are skilled in lamentation,
> and in all vineyards there shall be wailing,
>   for I will pass through the midst of you," says the LORD.

The remainder of the sermon is taken up by a series of woes. One oracle after another pronounces the judgment of God. Israel will be destroyed by a foreign nation. The oracle directed against the worship of Bethel is especially eloquent:

56

"I hate, I despise your feasts,
  and I take no delight in your solemn assemblies.
Even though you offer me your burnt offerings and cereal offerings,
  I will not accept them,
and the peace offerings of your fatted beasts
  I will not look upon.
Take away from me the noise of your songs;
  to the melody of your harps I will not listen.
But let justice roll down like waters,
  and righteousness like an overflowing stream."

(5:21-24)

Many have wondered if Amos is denouncing formal worship in general here.[56] That does not seem to be his intention, however. What he is denouncing is a worship that has been Canaanized, as James Luther Mays has put it.[57] Bethel had put a strong emphasis on the kind of elaborate sacrifices characteristic of Canaanite religion and had neglected the teaching of the Law and the remembrance of the traditions of Sinai. The solemn assemblies no longer taught faithfulness and justice. Rather than being assemblies for remembering the sacred traditions and passing on the commandments of the covenant, they had become bacchanals. And the wicked seemed to revel in these religious rites; those who were most guilty of ravaging the poor seemed the most enthusiastic about the elaborate celebrations.

God demanded of his covenant people not rites but righteousness. The worship at Bethel in no way served God's glory. Far from it, it beclouded God's glory. It was an offense to God, as Amos's sermon made vividly apparent.

All this sermonic material, however abbreviated it may be, is enough to give us the impression of a powerful preacher. Amos was a master orator

---

56. This question has generated an extensive literature. See particularly Th. Chary, *Les prophets et le cult à partir de l'Exil* (Paris: Desclée, 1955); H. W. Hertzberg, "Die prophetische Kritik am Kult," *Theologische Literaturzeitung* 75 (1950): 219-26; and Masao Sekine, "Das Problem der Kultpolemik bei den Propheten," *Evangelische Theologie* 28 (1968): 605-9.

57. This memorable phrase is found in Mays's commentary on Micah: James Luther Mays, *Micah: A Commentary,* The Old Testament Library (Philadelphia: Westminster Press, 1976), p. 45. In Mays's commentary on Amos he zeros in on Israel's self-centered worship. The worship is rebellious because it serves the desires of the worshipers rather than God. See particularly *Amos,* pp. 73-76 and 105-10.

who plainly understood a great deal about what it meant to preach the Word of God.

A thousand years after Amos preached, Augustine, living in the last days of the Roman Empire, brought up in a very different kind of culture and being the master of the very sophisticated rhetoric of his day, recognized the oratorical brilliance of the prophecies of Amos. In his *De doctrina christiana,* as we shall see in our second volume, Augustine analyzes point by point the beauty of the prophet's speech. Again and again modern scholars have expressed amazement at the sophistication of this preacher who was supposed to be a rude country boy. It is hard to escape the conclusion that there must have been a considerable preaching culture in eighth-century Israel and Judah. One does not learn to preach like Amos obviously did unless one has practice, and one does not get that kind of practice unless preaching is a regular feature of the religious life of the community.

The preaching of Amos raises an important question for today's preacher. Brevard Childs put his finger on it when he said that the purpose of the book of Amos is "not to provide a model of how the modern clergyman is to become a prophet like Amos for his day."[58] Childs goes on to make it clear that the prophets, like the apostles, had a unique ministry: God called them to put his Word in written form. The task of the minister of today, on the other hand, is to bring the written Word to living speech. The Word of God written is not the same thing as the Word of God preached. That is why in both the synagogue and the church the Word is read as well as preached. Interestingly enough, in the synagogue there is a whole body of oral tradition intended to make clear the importance of *reading* the text of the Scriptures during worship, not reciting Scripture from memory. In public worship the Scriptures are supposed to be both read and preached. The two are not the same.[59]

In the strictest sense of the word, the Church has neither prophets nor apostles today; the canon of Scripture is closed. In a larger sense, however, both the word "prophet" and the word "apostle" are used today. Surely today's ministers are called to be prophets as well as apostles, and

58. Brevard S. Childs, *Introduction to the Old Testament as Scripture* (Philadelphia: Fortress Press, 1979), p. 410.

59. Birger Gerhardsson, *Memory and Manuscript: Oral Tradition and Written Transmission in Rabbinic Judaism and Early Christianity* (Uppsala: C. W. K. Gleerup, 1961), pp. 68-70.

surely the Church of today, as always, needs prophetic preachers. During the last half of the twentieth century, Americans have heard plenty of preaching that claims to be prophetic. We have had a whole generation of amateur social critics in our pulpits who thought they were following the example of Amos by denouncing everything from the Vietnam War to smoking marijuana. By a sort of typology they imagined that President Johnson or President Nixon, or President Reagan or President Clinton, was the contemporary Jeroboam. Few of these sermons even came close to those of Amos. Their social criticism may or may not have been justified, but that is not the point. The problem was that they imagined that one line of social criticism or another was the Word of God for our time. They used the prophets to justify some economic program or social ideology and thought they had done their job.

One of the traditional topics of systematic theology is the doctrine of the inspiration of Scripture. The Nicene Creed tells us that the Holy Spirit spoke through the prophets. It is also true that the Holy Spirit inspires preachers to interpret those Scriptures today. As similar as the two may be, they are not exactly the same. Preaching, especially prophetic preaching, demands a special charisma. It is not always easy to tell when preachers have this special grace. In time, however, we will know them by the fruit of their preaching.

It is the job of the preacher to make the Word of God, the Word the prophets put into writing, a living reality for the congregation. Amos himself, along with his immediate disciples, saw the need for this — or at least that is the way some recent scholars have explained it. Redaction criticism explains much in the canonical form of Amos as the attempt of Amos and his disciples to reinterpret the material he preached in the Northern Kingdom for the needs of a later day in the Southern Kingdom. If these scholars have it right, then we find in Scripture itself an example of the need and the value of hermeneutic. It is not enough simply to read Scripture. Scripture has to be interpreted. It must be preached as well as read. Preaching is a special charisma.

What Childs put negatively he also put positively. The book of Amos "serves as a faithful witness to the God of Israel whose will we now understand more clearly through the medium of Scripture. This living God calls his people into obedient worship which is tested by the standard of God's justice and righteousness."[60] To this Childs appends a reference

60. Childs, *Introduction*, p. 410.

to Amos 5:24, "'But let justice roll down like waters, and righteousness like an everflowing stream.'" To preach prophetically is far more than to exercise social criticism, be that social criticism from the right or the left. To preach prophetically is to witness to the righteousness and justice of God. Here is where preaching goes beyond social criticism and becomes worship. As we have said, the worship of the wicked beclouds God's holiness; and that is why God hated the feasts and solemn assemblies, the hymns and the sacrifices of Bethel. The sermons of Amos, on the other hand, are punctuated with hymns that make clear that these sermons are true worship because they insist on God's holiness and press the claims of God's justice and righteousness.

C. Isaiah

Now let us look at the prophecies of Isaiah.[61] With Isaiah we glimpse some other facets of the preaching of the prophets. We begin with chapter 6 where Isaiah recounts the circumstances of his receiving a prophetic oracle that he understood as central to his whole ministry. The giving of this oracle took place during the course of a sacrifice at the Temple. The eye of the prophet penetrates the inner reality of the traditional worship.[62] He sees God seated upon the ark of the covenant, enthroned upon the praises of Israel; the smoke of the sacrifice fills the heavenly sanctuary, and the coals of the altar glow in purifying fire. This was the most propitious time for an oracle. The sacrifice had been immolated, the psalms had been sung, and the prayers of the people had been offered. It was often the case that at this point in the worship one

61. Particularly important for the following study have been the commentaries of Otto Kaiser, *Isaiah 1–12*, The Old Testament Library (Philadelphia: Westminster Press, 1972); J. N. Oswalt, *The Book of Isaiah 1–39*, The New International Commentary on the Old Testament (Grand Rapids: Wm. B. Eerdmans Publishing Co., 1986); R. B. Y. Scott, "The Book of Isaiah, 1–39: Introduction and Exegesis," *Interpreter's Bible*, 5:151-381; John Skinner, *The Book of the Prophet Isaiah I–XXXIX*, Cambridge Bible for Schools and Colleges (Cambridge: University Press, 1954); George Adam Smith, *The Book of Isaiah*, 2 vols. (New York: Harper and Brothers, 1927); John D. W. Watts, *Isaiah 1–33*, Word Biblical Commentary, vol. 24 (Waco, Tex.: Word Books, 1985); Hans Wildberger, *Jesaja Kapital 1–12*, Biblischer Kommentar altes Testament, vol. X/1 (Neukirchen-Vluyn: Verlag des Erziehungsvereins, 1980).

62. R. B. Y. Scott puts it very well: "The prophet present in the temple . . . , in the intensity of his spiritual absorption *saw* the reality symbolized by its ritual and ceremonial." "The Book of Isaiah, 1–39: Introduction and Exegesis," *Interpreter's Bible*, 5:206.

of the prophet-priests of the Temple would be inspired with an oracle from God. At this particular sacrifice God gave a prophetic Word to Isaiah that made clear to him that he was called to a prophetic ministry.

It is often suggested that Isaiah was one of the priests in the Temple at Jerusalem and that he exercised his prophetic ministry and his priestly service in close connection with each other. In this case he would have been quite different from Amos. Isaiah may well have been both priest and preacher.[63] The tremendously vivid account of how Isaiah received the constituting oracle of his ministry is perhaps typical of his ministry, and it may indicate that his oracles normally had a strong connection with the worship of the sanctuary.[64] On the other hand, the record that has been preserved for us does not specifically tell us that this was the case. In fact, a number of other texts seem to want to make the point that God can give an oracle when and where and how he pleases.

This is quite clearly the case in the story of the oracle that occurs in the following chapter.[65] Isaiah must have received this oracle quite some time after the one recorded in chapter 6, for the chapter begins by telling us that it happened in the days of Ahaz, the grandson of Uzziah. Ahaz had been alarmed by the news that Rezin, king of Assyria, and Pekah, the son of the king of Israel, were planning to make war on his kingdom. The text does not tell us anything about how Isaiah received the oracle. We are only told that Isaiah was directed to go to a particular place, "'at the end of the conduit of the upper pool on the highway to the Fuller's Field'" (Isa. 7:3), and that there he was to confront the king with his oracle. We are given the text of the oracle itself. Possibly the prophet framed the oracle in a certain amount of homiletical material, for we find an admonition that has been preserved in prose: "'"Take heed, be quiet, do not fear, and do not let your heart be faint because of these two smoldering stumps of firebrands, at the fierce anger of Rezin and Syria and the son of Remaliah. Because Syria, with Ephraim and the son of Remaliah, has devised evil

---

63. It should be noted that while von Rad often speaks of Isaiah as a preacher, e.g., *Old Testament Theology*, 2:147, 151, 167, and 174, he leaves open whether Isaiah had any official position in the Temple. *Old Testament Theology*, 2:147. On the other hand, see Scott, "The Book of Isaiah, 1–39: Introduction and Exegesis," *Interpreter's Bible*, 5:162ff., 207.

64. John D. W. Watts suggests that the experience in Isaiah 6 may well be intended to indicate that all of the oracles of Isaiah originated in this kind of experience. *Isaiah 1–33*, pp. 74, 76.

65. On the nature of Isaiah's prophetic oracles, see Scott, "The Book of Isaiah, 1–39: Introduction and Exegesis," *Interpreter's Bible*, 5:154ff.

against you" ' " (7:4-5). This is then followed by a text in poetic form, which is apparently the oracle itself. It is introduced by the usual formula for introducing an oracle: "Thus says the Lord GOD."

> " 'It shall not stand,
> and it shall not come to pass.
> For the head of Syria is Damascus,
> and the head of Damascus is Rezin. . . .
> And the head of Ephraim is Samaria,
> and the head of Samaria is the son of Remaliah.
> If you will not believe,
> surely you shall not be established.' "
>
> (7:7-9)

Apparently Ahaz spurned the message of the prophet, for we read: "Again the LORD spoke to Ahaz, 'Ask a sign of the LORD your God; let it be deep as Sheol or high as heaven.' But Ahaz said, 'I will not ask, and I will not put the LORD to the test.' " Isaiah replied, " 'Hear then, O house of David! Is it too little for you to weary men, that you weary my God also? Therefore the Lord himself will give you a sign' " (7:10-14). The prophecy then goes on to speak of the birth of Immanuel. The ultimate prophetic sign is the birth of the long-promised messianic prince of the house of David.

> " 'Behold, a young woman shall conceive and bear a son, and shall call his name Immanuel. He shall eat curds and honey when he knows how to refuse the evil and choose the good. For before the child knows how to refuse the evil and choose the good, the land before whose two kings you are in dread will be deserted. The LORD will bring upon you and upon your people and upon your father's house such days as have not come since the day that Ephraim departed from Judah — the king of Assyria.' " (7:14-17)

God will be faithful to his promises in spite of Ahaz, the prince of the house of David who was so clearly not the promised one. The passage concludes in verses 18-25 with four prophecies expounding this sign, each beginning with the phrase "In that day."

To be sure, as anyone who has given time to the study of this passage by contemporary biblical scholars is aware, much attention has been given to figuring out what the original prophecy was. The passage itself tempts us to distinguish between the original oracle given to Isaiah and the homiletical expansion of that oracle either by Isaiah himself or by his prophetic interpreters of later times. Yet the passage also seems to imply that the whole thing is the Word of the Lord, even its homiletical development. While the prophet delivers a formal oracle, he delivers an interpretation of that oracle as well. Clearly the text implies that this interpretation of the original oracle has authority, too.[66]

This has tremendous implications for the nature of the ministry of the Word as it was performed by the prophets. The prophet is not merely the mouthpiece of God, who in some sort of trance utters the words of God quite apart from his own intelligence. The prophet understands the oracle; he is a witness to its truth and an advocate of its application. The faith of the prophet in the word he utters is an essential component of this ministry. Here is an important point of difference between the canonical prophets and the frenzied ecstatics of the ancient Near East. Here is the difference between Isaiah and Balaam.[67]

Another point we want to make clear here is that this prophetic word was not preached in the Temple, nor was it specifically connected with the regular worship of Israel. While there are indications in the text that Isaiah may well have been a priest who ordinarily carried out his prophetic ministry in the regular services of the Temple, we are not specifically told this. If indeed Isaiah was officially acknowledged as one of the prophets of the Temple and was already recognized to have a powerful prophetic ministry by the people, his appearance at this unusual time and place would have been all the more significant. God may have revealed this word to Isaiah in the context of the regular worship of the Temple, but again the text does not indicate this. On the other hand, the place where this word was pronounced is not irrelevant. God gave Isaiah specific instructions as to where he was to confront the king with this message. It was a particular word for a particular time and a particular place. The ministry of Isaiah was charismatic but not erratic.

In the fifth chapter of Isaiah we find what may be regarded as a prophetic sermon. It appears to be a sermon in the more usual sense of the word and may well have been a formal address given in the course of

66. Again Scott's remarks on Isaiah's oracles are helpful. "The Book of Isaiah, 1–39: Introduction and Exegesis," *Interpreter's Bible,* 5:154ff.

67. Scott puts it very well: "The ecstasy of the great prophets differed profoundly from the crude psycho-physical manifestations of the older and contemporary professional 'holy men' (cf. 1 Sam. 19:23-24; Mic. 3:5); it was the intensified spiritual perception of noble minds. This is not to say that the visions and oracles originated with these men; they themselves were sure that God had spoken to them." "The Book of Isaiah, 1–39: Introduction and Exegesis," *Interpreter's Bible,* 5:206.

a service of worship. It is an oracle or a series of oracles, addressed to the inhabitants of Jerusalem and the people of Judah, joined together with a definite homiletical intent. It has often been suggested that it was delivered at the feast of tabernacles, which was celebrated in the fall at the time of the vintage, because this sermon begins with the famous song of the vineyard:

> Let me sing for my beloved
>   a love song concerning his vineyard:
> My beloved had a vineyard
>   on a very fertile hill.
> He digged it and cleared it of stones,
>   and planted it with choice vines;
> he built a watchtower in the midst of it,
>   and hewed out a wine vat in it;
> and he looked for it to yield grapes,
>   but it yielded wild grapes.
>
>   (5:1-2)

The song of the vineyard goes on to call on the congregation to judge between the vine grower and his vineyard. What more could he do? What other alternative did he have but to root out the vines and clear the land? The song goes on to apply this parable. Judah is the vineyard of the Lord. God planted his people in the land that justice might flourish, but instead injustice became rampant.

This parable forms the introduction to the sermon, an introduction cleverly devised to win the attention of the festal assembly. The main body of the sermon is a series of indictments against the land of Judah. It unfolds as a series of woes. There is a woe against those who join house to house, who add field to field, driving out the small landholders from their patrimony in order to build large estates. There is a woe against revelry and those idle fellows who waste their time in drinking and carousing. Instead of celebrating the mighty acts of God in their feasts, they simply become inflamed with wine. Therefore they will go into exile. There is a woe against the sophists who call evil good and good evil. This series of denunciations is then brought to a close by a powerful threat of wrath: "For all this his anger is not turned away / and his hand is stretched out still" (5:25b). The sermon then concludes with a description of the approach of the troops of the enemy, the enemy who will destroy Judah, the vineyard of the Lord:

He will raise a signal for a nation afar off,
    and whistle for it from the ends of the earth;
. and lo, swiftly, speedily it comes!
None is weary, none stumbles,
    none slumbers or sleeps,
not a waistcloth is loose,
    not a sandal-thong broken;
their arrows are sharp,
    all their bows bent,
their horses' hoofs seem like flint,
    and their wheels like the whirlwind.

(5:26-28)

Some would contest the literary unity of this chapter, but there is much to be said for it nevertheless. The song of the vineyard is a skillful introduction to the denunciation that follows. The series of woes logically unfolds this charge. The theme of vineyards, grapes, and drunkenness constantly recurs in this series of woes. The conclusion then contrasts the sobriety of the approaching conqueror with the confused carousing of a fallen Israel. From a literary standpoint this sermon is a masterpiece! What a sermon outline! From the standpoint of the art of public speaking, what clever strategy! Isaiah knew how to awaken the conscience of his people. Here we see a preacher who knew how to use rhetoric with great mastery and power — all the more so if it was uttered as a prophetic oracle at the height of the sacrifice during the feast of tabernacles, the dramatic moment when the Temple prophet was expected to pronounce an oracle of blessing on the festal congregation.

Another thing about Isaiah's preaching that we should mark is that here is a prophet who knows how to inspire his congregation with the sheer beauty of his vision. In chapter 11 we seem to have another oracle that is not only pronounced but preached as well. The beauty of Isaiah's prophetic vision has inspired God's people generation after generation.

There shall come forth a shoot from the stump of Jesse,
    and a branch shall grow out of his roots.
And the Spirit of the LORD shall rest upon him,
    the spirit of wisdom and understanding,
    the spirit of counsel and might,
    the spirit of knowledge and the fear of the LORD.
And his delight shall be in the fear of the LORD.

He shall not judge by what his eyes see,
    or decide by what his ears hear;
but with righteousness he shall judge the poor,
    and decide with equity for the meek of the earth;
and he shall smite the earth with the rod of his mouth,
    and with the breath of his lips he shall slay the wicked.
Righteousness shall be the girdle of his waist,
    and faithfulness the girdle of his loins.

The wolf shall dwell with the lamb,
    and the leopard shall lie down with the kid,
and the calf and the lion and the fatling together,
    and a little child shall lead them.
The cow and the bear shall feed;
    their young shall lie down together;
    and the lion shall eat straw like the ox.
The sucking child shall play over the hole of the asp,
    and the weaned child shall put his hand on the adder's den.
They shall not hurt or destroy
    in all my holy mountain;
for the earth shall be full of the knowledge of the LORD
    as the waters cover the sea.

(11:1-9)

Isaiah's visions of the promised Messiah are extremely important from a theological standpoint, but surely one of the reasons for their importance is their ability to inspire. Their beauty lifts up our thoughts. That is the function of beauty. It is one thing for the prophet to criticize and another for him to inspire. Some who would be prophets never get much further than destructive criticism. They are thoroughly able to expose the corrupt and tear down the decadent, but they seem unable to build up something better in its place. It is here that Isaiah excels. More brilliant than his social criticism is his vision of the transcendent purposes of God. His vision of the promised Messiah and the kingdom of God that he will establish has never ceased to lift people's sights.

In the opening words of the oracle we are given a metaphor for the Davidic origins of the promised Messiah: "There shall come forth a shoot from the stump of Jesse, and a branch shall grow out of his roots." It is hard to say whether this metaphor was new to Isaiah's congregation or whether it was already a conventional term for the Messiah. By the time

66

of Jesus the shoot from the stump of Jesse was standard terminology for those who preached the messianic promise, a metaphor that was of the essence of the proclamation of the coming of the Messiah. Sometimes, at least, God's Word comes to us in metaphors and similes. We noticed this in the preaching of Moses. One great metaphor is worth ten thousand words. How often through the whole history of God's people this metaphor, the root of Jesse, has been picked up and expanded. The messianic hope was expressed in a whole host of prophetic metaphors: Root of Jesse, Rose of Sharon, Lamb of God, Star of Jacob, Prince of Peace. This formulation of metaphors is one of the basic arts of preaching.

After this opening metaphor Isaiah goes on to develop the meaning of the anointing God promised to the prince of the house of David. So many princes of the house of David had come and gone since God first gave the messianic promise. With one after another it had become clear that the promised one was yet to come. The kings of Judah again and again disappointed the messianic hope. Some preachers would have been content to call attention to the failures of the Davidic monarchy, but the word of the Lord that God gave Isaiah went beyond criticism of what was wrong and presented a vision of what it was to be the Messiah — that is, to be the Lord's anointed. "And the Spirit of the LORD shall rest upon him, the spirit of wisdom and understanding, the spirit of counsel and might, the spirit of knowledge and the fear of the LORD." The true Messiah would be a prince endowed with an abundance of spiritual and intellectual gifts. These are actually the highest of gifts, and in the end they have infinitely more power than all the sanctions and mandates of statecraft.

We notice here one of the techniques of Hebrew rhetoric. By the use of repetition and parallel constructions a sense of solemnity is conveyed. The word "spirit" is repeated four times. The first time we are told that "the Spirit of the LORD" anoints the Messiah. This declaration is unfolded with an enumeration of the spiritual gifts conferred by the Spirit of the LORD, using three parallel phrases. Each phrase mentions a different pair of spiritual gifts. From the standpoint of Hebrew rhetoric this constitutes a majestic utterance appropriate to the proclamation of a royal personage.

The description of the spiritual gifts of the Messiah is followed by a description of his moral character. The Messiah is to be distinguished by his justice, his righteousness, his equity, and his faithfulness. Again there is a rich use of metaphorical language. The high tone of this vision of the Messiah is impressive. The emphasis is clearly on the spiritual, intellectual, and moral gifts of the prince.

Isaiah continues, relating to us a vision of the kingdom over which the prince will preside. Here, too, we have a vision that has inspired the faithful with its beauty ever since it was first preached. Preachers have preached it again and again. Artists have painted it, and musicians have sung it. The peaceable kingdom Isaiah spreads out before us is impossibly naive. "The wolf shall dwell with the lamb, and the leopard shall lie down with the kid . . . and a little child shall lead them." That, of course, is part of its beauty — its utter naiveté.

Old Testament commentators tell us that those who heard this oracle preached by the prophet himself probably understood this as a restoration of the Garden of Eden: "They shall not hurt or destroy in all my holy mountain." Paradise in the ancient Near East was often thought of as a mountain. Here again we must draw attention to the strong use of metaphor. Paradise is represented as a holy mountain. Its height suggests the possibility of communion with God, contemplation of the divine, and at the same time a vista of the world below, at a distance that allows one to sense its order and harmony.

This passage is just one example of metaphorical preaching by an Old Testament prophet. The prophets preached metaphorically because metaphors allowed them to intimate what in normal language would sound ridiculous. We gather from the texts they left behind them, texts that surely echo their preaching, that the prophets were masters of metaphor.

The same thing can be said of similes.[68] The finishing touch to this picture of the peaceable kingdom is a beautiful simile: "For the earth shall be full of the knowledge of the LORD as the waters cover the sea." The beauty of a simile is that it has the power of suggestion. Isaiah has always been a favorite book of the Bible even though it recounts little in the way of stories, and even though it is long and rather complicated to untangle. Surely one of the reasons for its popularity is the sheer beauty of its visions. It is filled with word pictures. Isaiah, like the Old Testament prophets generally, abhorred the use of idols, and yet his preaching is remarkably visual. His use of words was so skillful that he let his congregation see what is essentially invisible.

---

68. Von Rad makes the point that the similes of Isaiah are characteristic of his rhetoric. *Old Testament Theology,* 2:147 n. 1.

D. Deutero-Isaiah

For several generations now Old Testament scholars have reckoned Isaiah 40–66 as the work of an unknown prophet of the exile.[69] Little is known about this hypothetical prophet. Some go on to speak not only of a Deutero-Isaiah but of a Trito-Isaiah as well. Others have suggested that these chapters are the work of an order of prophets who saw themselves as carrying on the work of Isaiah.[70] Whoever wrote or preached these chapters, they are among the most inspiring in all Scripture. Like the first thirty-nine chapters of Isaiah, these chapters contain the same exalted vision of the messianic promise. It is hard to imagine that a prophet of such importance to the shaping of Israel's faith should be completely hidden by obscurity.

With such uncertainty about the author of these chapters, one can hardly insist that he was a preacher.[71] If the lines we have in Isaiah 40–66 originally came from sermons, they must have been some of the most inspiring sermons ever preached. It is hard to say how these prophecies first originated, but two passages clearly claim that the author has been called to preach.

The first is Isaiah 40:1-11, the first of the servant songs:

Comfort, comfort my people,
    says your God.
Speak tenderly to Jerusalem,
    and cry to her
that her warfare is ended,
    that her iniquity is pardoned,
that she has received from the LORD's hand
    double for all her sins. . . .

69. Recently Old Testament scholars have recognized the need to treat the book of Isaiah in its canonical form. John D. W. Watts in the introduction to his commentary makes a most impressive argument for taking all sixty-six chapters as a literary whole. *Isaiah 1–33*, pp. xli-xliv.

70. For a good summary of this attempt to discover the historical context of Isaiah 40–66, see Childs, *Introduction*, pp. 316-38.

71. Even at that we notice that Claus Westermann constantly calls Deutero-Isaiah a preacher. *Isaiah 40–66: A Commentary*, The Old Testament Library (Philadelphia: Westminster Press, 1969), pp. 6ff. et passim. Possibly we owe the whole book of Isaiah to a group of preachers who collected these oracles with the intention of their being read as Scripture in worship in the way Lohfink suggests Deuteronomy was composed. Cf. James Muilenburg, "The Book of Isaiah, 40–66: Introduction and Exegesis," *Interpreter's Bible*, 5:386.

A voice says, "Cry!"
    And I said, "What shall I cry?"
All flesh is grass,
    and all its beauty is like the flower of the field.
The grass withers, the flower fades,
    when the breath of the LORD blows upon it;
    surely the people is grass.
The grass withers, the flower fades;
    but the word of our God will stand for ever.

Get you up to a high mountain,
    O Zion, herald of good tidings;
lift up your voice with strength,
    O Jerusalem, herald of good tidings,
    lift it up, fear not;
say to the cities of Judah,
    "Behold your God!"
Behold, the Lord GOD comes with might,
    and his arm rules for him;
behold, his reward is with him,
    and his recompense before him.

(40:1-2, 6-10)

Here the Servant of the LORD is called once more to enter upon a ministry of preaching. It is a very different message from the message given to Isaiah in chapter 6. This time the preacher is to preach good news. He is to be a herald of good tidings. He is to be a preacher of the gospel. One notices a certain ambiguity here. Is an individual Servant of the LORD called to preach or is the servant people of God called to preach? In verse 9 we read that it is Zion, Jerusalem, who is to be the herald of good tidings. Perhaps both are meant. Both the Servant of the LORD and the servant people of God are to proclaim the good news. Perhaps both preacher and congregation bear the responsibility in their worship to give witness to the Word of God. The passage tells us that the Word of God stands forever, and when God's people hear and receive that Word the salvation of God is revealed and God is glorified.[72]

The second passage, found in Isaiah 61, gives us a very high sense

---

72. Cf. Karl Elliger, *Deuterojesaja,* Biblischer Kommentar altes Testament, vol. XI/1 (Neukirchen-Vluyn: Verlag des Erziehungsvereins, 1978), pp. 27-29.

of preaching as worship. As we find in the Gospel of Luke, Jesus himself used it to speak of his own preaching ministry. Surely it should be studied as a major passage on the nature of preaching.

> The Spirit of the Lord God is upon me,
>   because the Lord has anointed me
> to bring good tidings to the afflicted;
>   he has sent me to bind up the brokenhearted,
> to proclaim liberty to the captives,
>   and the opening of the prison to those who are bound;
> to proclaim the year of the Lord's favor,
>   and the day of vengeance of our God;
>   to comfort all who mourn;
> to grant to those who mourn in Zion —
>   to give them a garland instead of ashes,
> the oil of gladness instead of mourning,
>   the mantle of praise instead of a faint spirit;
> that they may be called oaks of righteousness,
>   the planting of the Lord, that he may be glorified.
> They shall build up the ancient ruins,
>   they shall raise up the former devastations;
> they shall repair the ruined cities,
>   the devastations of many generations.
>
> (61:1-4)

Several things should be noticed about this passage. In the first place, it speaks of the messianic ministry of preaching. Exercising the ministry of the Word is of the essence of being the Lord's anointed.[73] The text is very specific about this. The anointed one has been anointed to preach the good news. Central to the messianic ministry is the proclamation of the gospel. Even if one is hesitant to claim that this was indeed a messianic prophecy or that Jesus fulfilled this prophecy, what the passage says about the messianic office and the place of preaching in that office is as clear as can be. When the Messiah comes, whoever he might be, he will proclaim a message of deliverance and redemption. He will be a preacher, and a preacher of good news.

73. We find throughout these chapters a very basic assumption that God reveals himself through his Word. James Muilenburg points out that Deutero-Isaiah is rich in its vocabulary of revelation. There are a great number of words for speaking and hearing. It is through proclaiming, announcing, declaring, foretelling, and predicting that God reveals himself. "The Book of Isaiah, 40–66: Introduction and Exegesis," *Interpreter's Bible*, 5:404.

The usual commentary on this passage gives first attention to the content of this proclamation.[74] The text tells us that messianic preaching is to be a message of hope, assurance, and healing. Prominent in the text is the word "proclaim," a word used to speak of the announcement of a herald, especially the herald of a prince, or the announcement of an official decree or edict from the sovereign.[75] In the New Testament this word will become increasingly prominent when speaking of Christian preaching. The use of this word "proclaim" implies a positive message. Prophetic preaching was not always a matter of threatening doom, even though in the Old Testament so much of the message of the prophets concerned the consequences of Israel's sin, especially the coming of military defeat at the hands of Assyria, the destruction of Jerusalem, and the exile in Babylon. All of these prophets, at least in their canonical form, had positive messages as well, but in Isaiah 61 we have the prototype of a prophetic gospel. Here the Word of God is a liberating Word, a constructive Word, a word of promise and a word of comfort.

We have already spoken of the high literary refinement of the preaching of the prophets. Isaiah and especially Deutero-Isaiah bring this to a pinnacle of perfection. The proclamation of the gospel as we find it in Deutero-Isaiah is done in the most beautiful rhetoric.[76] A great variety of rhetorical devices is used, but above all these oracles or sermons, if indeed they are sermons, are poetry. They are a lyrical sort of poetry that delights in the Word of God. The beauty of Isaiah's word is a witness to the sacredness of his message. It is an intimation that what he says is indeed the Word of the Holy One of Israel.

The preaching found in Deutero-Isaiah gives us yet another insight into how prophetic preaching can be worship. The messianic preaching

---

74. For commentaries on Isaiah 40–66, cf. James Muilenburg, "The Book of Isaiah, ch. 40–66: Introduction and Exegesis," in the *Interpreter's Bible*, 5:708ff.; John Skinner, *The Book of the Prophet Isaiah XL–LXVI*, Cambridge Bible for Schools and Colleges (Cambridge: University Press, 1954), pp. 203-9; Smith, *The Book of Isaiah*, 2:472-79; John D. W. Watts, *Isaiah 34–66*, Word Biblical Commentary, vol. 25 (Waco, Tex.: Word Books, 1987), pp. 302-5; Westermann, *Isaiah 40–66*, pp. 364-67.

75. Cf. Muilenburg, "The Book of Isaiah, 40–66: Introduction and Exegesis," *Interpreter's Bible*, 5:708ff.

76. Muilenburg gives us a most perceptive study of the art of rhetoric as it is found in Deutero-Isaiah."The Book of Isaiah, 40–66: Introduction and Exegesis," *Interpreter's Bible*, 5:386-92.

of the gospel of redemption to the exiles in Babylon was worship because it proclaimed God's faithfulness to his people. It revealed the goodness, the patience, and the love of God. When preaching witnesses to God's faithfulness, then it serves God's glory. Even further, when the Word of God comforts his people, when it opens the eyes of the blind and makes the prisoner free, then God is truly glorified.

When the people of God live in peace and justice, then the glory of God is manifested in the world. "They may be called oaks of righteousness, / the planting of the LORD, that he may be glorified" (61:3). If God's planting prospers, then God is magnified. We found this theme in Isaiah 5, where the planting of the LORD was a vineyard. Here the theme has become even richer. The prosperity of God's people praises God. When God's people wear the mantle of praise and their faces shine with the oil of gladness, then God is glorified. God is honored by nothing quite so much as the righteousness of his people. There is nothing Donatist or Pelagian about this at all. When God's people proclaim his Word, listen to his Word, and live by his Word, then the glory of God is served most eloquently.

The universalism of Deutero-Isaiah is often mentioned. God is recognized not only as the God of Israel but as the God of all peoples. Not only the Jews but all nations will eventually come to worship the one true God. Just as in certain of the psalms, we find in the prophecies of the final chapters of Isaiah the expectation that eventually even the heathen will recognize the sovereignty of God. In chapter 60 we read: "And nations shall come to your light, / and kings to the brightness of your rising" (60:3). Then at the end of chapter 61 we find these words: "So the Lord GOD will cause righteousness and praise / to spring forth before all the nations" (61:11). When Israel recognizes God's sovereignty, then God is worshiped by his people; but when all nations come to recognize God's sovereignty, then the worship of God is universal. The praise of God is universal in extent, just as it is eternal in duration. The prophetic doxology, as I have written elsewhere, leads us inevitably to a kerygmatic doxology.[77] Through evangelism, the claim of God's rule over all peoples is proclaimed. Evangelism is worship because it witnesses to God's universal sovereignty.

---

77. See my work *Themes and Variations for a Christian Doxology* (Grand Rapids: Wm. B. Eerdmans Publishing Co., 1992).

E. Jeremiah

Jeremiah, like Isaiah, is to be reckoned among the greatest of the preaching prophets. He, too, may have been a priest who had a preaching ministry.[78] Both these prophets had long public ministries in which they often presented to the people the oracles they had received from God in sermons of a more or less formal nature. Jeremiah, along with Amos, Micah, Isaiah, and others, belongs to the literary prophets, and yet these prophets exercised a ministry of public preaching. Prophecy had not become primarily literary. Jeremiah's oracles were committed to literary form because at a certain time in his ministry he was denied the pulpit. He was forced into writing.[79] No doubt Jeremiah considered himself a preacher rather than a writer.

The question we have at this point is where and in what sort of setting did Jeremiah exercise his ministry of preaching? Was it a matter of preaching only on unusual occasions, as with Elijah and Amos, or was there some regular time and place in the life of Israel when preaching normally took place? The sermons and sermonic material that have come down to us from this period are of very high quality and indicate a rather sophisticated preaching culture, the sort of preaching culture that develops only when there is a great deal of preaching going on. Where was this preaching done? We have a certain amount of biographical information concerning Jeremiah — considerably more, at least, than we have for Isaiah. With Jeremiah we are able to put together certain hypotheses,

---

78. To what extent Jeremiah's preaching ministry may have been recognized by the priesthood in Jerusalem is not known. While the older scholarship tended to regard priesthood and prophecy as contending ministries, more recent scholarship has tended to see them as complementary. Cf. Kraus, *Gottesdienst in Israel*, pp. 122-33. Kraus makes a strong case for a prophetic element in the worship of the Temple. On the other hand, Rowley, *Worship in Ancient Israel*, pp. 153ff. and 159ff., is not convinced, and de Vaux, *Ancient Israel*, 2:384-86, is even less so. Kraus, building on his study of the psalms, argues that a charismatic or prophetic ministry was recognized in the worship of the Temple. The traditions of the Temple included a place for a prophet like Jeremiah to exercise his ministry in the context of the liturgy of the Temple. The fact that Jeremiah was of priestly lineage could only be regarded as strengthening his reputation for having genuine charismatic gifts.

79. On the rather complicated subject of how the Jeremiah traditions were committed to writing see Bright, *Jeremiah*, pp. 55-85; and J. A. Thompson, *The Book of Jeremiah*, The New International Commentary on the Old Testament (Grand Rapids: Wm. B. Eerdmans Publishing Co., 1980), pp. 33-50. See further Sigmund Mowinckel, *Preaching and Tradition* (Oslo: I kommisjon hos J. Dybwod, 1946); and E. W. Nicholson, *Preaching to the Exiles* (Oxford: B. Blackwell, 1970).

certain educated guesses, as to where preaching regularly took place in the religious life of Israel.

One suggestion I would like to make is that it was a regular practice to have preaching at the Temple gates before the worshipers entered for Sabbaths and feasts. A number of Old Testament scholars who have given special attention to the psalms have pointed out that several psalms give us some good hints about how a typical Temple service began.[80] The most obvious example is Psalm 24, which apparently contains parts of an entrance liturgy:

> The earth is the LORD's and the fulness thereof,
>   the world and those who dwell therein;
> for he has founded it upon the seas,
>   and established it upon the rivers.
>
> Who shall ascend the hill of the LORD?
>   And who shall stand in his holy place?
> He who has clean hands and a pure heart,
>   who does not lift up his soul to what is false,
>   and does not swear deceitfully.
> He will receive blessing from the LORD,
>   and vindication from the God of his salvation.
> Such is the generation of those who seek him,
>   who seek the face of the God of Jacob.
>
> Lift up your heads, O gates!
>   and be lifted up, O ancient doors!
>   that the King of glory may come in.
> Who is the King of glory?
>   The LORD, strong and mighty,
>   the LORD, mighty in battle!
> Lift up your heads, O gates!
>   and be lifted up, O ancient doors!
>   that the King of glory may come in.
> Who is this King of glory?
>   The LORD of hosts,
>   he is the King of glory!

---

80. Mowinckel, *The Psalms in Israel's Worship*, 1:177ff.; Hans-Joachim Kraus, *Psalmen*, 2 vols. (Neukirchen-Vluyn: Neukirchener Verlag, 1961), 1:194ff. See especially the same author's reconstruction of a service of worship in the Temple, in *Gottesdienst in Israel*, pp. 242-57.

From this psalm it would appear that one approached the Temple gates with hymns of praise. Upon arriving there, one would go through a time of repentance. The question is asked, "Who shall ascend the hill of the LORD? And who shall stand in his holy place?" The answer is given, "He who has clean hands and a pure heart. . . ." While in the psalm this penitential portion of the service is given in very compact form, just as the hymn of praise is given in an equally compact form, we can well imagine that in actual fact the penitential rites that Israelites were expected to perform before entering the Temple took more time. At what more appropriate time and place could a prophet or priest instruct worshipers on how one should approach God? Clues given in the psalm suggest that a penitential sermon was part of the entrance liturgy of the Temple. Perhaps this was done every Sabbath, perhaps only at the major feasts.

It was on such an occasion, I would like to suggest, that Jeremiah preached his famous Temple sermon.[81] As this sermon is reported in chapter 7, God sent Jeremiah to preach a particular message to the people of Israel on that particular occasion.

> The word that came to Jeremiah from the LORD: "Stand in the gate of the LORD's house, and proclaim there this word, and say, Hear the word of the LORD, all you men of Judah who enter these gates to worship the LORD. Thus says the LORD of hosts, the God of Israel, Amend your ways and your doings, and I will let you dwell in this place." (Jer. 7:1-3)

It is possible that Jeremiah was the prophet who in the course of things was appointed to preach the regular penitential sermon at the opening of the gates that particular Sabbath or feast day. Jeremiah had a strong sense of providence. But however regular or irregular it may have been that Jeremiah should preach on that occasion, God spoke to Jeremiah, sent him there, and gave him a particular message, a message that was quite irregular — namely, that if the men of Judah did not repent in earnest, the Temple itself would be destroyed. The holiness and inviolability of the Temple was an article of faith to the Israelites. The word God gave Jeremiah to preach at that central moment in the worship of the community was

---

81. Two versions of this sermon appear in Jeremiah, one in chapter 7, the other in chapter 26. For various attempts to reconstruct the sermon, see Bright, *Jeremiah*, pp. 52-59; Robert P. Carroll, *Jeremiah* (Sheffield: JSOT Press, 1989); Wilhelm Rudolph, *Jeremia*, Handbuch zum alten Testament (Tübingen: J. C. B. Mohr [Paul Siebeck], 1958), pp. 47-50; and Thompson, *The Book of Jeremiah*, pp. 271-96.

no doubt received as verging on heresy.[82] Its shock effect would only be heightened if, as I have suggested, the penitential sermon at the opening of the gates was an important occasion and was normally filled with an able preacher.

One can hardly help but notice the way the Hebrew word דבר is used in these three verses. It refers first to the Word revealed to Jeremiah and then to the Word Jeremiah preached to his congregation. Thus the Word of God can be spoken of as the revealed Word and as the preached Word, suggesting that there are different moments in revelation.

Going along with our hypothesis a bit further, we note that the sermon contains some very traditional material. We have noticed in Psalm 24 that after the opening hymn of praise there is a call to self-examination and repentance. It may well have been traditional in these penitential sermons at the gates of the Temple to have instructed the people in the Law and in the nature of true purity, to have fleshed out what it means to have "clean hands and a pure heart" (Ps. 24:4). In Jeremiah's sermon a number of provisions of the Law are mentioned specifically: "'Will you steal, murder, commit adultery, swear falsely . . . ?'" (Jer. 7:9). This sermon could even be spoken of as a sermon on the Ten Commandments; and it could very well be that it was a regular tradition to preach on the Ten Commandments before entering worship. Perhaps it was here, on entering the Temple, that the priests were supposed to instruct the people in the Law. Down through the history of worship, more than one liturgical tradition has found this appropriate.

Like several of the prophetic oracles of Amos and Isaiah, this oracle is presented in sermonic form. It is a call for repentance addressed to a particular congregation.

> "For if you truly amend your ways and your doings, if you truly execute justice one with another, if you do not oppress the alien, the fatherless or the widow, or shed innocent blood in this place, and if you do not go after other gods to your own hurt, then I will let you dwell in this place, in the land that I gave of old to your fathers for ever." (7:5-7)

There is even what might be called a sermon illustration. The preacher reminds his congregation of the sanctuary at Shiloh and how Shiloh

---

82. What Jeremiah had to say was only the logical implication of his deep understanding of worship. Cf. Thompson's magnificent paragraph on the theology of worship, *The Book of Jeremiah*, p. 275.

came to ruin because of the wickedness of Israel. That is what will happen to the Temple in Jerusalem, the preacher warns, if the people continue in their sin. Here we find a sermon in all its essential features. It is a prophetic oracle to be sure, but a prophetic oracle delivered as a sermon.

In addition to the opening of the Temple gates, there is a second point in the Temple service at which prophets might have exercised their preaching ministry — namely, at the conclusion of a sacrifice. In chapter 14 we find a set of prayers meant to accompany the sacrifice for a fast day.[83] The fast day had apparently been called during a drought. The chapter begins with a psalm of lamentation that cries before God about the drought:

> "Judah mourns
>   and her gates languish;
> her people lament on the ground,
>   and the cry of Jerusalem goes up.
> Her nobles send their servants for water;
>   they come to the cisterns,
> they find no water,
>   they return with their vessels empty;
> they are ashamed and confounded
>   and cover their heads.
> Because of the ground which is dismayed,
>   since there is no rain on the land,
> the farmers are ashamed,
>   they cover their heads.
> Even the hind in the field forsakes her newborn calf
>   because there is no grass.
> The wild asses stand on the bare heights,
>   they pant for air like jackals;
> their eyes fail
>   because there is no herbage."

(14:2-6)

---

83. Mowinckel pointed out the possibility of a liturgical origin of these lines. *The Psalms in Israel's Worship,* 1:28 and 197. Cf. also J. Begrich, "Die priesterliche Tora," *Beihefte zum Zeitschrift für die alttestamentliche Wissenschaft* 66 (1936): 81 ff.; Bright, *Jeremiah,* pp. 102 ff.; and Thompson, *The Book of Jeremiah,* pp. 377-81.

This lamentation is followed by a prayer of confession of sin and supplication for mercy.

> "Though our iniquities testify against us,
>   act, O LORD, for thy name's sake;
> for our backslidings are many,
>   we have sinned against thee.
> O thou hope of Israel,
>   its savior in time of trouble,
> why shouldst thou be like a stranger in the land,
>   like a wayfarer who turns aside to tarry for a night?
> Why shouldst thou be like a man confused,
>   like a mighty man who cannot save?
> Yet thou, O LORD, art in the midst of us,
>   and we are called by thy name;
>   leave us not."
>
> (14:7-9)

These two elements follow the pattern of several psalms of lamentation that have come down to us in the canonical book of Psalms.[84] Contemporary Old Testament scholars claim that this was the customary liturgical order for the prayers that would have accompanied the sacrifices of a fast day. It was expected or hoped that a prophet or priest would be inspired at this point to deliver an oracle announcing God's acceptance of the prayer. In the particular liturgy that unrolls before us, it was Jeremiah who was inspired to deliver the oracle. But the word God gave to Jeremiah was not an assurance of pardon; it was rather an assurance of judgment.

> Thus says the LORD concerning this people:
> "They have loved to wander thus,
>   they have not restrained their feet;
> therefore the LORD does not accept them,
>   now he will remember their iniquity
>   and punish their sins."
>
> (14:10)

Here, I suggest, was the liturgy in its simplest form. The oracle is straightforward and short, but perhaps on this occasion or on similar occasions

---

84. On prayers of lamentation and confession, see Mowinckel, *The Psalms in Israel's Worship*, 1:193-224 and 2:1-25.

the prophet might have elaborated the oracle with the same sort of homiletical features we found in the Temple sermon.

The remainder of the chapter and the beginning of the following chapter contain quite a bit of homiletical material. Verses 11 and 12 give an explanation of the oracle: God had told Jeremiah that he would pay no attention to their fasts. Verses 13-16 explain why other prophets had assured the congregation that God would come to their rescue, but now Jeremiah had delivered an oracle contradicting the other prophets. It is quite understandable that a prophetic oracle such as the one we have in verse 10 would demand some sort of explanation or prompt some sort of exhortation. Some have explained this homiletical material following the oracle as the work of disciples of the prophet who preached the Jeremiah traditions during the exile. At any rate, in these verses we see a sermon being used to expand the highly condensed material delivered in an oracle that was given in the Temple ministry of a prophet who was perhaps also a priest.[85]

There is no reason why the preaching ministry should have been confined to the entrance liturgy. In fact, I would suggest that it was often exercised at the very height of the liturgical action.[86] There are those who like to think that preaching is not worship so much as preparation for worship; the preachers of the Anglican High Church movement in the nineteenth century — among them John Henry Newman, for example — saw things this way. Jeremiah would certainly have disagreed with this view. The prophetic oracle occasioned by the sacrifices was not ordinarily expected to be read from the prayer book, so to speak. In fact, if any part of the liturgy was left to the inspiration of the moment it was this. That is why a number of psalms give the lamentation and the supplication, leave out the oracle, and then conclude with a thanksgiving for the hearing of the prayers.[87] The other parts of the liturgy could use long-established liturgical texts, but it was always hoped that God would indeed give

---

85. When Josiah suppressed the sanctuaries in outlying cities and towns, he brought their priests to Jerusalem and gave them a place in the Temple ministry. John Bright, *A History of Israel* (Philadelphia: Westminster Press, 1976), p. 318. This may explain how Jeremiah, a priest of Anathoth, had priestly stature in Jerusalem.

86. Cf. Kraus, *Gottesdienst in Israel*, pp. 242-54; and Mowinckel, *The Psalms in Israel's Worship*, 2:58ff.

87. Mowinckel particularly makes this point. *The Psalms in Israel's Worship*, 1:219 and 2:58. For psalms that have a lamentation and a thanksgiving but have left out the prophetic oracle, see Psalms 6; 28; 31; and 62.

through the ministry of a prophet a particular word of blessing, specifically suited to the needs of the time. That was what happened here; lamentably, however, it was not the message the congregation wanted to hear.

Finally, it seems highly likely that there was regular teaching in the courts of the Temple on a day-to-day basis. In New Testament times, after the morning sacrifices were finished, it was a regular practice for the rabbis to teach any who might want to stay around and listen. We hear of Jesus doing this, and it apparently was an old custom that may have gone far back into antiquity. There is some very good evidence that already in the days of Jeremiah this was a well-established practice. It was evidently in the courts of the Temple that Jeremiah appeared wearing the yoke God commanded him to bear (Jeremiah 27–28). It was there also that Hananiah, the prophet from Gibeon, proclaimed his oracle and broke the yoke of Jeremiah (28:2-4, 10). Surely the courts of the Temple would have been an appropriate place for a forum of religious discussion, for that was where one could count on finding people who were interested in hearing the Word of the Lord. Amos was surely not the first or the last to have thought of that. Surely it was not only the prophets who preached there. It was the logical place for the priests to have taught the Law. That was where those who were interested in things religious would be most apt to gather.

Of interest in this regard is the story of Jeremiah sending Baruch to the Temple to read a scroll containing all the words of the LORD that God had spoken to him (Jer. 36:1-10).[88] The reason given is that Jeremiah himself had been debarred from going to the Temple. We might take this to imply that it was at the Temple that Jeremiah ordinarily taught. Just how formal or informal this teaching may have been we hesitate to say.[89] Obviously many of the oracles of Jeremiah were not given in the Temple; but if it had not been Jeremiah's usual practice to teach in the Temple, why was he debarred specifically from going there? We note from the text that Jeremiah sent Baruch to read his prophecies "on a fast day in the hearing of all the people" (36:6), presumably because a large congregation would usually be present on such an occasion. It might also be the case that such an occasion would include readings from the Law in the regular

---

88. See John Bright's comments on this passage, in *Jeremiah*, pp. 181-83.

89. Even today there are still places in cities where voluntary speakers take it upon themselves to address anyone who might care to listen. No one organizes such speeches or draws up a schedule.

course of the service and perhaps even teaching on the Law. If that was indeed so, the reading of Jeremiah's prophecies from a scroll might have fit very well into the accustomed procedures of the liturgy of the fast day. We have already spoken of this possibility in relation to the festal celebrations at the sanctuary of Shiloh.

We should note that it was not very long before this time that the scroll of Deuteronomy was rediscovered in the Temple, contributing to an important revival during the reign of Josiah. A good number of passages in Deuteronomy would have been appropriate for public reading at a fast day assembly. The public reading and preaching of such Scriptures could very logically have fit into such an occasion. Those who came to the Temple to pray at the time of a national catastrophe quite naturally sought an understanding of what had befallen them, and the reading and preaching of the Scriptures would have ministered to that need.[90]

Our word-weary generation sometimes forgets how our grandparents before the days of telecommunications considered it a great privilege to go into town to attend a public meeting at which someone would give a public address. One of the features of the Chautauqua movement was preaching, teaching, and lecturing all day long. Especially for people who lived in the country, public speaking would draw a crowd just as much as a concert or a sports event. At a feast day or a fast day in Jeremiah's time, good speakers who could be expected to hold forth on subjects of current interest would draw large crowds. In an oral culture public addresses would be even more important. Any national emergency that would call for a fast would call for discussion as well.

Whatever might have been the customary procedure, Baruch's reading of the collected prophecies of Jeremiah surely established a precedent that would make the reading of the prophets a feature of worship in centuries to come. If Josiah's public reading of the rediscovered book of the Law is one of our first records of such reading of the Law in the worship of the Temple (II Kings 23:2), then Baruch's reading of the scroll of Jeremiah's oracles may be regarded as one of the oldest records we have of the public reading of the prophets.

One noticeable aspect of the sermons of Jeremiah is how often they

90. On the role of the rediscovery of the book of the Law in the reform of King Josiah, see H. B. MacLean, "Josiah," *Interpreter's Dictionary of the Bible*, 2:996-99; and Bright, *A History of Israel*, pp. 316-23.

are sealed with a sign.[91] Other prophets had done the same thing, but the signs we find in Jeremiah are particularly clear. Perhaps this is because the book of Jeremiah has come down to us with more biographical material than most of the other prophets. His prophecies are often put in their historical setting.

One of the clearest examples of a prophetic sign is found in chapter 19, where God tells Jeremiah to buy a potter's earthen flask and to take some of the elders and the priests and go out to the Valley of Hinnom. God gives Jeremiah a rather lengthy word to preach to those representatives of the people. The kings of Judah and the inhabitants of Jerusalem have abused God's patience too long. Too long they have sacrificed to other gods in this spot. They have openly committed idolatry, burning incense to gods unknown to their fathers. They have built high places to Baal and sacrificed their sons on his altars, something completely contrary to God's commands. Therefore God was about to abandon his people. He was giving them up to the sword of their enemies. After proclaiming these words Jeremiah was commanded to smash the potter's vessel in the sight of those he had brought with him. To accompany this action he was given this word: " ' "Thus says the LORD of hosts: So will I break this people and this city, as one breaks a potter's vessel, so that it can never be mended" ' " (19:11). Both the word and the sign were specifically given by God to Jeremiah. The sign was not some clever illustrative gesture thought up by Jeremiah to help him make his point; rather, like the fire that descended from heaven to consume Elijah's sacrifice on the top of Mount Carmel, it was a divinely given sign that confirmed the message of the prophet.

In chapter 27 we find another prophetic sign. In this case God tells Jeremiah to take a yoke, the sort of yoke used to hitch an ox to a cart, and to put it around his own neck. He was then to go out and announce that God had given the rulership to Nebuchadnezzar; if the king of Judah and his people would bring their necks under the yoke of the king of Babylon it would go well with them, but if they would not they would perish. Jeremiah did as God had directed him. He appeared in the courts of the Temple with the yoke about his neck, and there he delivered his message just as God had directed him. The false prophet Hananiah, understanding full well the importance of a prophetic sign, uttered a

---

91. On the subject of prophetic signs, see G. Fohrer, *Die symbolischen Handlungen der Propheten* (Zurich, 1953); von Rad, *Old Testament Theology*, 2:95-98; and K. H. Rengstorf, "σημεῖον," *Theological Dictionary of the New Testament*, 7:217ff.

counter oracle and took the yoke off Jeremiah's neck and broke it. Hananiah claimed that God had revealed to him that the yoke of Nebuchadnezzar would be broken off the necks of the subject peoples and that within two years all the vessels of the house of the LORD would be returned to Jerusalem. Jeremiah's only reply was that history would show who was right — as indeed it did.

Another prophetic sign is found in chapter 32. This is a sign of restoration, like the sign of the rainbow after the flood. God tells Jeremiah that before long some of his relatives from Anathoth will come to him and offer to sell him a field that apparently was part of the family patrimony. Jeremiah had a right to the property. It had to be offered to him before it could be offered to anyone outside of the family, but if he wanted to keep it within the family he would have to buy it. One can well imagine that with the Babylonian invasion real estate prices had tumbled. No one in his right mind was buying real estate. Cash was no doubt in short supply. Those who had cash had fled or were fleeing. But God told Jeremiah to buy the property as a sign that the time would finally come when God's people would be reestablished in their own land. This sign has always interested me because it is so persuasive. There is nothing miraculous about it; it was simple good business sense. A wise man puts his money in something that he feels has a future. To use a popular expression, Jeremiah put his money where his mouth was, and that was surely convincing.

What is important to notice in these prophetic signs is the way they are related to the word given by God. They do more than simply illustrate the word; they confirm and seal the word. Furthermore, there is a clear analogy between the way these prophetic signs sometimes signed and sealed the message of the prophets and the way the New Testament sacraments sign and seal the preaching of the gospel.

III. The Ministry of the Word as Understood by the Wisdom School

It is only in the last few decades that the distinct insights of the Wisdom school have gotten the attention of biblical scholars.[92] The Wisdom school

92. Among the more important works that have contributed to this recovery are James L. Crenshaw, *Studies in Ancient Israelite Wisdom* (New York: KTAV Publishing

claimed Solomon as its founder. Surely the claim is not without foundations. Large portions of the material must go back at least to Solomon, and some of it may be even older. Just how far back in the history of Israel its roots can be traced has been debated for years.

A text from the book of Jeremiah indicates that already in preexilic days it was possible to speak of a threefold spiritual leadership in Israel, a leadership that had existed for a long time and would continue to exist for a long time: " 'for the law shall not perish from the priest, nor counsel from the wise, nor the word from the prophet' " (Jer. 18:18). In preexilic days the term "the wise" may have designated royal counselors who advised the king or perhaps the elders who sat at the gate. The wise along with the priest and the prophet had a distinct contribution to the ministry of the Word. A passage in Proverbs (25:1) claims that it was "the men of Hezekiah king of Judah" who collected the proverbs of Solomon. Presumably they were men versed in sacred tradition as well as the affairs of state.

Just as certain books of Scripture come to us from the priestly tradition and others from the prophetic tradition, so several biblical books come to us from the Wisdom tradition. Such Wisdom books as Proverbs and Job seem to have taken canonical form in the fourth and fifth centuries before Christ. Others, including several that were never taken into the canon, appeared as late as the second century before Christ. The Wisdom school flowered later than did the priestly or prophetic schools, or at least it is only from a later period that we are able to get a clear picture of how it functioned. It is often suggested that the Wisdom literature was the product of the school rather than the Temple or even the synagogue, yet a number of psalms seem to have been produced by the Wisdom writers. The schools were closely connected with both Temple and synagogue, however, for in those days there was little distinction between sacred knowledge and secular knowledge. It is really in the postexilic period that the Wisdom school began to have its greatest influence.

House, 1976); Jean Daniélou, *Origène* (Paris: La table ronde, 1948); Jean Leclercq, *The Love of Learning and the Desire for God: A Study of Monastic Culture*, trans. Catharine Misrahi (New York: Fordham University Press, 1961); Pierre Nautin, *Origène, sa vie et son oeuvre* (Paris: Beauchesne, 1977); *Odes of Solomon*, ed. and trans. James H. Charlesworth (Chico, Calif.: Scholars Press, 1977); Gerhard von Rad, *Wisdom in Israel*, trans. James D. Morton (Nashville: Abingdon Press, 1972); O. S. Rankin, *Israel's Wisdom Literature* (Edinburgh: T. & T. Clark, 1936); and Robert B. Y. Scott, *The Way of Wisdom in the Old Testament* (New York: Collier Books, 1986).

Even if Solomon was the prototype of the school, Jesus ben Sirach was its best example.[93] Ben Sirach was a devout man, although he was neither priest nor prophet. He was a teacher in the schools rather than a specifically religious functionary. In his writings Jesus ben Sirach gives us an idealized portrait of the ministry of the wise man. The wise man is above all a biblical scholar:

> On the other hand he who devotes himself
>   to the study of the law of the Most High
> will seek out the wisdom of all the ancients,
>   and will be concerned with prophecies;
> he will preserve the discourse of notable men
>   and penetrate the subtleties of parables;
> he will seek out the hidden meanings of proverbs
>   and be at home with the obscurities of parables.
> He will serve among great men
>   and appear before rulers;
> he will travel through the lands of foreign nations,
>   for he tests the good and the evil among men.
> He will set his heart to rise early
>   to seek the Lord who made him,
>   and will make supplication before the Most High;
> he will open his mouth in prayer
>   and make supplication for his sins.
>
> If the great Lord is willing,
>   he will be filled with the spirit of understanding;
> he will pour forth words of wisdom
>   and give thanks to the Lord in prayer.
> He will direct his counsel and knowledge aright,
>   and meditate on his secrets.
> He will reveal instruction in his teaching,
>   and will glory in the law of the Lord's covenant.
>
> (Sir. 39:1-8)

The biblical scholar in this portrait devotes himself not only to the teachings of the wise men of antiquity but perhaps even more to the study of the Law and the prophets. He is concerned with the memorization of

---

93. For a study of Jesus ben Sirach, see von Rad, *Wisdom in Israel,* pp. 240-62.

Scripture, its preservation, the copying of its manuscripts, and its interpretation. He may well be a civil servant. He has traveled abroad and studied the philosophies and religions of other lands and peoples. Yet this biblical scholar is a man of prayer who participates in the worship of both synagogue and Temple. He takes his turn preaching in the synagogue and may even be a teacher in the schools. By the grace of God he has been given the gift of understanding, but above all he is one who loves the Law of the LORD. All that Sirach says is perhaps best summed up in a line from Psalm 1: "His delight is in the law of the LORD, / and on his law he meditates day and night" (v. 2).

In the earlier days, as we have said, when Solomon's Temple still stood, the priests had a ministry of the Word that to a large extent was concerned with the preservation of an oral tradition, although surely much had already been committed to writing. Similarly, the prophets were concerned with uttering the oracles of God in a living voice. In Sirach's time those who were entrusted with the ministry of the Word were much more concerned with the written Word — that is, with sacred Scripture. The Word had become the written Word. Memorizing the sacred text, copying the scrolls, and interpretation of a primarily written Word came to have increasing importance. The ministry of the scribe came to be more and more appreciated. That Ezra, for example, one of the leaders of the Jewish community in the days of the exile, understood himself as a scribe became emblematic of a new situation. The very word "scribe" implies one whose primary attention is to a written word. A scribe is one who passes on a written tradition. Study inevitably became an important aspect of piety.

Among these scribes, these biblical scholars, love for the Word of God became a brilliant facet of love for God. It was manifested in a fascination with every detail of Scripture and its meaning. This scholarly service of the Word — memorizing it, copying it, understanding it, interpreting it, and teaching it — was a form of worship. Delighting in the Scriptures was praise in the same way that the psalmists delighted in Zion and exulted in the service of the Temple. In fact, several of the psalms express this scholarly worship. That the very study of Scripture is worship is made clear, for example, in Psalm 19:

> The law of the LORD is perfect,
> reviving the soul;
> the testimony of the LORD is sure,
> making wise the simple;

the precepts of the LORD are right,
    rejoicing the heart;
the commandment of the LORD is pure,
    enlightening the eyes;
the fear of the LORD is clean,
    enduring for ever;
the ordinances of the LORD are true,
    and righteous altogether.
More to be desired are they than gold,
    even much fine gold;
sweeter also than honey
    and drippings of the honeycomb. . . .
Let the words of my mouth and the meditation of my heart
    be acceptable in thy sight,
    O LORD, my rock and my redeemer.

(vv. 7-10, 14)

When we read and study the Law, the words of our mouths and the meditations of our hearts are worship at its most essential. We find the same thing in Psalm 119:

I will praise thee with an upright heart,
    when I learn thy righteous ordinances.

(v. 7)

With my lips I declare
    all the ordinances of thy mouth.

(v. 13)

Seven times a day I praise thee
    for thy righteous ordinances.

(v. 164)

If there were those who could pray, "How lovely is thy dwelling place, / O LORD of hosts!" (Ps. 84:1), then there were also those who could pray, "Open my eyes, that I may behold / wondrous things out of thy law" (119:18).

Much more may be said about the sheer love of Scripture that developed among biblical scholars of the centuries before the coming of Christ. Already in the book of Proverbs one finds that wisdom invites the love of the devout. The Wisdom school developed this line of thought profoundly. Sacred wisdom, whether revealed in creation or in the Law, became a wondrous object of contemplation to the faithful Jew. Again, Psalm 19 witnesses eloquently to this. Gerhard von Rad has helped us understand this sapiential theology as producing a piety that was both moral and literate. More and more the biblical scholar understood his work as a faithful response to the call of wisdom to forsake foolishness and devote himself to sacred learning.

The book of Proverbs unfolds at some length the piety of the Wisdom school. It opens with a short poem on the ideals of the teaching of wisdom:

That men may know wisdom and instruction,
    understand words of insight,
receive instruction in wise dealing,
    righteousness, justice, and equity;
that prudence may be given to the simple,
    knowledge and discretion to the youth —
the wise man also may hear and increase in learning,
    and the man of understanding acquire skill,
to understand a proverb and a figure,
    the words of the wise and their riddles.

The fear of the LORD is the beginning of knowledge;
    fools despise wisdom and instruction.

(Prov. 1:2-7)

The teaching that this school intends to impart is sacred wisdom.[94] The foundation for such wisdom is the fear of the LORD, as we are told here and in a number of other Wisdom texts. "The fear of the LORD" is a biblical idiom for reverence. What this often repeated phrase would teach is that the practice of piety is the way to wisdom. The best-known statement of this proverb comes a little further on in the book:

The fear of the LORD is the beginning of wisdom,
    and the knowledge of the Holy One is insight.

(9:10)

94. William McKane says quite well that the robust combination of intellectual interest, technical ability, and piety revealed in this introductory poem is characteristic of Wisdom. *Proverbs: A New Approach,* The Old Testament Library (Philadelphia: Westminster Press, 1975), pp. 262ff.

Clearly there is a world of difference between the learning taught by the Wisdom school and the learning taught by today's secular humanism. There is also a world of difference between this kind of piety and the pietism of some Christian groups that consider learning a hindrance to godliness. The religion of the Wisdom school was a religion of the book, and a religion of the book is bound to be a religion devoted to sacred learning. The pious are constantly at their books, just as they are constantly at their prayers.

The learning of the Wisdom school was devoted to high moral and ethical ideals. Wisdom involved not just practical know-how but justice, equity, and righteousness as well. Wisdom concerned developing insight. The Wisdom school firmly believed that the higher principles of the Law of God gave "instruction in wise dealing," prudence, and discretion. We might put it this way: Sacred knowledge proved itself in the world of business and industry as well as in the individual's religious life. As we find again and again in Proverbs, sacred wisdom helps both king and nobles to govern their states well (8:15-16). It is more precious than gold or silver, rubies or sapphires, but it is also useful in bringing prosperity and wealth to those who make wisdom their guide (8:18-19).

The teaching of the Wisdom school was the sort of literary education that taught one to understand sacred texts, "to understand a proverb and a figure, / the words of the wise and their riddles" (1:6). This education involved quite a bit of what we might call philosophical speculation. Both Job and Ecclesiastes are good examples of speculative thought. The Wisdom hymn in Proverbs 8, for instance, goes into the question of the origins of Wisdom. There we are told that Wisdom was the first of God's creations.

"The LORD created me at the beginning of his work,
　　the first of his acts of old.
Ages ago I was set up,
　　at the first, before the beginning of the earth.
When there were no depths I was brought forth,
　　when there were no springs abounding with water.
Before the mountains had been shaped,
　　before the hills, I was brought forth;
before he had made the earth with its fields,
　　or the first of the dust of the world.
When he established the heavens, I was there,
　　when he drew a circle on the face of the deep,
when he made firm the skies above,

> when he established the fountains of the deep,
> when he assigned to the sea its limit,
>   so that the waters might not transgress his command,
> when he marked out the foundations of the earth,
>   then I was beside him, like a master workman;
> and I was daily his delight,
>   rejoicing before him always,
> rejoicing in his inhabited world
>   and delighting in the sons of men."
>
> (8:22-31)

God's delight in Wisdom is especially noticeable here, which surely has major implications for our understanding of worship. God rejoices in the worship of intelligent human beings. God is not threatened by our intelligence; quite to the contrary, he delights in it. Learned, scholarly handling of his Word pleases God far more than naive, credulous, or careless handling of his Word.

In chapter 9 we find a short poem on the openness of divine Wisdom. Wisdom does not hide from us or resist our attempts to understand. Quite to the contrary, Wisdom is a gracious hostess who invites even the most simple to enter into her feasts.

> Wisdom has built her house,
>   she has set up her seven pillars.
> She has slaughtered her beasts, she has mixed her wine,
>   she has also set her table.
> She has sent out her maids to call
>   from the highest places in the town,
> "Whoever is simple, let him turn in here!"
>   To him who is without sense she says,
> "Come, eat of my bread
>   and drink of the wine I have mixed.
> Leave simpleness, and live,
>   and walk in the way of insight."
>
> (9:1-6)

The source of this imagery has been much discussed; but however exotic the sources might be, the meaning of the passage is quite plain.[95] The

---

95. Berend Gemser, *Sprüche Solomons* (Tübingen: J. C. B. Mohr [Paul Siebeck], 1963), pp. 48ff.; and McKane, *Proverbs*, pp. 359-65.

festive meal prepared by Lady Sophia is a banquet of knowledge and insight, and yet it is a sacred communion. As I have written elsewhere, here is a good text for a sapiential understanding of the Lord's Supper.[96] Even more to the point, here we have a good text for a sapiential understanding of worship in general. It suggests that in sacred learning we enter into communion with God.

Finally, we must say something about the Song of Solomon. These beautiful love songs may well have been written without any religious thoughts at all; but be that as it may, they were included in the canon of Scripture because these poems can be understood in terms of a sacred passion for the divine Wisdom.[97] The Wisdom of God is served not by a cold objectivity but by a holy passion, by an all-consuming love for God himself.

The Wisdom school could not help but have a profound influence on the place of the reading and preaching of the Word in Jewish worship. If there is a covenantal theology of preaching and if it is complemented by a prophetic theology of preaching, then we must add to this a sapiential theology of preaching.

The theology of preaching of the Wisdom tradition is clear. Just as the heavens declare the glory of God, so the very reading of the Law declares the glory of God. If the shining of sun, moon, and stars in the heavens glorifies God, then in the same way God is glorified when Israel reads the Torah. When the scrolls of sacred Scripture are lifted from the ark of the covenant, solemnly unrolled, and read in the midst of the assembly of God's people; when scholars who have devoted their lives to cultivating the sacred text then step forward and read the sacred text, distinguishing between *katib* and *karre*, which only those who have spent years in sacred studies can do correctly; when the passage is then commented upon and applied to the lives of the faithful — when all of this is done, God is glorified.

Even more than the careful rendition of sacred music, which was cultivated in both Temple and synagogue, the reading and preaching of the Scriptures became a matter of highly specialized training. If today in

96. Hughes Oliphant Old, "Biblical Wisdom Theology and Calvin's Understanding of the Lord's Supper," *Calvin Studies* 6 (1992): 111-36.

97. On the roots of this approach to the interpretation of the Song of Solomon, cf. von Rad, *Wisdom in Israel;* and Olivier Rousseau, *Origène, Homélies sur le Cantique des Cantiques* (Paris: Éditions du Cerf, 1966), pp. 7-57.

our secularized society we devoutly cultivate the musical arts, give tremendous amounts of time and energy to developing musical talent, and appreciate the most exacting kind of technical virtuosity, the Jewish culture of the centuries just before Christ gave no less devotion to the cultivation of the arts and sciences of reading and preaching the Scriptures. Because of the nature of the Hebrew language and the way it came to be written, there was often a certain amount of latitude in the way a written text could be read. The *katib* was the way a text was written and the *karre* was the way it was read. Very exacting traditions developed about the correct *karre*, and those who read the Scriptures in public were expected to know these traditions. In the same way traditions developed about the interpretation of Scripture. The interpretation of Scripture was strictly governed by tradition; it was never dreamed that each individual might have a right to his or her own interpretation or that one man's or woman's interpretation was as good as another's. The Scriptures were worthy of careful study. They deserved to be handled with competent hands. Their preservation was entrusted to the most intelligent and devout men of the community. All these things belonged to what might be called a scriptural piety, recognizing that when God's Word was read with clarity and heard with understanding, God was glorified.

This sapiential piety had its effect on the style of preaching that became popular in the centuries just before the Christian era, the time when the expository sermon came into its own. Preaching was not simply a matter of moral or theological teaching, merely inculcating the moral principles of the community, or telling again the old traditions of the community — how it came into existence and how it had maintained itself in times of trial. All this was done, to be sure, but expository preaching was also more. Preaching was the presentation of the Scriptures in which these traditions and principles had received their canonical form. Sermons therefore gave primary attention to what Scripture actually says. Expository preaching discussed the text, its grammar and vocabulary. All kinds of philological investigations were undertaken in trying to hear the Scriptures. Preachers studied the Scriptures in the original language and cultivated a knowledge of the classical Hebrew. The results of all of this study provided material for the sermon.

Preaching presented the Scriptures because the Scriptures themselves had authority. Preaching was not just concerned with learning about the events of the past; the concern of preaching was far more with how Scripture presented the past. The Wisdom school did not want to hear sermons on the history of the Jewish community or on its cultural traditions; it wanted to hear what Scripture taught about God's gracious acts of salvation and God's will for their lives. Preachers were not asked to be historians or even moral philosophers, but to be interpreters of Scripture.

IV. The Ministry of the Word in the Synagogue

The origins of the synagogue are obscure.[98] It is most often suggested that the synagogue originated during the Babylonian exile, when the Temple in Jerusalem had been destroyed and the Jews needed a place to worship during their exile. Since the Deuteronomic reform there had been a strong sense of the uniqueness of the worship of Solomon's Temple, and so the Jews who gathered in Babylon for worship were careful not to reproduce the worship of the Temple, and particularly not its sacrificial service, when they came together each Sabbath for worship. The synagogue was clearly not a miniature Temple, but rather an alternative to the worship of the Temple. The worship of the Temple was tied to Mount Zion — to the holy city, Jerusalem.

There is another possibility, however. Perhaps the synagogue goes back to the time of the Deuteronomic reform, when the sacrificial worship was centralized in Jerusalem. Some sort of worship would have to have been provided for the outlying towns and cities of Judah to replace the worship of the local shrines whose sacrificial service was supposed to have been discontinued under the Deuteronomic reform. This suggestion was put forward with particular force by Julius Morgenstern. The trouble with this suggestion is that it seems to envision the founding of the synagogue at this particular time, but this seems unlikely.

Perhaps it should be argued that the synagogue goes back to the survival of the local Sabbath day assemblies, which had existed for generations before the Deuteronomic reform had demanded the discontinuance of such sacrifices. One of the psalms mentions the "meeting places of God" throughout the land (Ps. 74:8). One hesitates to construct too large an edifice on such a small piece of evidence, but there must have been some place for sacred assemblies in the smaller cities and towns. There must

---

98. On the origins of the synagogue, see Moore, *Judaism in the First Centuries,* 1:283ff.; Rowley, *Worship in Ancient Israel,* pp. 213ff.; and I. Sonne, "Synagogue," *Interpreter's Dictionary of the Bible,* 4:476-91, especially pp. 478ff.

have been houses of prayer and meeting places where the Scriptures were read and the guardians of sacred tradition recounted their stories and interpreted their laws and customs. If all this oral tradition was passed on for centuries, where was it passed on? When was it told and retold? Was it something carried on privately within the priestly caste? Probably not. Much more likely it was something done at the Sabbath assembly, where people eagerly listened to their storytellers and their preachers.

It is hard to imagine how the Ten Commandments could give such prominence to Sabbath day worship if in fact the three pilgrimage feasts were the only times the people assembled together for worship. There must have been some sort of Sabbath assembly in the cities of Judah outside Jerusalem. Reading through the Law Sabbath by Sabbath may well have been part of public worship long before the Deuteronomic reform. It may well have been the case that in every town and village there was a regular Sabbath day assembly at which sacrifices were made, prayers were offered, the Law read and preached, the sacred traditions recounted, the oral traditions passed on and discussed, and perhaps even a common meal shared. The synagogue service may have been what was left of the old Sabbath day service once the sacrifices had been discontinued.

The reading and preaching of the Law may not have been systematic. Not every one of these meeting places may have had the complete Pentateuch as we have it today. The priest may have made his own choice of what part of the Law he wanted to read or what part of the oral tradition he wanted to recount. Such matters may have been structured more formally at Jerusalem and with considerably less formality in outlying towns. To be sure there would have been major shrines, but many local assemblies would have taken place as well. Just how all of this may have been related to the high places we hesitate to say. Perhaps the Sabbath assemblies were separate from the worship of the high places, but it could also be that the high places were not totally dominated by the liturgical traditions of Canaan. The traditions of Sinai may have had their influence as well. Unfortunately, too little trace has been left in our historical records for us to be sure just how or when the synagogue became an important place for devout Jews to worship. At least it can be said that within a short time after the exile the synagogue was a firmly established institution.

However far along the development of the synagogue may have been when Ezra returned to Jerusalem, the account given of the reading of the Law in Nehemiah 8 can safely be regarded as the oldest description we have of a liturgy of the Word.[99] It seems certain that this service over which Ezra presided was anything but a novelty at the time.[100] The description seems to suggest that there were already accustomed ways of doing some of these things, but we can only speculate about what was already established custom and what was unique. Whatever else may be said about this service, it is clear that the order of worship here is essentially the order that has become traditional in the synagogue. Whether the traditions of the synagogue shaped what is here reported of Ezra's service or whether it was Ezra who shaped the synagogue tradition is not completely clear. Be that as it may, the account is most helpful for understanding the ministry of the Word as it was exercised by the Judaism that gave birth to the Christian Church.

When we look at some of the details of the service, we notice that this reading is very specifically from "the book of the Law of Moses." We understand this to mean the Torah in its canonical form or at least very close to its canonical form. John Bright tells us that this "book of the Law of Moses" was the Pentateuch as it was put together during the exile and that the effect of Ezra's reform was the canonization of the Pentateuch.[101] There has been considerable discussion of this point. There are those who envisage a much smaller collection of purely legal material.[102] It seems more likely, however, that this "book of the Law of Moses" was pretty much what we have today. In fact, this reading may have been the de facto canonization of the Torah. At least with this reading, if not before, "the book of the Law of Moses" became the standard worship text; once it was given the authority it has obviously been given here, it had in fact become sacred Scripture, and it would have been difficult to alter it after that point.

One cannot help but ask just how much of the Law could have been

---

99. Antonius Gunneweg sums it up very well when he tells us that the passage offers us what the synagogue later understood to be a story that explained its beginnings, its etiology — in particular the origins of Torah reading and Torah teaching. *Nehemia, Kommentar zum alten Testament*, vol. XIX/2 (Gütersloh: Gerd Mohn, 1987), p. 112.

100. Gerhard von Rad surely is correct when he suggests that instructing the congregation by reading Scripture lessons and then interpreting them in a sermon was already an established procedure well before the time of Ezra, even if we have no record of it. *Studies in Deuteronomy*, pp. 13ff.

101. Bright, *A History of Israel*, pp. 391ff.

102. Gunneweg insists that the Chronicler had in mind the whole of the Law of Moses, but that he was speaking of an ideal situation. *Nehemia*, p. 110.

read in the course of seven or eight mornings.[103] But in the last analysis, this question, as interesting as it is to the contemporary biblical scholar, probably does not help us understand the text. The idea seems to be that the whole book of the Law of Moses was read through in the course of this eight-day feast. The meaning of this, as Brevard Childs has pointed out, is that the restored Israel is characterized by the reading and understanding of the Law.[104] The Torah was Israel's greatest treasure. It was a gift from God that Israel was to cherish. Our text makes a specific point of this: "and they told Ezra the scribe to bring the book of the law of Moses which the LORD had given to Israel" (Neh. 8:1). One of the essential functions of Israel, one of the functions that makes Israel what it is, is the hearing and understanding of the Law. Israel was called out from among the nations for this purpose, that she might hear the Law and live the Law. The point Ezra-Nehemiah wants to make is that the systematic reading through of the Law is essential to the worship of the restored Israel.

A second point to be noticed in this report is that this reading is clearly worship. We read that a wooden platform or pulpit was built on which Ezra stood when he read. On each side of him stood leaders of the community, indicating that this was an official act of the community. The text further reports that Ezra opened the book in the sight of the people and that when he opened it the people stood. Perhaps this means that the Torah was held up at this point, as it is in the synagogue today. These two actions make it very clear that this is a liturgical act. If there is any doubt about the liturgical nature of this assembly, what follows makes it even more certain. We read, "And Ezra blessed the LORD, the great God; and all the people answered, 'Amen, Amen,' lifting up their hands; and they bowed their heads and worshiped the LORD with their faces to the ground" (Neh. 8:6).

103. Jacob Myers, *Ezra, Nehemiah,* The Anchor Bible, vol. 14 (Garden City, N.Y.: Doubleday, 1965), raises the question of how much of the Pentateuch could be read in one morning. He considers the study of the Law that followed the next day as something different. According to Myers, Ezra read *from* the Law — that is, selections from the Law rather the Law in its entirety. Myers is followed by F. Charles Fensham, *The Books of Ezra and Nehemiah,* The New International Commentary on the Old Testament (Grand Rapids: Wm. B. Eerdmans Publishing Co., 1982). Antonius Gunneweg, on the other hand, insists that the author was not interested in such questions regarding the extent of the reading; rather, what interested him was the fact of the reestablishment of the liturgical reading of Scripture. *Nehemia,* p. 110.

104. Childs, *Introduction,* p. 638.

This account of the reading of the Law indicates that already at the time of the writing of this text there was a considerable amount of ceremonial framing of the public reading of Scripture. This ceremonial framing is a witness to the authority of the Bible. In all this ceremonial it is clear that Ezra blessed the LORD and that the people worshiped the LORD. In the reading of the Word of God, God himself is glorified. This liturgical framing or ceremonial with which the Law is publicly read as an act of worship was surely not an invention of Ezra, nor even an invention of the synagogue of the exile. This kind of ceremonial would not be invented out of nothing. Surely there were already old traditions about this sort of thing.[105] The fact that it was the Levites who stood by and took turns reading the Law would indicate that these traditions went back at least to the Temple. The Levites had exercised a ministry of preaching in the Temple, and surely the Scriptures had been ceremonially read as part of their ministry. One wonders if in the Jerusalem Temple, or even in Shiloh, the tablets of the Law were ever taken from the ark of the covenant and held up in the sight of the people and then read.

Another thing to point out is that after the Scriptures are read they are explained: "And they read from the book, from the law of God, clearly; and they gave the sense, so that the people understood the reading" (Neh. 8:8). Some suggest that all we have here is an indication that after the text in classical Hebrew had been read it was translated into Aramaic passage by passage. According to Jewish tradition, this was the origin of the Targum.[106] We know that this practice was followed at one point in the history of Jewish worship. Others insist that something more than a simple translation is implied by "reading clearly" and "giving the sense."[107] More than a translation would surely be needed "so that the people understood the reading." Nevertheless, whether the text is reporting the giving of a Targum or the preaching of a sermon, what we seem to have here can at

---

105. Cf. von Rad, *Studies in Deuteronomy,* p. 14, on the antiquity of the procedures mentioned in Nehemiah 8. This ceremonial may go back to Shechem, as von Rad suggests, but in order for it to have influenced Ezra it would have to have had a far greater currency. The assertion that this was established ceremonial in Ezra's day implies that the reading and preaching of Scripture was a regular feature of Jewish worship not only at feasts but at regular Sabbath services as well.

106. Mann, *Bible as Read and Preached,* 1:xiv; Elbogen, *Der jüdische Gottesdienst,* pp. 187ff.

107. Gunneweg, *Nehemia,* pp. 110-12, asserts strongly that more than a mere translation is intended here; an exegesis or exposition is what is meant.

least be regarded as the embryo of the sermon. In the end, the point of the sermon was to make clear the reading of the Scriptures.

Jewish tradition always gave impressive authority to Ezra. More recent critical historians have shown considerably less deference to him. Nevertheless, the Jewish tradition may well be a better guide to understanding him than some have thought. A number of more recent scholars believe that the Chronicler who composed the books of Ezra and Nehemiah in addition to I and II Chronicles may have been Ezra himself. Be that as it may, John Bright has surely summed up Ezra's goal fairly well when he tells us that the focus of Ezra's reform was to reorganize the Jewish community around the Law.[108] The liturgical aspect of this reorganization was to regularize the reading and preaching of the Law in the synagogue each Sabbath. The least we can say is that the report found in Nehemiah no doubt reflects the liturgical practice of the synagogue from the time of Ezra's reform on.

If the basic shaping of the liturgy of the Word in the synagogue was a result of Ezra's reform, then we can date it, following John Bright, around the year 428 B.C. A number of important developments took place after that time. Let us look at several of these in turn.

1. The first of these is the development of a system for the reading of the Scripture lessons. Eventually the passage of the Law to be read publicly each Sabbath was fixed so that in the course of a year, as was the custom in Babylon, or three years, as was the custom in the synagogues of Palestine, the whole Law was completed. That was not the way it was done at first, however. The older approach was to read a passage of appropriate length each Sabbath, beginning with Genesis, continuing each Sabbath where one had left off the Sabbath before, until one reached the end of Deuteronomy. There was no set time in which this had to be accomplished. One synagogue might take four years, another three and a half, another two, and another even less. Systematizing the reading of Scripture was a logical reform for Ezra to institute if indeed he was concerned to organize the new Judaism around the Torah. It assured that the faithful would hear the whole of the Law on a regular basis and provided for a systematic preaching of the Law in its entirety.

The story we find in Nehemiah 8 tells us that the Law was read in its entirety by Ezra and his colleagues. While the book of Deuteronomy stipulates that this was to be done as a regular procedure every seven years

---

108. Bright, *A History of Israel*, p. 391.

at the feast of tabernacles, it was not in fulfillment of this requirement that Ezra read the Law at that time; this is clear from the fact that Ezra's reading took place, not at the feast of tabernacles, but several weeks before it. Instead, the reading of the entire Pentateuch — the canonical Torah — in Nehemiah 8 and the worship and prayers that accompany the reading are presented as the prototype of the worship of Israel. That onetime reading of the Torah was then to be unrolled Sabbath by Sabbath in every Jewish synagogue. If worship in Solomon's Temple had included regular readings of the Scriptures, as seems very likely, Ezra now made this practice the characteristic feature of every worshiping assembly of every Jewish community either in the Palestinian homeland or in the Diaspora.[109] And Ezra systematized the reading and preaching of the Law, probably for the first time, so that from then on the Torah would be regularly read in worship in its entirety and in its full and complete form.

2. In the second century of the Christian era, or perhaps even later, this *lectio continua* was tied down to a particular cycle so that each Sabbath of the year had a prescribed lection. In fact these lections, or *parshiyoth*, as the Jews called them, were probably not developed until Masoretic times. Several traditions preserved from about this time imply that the lessons were not yet fixed. In the Babylonian Talmud we hear of a difference of opinion between two second-century rabbis. Rabbi Meir taught that Scripture readings were to follow a day-by-day pattern — that one begins reading at the Sabbath afternoon service at the place where one had ended in the Sabbath morning service, one begins on Monday at the place where one had left off in the afternoon service, one begins on Thursday at the place where one had left off on Monday, and one begins the following Sabbath at the place where one had left off on Thursday. Rabbi Judah, on the other hand, taught that Scripture reading should follow a Sabbath-by-Sabbath pattern — that one begins the reading each Sabbath at the place where one had ended on the previous Sabbath.[110] G. F. Moore reckons that if one follows the number of readers and the number of verses required by tradition, the Torah would

---

109. The *lectio continua* method of reading the Scriptures must have gone back well before Ezra. It is the natural way of reading a scroll. The wear and tear on the scrolls would be too great if readers skipped back and forth from one passage to another. In addition, it would have taken some time to roll and unroll the manuscript.

110. *Megillah* 31b, in *The Babylonian Talmud*, ed. I. Epstein (London: Soncino Press, 1938).

be completed in a bit more than two years following the system of Rabbi Meir and more than five years following the system of Rabbi Judah.[111]

3. The reading of the Torah by *lectio continua* accounted for the readings of most Sabbaths, but in addition to this there were also *lectio selecta* — that is, special lessons for special days. A list of these special readings is given in the Mishnah tractate *Megillah*.[112] The special days included Passover, Pentecost, New Year, Day of Atonement, each day of Tabernacles, Dedication, Purim, New Moons, the fast days, and the four Sabbaths before Passover. Moore is of the opinion that at least the readings for the major festivals antedate the fall of Jerusalem,[113] though others appear to be more recent.

Most of these readings are rather short. Rather than recounting the events that the feast celebrated, the passage gives the legislation on how the feast is to be celebrated. Behind these special readings is a very specific understanding of the function of the reading of Scripture in worship. It differs greatly from the idea of an earlier day, in which reading from Scripture was a means of thankfully recounting the mighty acts of God for the salvation of his people, thus serving as a covenantal confession that one belonged to the covenant people. These special feast day lessons belie a legalistic concern much narrower than the concern that formed and canonized the Pentateuch. Those who drew up these lessons for the feast days had lost sight of the eucharistic aspect of the reading of Scripture and had narrowed in on merely legalistic concerns. This fact alone would suggest that these lessons are not nearly as old as the tradition of reading the whole of the Pentateuch through in the course of time.

4. Another development, the reading of the lesson from the prophets, had a very different origin. Strangely enough it is in the New Testament that we find one of the earliest witnesses to the reading of the prophets in worship. No doubt it was a well-established practice before that time, but the story we find in the Gospel of Luke, which tells of Jesus preaching in the synagogue of Nazareth, gives a very good picture. We are told that Jesus stood up to read and that the book of the prophet Isaiah was given to him. He opened the book and found the passage that reads, "The Spirit of the Lord is upon me . . ." (Isa. 61:1-2). After reading several lines he closed the book, gave it back to the attendant, and sat down to preach (Luke 4:16-28).

111. Moore, *Judaism in the First Centuries*, 1:296-302.
112. *Megillah*, 3, 5-6.
113. Moore, *Judaism in the First Centuries*, 1:297ff.

We will take up the sermon of Jesus at another point, but here we want to draw attention only to the fact that all the details correspond with what we know from later sources about how the reading of the prophets was done in the synagogue. The book was handed to Jesus. He read standing. He handed the book back to the attendant and then sat down to preach. Apparently he chose his own lesson; although it is possible that Jesus found and read the lesson he was asked to read, that does not seem to be what the text has in mind. What the lesson from the Law might have been on this occasion is not indicated, but presumably Jesus would have followed the custom of choosing a lesson from the prophets appropriate to the lesson from the Law. Having read it aloud, he sat down and preached a sermon on the lesson he had read.

The lesson from the prophets was supposed to be chosen by the preacher. By means of this lesson the preacher opened up the passage that had been read from the Law earlier in the service. The principle that Scripture is to be interpreted by Scripture was already well established. The point in reading from the prophets was to explain the reading from the Law. Only much later, after the cycle of fixed readings from the Law had been established, was a cycle of fixed readings from the prophets developed.[114]

Now if it was indeed the case that the lesson from the prophets was supposed to lead into the sermon, this has an interesting implication for the nature of preaching. The sermon must have been understood as a continuation of the prophetic ministry. It was appropriate that the prophets be understood as the interpreters of the Law and therefore the prototype of the preacher.

5. By the beginning of the Christian era, preaching played a major role in the worship of the synagogue.[115] The art of preaching had been cultivated over the centuries so that one could expect of preachers both theological depth and literary refinement. While the synagogue did not limit preaching to a professional ministry, there was a large core of dedicated men who had given their lives to the study of the Scriptures, and who prepared themselves to preach when the leadership of the synagogue invited them to do so.

The preaching of the synagogue had as its aim the interpretation

114. Cf. Mann, *Bible as Read and Preached*, 1:xx-xxvii.

115. On preaching in the synagogue, cf. Moore, *Judaism in the First Centuries*, 1:306ff.

and application of the lessons read in worship. It was understood that interpretation of the Scriptures had to be at two levels. The first level involved the more straightforward matter of interpreting the classical Hebrew into the language of the people.[116] This presented different problems at different times and places, depending on how well the classical Hebrew was understood by the congregation. In Egypt there was no problem because the Scriptures were read in Greek, but in many places the Hebrew text had to be translated into Aramaic by a special translator who translated the lesson from the Law verse by verse. Care was taken so that the translator did not become a commentator. The translation was not supposed to be so much a literal rendering as a free paraphrase. It was not to be read although it could be prepared beforehand as long as it was not written out. Even at this, these translations did eventually develop into the Targum, a semiofficial translation of the Torah.

The translation was only the first level of the interpretation. The second level was the sermon.[117] The sermon was supposed to be a learned interpretation and application of the text. It was supposed to teach, admonish, inspire, and comfort the congregation. Paul Billerbeck, in his monumental commentary on the New Testament from Talmud and Midrash, has provided a wealth of information on the worship of the synagogue at the beginning of the Christian era, including a considerable number of reports of sermons by rabbis from those early days.[118] While these reports are often very short, they do give us some insight into how Scripture was expounded in a typical sermon of the period.

A number of different sermon methods were used. The first method was simply to take a passage from the Law and explain it phrase by phrase. Billerbeck quotes a report of a sermon of Eleazar ben Azariah from the

116. On the liturgical translation of the Scripture lesson in the synagogue and the development of the Targum, cf. Moore, *Judaism in the First Centuries,* 1:304ff. For the important recent developments in the study of the Targum, cf. M. McNamara's article, "Targums," *Interpreter's Dictionary of the Bible,* Supplementary volume, pp. 856-61.

117. Most of what we know about the preaching of the synagogue in the days of Jesus and the apostles is found in very concentrated form in the Midrashim. Cf. further on the subject Hermann L. Strack, *Introduction to the Talmud and Midrash* (New York: Harper & Row, 1965), pp. 201ff.

118. Paul Billerbeck, *Kommentar zum Neuen Testament aus Talmud und Midrasch,* 6 vols. (Munich: Beck, 1961-65), 4:174-88.

end of the first Christian century that was preached on Deuteronomy 31:12: "'Assemble the people, men, women, and little ones . . . that they may hear and learn to fear the LORD your God.'" The rabbi first explained that men come to the synagogue in order to learn. The second point of the sermon was that women come in order to hear. The third point explained that children were to come to the synagogue in order that those who brought them might be rewarded. Modern readers would no doubt like to ask a number of questions about this sermon, none of which the report that has come down through the centuries satisfies in the least. Be that as it may, we all recognize the classic three-point sermon, each point taking off from a phrase in the text. Sermons of this sort might well develop a considerably greater number of phrases in any passage, but the method is as old as it is familiar.

Another method, used particularly with difficult or problematic texts, was to bring to the principal text a number of secondary texts that dealt with the matter more clearly. Billerbeck gives us the report of a sermon by Rabbi Eleazar ben Jose (ca. A.D. 180) on Exodus 19. The sermon dealt with the question of why God should choose Israel when he knew that Israel would not always be faithful. The passage from the prophets by which he opened up the text was Isaiah 63:9: "In all their affliction he was afflicted." This is a rather startling text for those who have been schooled in the impassable transcendence of God. The preacher developed this text with references to Psalm 78:36-38 and Isaiah 6:10 to show that God is prepared to deal with the hardness of human hearts. The sermon taken as a whole must have been a profound statement of the depth of God's patient and forgiving mercy. Again we find here a classic method of expounding Scripture.

Another method very closely related to this was called the string of pearls. One began with a text from the lesson and then added to it text after text on the same theme. When this was done with skill, each new text added different colors and shades of meaning to those which had gone before; each new text brought another perspective to the primary theme. As an example Billerbeck tells us of a sermon of the famous second-century preacher Rabbi Meir on the text, "'Give ear, O heavens, and I will speak; / and let the earth hear the words of my mouth'" (Deut. 32:1). The report of this sermon mentions thirty-two auxiliary texts, all of which tell of aspects of the creation that give their witness to the truth of God's judgments. These texts are gathered from a wide range of earlier and later prophets as well as the Hagiographa.

A favorite means of expounding the text among the rabbis was the parable. The homiletic parable took the central teaching of the text and illustrated it by means of an imaginative story that made the same point as the text. True stories from the lives of the godly who had gone before were also employed. Rabbinical tradition passed on a wealth of anecdotes concerning the virtues of the rabbis of days gone by, and no doubt these stories were recounted in sermons again and again. Rabbinical preaching made every effort to be interesting.

Sometimes the concern to keep the congregation interested prompted the preacher to add to the biblical account of Israel's history imaginative details that made the classic stories even more remarkable than they already were. We are told, for instance, of a sermon by Rabbi Nehori, preached in the middle of the second century, in which he enlivened the familiar story of the passage through the Red Sea by telling of a woman carrying her child. The child was hungry and began to cry, so the mother reached out and picked a pomegranate that God had graciously provided in that unlikely place. The good rabbi assured his congregation that he was doing no injustice to Scripture. Had not Moses himself said that during the forty years from the time they left Egypt to the time they entered the Promised Land God had provided for all their needs? This story probably raised many eyebrows at the time, as it would today, but the history of preaching, let us never forget, is filled with fun and fancy. It has always been so, and as long as God is gracious it will always continue to be so until the last laugh is absorbed in eternal hallelujahs.

V. The Ministry of the Word in the Rabbinical Schools

The Judaism from which Jesus and the apostles came exercised the ministry of the Word not only in the reading and preaching of the Scriptures in the synagogue but also in the regular study sessions of the rabbinical schools.[119] The prototype of the rabbinical school was the teaching sessions of the rabbis in the courts of the Temple. This kind of rabbinical teaching is frequently mentioned in the New Testament, and therefore it must have been considered an important part of the religious life of Judaism at that time.

119. Cf. the excellent chapter on the Jewish rabbinical schools in Moore, *Judaism in the First Centuries*, vol. 1, chapter 6.

We will take this up again in the following chapter, but for the present I will mention only a few New Testament passages. The story of the boy Jesus discussing the Law with the doctors (Luke 2:41-51) is perhaps the most obvious example. Matthew, who always gives careful attention to typology, begins his Gospel by depicting Jesus as the true Moses in his Sermon on the Mount to show that Jesus was fulfilling a very ancient office. Then, in a lengthy passage toward the end of his Gospel (21:23–23:39, almost two and a half chapters), Matthew reports Jesus holding a teaching session in the Temple courts to show that Jesus was the fulfillment of the rabbinical office as it was exercised at the time. The different schools — Herodians, Pharisees, and Sadducees — come to him with their questions regarding how the Law is to be interpreted, and Jesus in good rabbinical form answers them. In these two and a half chapters Matthew gives us a perfect picture of how the higher level of the rabbinical schools operated, which is of particular interest because it has to do with the interpretation of the Law. A similar account of Jesus teaching in the Temple in the way rabbis usually taught, by the question and answer method, can be found in John 7 and 8.

The teaching that took place in the Temple had a special preeminence, but the same sort of teaching took place in every Jewish community of any size. The rabbinical schools differed in prominence and in level. There were elementary schools, which aimed at teaching children how to read the unpointed text of the Hebrew Scriptures. In practice this meant learning the text of the Bible by heart. Then there were higher schools, which taught the interpretation of Scripture. For centuries the rabbinical schools made a sharp distinction between the written Law and the oral tradition. The elementary schools were concerned with learning the written Law, while the higher schools were concerned with the transmission of the oral tradition regarding the interpretation of the Law.

The most prestigious of the higher schools was naturally the one held in the courts of the Temple, but others gained special prestige at one time or another. There were academies in Babylonia and in Palestine. An important academy was located at Tiberias on the shores of the Sea of Galilee. The academy at Jabneh succeeded that of Jerusalem after the destruction of the Holy City. In addition, there were schools that maintained the tradition of a particular teacher, such as the school of Hillel and the school of Shammai. Some of these schools had their own buildings, while others were held in the synagogue.

The oral tradition taught in the rabbinical schools was divided up into two kinds: (1) Midrash, that is, commentary on Scripture; and (2) Mishnah, the systematic interpretation of the Law that proceeds from one subject to another. Midrash is probably the easier to understand. Like modern commentaries, the Midrashim follow the course of a particular book of the Bible such as Genesis or Deuteronomy. The Midrash is a sort of digest of the history of rabbinical interpretation. For a particular passage of Scripture the interpretation of a number of leading rabbis is given. This interpretation is reported in a condensed form since the material has to be memorized.[120]

The earliest Midrashim were formulated in the second Christian century. These were Halachic Midrashim, commentaries on the legal parts of Scripture — for example, the *Mekilta* of Exodus, the *Sifra* of Leviticus, and the *Sifre* of Numbers and Deuteronomy. The Midrash on Genesis, on the other hand, is a Haggadic Midrash — a commentary on a narrative part of Scripture. This type of Midrash was formulated about a century later than the Halachic type. Among the most popular of the Midrashim were those on the five books of the *Megilloth:* the Song of Solomon, Lamentations, Ecclesiastes, Ruth, and Esther.

Mishnah, on the other hand, is a bit more difficult to understand, since there is nothing to which we can easily compare it. Mishnah is the oral interpretation of the Law studied systematically. Beginning with prayers, it proceeds to feast days, clean and unclean foods, inheritances, and marriage. All that the Law teaches is studied according to specific categories. If the Midrashim can be compared to our biblical commentaries, one might compare the Mishnah to a systematic theology, except that a systematic theology is not quite the same thing as a systematic discussion of the Law.

Toward the end of the second Christian century, Rabbi Judah the Patriarch made a collection of these oral traditions, organizing them into some sixty loci or tractates.[121] The published form of this Mishnah preserved many of the interpretations of the Law that were discussed at the time of Jesus and the apostles.[122] The famous Rabbis Akiba, Hillel, Shammai, Johanan ben Zakkai, Gamaliel I, Gamaliel II, Eliezer ben Hyrcanus, Meir, and Judah the Patriarch are frequently quoted in it.

---

120. For further discussion of Midrash, see Strack, *Introduction,* pp. 201-34.

121. For an English translation, see *The Mishnah,* trans. Herbert Danby (Oxford: Oxford University Press, 1933).

122. On the way in which a collection of oral material was published, cf. Gerhardsson, *Memory and Manuscript,* pp. 119-21.

The Mishnah as arranged and published in the second century became the nucleus of all further study of the oral tradition of the Law. Eventually, starting around the sixth century of the Christian era, commentary on the Mishnah was formulated in the Talmud so that the Talmud is an elaboration of the Mishnah. Two forms of the Talmud were developed. The shorter form is known as the Talmud of Jerusalem, while the longer form is called the Talmud of Babylonia. During that period a number of rabbinical schools flourished in Babylonia, making it a center of Jewish learning.

The sessions of rabbinical schools were quite different from Sabbath day services at the synagogue. They performed a ministry of the Word — a very different ministry, and yet one that was clearly understood as a ministry of the Word.[123] After students had mastered the text of Scripture and learned by heart the major collections of oral tradition, either Midrash or Mishnah, they were ready to take part in the sessions of the higher rabbinical schools, which consisted of both lectures and discussion.[124] Having studied Scripture and memorized the oral tradition, students at this higher level of study were supposed to learn how to interpret and apply it.

A typical session might go something like this. The rabbi would propose that a certain subject be discussed. He might make a few introductory remarks, after which he would call on one of his disciples to repeat the relevant passages from the oral tradition, which would include the interpretation of various passages of Scripture that had been applied to the problem in the past. The publication of the Mishnah in the second century greatly facilitated this for disciples, since they could simply recite the appropriate tractate, but before that time disciples demonstrated their thoroughness by coming up with the most relevant material. Other disciples might add further bits of material. The rabbi might then ask several students what was meant by the tradition that had been recited, and he would respond to their answers. The rabbi might continue the discussion by presenting a hypothetical case and asking the students how it might be solved. Different students might give different solutions, and a debate would ensue. The rabbi would guide the discussion by questions and

123. On the use of the phrase "ministry of the Word" both in rabbinical circles and in Acts 6:4, cf. Gerhardsson, *Memory and Manuscript*, pp. 234ff.
124. On the lecture procedures of the rabbinical schools, cf. Gerhardsson, *Memory and Manuscript*, pp. 103ff., 118, 140.

remarks. Finally he would give his solution to the problem, often illustrating his answer by telling a parable, interpreting a passage of Scripture, or recounting a story about a rabbi of the past. The central theme of the teaching session would then be formulated in a simple, easily memorized dictum. Day by day the school would proceed from one topic to the next with the intention of going through the whole body of oral tradition over a given period of time.

The point of this discussion of Jewish sacred learning is to show that the ministry of the Word as it was exercised in the rabbinical schools was the source of a very distinct genre of Christian preaching — namely, catechetical preaching. Further on in our study we will see how the Church developed its own systematic moral teaching. Modern scholars often refer to this as the primitive Christian catechism or, to use the term current in German circles, the early Christian *Haustafel*. Perhaps one could just as well call it the Christian Mishnah. We will have more to say about this later. What I have tried to show here is how this facet of the ministry of the Word functioned in the rabbinical schools and how it shaped the religious world in which Jesus and the apostles lived.

Finally, it is important to see that, just as the continual exposition of the Scriptures in the synagogue sermon was a form of worship, for the devout Jew the systematic study of the Law was also worship. The very fact that the ideal place for this systematic study of Scripture was in the courts of the Temple certainly indicates that this kind of intellectual activity was thought of as worship. The fact that among Jews living in the Diaspora this study took place in a school, or a special house of study, need be no hindrance. The Jews were quite adept at dealing with this kind of problem.

For the Jews, study was an important part of worship. Great numbers of people devoted their lives to memorizing the Scriptures and to memorizing and discussing the oral tradition. For Judaism the Word of God was not a dead document but a living Word, written not on pages of paper but in the lives of God's people, not on tablets of stone but on the hearts of human beings. The study of Scripture and tradition was not a task reserved to the priesthood or to the rabbis, or to any kind of professional office. It was both the sacred duty and the heavenly delight of every devout Jew.[125] It was a lifetime pursuit for those who wished to give themselves to it. Hours and hours over years and years had to be given to memorizing

125. On the place of study in Jewish piety, cf. Moore, *Judaism in the First Centuries,* 2:239-47.

the texts of Scripture and then the oral tradition as well. Rabbinical scholars were not pedants who knew only what they had memorized; they were living libraries who preserved in their minds a vast tradition of learning. This learning was sacred learning. It was a holy service performed to the honor and glory of God. It was begun with prayers and ended with prayers.[126] It was, very simply, worship.

126. Gerhardsson, *Memory and Manuscript*, p. 116.

CHAPTER II

The Preaching of Christ and the Apostles

Jesus was preeminently a preacher of the Word. To be sure, as the Church has always taught, Jesus is the Word, the Son of God and the Savior of the world, yet when we look at Jesus during his ministry in Galilee and then in Jerusalem we see a preacher. He was the Christ, the Messiah, whom God anointed with his Spirit to preach glad tidings. He was, in fact, an itinerant preacher of the gospel. His three-year ministry was above all a preaching ministry. Those who continued his ministry, the apostles, were preeminently preachers as well, as evidenced by the Acts of the Apostles and the New Testament Epistles. Christianity from its earliest beginnings was a preaching religion. At the center of its worship was the reading and preaching of Scripture. It was by preaching above all that it witnessed to the glory of God in the risen Christ. The kerygmatic dimension of its worship was characteristic. All of which went back to the fact that Jesus was preeminently a preacher.

Again and again revivals of preaching have begun with the recognition of this fundamental fact: Jesus was a preacher and he gave a major portion of his energy to preaching. In the High Middle Ages the preaching orders, the Franciscans and the Dominicans, brought about a major spiritual revival by emphasizing the preaching ministry of Jesus. On the American frontier the Methodist circuit riders took the preaching of Jesus as their pattern. Again and again the Church has returned to the preaching ministry of Jesus for its example.

111

In this chapter we will examine the preaching of Jesus and his disciples as a school of preaching. Just as we will eventually come to speak of a Cistercian School, a Franciscan School, a Puritan School, or a Pietist School, we will try to see the preaching of Jesus and the apostles as a school which took certain approaches to and had certain convictions about the nature, content, and purpose of preaching. It was a school which was formed by certain practical problems and had several unique privileges. Yet even if there was a uniqueness about the preaching of Christ and the apostles, it nevertheless established the pattern of Christian preaching.

Inevitably we will ask questions of the New Testament text which are a bit different from those commonly asked by contemporary New Testament scholars. Our basic question is, how did Jesus exercise the ministry of the Word? We will also ask such obvious questions as how the earliest Christian preaching related to the preaching of the synagogue, and how and to what extent the sermons of Jesus and the apostles have been preserved by the text of the New Testament.

New Testament scholars have done much work on this in recent years, and naturally we assume the work of contemporary biblical research. The footnotes, which we tried to leave very brief, indicate only the New Testament scholarship we found most helpful. The bibliography for this chapter could be overwhelming; and we have resisted the temptation to unroll it all. We cannot go into these subjects at the same level which proper New Testament scholars would want; we can only, with due modesty, point out certain possibilities which appear to those primarily interested in the history of Christian worship. We cannot really do more than look back at the origins of Christian preaching through its two thousand years of development and try to understand the New Testament in light of the possibilities that did in fact develop. But surely there is value in that. If nothing else, it helps us understand who we are and what we are doing, here and now. Even at that, whenever we submit to a conscientious study of Scripture, things open up to us that we had never understood before. We find ourselves ever called to a new obedience. So once again we will turn to the Bible, as the Fathers and the Schoolmen and the Reformers before us have, to help us understand where we want to go and how we might get there.

We begin with a brief look at the preaching ministry of Jesus as reported by each of the four Gospels. Then we will look at the apostolic preaching as reported in the Acts of the Apostles and finally at the approach to preaching we find in various New Testament Epistles.

I. The Ministry of Preaching in the Synoptic Gospels

A. The Gospel of Mark

1. Preaching in Galilee

The Gospel of Mark for all its brevity shows us very distinctly that Jesus was a preacher.[1] Mark starts out his account of the ministry of Jesus by telling us, "Jesus came into Galilee, preaching the gospel of God, and saying, 'The time is fulfilled, and the kingdom of God is at hand; repent, and believe in the gospel'" (Mark 1:14-15).[2] Often Mark tells us that Jesus preached in the synagogues (1:21; 1:39; 3:1-6; 6:2). Several summary statements indicate that he preached all through Galilee, Judea, and the country across the Jordan. He must have preached regularly in the synagogues of these different regions. We read at one point, "And he went . . . preaching in their synagogues" (1:39). He did not limit himself to formal sermons in the synagogues, to be sure, but seems to have preached wherever he could gather a crowd. Very simply put, Jesus did a considerable amount of preaching. From the picture Mark draws we get the impression that preaching was the primary emphasis of his ministry.

When we ask what Jesus preached, we are given a very precise summary. He came "preaching the gospel of God, and saying, 'The time is fulfilled, and the kingdom of God is at hand; repent, and believe in the gospel'" (1:14). This makes it clear that first of all his preaching was the proclamation of the good news that the promises of Scripture are fulfilled and the long-promised kingdom is at hand; therefore the people were to repent of their sins and believe this gospel. About all this Mark is very clear and straightforward.

Furthermore, Mark preserves for us a good number of sayings of Jesus which no doubt reflect the material he ordinarily preached, as well

---

1. William Lane takes very seriously the tradition passed on by Papias that Mark has passed on to us the material preached by Peter, *The Gospel of Mark*, New International Commentary on the New Testament (Grand Rapids: Wm. B. Eerdmans Publishing Co., 1970), pp. 8-12. From a very different perspective, see Willi Marxsen, *Mark the Evangelist, Studies on the Redaction History of the Gospel*, trans. Roy A. Harrisville et al. (Nashville: Abingdon, 1969).

2. On the significance of this summary statement, see Robert A. Guelich, *Mark*, 2 vols., Word Biblical Commentary (Dallas: Word Books, 1989), 1:40-46; Ernst Lohmeyer, *Das Evangelium des Markus*, Meyers Kritisch-exegetischer Kommentar über das neue Testament (Göttingen: Vandenhoeck & Ruprecht, 1963), pp. 29-31; Vincent Taylor, *The Gospel according to St. Mark* (London: Macmillan, 1955), pp. 164-67.

as a number of parables which probably were an important feature of his sermons. Like the typical rabbi of his day, Jesus doubtless filled his sermons with this kind of material. Much of this homiletical material we can imagine is the crystallization of his preaching. We will look more carefully at the homiletical material preserved in the Gospels as our story develops, but for the present we simply want to note that not only does Mark tell us very specifically that Jesus gave much time to preaching, but he reports to us as well a substantial amount of the homiletical material Jesus used.

As we find it in the Gospel of Mark, the preaching of Jesus followed from the preaching of John the Baptist. This seems to have been a significant fact for the earliest Christians, since all four Gospels make a point of it. One reason, no doubt, was that the connection with John the Baptist implied a connection with the prophets.[3] The preaching of John the Baptist followed in the tradition of the preaching of the prophets. The Gospels make this quite explicit, too.

As it is written in Isaiah the prophet,

> "Behold, I send my messenger before thy face,
> who shall prepare thy way;
> the voice of one crying in the wilderness:
> Prepare the way of the Lord,
> make his paths straight — "

John the baptizer appeared in the wilderness, preaching a baptism of repentance for the forgiveness of sins. (Mark 1:2-4)

It is in that tradition that Mark would have us understand Jesus. The place of preaching in the worship of Israel, as we have said, was well established when Jesus began his ministry. It was a strong foundation on which Jesus built. How striking that right at the beginning of Mark's Gospel we have this statement of how the preaching of Jesus fit into the preaching of Israel! Mark wants us to understand right from the beginning that Jesus was a preacher in the succession of John the Baptist, and therefore the whole prophetic tradition.

3. Some manuscripts tell us that the preaching of John the Baptist was in accordance with the prophets without naming any specific prophet. The generally accepted reading names Isaiah alone, and then gives a quotation. Actually this is a composite allusion to two prophets, Isaiah 40:3 and Malachi 3:1. Cf. C. S. Mann, *Mark*, The Anchor Bible, vol. 27 (Garden City, N.Y.: Doubleday, 1986), pp. 193-97, and R. Guelich, *Mark*, 1:7ff. This would imply that the interest in connecting Jesus with the ministry of John the Baptist was to place Jesus squarely in the prophetic tradition.

The following paragraphs of chapter 1 tell how Jesus entered the synagogues and preached. The point seems to be that Jesus followed the usual practice supplied by the institution of the synagogue. Later in the Gospel we read how Jesus followed the customary practice of teaching in the Temple. When we look at the continuity between Jesus and John the Baptist, however, we see that something more charismatic and spontaneous inspired the preaching of Jesus. Jesus fit into the tradition of Jewish preaching, but not as the parish priest, as it were. John the Baptist was not an institutional preacher who preached because society had given him that responsibility and had provided for him a parish, a pulpit, and a parsonage. John the Baptist was a charismatic preacher whom God's Spirit raised up as he had the prophets, to preach a unique message for a very particular time. Like the Methodists and the Franciscans, like the hermit preachers in the Eastern Orthodox churches, like the Pentecostal preachers of today, John the Baptist preached out-of-doors. He preached in the wilderness and people went out to hear him. The voice crying in the wilderness was a very special kind of preaching, and John the Baptist is the biblical figure for this kind of preaching. The voice crying in the wilderness has a special intensity because it is called forth directly by the Holy Spirit. It came from the white-hot burning bush of God's presence. Jesus, too, was a charismatic preacher, a voice crying in the wilderness. Jesus could preach in the marketplace, on the mountainside, and beside the sea. Not everyone can do that. It takes a special charisma. Jesus could do it as John the Baptist could.[4]

As much as the preaching of John the Baptist may have prepared the way for the Messiah and anticipated the gospel, it was not the preaching of the gospel. All four Gospels make it quite clear — John preached repentance, and that is not the same thing as the gospel. He, as the prophets before him, preached the coming of the Messiah. The messianic promises had been an important part of the preaching of the prophets, and in the days of John the Baptist the messianic hope engendered by this preaching was especially vivid, but preaching that hope was not the same as preaching the gospel. When the ministry of John the Baptist was finished and he had been imprisoned, Jesus began to preach that now the promises were being realized, " 'The time is fulfilled, and the kingdom of God is at hand; repent, and believe in the Gospel' " (Mark 1:15). There was a continuity between the preaching of Jesus and the preaching of Israel as it was

4. M. Hengel, *The Charismatic Leader and His Followers,* trans. J. Greig (New York: Crossroads, 1981).

institutionalized in both the synagogue and the Temple, and there was a continuity with the noninstitutional, that is, the charismatic preaching of Israel. But there was more. The preaching of Jesus took a very important step beyond the preaching of Israel. Jesus preached the gospel, the proclamation that the promises of God had been fulfilled. All this the Gospel of Mark makes abundantly clear, but there is still something else.

Not only do we find that the preaching of Jesus was in a distinct continuity with the preaching of Israel, but also that the preaching of Jesus initiated the preaching of the apostles. Jesus carried on a ministry of preaching himself, but he also made a point of calling to himself disciples whom he trained to continue this ministry and sent out into all the world to preach the same gospel.[5] Mark, as do the other Gospels, makes this very clear.

> And he went up on the mountain, and called to him those whom he desired; and they came to him. And he appointed twelve, to be with him, and to be sent out to preach and have authority to cast out demons: Simon whom he surnamed Peter; James. . . . (3:13-17)

This text shows that Jesus was not only a preacher, but also a trainer of preachers. Jesus established a ministry which was to continue his preaching and work, but that ministry included more than preaching. Of the essence of that ministry is to abide in the presence of Jesus. "And he appointed twelve, to be with him. . . ." Without this the preaching lacks not only its inspiration but its authority as well. The mention of casting out demons here seems to have been understood by Mark as a sign which confirmed the Word. Just as God often gave signs to seal the preaching of the prophets, so Christ has given signs to confirm the preaching of the gospel. Mark specifically mentions casting out demons, but other mighty works would have had the same purpose. In a more formal way the signs of baptism and the Lord's Supper would be included. Biblical preaching is often introduced by signs and often followed by signs which open our ears to the Word or seal the Word in our hearts.

A bit further on we again read of Jesus sending out his disciples to preach (6:7-13).[6] Here quite a bit is said about how the disciples were to

---

5. Cf. Guelich, *Mark*, 1:318-24; Lane, *The Gospel of Mark*, pp. 132-33.

6. Guelich, *Mark*, 1:318-24; Lane, *The Gospel of Mark*, pp. 206-10; Ulrich Mauser, *Christ in the Wilderness* (Naperville, Ill.: A. R. Allenson, 1963); Robert P. Meye, *Jesus and the Twelve: Discipleship and Revelation in Mark's Gospel* (Grand Rapids: Wm. B. Eerdmans Publishing Co., 1968).

carry out this ministry. For the support of their ministry they were to depend completely on the providence of God. "He charged them to take nothing for their journey except a staff; no bread, no bag, no money in their belts; but to wear sandals and not put on two tunics" (6:8-9). From meal to meal they were to be dependent on what God provided, just as Elijah was dependent on what the birds brought him. Night by night they were to be dependent on the hospitality of those who heard them. If people received their message, that was fine, but if they did not, they were to go on to those who would. Apparently they were to rely completely on the work of the Spirit.

2. Preaching in the Temple

We can perhaps find an even more fully developed reflection of the sermons of Jesus in the report Mark gives us of the teaching of Jesus in the Temple. As Mark presents it, in the course of the feast of Passover Jesus presented several different sermons. In chapters 11 and 12 we are told of how Jesus, after his triumphal entry into Jerusalem, went to the Temple, drove out the money changers, and then "taught" by explaining two texts of Scripture, Isaiah 56:7 and Jeremiah 7:11.[7] Chapters 11 and 12 bring together a considerable amount of material which Jesus taught in the Temple.[8] When regarded from the standpoint of the subjects treated, this material fits into the Markan narrative very well. It reads as an ongoing disputation lasting for several days, but it could also be understood as a series of sermons beginning with one on the house of prayer for all peoples.[9] The prophets frequently performed some sort of symbolic act as an introduction to their preaching, and what we apparently have here is the same sort of preaching, for we are told that the multitudes were

---

7. William Lane remarks concerning this passage that it is clear that Jesus was teaching in the Temple but that only the briefest summary of that teaching has been preserved. Lane, *The Gospel of Mark*, p. 408. Vincent Taylor remarks that verse 17 may indicate that Jesus taught at considerable length and that much more was said than is recorded. Taylor, *Gospel according to St. Mark*, p. 463.

8. On the arrangement of chapters 11 and 12 into different days and different sermons, see Lohmeyer, *Das Evangelium des Markus*, pp. 227-87, who treats chapters 11–13 as a unit under the heading, "Jesu Botschaft in Jerusalem." Vincent Taylor follows Lohmeyer, *Gospel according to St. Mark*, pp. 106-12 and 450-524. Mann, *Mark*, pp. 432-511 and especially pp. 432ff., treats chapters 11 and 12 as one unit and chapter 13 as another.

9. For commentary on this sermon, see Lane, *The Gospel of Mark*, pp. 406-7.

"astonished at his teaching" (11:18). Surely that implies that there was considerably more teaching than a few words explaining his actions. What we seem to have here is a brief report of a sermon introduced by a sign. The sign was certainly astonishing, and, Mark assures us, the sermon was equally astonishing.

We have already mentioned that there must have been a great amount of teaching or preaching in the courts of the Temple.[10] Surely there were accustomed ways of doing this; unfortunately we do not know what traditions or regulations governed this practice. We would like to know who was allowed to teach in the Temple and under what conditions, how the subject material was selected, and how the rabbis in Jesus' day might have distinguished between preaching in the synagogue and teaching in the Temple. The words "teach" and "preach" seem to be synonymous in the Gospel of Mark. While we might draw some clear distinctions between preaching and teaching elsewhere in the New Testament, these distinctions are probably not applicable here. We are no doubt to understand this teaching on the two texts from Isaiah and Jeremiah as part of the daily teaching Jesus conducted in the Temple when he was in Jerusalem. Later in the story Jesus reminds those who came to take him captive, " 'Day after day I was with you in the temple teaching' " (14:49).[11]

The following day Jesus again came to the Temple to teach. The question is, How formal was this teaching? Are we to understand that Jesus actually held lectures, preached sermons, or what in those days was considered an exercising of the ministry of the Word? Not all this material implies it came from formal teaching sessions, much less from sermons, yet much of it is homiletical material. In some cases a more formal teaching or preaching situation is assumed. In 12:1 we read, "And he began to speak to them in parables," and then in 12:35, "And as Jesus taught in the temple, he said. . . ." Some of the material implies a more informal sort of teaching. In 11:27 we read that while Jesus was walking in the Temple, the priests, scribes, and elders questioned him on his authority. As Mark presents the material, a number of people came up to Jesus and presented questions. This was perhaps an established way of teaching among the rabbis who taught in the Temple. It is interesting that in this material Jesus is repeatedly addressed as Teacher. We hesitate to draw too many conclusions about the formality or

10. See above, chapter 1.
11. Lane suggests that Jesus maintained his teaching ministry in the Temple during that particular visit for something like two weeks, *The Gospel of Mark*, p. 526.

informality of this teaching; nevertheless, we can say something about how Jesus taught and preached from the material presented here.

We point first to the expository material. After cleansing the Temple Jesus explained his action in terms of Isaiah 56:7. This was a key passage of Scripture for Jesus. It spoke of the gathering in of the Gentiles and of the purified worship of the messianic age.

> "These I will bring to my holy mountain,
>   and make them joyful in my house of prayer;
> their burnt offerings and their sacrifices
>   will be accepted on my altar;
> for my house shall be called a house of prayer
>   for all peoples."

Jesus had evidently taught extensively on the nature of the Temple in the days before his Passion. In fact, at his trial he was charged with threatening to destroy the Temple and to build it up in three days (Mark 14:58). Furthermore, the Gospel of John connects these sayings about destroying the Temple with a considerable amount of other material about how Jesus understood his body to be the fulfillment of the Temple. Yves Congar has done a beautiful job of putting all this material together and showing that this line of interpretation is found all through the literature of the New Testament and the ancient Church.[12]

A second passage of Scripture on which Jesus must have preached in the Temple was Psalm 118.

> The stone which the builders rejected
>   has become the head of the corner.
> This is the LORD's doing;
>   it is marvelous in our eyes.
>
> (vv. 22-23)

Psalm 118 was a classic text for the feast of Passover,[13] and it would have been more than appropriate to preach on it. In fact, the crowds sang the

---

12. Yves Congar, *Le mystère du Temple*, 2nd ed. (Paris: Les Éditions du Cerf, 1963). An equally important work on the relation of the worship of the Temple and the Christian gospel is Ernst Lohmeyer, *Lord of the Temple: A Study of the Relation between Cult and Gospel*, trans. Stewart Todd (Richmond: John Knox Press, 1962), especially pp. 34-52.

13. On the importance of the psalm for the earliest Christian, see Hans-Joachim Kraus, *Psalmen*, 2 vols. (Neukirchen: Neukirchener Verlag, 1961), 2:809.

psalm as Jesus entered Jerusalem (Mark 11:9). As Mark presents it, the exposition of this psalm is connected with the parable of the tenants of the vineyard who killed the owner's son (12:1-12). According to Mark, Jesus uses the parable to introduce the text from Psalm 118. Whether it was Mark or one of his sources who connected the parable and the text[14] will have to be left to New Testament scholars, but for those interested in the history of preaching this joining of parable and text suggests that what we have here is a crystallized sermon. All three Synoptic Gospels connect Psalm 118 with this parable, although other Gospels tell us more about how Jesus was accustomed to interpreting this psalm. In fact this psalm, too, had a very specific Christian interpretation which is found in all strata of the New Testament. This Christian interpretation was not something discovered after the fact by early Christians trying to find proof texts to show that Jesus was the Messiah. Could it not be that the Christian interpretation of this psalm goes back to the preaching of Jesus? Could it have been Jesus who took the favorite Passover psalm, which in his day was sung as a hymn of victory for the Messiah who was surely about to come, and showed that this promised Messiah would be rejected by both the Jewish priests and Roman governors but would in spite of it all be victorious because in God's sight he was chosen and precious?

A third passage of Scripture which Jesus expounded by his preaching in the Temple is Psalm 110.

> The LORD says to my lord:
>   "Sit at my right hand,
> till I make your enemies your footstool."
>
> (v. 1)

As Mark presents this, Jesus interprets the psalm by putting it in the form of a riddle. How is it that if the Messiah is David's son he calls him Lord? The obvious answer is that while the Messiah is indeed David's son he is also God's Son and therefore David's Lord. This is an audacious interpretation of Scripture which the Enlightenment theologians of several generations ago could never believe went back to Jesus. Today, with Paul

---

14. Taylor, *Gospel according to St. Mark,* pp. 476-77, figures that the interpretation of Psalm 118 does go back to Jesus. "Primitive Christianity [in its teaching about Christ as the stone rejected by men, but made by God the cornerstone of a new Temple] is based upon the memory that he used Psa cxviii. 22f. in a devastating attack upon the Jewish hierarchy." See as well Mann, *Mark,* pp. 466ff.

Billerbeck on one hand and Sigmund Mowinckel on the other, this bit of biblical exposition appears quite differently. In terms of the way the rabbis interpreted Scripture it was brilliant. But again we must point out that this interpretation of Psalm 110 appears repeatedly in the New Testament and in the literature of the ancient Church.[15] It is one of those fundamental Christian interpretations of Scripture which goes back to the preaching ministry of Jesus. The teaching ministry of Jesus, as the teaching ministry of any other rabbi of this time, was based on the interpretation of Scripture. These interpretations of Scripture were at the core of the teaching ministry of Jesus and of his disciples for generations to come.

Before we go further, we must point out that this brief exposition of Psalm 110 as reported by Mark shows considerable rhetorical sophistication. As mentioned above, Jesus makes his point by making a riddle of his text: If the Messiah is the son of David, how then does David call him Lord? Jesus knew how to stimulate thought. If the exposition was brilliant, so was the rhetoric. Jesus did not start out by assuming his hearers had only a high school education and that he therefore had to limit himself to the simple and the easy. Jesus was a brave teacher, willing to take the risk of confronting his hearers with the profound. One thing is abundantly clear from this exposition of Psalm 110, as it is from a number of Jesus' other expositions: Expository preaching for Jesus is above all proclamation. It proclaims that the promises of God have been kept and the Scriptures have been fulfilled, for the kingdom is at hand.

Another significant element in this series of sermons is dialogue. Various people brought questions to Jesus, and Jesus gave them answers. We in our day do not associate this sort of dialogue with preaching. In fact, in our day even teaching, with its formal lectures, is often far removed from dialogue. That does not seem to be the case with many of the sermons reported to us in both Old Testament and New Testament. The daily teaching of Jesus in the Temple as it is reported in all four of the Gospels obviously allowed for questions. How this was done we hesitate to say. Were the listeners allowed or even expected to ask questions after the preaching of a formal sermon, or were they given that liberty during the course of the sermon?

However these questions fit into the teaching and preaching ministry of Jesus, it is clear that Jesus was glad to take up the topics of the day and

---

15. Oscar Cullmann, *The Christology of the New Testament*, trans. Shirley Guthrie and Charles Hall (London: SCM Press, 1963), p. 88.

discuss them. Four such topics, according to Mark, were taken up during this series of sermons in the courts of the Temple. First is the question of paying taxes to Caesar. This was addressed to Jesus, we are told, by the Pharisees and Herodians, to which Jesus gave a somewhat evasive answer. Here, as elsewhere, we see that Jesus knew how to stay clear of issues that would embroil him in mundane concerns. To be sure, Jesus was no current events preacher, waving a newspaper in his hand.

The next question was advanced by the Sadducees. It was a question that came out of the furnace of the theological controversy of the day: Are the dead raised up to eternal life? To this question Jesus gave a clear and precise answer which decided against the Sadducees and for the Pharisees. He supported his answer with an interpretation of Scripture, " 'Have you not read in the book of Moses, in the passage about the bush, how God said to him, "I am the God of Abraham, and the God of Isaac, and the God of Jacob"? He is not God of the dead, but of the living' " (Mark 12:26-27).

Finally, a scribe posed a question as to which is the most important commandment. Here we have a question — in fact, a cardinal question — on how Scripture is interpreted. It asks very simply, What does Scripture all boil down to, if we might use a common expression of our day? It is first to love God and second to love the neighbor. There was, as we have already pointed out, a long tradition of theological discussion within the precincts of the Temple. One talked continually about what the Law meant and how the Law was to be obeyed. The scribes were the experts on the subject, and it is significant that a scribe asked this question.

We have already mentioned that in the courts of the Temple there seems to have been a continuing forum of religious teaching, theological debate, and biblical interpretation. It was almost as though one had in the Temple all at the same time the preacher's pulpit, the professor's lectern, and the judge's bench. All this belonged to the ministry of the Word. It was this whole ministry of the Word with all its facets that Jesus fulfilled when he preached daily in the Temple.

3. Mark's Words for Preaching

Let us look briefly at the vocabulary of the Gospel of Mark as it relates to preaching. Mark's choice of words demonstrates some fundamental things about the way the early Christians understood the preaching ministry of Jesus. To be sure, we are dealing not so much with the vocabulary of Mark himself as with the usage of the primitive Church as we find it reflected in Mark.

First we look at the word κηρύσσειν,[16] usually translated by "preach" or "proclaim." Very specifically it refers to what a herald does with an official announcement. He makes public a proclamation, announces the arrival of an official personage, or publishes good news. As Friedrich puts it, the preaching of Jesus was a trumpet blast which awakened the whole land to a new reality. The doors of the prison were opened and the prisoners released. As a result a new order came into existence, for the proclaimed word is a creative power and brings about what it announces.[17] The noun κῆρυξ indicated a herald, and the verb the work of the herald.[18]

Among the more significant uses of the word in the Gospel of Mark we find this statement:

> Now after John was arrested, Jesus came into Galilee, preaching the gospel of God, and saying, "The time is fulfilled, and the kingdom of God is at hand; repent, and believe in the gospel." (1:14-15)

This text is probably a good reflection of how the earliest Christians perceived the ministry of the Word. In fact we will return to this text again and again. Jesus was the prototype of the minister of the Word. Mark, as was true of the primitive Church generally, perceived Jesus as a herald of God announcing the final establishment of God's kingdom. His mission was to announce the arrival of that eschatological event. His ministry of preaching and teaching set the example of how the preachers of the early Church worked. In these two verses we get a good picture of how the early Church understood the word κηρύσσειν: It meant to proclaim that the kingdom was at hand but also implied a call to repentance and an invitation to faith. The word referred to the proclamation of the whole of the Christian message, not just the initial announcement.

Another text which exemplifies the Markan use of this word comes in what is often called the Little Apocalypse. In speaking of the tribulations

---

16. G. Friedrich, "κῆρυξ," *Theological Dictionary of the New Testament*, 3:697-717. See the concise article of Philippe-Henri Menoud, "Preaching," *Interpreter's Dictionary of the Bible*, 3:868-69; K. Goldammer, "Der Kerygma begriff in der ältesten christlichen Literatur," *Zeitschrift für die neutestamentliche Wissenschaft* 48 (1957): 77-101.

17. Friedrich, "κῆρυξ," *Theological Dictionary of the New Testament*, 3:706-7.

18. Friedrich, "κῆρυξ," *Theological Dictionary of the New Testament*, 3:696ff.

of the last day, Jesus says, "And the gospel must first be preached to all nations." Evangelism of the Gentiles was a major dimension of what was meant by κηρύσσειν. Preaching had to announce the kingdom of God to those who had never heard, who had had no previous relation to the people of God. The obvious eschatological flavor of this word is evident. To preach is to announce the coming day of the Lord.

We find this emphasis again in the conclusion to the Gospel as found in some manuscripts: "And he said to them, 'Go into all the world and preach the gospel to the whole creation'" (Mark 16:15). This Markan version of the Great Commission makes particularly obvious the connection of the Christian understanding of preaching with the evangelism of the Gentiles. Missionary preaching is at the heart of Christian preaching. The usage of the word κηρύσσειν gives a particular flavor to preaching. This is especially so when this verb takes as its object the noun εὐαγγέλιον, as it so often does in the Gospel of Mark.

Let us look for a moment, therefore, at this word εὐαγγέλιον.[19] The noun is usually translated "gospel." Quite literally the Greek word means good news. The prefix "eu" indicates something good; "angelion" indicates a message. Put together it simply means good news. Looking at the usage of this word in the Greek text of Mark, we notice that the first line of the Gospel reads, "The beginning of the gospel of Jesus Christ, the Son of God." This usage would imply that one could mean by the word εὐαγγέλιον simply the story of Jesus or even the message of Jesus.[20] This sentence implies that the two were closely related. The gospel is the story of the Savior, the culmination of the history of salvation. It is a message, a saving message. This rather strange statement, "The beginning of the gospel of Jesus Christ," implies that what is found in the Gospel of Mark is a summary of what the Church preached when it preached the gospel. Just as the Law of Moses told the story of redemption and also set down the stipulation for the life of the covenant community, so the Gospel of Mark both tells the story of redemption and teaches the way of life to be lived in the congregation of the New Covenant. By εὐαγγέλιον is obviously meant the total content of the message. This would be true of the gospel as it was preached both by Jesus and his disciples.

---

19. Cf. G. Friedrich, "εὐαγγελίζομαι," *Theological Dictionary of the New Testament*, 2:707-37. Cf. Guelich's excursus on the word "gospel," *Mark*, 1:13ff.
20. Cf. Guelich, *Mark*, 1:5-12.

Once again Mark 1:14-15 sheds significant light on what the early Church meant by the preaching of the gospel.

> Now after John was arrested, Jesus came into Galilee, preaching the gospel of God, and saying, "The time is fulfilled, and the kingdom of God is at hand; repent, and believe in the gospel."

As Mark understands it this was characteristic of the ministry of Jesus: He preached the gospel. He preached, "The time is fulfilled, the kingdom of God is at hand." "Fulfillment" is the key word. The good news is that the Scriptures have been fulfilled. The rabbis of the time taught the Scriptures, but Jesus preached the gospel. Teaching the Scriptures was evidently an important element in preaching the gospel, but preaching the gospel was more. What Christ did was to recount the promises of God and their fulfillment in himself. This recounting was a matter of teaching the Scriptures, to be sure, and also an announcement of the good news that they were being fulfilled, but beyond that, this announcement demanded repentance and faith. The preaching of the gospel called its hearers to faith and to faithfulness.

Moreover, twice in the Gospel of Mark we find the phrase "for my sake and the gospel." One instance is found in the famous saying of Jesus in 8:34-35:

> And he called to him the multitude with his disciples, and said to them, "If any man would come after me, let him deny himself and take up his cross and follow me. For whoever would save his life will lose it; and whoever loses his life for my sake and the gospel's will save it."

The point of the second saying, 10:29, is very similar. Both give the impression that the cause of Christ and the cause of the gospel are much the same. To preach the gospel is to preach Christ.

Gerhard Friedrich discusses at some length whether Jesus ever used the word "gospel." He admits that one could make a case that the word "gospel" was never on the tongue of Jesus, but on the other hand there is no reason for thinking that the concept was foreign to him.[21] The word does have a tendency to appear more in words about Jesus than in the words of Jesus, but at the end of the twentieth century it is not altogether clear why one should deny such sayings as Mark 8:35; 10:29; and 13:10

---

21. Friedrich, "εὐαγγελίζομαι," *Theological Dictionary of the New Testament*, 2:727-29.

to Jesus. Quite to the contrary, the picture Mark gives us of Jesus would indicate that this concept of preaching the gospel as it is so well expressed in the Greek word εὐαγγέλιον would come quite naturally to him. We will say more about this further on.

We turn now to the word διδάσκειν,[22] usually translated by the English word "teach." It is a simple Greek verb which belongs to the basic vocabulary and, unlike κηρύσσειν, has no special flavor to it. It is a very comprehensive word. As we have already mentioned, it appears in the Gospel of Mark as a synonym for the verb "to preach." But whereas the phrase "to preach the gospel" meant something done in a special way by Jesus and his disciples, the word "teach" when used as a synonym for "preach" tends to designate the ordinary ministry of the Word in its similarity to the ministry of the rabbis.[23] When we read, for example, in Mark 1:21 that on the Sabbath Jesus "entered the synagogue and taught," we must first understand that Jesus taught in the same way that the rabbis taught. What was different was that the teaching of Jesus had authority. We read:

> And they went into Capernaum; and immediately on the sabbath he entered the synagogue and taught. And they were astonished at his teaching, for he taught them as one who had authority, and not as the scribes. (1:21-22)

It is not clear how Jesus was so successful at catching the attention of his listeners. He preached much as other preachers in his day. He was learned in the Scriptures and interpreted his text in the way other learned preachers did. His teaching, however, had authority. Possibly in his preaching Jesus did not appeal to other authorities, those traditionally quoted from the oral tradition. Much more importantly, however, this seems to have meant that the message of Jesus was self-authenticating. When people heard it they knew it was true.

22. Rendtorff, "διδάσκω," *Theological Dictionary of the New Testament*, 2:135-65; George Foot Moore, *Judaism*, 2 vols. (New York: Schocken Books, 1971), 1:308ff.; C. H. Dodd, "Jesus as Teacher and Prophet," *Mysterium Christi* (1930): 53-66; Floyd V. Filson, "The Christian Teacher in the First Century," *Journal of Biblical Literature* 60 (1941): 317-28; E. L. Dietrich, "Rabbiner," *Die Religion in Geschichte und Gegenwart*, 6 vols., 3rd ed. (Tübingen: J. C. B. Mohr-Paul Siebeck, 1957-65), 5:759; P. Parker, "Rabbi," *Interpreter's Dictionary of the Bible*, 4:3 and "Teacher," *Interpreter's Dictionary of the Bible*, 4:522-23; Vernon K. Robbins, *Jesus the Teacher: A Socio-Rhetorical Interpretation of Mark* (Philadelphia: Fortress Press, 1984).
23. On the teaching of Jesus in comparison with the teaching of the rabbis, see Guelich, *Mark*, 1:55ff.

At the beginning of chapter 4 we again find this very simple word "teach" used to speak of the preaching of Jesus.

> Again he began to teach beside the sea. And a very large crowd gathered about him, so that he got into a boat and sat in it on the sea; and the whole crowd was beside the sea on the land. And he taught them many things in parables. (4:1-2)

The usage of the verb διδάσκειν here seems to make it very clear that the preaching ministry of Jesus put an emphasis on teaching and had a strong teaching content. The setting was informal — he preached beside the sea. Perhaps that meant he preached on the beach or in the port along the quay where the boats were tied up. Yet, however informal the setting may have been, the teaching content of Jesus' sermons must have been strong. In our day with such an abundance of cheap education even the common people are a bit jaded when it comes to learning. It is no doubt because of this that didactic preaching is so often deprecated. We forget that in a day when there were no free public schools, great crowds of people would eagerly gather to be taught. Even the common people were eager to learn. They loved Jesus because he was willing to teach them.

This would seem to be borne out by the next word to which we direct our attention, διδάσκαλος. At least ten times in the Gospel of Mark Jesus is addressed as Teacher. This is no doubt simply Mark's translation of the Hebrew honorific Rabbi. Even at that, the fact that Mark translates the term into Greek would certainly indicate he saw in this title more than an empty formality. At the bare minimum the use of the title would indicate that the people of his day saw Jesus in terms of the learned leadership the Jewish rabbis of the day gave to their people. But we can take the fact that Mark presents Jesus as one who was commonly addressed as Teacher to indicate that those to whom Jesus ministered understood him as their teacher. In his preaching they understood that they were being taught the truth of God, and they were glad to receive his teaching.

As we have seen, the Jesus we meet in the Gospel of Mark was a strong preacher. This was apparently the impression he left on the earliest Christians. As we go through the other Gospels we will get the same idea. The initial impression will be confirmed again and again.

B. Gospel of Luke

In the last generation New Testament scholars have done much to delineate the particular genius of the Gospel of Luke.[24] An interesting facet of Luke was his concern to explain how it came about that the Word of God, which for generations had been preached to the Jews alone, was now being received by the Gentiles. Luke opens his Gospel by telling us that he wants to pass on this story which Christians had received from those who were "eyewitnesses and ministers of the word" (Luke 1:2). He closes the Acts of the Apostles by telling us of how Paul lived in Rome, "preaching the kingdom of God and teaching about the Lord Jesus Christ quite openly and unhindered" (Acts 28:31). For Luke it is a wondrous sign of God's grace that the Word of God is both preached to and received by the Gentiles. How it came about that the gospel was preached to the Gentiles is therefore of special interest to Luke. He gives special attention to the proclamation of the gospel, to what was proclaimed and how it was proclaimed.[25] While Luke retains much of the same material as Mark, he preserves several traditions which add substantially to our picture of Jesus as preacher. The first is the story of the boy Jesus confounding the doctors in the courts of the Temple.

1. The Boy Jesus in the Temple

Only Luke tells us the story of the boy Jesus in the Temple. While some quickly relegate it to those legendary tales which grow up around the great figures of history, the story may very well preserve reliable material.[26] Much about it rings true, especially if one goes along with the theory that Luke got this material from Mary herself.[27] The family circle has a way of

---

24. Particularly important for this discussion is Hans Conzelmann, *The Theology of St. Luke*, trans. Geoffrey Buswell (New York: Harper & Row, 1961). Two commentaries which follow out the implications of this discussion are: Joseph A. Fitzmyer, *The Gospel according to Luke*, 2 vols., The Anchor Bible, vols. 28 and 28A (Garden City, N.Y.: Doubleday, 1981 and 1985); John Nolland, *Luke*, 3 vols., Word Biblical Commentary (Dallas: Word Books, 1989-93). For an evaluation of Conzelmann's contribution, see W. C. Robinson, Jr., "Luke, Gospel of," *Interpreter's Dictionary of the Bible*, supp. vol., pp. 558-60.

25. Cf. Fitzmyer on Luke's theology of proclamation, *The Gospel according to Luke*, 1:145-62.

26. Fitzmyer, *The Gospel according to Luke*, 1:437.

27. Norval Geldenhuys, *The Gospel of Luke*, The New International Commentary on the New Testament (Grand Rapids: Wm. B. Eerdmans Publishing Co., 1951), p. 125.

remembering stories of how children get lost on a trip to the big city, stories the children would just as soon forget when they get older. If we take the account just as Luke has preserved it, we do indeed get an important insight into how Jesus prepared for his ministry of preaching and teaching.[28]

Jesus prepared for this ministry in the same way any good Jewish boy would have in first-century Galilee.[29] Twelve years old was about the age at which higher education began in those days. Incredible as this may seem to us in our day, we need only remember that at about the same age Calvin was sent off to the College Montague in Paris or Bullinger was sent off to the University of Cologne. Latimer is supposed to have been sent off to Cambridge at thirteen. The center of Jewish theological education was the teaching held in the courts of the Temple at Jerusalem. This remained true as long as the Temple stood. For a devout and precocious Jewish boy the temptation to hear the leading rabbis lecture must have been very great, and since the courts of the Temple were the lecture halls of the University of Jerusalem the lectures of its great professors were open to all. His whole education up to that point pushed him to go seek out the sessions of study conducted by the most famous rabbis of the time.

It is rather surprising that a boy of twelve actually spoke in one of those sessions, but the precocious have a way of doing that and people have a way of being fascinated by the precocious. Sometimes they find themselves in the center of attention in spite of themselves. Evidently even the leading rabbis were fascinated by this adolescent prodigy. This story makes quite a bit of sense if we assume that Jesus had listened to the study sessions of the rabbis and their disciples, which were undoubtedly held in the synagogue of Nazareth. We spoke of these daily study sessions at length in the previous chapter. Jesus was no doubt fully familiar with how rabbinical discussion proceeded and was able to enter into that discussion with enough skill to command the amazement of even the mature professors. The story suggests that Jesus had a full rabbinical education. The fact that later in life he was regularly addressed as Rabbi or as Teacher and was allowed to teach in the synagogue would

---

28. Fitzmyer, *The Gospel according to Luke,* 1:438, tells us that Luke intends to convey by this story that Jesus "was one trained in the Torah and its requirements."

29. On Jewish education in the time of Jesus, see Birger Gerhardsson, *Memory and Manuscript* (Lund: C. W. K. Gleerup; Copenhagen: Ejnar Monksgaard, 1961), pp. 85-92.

certainly lead in that direction.[30] Here again we find evidence of a strong continuity between the way the ministry of the Word was exercised in the Church and the way it had been exercised in the Temple and the synagogue.

2. The Sermon at Nazareth

A second passage which adds substantially to the knowledge of the way Jesus exercised the ministry of the Word is the story of Jesus preaching in the synagogue of Nazareth.[31] The text tells us that on the Sabbath Jesus went to the synagogue as was his custom. Quite naturally he was asked to preach. We need not assume that this was an impromptu invitation. Normally preachers were expected to prepare and were therefore given the time necessary to do so. What Luke reports about the procedure fits well into what is known about the liturgical customs of the synagogue. Luke does not mention the reading of the Law, but we can assume that a rather lengthy passage from the Law was read before the preacher of the day stood up to read a passage from the prophets. Usually the passage the preacher chose served as a key of interpretation for the passage from the Law, the point being that Scripture was supposed to be interpreted by Scripture. So Jesus stood up to read the lesson from the prophets, and, as Luke recounts the story:

> There was given to him the book of the prophet Isaiah. He opened the book and found the place where it was written,
>
>> "The Spirit of the Lord is upon me,
>> because he has anointed me to preach good news to the poor.
>> He has sent me to proclaim release to the captives
>> and recovering of sight to the blind,

---

30. There are also suggestions that Jesus lacked a formal education. In the light of such texts as John 7:15 and Mark 1:22 one has to be very tentative about how Jesus learned the interpretation of Scripture. At the least, however, this passage from Luke should warn us against assuming that Jesus had no formal training in Scripture at all. The text from John 7:15 may mean nothing more than that Jesus had never spent a prolonged period as a disciple of one of the great rabbis as, for example, Paul had. Cf. Brooke Foss Westcott, *The Gospel according to St. John* (Grand Rapids: Wm. B. Eerdmans Publishing Co., 1954), p. 118.

31. Fitzmyer, *The Gospel according to Luke*, 1:434-48; Geldenhuys, *The Gospel of Luke*, pp. 125-32; Nolland, *Luke*, 1:126-32.

to set at liberty those who are oppressed,
to proclaim the acceptable year of the Lord."

And he closed the book, and gave it back to the attendant, and sat down. (Luke 4:17-20)

The chances are, given what we know about the liturgical customs of the day, that Jesus did in fact choose his own lesson from the prophets and that it was appropriate to the lesson from the Law which would inevitably have been read that Sabbath. Nevertheless, there is the possibility that it was an appointed lesson, and in this case we find the trace of an intimation that the choice of the lessons was providential.[32] The brevity of the text unfortunately does not allow us to press either interpretation.

Be that as it may, one could hardly find a better text on which to preach a sermon on the messianic preaching ministry. Here we see Jesus preaching on preaching. The text from Isaiah makes the point that the Messiah is anointed to preach good news to the poor, release to the captive, recovery of sight to the blind, and liberty to the oppressed. The Greek text contains the rich words Christian theologians have always understood to speak of the essence of preaching: εὐαγγελίζεσθαι, to proclaim the good news, and κηρύσσειν, to herald glad tidings. Furthermore, this text understands the preaching ministry of the Messiah in much the same way as Mark had summarized it: "Jesus came . . . preaching (κηρύσσων) the gospel (τὸ εὐαγγέλιον) of God, and saying, 'The time is fulfilled, and the kingdom of God is at hand; repent, and believe in the gospel'" (Mark 1:14-15). In both texts we find the idea that the appointed or acceptable time has come and the promises of God are being fulfilled.[33] The fulfillment theme is prominent. In fact, Jesus' sermon is basically the announcement that the prophecy which he read had been fulfilled. "'Today this scripture has been fulfilled in your hearing'" (Luke 4:21).

Several observations can be made about the way the sermon is put

32. It would depend on whether Luke and his readers considered that the lesson from the prophets was normally appointed. Most authorities figure that it was not until after the emergence of the Christian Church that lists of appointed lessons were drawn up. Cf. Jacob Mann, *The Bible as Read and Preached in the Old Synagogue*, vol. 1 (New York: KTAV Publishing House, 1971), vol. 2 (Cincinnati: Hebrew Union College, 1966); Nolland, *Luke*, 1:194 and 196.

33. On the relation of Luke's terminology for preaching to the terminology of the other Gospels, cf. Augustin George, *Études sur L'oeuvre de Luc* (Paris: J. Gabalda, 1978), p. 388.

together. First of all, Luke tells us nothing about how the sermon treated the reading from the Law, which we can assume was read, but we need not deduce from that that Jesus' sermon was unrelated to the lesson from the Law appointed for that Sabbath. We do find, however, that Jesus used two passages from the former prophets to interpret the lesson from Isaiah. First he reminds his listeners of the way Elijah was sent to the aid of the widow of Zarephath (I Kings 17:8-16), and second he illustrates the same point with the story of the healing of Naaman the Syrian in the time of Elisha (II Kings 5:1-14). As Luke presents the sermon, extensive use is made of the principle that Scripture is to be interpreted by Scripture. When Jesus preached in the synagogue on the Sabbath he was an expository preacher. His sermon was an interpretation of Scripture.

Another interesting point about the way this sermon is put together is that it reflects the uniqueness of the situation. Jesus is preaching in his hometown synagogue and recognizes that his congregation has special expectations of him and of what he should say and do for them. The congregation was delighted with Jesus' impressive opening announcement that the Scriptures were even then being fulfilled among them.

> And all spoke well of him, and wondered at the gracious words which proceeded out of his mouth; and they said, "Is not this Joseph's son?" And he said to them, "Doubtless you will quote to me this proverb, 'Physician, heal yourself; what we have heard you did at Capernaum, do here also in your own country.'" (Luke 4:22-23)

We notice evidence that the congregation was not completely passive nor altogether silent during the preaching of a sermon. We see here the give-and-take that is of the essence of public oratory. This sermon is no monologue. Jesus plays on the response of the congregation and even anticipates their thoughts by quoting a folk parable from the popular wisdom of the day, "Physician, heal yourself." Evidently Jesus had nothing against using illustrative material from all kinds of sources in his sermons. The use of this proverb is only one example; we will find plenty of others throughout the New Testament. The records we have of the sermons of the earliest Christians show a variety of different kinds of illustrative material. Early Christian preaching was sensitive to the congregation, and Jesus' illustrations here are appropriate to this particular congregation and only to this congregation. It is important to point out this feature. The sermon is thoroughly expository and yet at the same time takes up into it the concerns, capacities, and interests of the congregation. It is an interpretation of Scripture and also an interpretation of the congregation.

This sermon as Luke reports it is indeed marvelously instructive. The question is, Are we dealing here with a sermon of Jesus or with a literary construction of Luke? The question is made forceful in view of the fact that Luke has included in the Acts of the Apostles a number of sermons from the leading characters of the book — Peter, Stephen, and Paul — which, as is often pointed out, was considered the appropriate thing for Greek historians to do. They were forever constructing appropriate speeches for the leading characters of history at the crucial moments of history. We leave to others a thorough discussion of the problem, and only point out that there are reasons for regarding Luke's record as a good reflection of the preaching of Jesus. C. H. Dodd in his famous study on the apostolic preaching has shown that the sermons recorded in Acts are quite reliable witnesses to the preaching of the earliest Christians.[34]

It also needs to be pointed out that Isaiah 61, the passage Luke tells us Jesus used as his text, is another of those passages which appear again and again in the New Testament and, we are convinced, is one of the fundamental passages the interpretation of which Jesus taught his disciples.[35] It was only natural that at the center of the work of any teacher who stands in the biblical tradition there would be certain fundamental interpretations of Scripture. The message of any true biblical preacher is always based on certain key passages of Scripture. This is surely true of Jesus. Such characteristic interpretations of Scripture are at the center of the tradition of preaching which Jesus passed on to his disciples. We have already spoken of Jesus' interpretation of Psalms 110 and 118. His interpretations of Isaiah 53 and the Passover narrative in Exodus would be other examples. It was not just a method of preaching which Jesus passed on; it was a message as well. Jesus was an expository preacher, and certain expositions which he preached were essential to his ministry. That Scripture be fulfilled in what he did and what he preached was at the heart of his ministry.

---

34. C. H. Dodd, *The Apostolic Preaching and Its Development* (London: Hodder & Stoughton, 1936); also Gerhardsson, *Memory and Manuscript*, pp. 208-61.

35. Nestle-Aland, *Novum Testamentum Graece* (Stuttgart: Deutsche Bibelstiftung, 1979), identifies ten passages of the New Testament which either quote or allude to these verses, p. 761.

3. The Mission of the Seventy

Let us look at a third passage of the Gospel of Luke, namely, the story of the mission of the Seventy (Luke 10:1-16).[36] Again only this Gospel records the story. Much of the material found in it is found in the other Gospels, for example, in the stories of the training of the Twelve (Matt. 9:34-38; 10:7-16; Mark 6:6-13; and John 4:31-38); nevertheless, the way Luke puts this material together is quite unique. For the Gospels generally this was obviously significant material.

What seems to stand out in this material is that Jesus put a strong emphasis on the ministerial nature of the ministry of the Word.[37] God governs his kingdom by his Word and it is the responsibility of the minister of the Word to serve God in hearing the Word, in reading the Word, in interpreting the Word, and in witnessing to the Word. No one of us performs the whole of this ministry; we enter into the labor of other ministers (John 4:37-38). Just as the apostle Paul may have planted and Apollos watered but God gave the increase, so we find here that the ministry of the Word demands that a fellowship of ministers work together. The disciples are sent out two by two (Luke 10:1; Mark 6:7).[38] Each has his own talents, his own gifts of ministry, but in the end it is God who brings in the harvest. God, and God alone, is the Lord of the harvest (Luke 10:2). In one village the time may not be ripe, but it is important that the gospel be preached nevertheless. The preacher should not be frantic if there is little or no response because the fruition is in God's hands. There will be sons of peace who will receive the message and the blessing (Luke 10:6). There will be those who will not receive it, but it is important that they know that they had a chance, that the kingdom of God had come near to them (Luke 10:11).

Evidently Jesus had been very clear that the Church was to provide for her ministers. " 'The laborer deserves his wages' " (Luke 10:7). The preachers were to take little in the way of money or baggage (Luke 9:3 and Mark 6:8-9). Those who received the message were to take care of the messengers. If the

---

36. Fitzmyer, *The Gospel according to Luke,* 2:841-50; Geldenhuys, *The Gospel of Luke,* pp. 298-305; Nolland, *Luke,* 2:545-60.

37. Augustin George makes the point that the Gospel of Luke presents Jesus as the original minister of the Word, who prepares the disciples to continue his ministry. *Études sur L'oeuvre de Luc,* pp. 387-94.

38. Joachim Jeremias, "Paarweise Sendung im Neuen Testament," in *Abba. Studien zur neutestamentlichen Theologie und Zeitgeschichte* (Göttingen: Vandenhoeck & Ruprecht, 1966), pp. 132-39.

provision is modest the preachers are to be content, but they are presumably not to be distracted by lavish provision either. They are to eat and drink what is provided and remain with the same host as long as they labor in the same locality (Luke 10:7 and Mark 6:10). It is well known that Francis of Assisi took these sayings of Jesus as the prototype of the Franciscan Rule. He probably interpreted them as profoundly as anyone and well illustrated the meaning of these teachings. As he saw it the simplicity Jesus prescribed for his preachers had as its purpose complete dependence on divine providence. God would provide for the preachers of the gospel.

Another very important point in Jesus' instructions to his disciples is the tremendous authority God gave to his preachers. Through their teaching Satan would be bound, demons cast out, and the sick healed (Luke 9:1; 10:9, 17; Mark 6:13). These mighty works were to be God-given signs confirming the gospel they preached. They were to show that indeed the kingdom of God had come near (Luke 10:9). Even with the signs, however, it was in the last analysis the Word itself which won the hearts of the first Christians. The Word has self-authenticating power. The sheep know the voice of the shepherd, as we find it in the Gospel of John (John 10:4). It is this creative, enlightening Word which Jesus entrusted to the disciples. This gave them authority, all the authority they really needed.

> "He who hears you hears me, and he who rejects you rejects me, and he who rejects me rejects him who sent me." (Luke 10:16)

Here is a saying which even the most radical critics figure may well go back to Jesus himself. Be that as it may, the point seems to be that in the preaching of Christian preachers the congregation comes into close communion with Christ himself. Christ is present in the preaching of his Word. "He who hears you hears me." Once again we have an intimation of the doctrine of the kerygmatic presence.

4. On the Road to Emmaus

In the final chapter of the Gospel of Luke[39] we find the interesting account of Jesus meeting two disciples on the road to Emmaus[40] and interpreting

---

39. P. Shubert, "The Structure and Significance of Luke 24," Neutestamentliche Studien für Rudolf Bultmann, Beihefte zur Zeitschrift für die neutestamentliche Wissenschaft 21 (1954): 165-86.

40. C. H. Dodd, in building his case for a realized eschatology, makes the point that

the Scriptures for them. It makes very clear what we have already suggested: It is Jesus who taught the earliest Christians their characteristic interpretations of Scripture.

> And he said to them, "O foolish men, and slow of heart to believe all that the prophets have spoken! Was it not necessary that the Christ should suffer these things and enter into his glory?" And beginning with Moses and all the prophets, he interpreted to them in all the scriptures the things concerning himself. (Luke 24:25-27)

It was not that Jesus had not, even before the Passion and resurrection, taught his followers his interpretation of the Scriptures. It was far more that now his interpretation was beginning to make sense to them. After Christ's passion and resurrection the disciples could understand what they had not been able to understand before. Luke preserves quite a bit of the same material the other Gospels preserved about how Jesus interpreted the Scriptures, among the most important of which would be Isaiah 53, Isaiah 54, Isaiah 61, Psalm 110, and Psalm 118. The point the Gospel writers are obviously intent on making is that Jesus himself gave attention to teaching his disciples the interpretation of Scripture. We read at the very end of the Gospel of Luke:

> Then he said to them, "These are my words which I spoke to you, while I was still with you, that everything written about me in the law of Moses and the prophets and the psalms must be fulfilled." Then he opened their minds to understand the scriptures, and said to them, "Thus it is written, that the Christ should suffer and on the third day rise from the dead, and that repentance and forgiveness of sins should be preached in his name to all nations, beginning from Jerusalem. You are witnesses of these things." (Luke 24:44-48)

For Luke the Great Commission was a charge to preach the gospel to all nations, as it is in the other Gospels as well, but in Luke essential to this preaching is to announce that the Scriptures of the Old Testament have been fulfilled. Jesus sends the disciples out to do expository preaching, to

---

the apostolic preaching gave great attention to the fact that early Christian preaching proclaimed that the Scriptures had been fulfilled. *Apostolic Preaching and Its Development*, pp. 13, 17 et passim. For commentary on this passage, see Fitzmyer, *The Gospel according to Luke*, 2:1567; Geldenhuys, *The Gospel of Luke*, pp. 633-37; Nolland, *Luke*, 3:1194-1209; and Alfred Plummer, *The Gospel according to Luke*, 5th ed. (Edinburgh: T. & T. Clark, 1922), p. 555. We find ourselves in agreement with Plummer and Geldenhuys rather than Fitzmyer.

explain the Scriptures as he himself had explained them. Essential to the preaching of the gospel is the proclamation that the Scriptures have been fulfilled, that Christ's victory over death was according to Scripture. Luke saw it about the same way Paul preached it: "that Christ died for our sins in accordance with the scriptures, that he was buried, that he was raised on the third day in accordance with the scriptures" (I Cor. 15:3-4).

C. The Gospel of Matthew

We find an equally strong picture of Jesus as preacher in the Gospel of Matthew.[41] For Matthew, Jesus is the preacher who completely fulfills the priestly role of teaching the Law of Moses and the prophetic role of proclaiming the Word of God. That Jesus fulfills the role of preacher from the standpoint of both the Law and the prophets is particularly clear from the story of the transfiguration (Matt. 17:1-8). What the disciples saw on the mountain at that illuminating moment was that Jesus was the one who spoke to Moses on Mount Sinai and from whom Elijah heard the still, small, prophetic voice on that same mountain.

Again, as was true of the Gospel of Luke, many of the same traditions about the preaching ministry of Jesus that we find in Mark are passed on in Matthew. What is characteristic of Matthew, however, is a balance achieved among many aspects of the ministry of the Word. Jesus is preacher in the synagogue and beside the sea. Privately he teaches his disciples the secrets of the kingdom, and publicly he enters into rabbinical discussion on the interpretation of the Law in the courts of the Temple.

It is customary to point out that Matthew has organized his Gospel in such a way that the sayings or teachings of Jesus are collected into several sermons, each on a particular subject. Rather than being scattered through

---

41. Especially helpful in the following study of Matthew have been the following works: Paul Billerbeck and Herman L. Strack, *Kommentar zum Neuen Testament aus Talmud und Midrasch*, 3rd ed., 4 vols. (Munich: Beck, 1951-56), vol. 1, *Das Evangelium nach Matthäus;* Günther Bornkamm, Gerhard Barth, and Heinz Joachim Held, *Überlieferung und Auslegung im Matthäus Evangelium*, 4th ed. (Neukirchen-Vluyn: Neukirchener, 1965); Donald A. Hagner, *Matthew*, 2 vols., Word Biblical Commentary (Dallas: Word Books, 1993); Adolf Schlatter, *Der Evangelist Matthäus, seine Sprache, sein Ziel, seine Selbständigkeit*, 6th ed. (Stuttgart: Calwer Verlag, 1963); Eduard Schweizer, *The Good News according to Matthew* (Atlanta: John Knox Press, 1975); Krister Stendahl, *The School of Matthew*, 2nd ed. (Philadelphia: Fortress Press, 1968).

the narrative of the life of Jesus, they are arranged as sermons and presented at fitting intervals throughout the Gospel.[42] The most easily recognized of these is obviously the Sermon on the Mount. It is usually pointed out that these collections of sayings are not really sermons but rather collections of formulated teachings of Jesus. It is sermonic or homiletical material, to be sure, but it is crystallized into the shortest form possible so that it can be memorized and passed on in oral tradition. Let us in the very briefest way look at some of these collections of sermonic material to see what they might tell us about the preaching of Jesus.[43]

1. Sermon on the Mount

The setting Matthew gives to the Sermon on the Mount[44] makes it clear that Jesus is a preacher in the rabbinical tradition. We read, "Seeing the crowds, he went up on the mountain, and when he sat down his disciples came to him. And he opened his mouth and taught them, saying: . . ." (Matt. 5:1-2). A preacher or teacher in the ancient Orient sat to teach; the disciples stood to listen. It was a matter of honor being given to the preacher, and for that reason Matthew makes this clear. But Matthew wants to say more by using this setting. The sermon is given on a mountain and somehow, as more than one New Testament scholar has pointed out,

42. The theory can be taken to unwarranted extremes. In some versions five sermons are identified, each one corresponding to the five books of Moses, and the Gospel as a whole is understood as a Christian Torah. See the criticism of this in J. D. Kingsbury, "Form and Message of Matthew," *Interpretation* 29 (1975): 13-23.

43. The basis of identifying five discourses in the Gospel of Matthew is the repetition of the phrase "And when Jesus had finished these sayings" at Matthew 7:28; 11:1; 13:53; 19:1; and 26:1. F. C. Grant in his article on the Gospel of Matthew in the *Interpreter's Dictionary of the Bible* identifies the five discourses as follows: first, Sermon on the Mount, chapters 5–7; second, the mission of the disciples, 9:55–10:42; third, the hidden teachings of the parables, 13:1-52; fourth, church administration, 17:24–18:35; and fifth, a sort of double discourse, criticism of the scribes and Pharisees, chapter 23, and the doctrine of the parousia, chapters 24–25. For our purposes it seems better to speak of the Sermon in the Temple (21:23–23:29) and the Sermon on the Last Things (chaps. 24–25). As we have already said, the different Gospels provide us with much homiletical material which Jesus is supposed to have taught in the Temple. From Mark we gather that Jesus taught frequently in the Temple. The Sermon on the Mount of Olives, however, seems to be a separate construction.

44. For the interpretation of the Sermon on the Mount, see Georg Eichholz, *Auslegung der Bergpredigt*, 2nd ed. (Neukirchen-Vluyn: Neukirchener, 1970); W. D. Davies, *The Setting of the Sermon on the Mount* (Cambridge: University Press, 1966).

one sees in this mountain a reference to Mount Sinai. The teaching of Jesus was prefigured by Moses' teaching Israel from the mountain; in fact the teaching of Jesus is the fulfillment of the Law of Moses, as Jesus makes very clear in this sermon: " 'Think not that I have come to abolish the law and the prophets; I have come not to abolish them but to fulfill them' " (5:17). The overarching theme of the sermon is fulfillment. The kingdom of God is at hand.

This theme is set by the Beatitudes. In each of them good news is proclaimed to the poor, to those who mourn, to the meek, to those who hunger and thirst for righteousness, to the merciful, to the pure in heart, to peacemakers and those who are persecuted. Matthew has organized this sermon in such a way as to make it clear that this material, which no doubt appeared and reappeared again and again in the preaching of Jesus, was the keynote of all Jesus' preaching.

The sermon moves on to a series of interpretations of Scripture, which again underlines the importance Jesus gave in his preaching to this matter. Here Jesus interprets a number of the cardinal precepts of the Law, the commandments of the Decalogue itself. There are interpretations of the commandments against killing, adultery, swearing falsely, and coveting. In his interpretation of the moral law Jesus makes clear that it is love which fulfills the Law. There are interpretations of the laws regarding prayer, almsgiving, and fasting.

Finally, the sermon contains admonitions to repentance from the ways of the world and admonitions to faith. We are to turn away from the concerns of the Gentiles — what we shall eat, what we shall drink, what we shall wear — and seek the kingdom of God and his righteousness. We are to enter by the narrow gate and build our house on the rock.

While the Sermon on the Mount may not be a report of any particular sermon, it contains a good digest of the material Jesus typically taught in his preaching. It proclaimed the coming of the kingdom. Furthermore, it interpreted Scripture and proclaimed the coming of the kingdom as the fulfillment of Scripture. Finally it urged repentance and faith. What we have in the Sermon on the Mount is a fleshing out of that summary of his preaching which we found one chapter earlier in Matthew: "Jesus began to preach, saying, 'Repent, for the kingdom of heaven is at hand' " (Matt. 4:17).[45]

---

45. Even better the Sermon on the Mount fleshes out Mark 1:14-15, "Jesus came into Galilee, preaching the gospel of God, and saying, 'The time is fulfilled, and the kingdom of God is at hand; repent, and believe in the gospel.' "

2. Sermon to the Disciples

Another of Matthew's collections of the sayings of Jesus is found in 9:35 to 10:42, where Jesus instructs the Twelve before sending them out on a preaching mission.[46] We might call this the Sermon to the Disciples. Several of these sayings bear directly on the nature of the preaching ministry,[47] and taken together they make a very strong point of preaching being a divine work and that the preacher is but an instrument in God's employ. The preacher need take neither gold nor silver, bag nor staff, because he is to rely on God's providence. Sometimes people will listen and sometimes they will not; if they do not then the preacher must move on to the next town. One should not be surprised if one is persecuted. In this persecution, which may or may not come, the preacher is upheld by God's protecting hand;[48] he has his providential eye on the preacher just as he does upon the sparrow. When called to give witness before a hostile Gentile court, a preacher need not be anxious as to what to say, for the Holy Spirit will supply the words. Such authority is bestowed upon the preacher by Jesus! Not only does Jesus promise divine inspiration, he even promises that in preaching is to be found a real presence. " 'He who receives you receives me, and he who receives me receives him who sent me' " (Matt. 10:40). We found this same kerygmatic presence in the Gospel of Luke. For our understanding of worship it is a fundamental insight.

Obviously Jesus gave much time to preaching himself, but he also spent much time teaching his disciples to be preachers. The apostolic ministry, at least as we find it in the Gospel of Matthew, is clearly to be a preaching ministry. The apostles are to be ministers of the Word.[49]

We have now looked at all three Synoptic versions of the Sermon to the Disciples,[50] and if modern New Testament studies have guided us properly these different versions give us the material Jesus frequently

---

46. The commentary of Donald Hagner is helpful: *Matthew,* 1:262-97. Notice as well Hagner's remarks about the structure of this passage: *Matthew,* 1:258-61.

47. James Stuart Stewart, professor of New Testament at the University of Edinburgh, was both one of the greatest preachers of our century and one of the greatest teachers of preachers. His chapter on the teaching method of Jesus is of special interest: *The Life and Teaching of Jesus Christ* (Nashville: Abingdon Press, n.d.).

48. Cf. Schweizer, *Good News according to Matthew,* p. 234.

49. Hagner, *Matthew,* 1:297.

50. On the relation of this passage to the rest of the Synoptic tradition, see Schweizer, *Good News according to Matthew,* pp. 233, 235, 241ff., and 245ff.

preached to the inner circle of his disciples. As we will frequently find throughout the history of preaching, some sermons are directed to the crowds who have little familiarity with the Christian message, and some are directed to those who know much about the Christian message and are deeply committed to the work of the kingdom. Evangelistic preaching assumes that the hearers have not made a commitment to Christ. Ideally, catechetical preaching assumes they have made an initial commitment but know very little about the faith they wish to live. Then there is a kind of preaching which in some circles has been called "spiritual catechism," which assumes the listeners have made a commitment and that commitment has grown over the years; nevertheless they still need to deepen that commitment. It is this kind of preaching that Matthew summarizes in what we have called the Sermon to the Disciples. As is evidenced by this sermon's several parallels and doublets, Jesus directed an important part of his preaching ministry toward the inner group of disciples. The Sermon on the Mount was directed toward the crowd, but the Sermon to the Disciples was directed toward the inner group.

The first point Jesus seems to make in this sermon is that a true preacher must be sent out by God himself, the Lord of the harvest (Matt. 9:38). Jesus himself called his disciples and gave them authority (10:1). This is followed by the naming of the twelve apostles. One gathers from this that the ministry of the Word, at least as Matthew understood Jesus, was a formal, ordered ministry. That is not the same thing as saying that it was institutionalized. That the ministry should be managed like a transnational business corporation does not seem to be quite what Jesus had in mind.

The second point is that Christian preaching must be gratuitous: " 'You received without paying, give without pay' " (10:8). Christian preaching has to spring from a grace-filled heart; it is therefore grateful preaching, and when it does this, it is graceful preaching. It does not count the cost because already God has blessed the preacher far beyond anything he can ever repay. Gracious preachers are those who have been overcome by the grace of God. The point Jesus seems to be making here is that gratuitous preaching has by its very nature a sort of simplicity to it. It is not accompanied by elaborate preparations, nor is it contrived or programmed. As Matthew has preserved these sayings they very pointedly teach that when the disciples go out to preach they are to take no gold or silver or copper in their belts, no bag for their journey, no extra suit of clothes or change of shoes, not even a staff, yet the laborer deserves his wages (10:9-10). Those who receive the message owe the messenger his keep.

141

As the disciples went out to preach they well remembered that Jesus had warned them that their preaching would meet opposition. They had come to understand that Jesus was the Lamb of God, and if they understood *how* Jesus was the Lamb of God, they understood what he meant when he told them they were being sent out as "'sheep in the midst of wolves'" (10:16). Jesus had met persecution and they would meet persecution. Judging by how often this thought is found in parallel passages and in doublets through all four Gospels, we can well imagine that this theme must often have been treated in the preaching of Jesus.

In Matthew's Sermon to the Disciples we find an important saying of Jesus which has had quite an effect on the history of preaching.

> "When they deliver you up, do not be anxious how you are to speak or what you are to say; for what you are to say will be given to you in that hour; for it is not you who speak, but the Spirit of your Father speaking through you." (10:19-20)

What did Jesus mean by this? We are all aware that many preachers have used this as a justification for impromptu preaching on all occasions. Is it a lack of faith or a failure of the anointing of the Holy Spirit which keeps some preachers in their studies preparing sermons all week? This is probably not what Jesus intended to convey. More likely the point of the saying is that when in the course of giving the apostolic witness we are faced with challenges beyond our abilities, we can be sure that the Holy Spirit will give us the insight to say what needs to be said. Whether we speak about the doctrine of the Holy Spirit or the doctrine of providence, it all amounts to the same thing: the Lord will provide. It is he and he alone who gives the increase. He and he alone is Lord of the harvest.

Finally, the Sermon to the Disciples makes the point that the preacher must devote himself to a fearless profession of faith and a wholehearted commitment. This is the peroration of the sermon. Here we have the admonition with which a well-designed sermon concludes:

> "So every one who acknowledges me before men, I also will acknowledge before my Father who is in heaven; but whoever denies me before men, I also will deny before my Father who is in heaven." (10:32-33)

While New Testament scholars will hasten to assure us that Matthew's Sermon to the Disciples was constructed by the Evangelist from various sources and hardly represents an actual sermon that Jesus preached at a particular time and place, there is nevertheless every reason to believe that it was a typical sermon, a sermon which in one variation or another Jesus often preached. Perhaps more precisely, it is a concentrated sermon, containing in abbreviated form the message of many different sermons which Jesus preached to the more intimate circle of disciples.

3. Sermon of the Parables

Let us pass on to yet another of these "sermons" Matthew offers us, what we might call the Sermon of the Parables (Matt. 13:1-52).[51] It illustrates at length Jesus' most famous homiletical technique, namely, the parable. In this discourse Matthew has arranged a series of parables which speak on the subject of the ministry of the Word.[52]

The parable of the sower teaches us of the marvelous fruitfulness of the preaching of the Word. In spite of the hardness of human hearts, of persecution, and of the cares of the world, by the grace of God the preaching of the gospel will have tremendous success. The parable of the wheat and the tares assures us that the preaching of the gospel will bear fruit even if competing gospels are proclaimed. The preaching of the Word of God is like the sowing of the grain of mustard seed, which produces the greatest of trees. The Word has a power in itself which may appear insignificant but like the yeast which is hidden in the lump of dough it has a tremendous effect. Obviously Jesus not only did a great amount preaching, but he also did a great amount of preaching about preaching.

One of the curious features of this sermon is that it works on two levels. It is a sermon to the crowds and a sermon to the disciples. Two of the parables, namely, the parable of the sower and the parable of the wheat and tares, are told to the crowds in the course of Jesus' regular preaching and then expounded to the disciples privately. It is not that they had both

---

51. On Matthew's collection of parables in chapter 13, see Hagner, *Matthew*, 1:361-407. The literature on the parables is vast. For New Testament scholarship, however, the following have been particularly important: C. H. Dodd, *The Parables of the Kingdom* (London: Nisbet, 1935; New York: Scribner's, 1936); Joachim Jeremias, *The Parables of Jesus*, trans. S. H. Hooke (London: SCM; Philadelphia: Westminster, 1972); Birger Gerhardsson, "The Seven Parables in Matthew XIII," *New Testament Studies* 19 (1972-73): 16-37; Birger Gerhardsson, "If We Do Not Cut the Parables Out of Their Frames," *New Testament Studies* 37 (1991): 321-35.

52. On Matthew's arrangement or rearrangement of the material, see Schweizer, *Good News according to Matthew*, pp. 275ff.

an apparent meaning and a secret meaning, nor were they so obscure that without an explanation they could not be understood. Christianity was not at all like the mystery religions that had a body of secret teachings which was passed on only to the initiates.[53] Surely we are to understand this to mean that Christian truth is not always grasped at first hearing; it has to be listened to carefully and repeatedly and then meditated upon. A disciple must give time to study and contemplation. If one is to become a true minister of the Word one must follow the lectures of the master, enter into the discussion, ask questions, and preach for a time under the supervision of the master. The apostles went through this kind of training. That is obviously what is being said in the Sermon of the Parables. The synagogue had trained its preachers that way and the Church was following suit. That Matthew has this in mind we gather from the rather surprising statement at the end of the Sermon of the Parables. Jesus asked the disciples:

> "Have you understood all this?" They said to him, "Yes." And he said to them, "Therefore every scribe who has been trained for the kingdom of heaven is like a householder who brings out of his treasure what is new and what is old." (13:51-52)

Here we find a rather unexpected reference to the minister of the Word as a Christian scribe. This is quite in character with what we know of Matthew, who has often been called a Christian scribe.[54] However that may be, the assumption conveyed here is that those the Church trains to be her ministers must be like the scholars of Israel: they must have stored up a great treasure of wisdom and knowledge so that they can bring it out as the occasion arises.

A careful examination of these parables brings out several considerations about their literary form. In the first place some of these parables are not really parables at all but rather similes. Comparisons of the kingdom of heaven to a treasure hid in a field and a merchant in search of

---

53. To be sure, we hear of the parables containing the mysteries of the kingdom, but in spite of the use of the word *mystērion*, that is not the sort of teaching practiced by the earliest Christians. Cf. Raymond E. Brown, *The Semitic Background of the Term "Mystery" in the New Testament* (Philadelphia: Fortress Press, 1968); Lucien Cerfaux, "La connaissance des secrets du royaume d'après Matt. xiii. II et par," *New Testament Studies* 2 (1956): 238-49.

54. Cf. Stendahl, *The School of Matthew.*

fine pearls are obvious similes. The literary form of the biblical parable is not quite the same thing as the literary form of the parable in the classical literature of ancient Greece and Rome, much less modern American literature. Although it functioned as a sermon illustration, a parable as it was used by Jesus is more than an illustration. It is not a story which explains and makes simple a doctrine or moral teaching. Sometimes a parable is something of a riddle; and it is not always simple. It is sometimes very complex, demanding both the meditation of the congregation and the elaboration of the preacher.

The biblical parable is a very specific literary form. As it was developed in the biblical tradition, a parable was a device used by preachers to epitomize a sermon. A whole sermon could be packed up into a parable and put away in the memory and then later brought out again when the occasion arose and unpacked by a process of explanation and elaboration.

What we have here in the thirteenth chapter of Matthew is a whole series of parables of the kingdom, a veritable series of sermons in miniature. As any preacher who has tried to do a series of sermons on the parables knows, there is no better way to get across to a congregation the teachings of Jesus than a parable. Unpacking these parables always has a way of getting ahold of people's ears. The reason is very simple: When we do this we are re-presenting the preaching of Jesus. These parables are part of the sermon barrel Jesus gave his disciples when he sent them out to preach. We will often speak of sermon barrels as we move through the history of preaching. We will see them being used by Gregory the Great, by Bernardino of Siena, by John Wesley, and by Billy Graham. Great preachers have often bequeathed to their disciples a collection of model sermons. It is a technique of the homiletical art, the art of which Jesus was the master.

There is something else which needs to be said about the way Jesus used parables in his preaching. It is probably the most important thing we have to say about the subject. Preaching in its very nature is parabolic, just as life in its very nature is parabolic. Life is filled with signs and intimations of a higher unseen reality. The sowing of seed, its growth, fruition, and harvest is one of those signs, as is the beauty of a pearl. The sharing of a meal is a powerful sign. The relation of sheep to a shepherd, the relation between mother and child, the marriage relationship, and by all means the marriage feast — all are signs of the fundamental realities of existence. They are not only fundamental but ultimate realities. For years I have thought about the fact that almost all the parables have to do with bread or wine, the growing of wheat for the bread or the grapes for the wine or the feast at which they are eaten. I have not yet decided what to make of it, but the least one can say is that parables and sacraments have something in common. Somehow in these simple things of life we discover eternal truth. When Jesus tells us his parables there is something very special. Many wisemen have spoken about these basic relationships. The parables have deep roots in Scripture. They seem to culminate a whole tradition of meditation which runs through Scripture. Take, for instance, the shepherd and the sheep. From Genesis to Revelation there is a constant interpretation and reinterpretation of the figure of the shepherd. There is something final, however, in the way Jesus portrays the shepherd. It sums up a whole tradition of biblical insight. One might say there is something canonical about the parables of Jesus.

What this says about preaching is that one of the tasks of the Christian preacher is to interpret these fundamental similitudes of life. We must interpret them as Jesus interpreted them, to be sure. It is not our job to discover new similitudes or invent new parables any more than it is our job to invent new sacraments. The parables are there, built into life. They are discovered, not invented, but it takes the gospel to recognize them.

It is the parabolic nature of life which points to the parabolic nature of preaching. Meaning is conveyed by similitude, by analogy, by example. Preaching must intimate more than it defines. The power of suggestion is one of preaching's greatest strengths. Sometimes a sermon accomplishes more by being indirect than by being direct. Even the best Christian preachers must be like John the Baptist. It is not our ministry to say the last word. The best we can do is point to Christ and say, "Hear ye him." When it comes to sacred things, being indirect is often a matter of reverence. This reverent indirection is a recognition of the essential role of the Holy Spirit. Jesus had a way of leaving things for the Spirit to finish. The very fact that Jesus taught us in parables should suggest a whole dimension of his preaching. We will see this again and again throughout the history of preaching.

4. Sermon in the Temple

Of all these sermons found in Matthew the most interesting for our purposes is the Sermon in the Temple.[55] As we see it, this sermon begins

---

55. We have left chapter 18, usually counted as the fourth discourse, out of our discussion. Hagner calls it the discourse on life in the community. *Matthew,* 2:514-41.

at Matthew 21:23, which tells of Jesus entering the Temple the day after his triumphal entry. It continues through chapters 22 and 23 where we hear of Jesus teaching in the Temple and answering the questions of the scribes and Pharisees.[56] This is not ordinarily regarded as one of the five sermons in Matthew since it does not conclude with one of the summary statements which concludes the other sermons, but Mark and Luke put this material in a sermon or series of sermons preached in the Temple. The Sermon in the Temple already had a well-established place in the tradition when Matthew put together his Gospel.[57] As with the Sermon on the Mount, the Sermon in the Temple is a primary focus of the Gospel of Matthew. These two sermons form as it were the two foci of the homiletical material in Matthew's Gospel. The basic shape of the Sermon in the Temple can be found in the Gospel of Mark, and Luke as well. Matthew, however, adds some material which brings to full expression what Mark had begun to show us.

In Matthew's version Jesus is shown once again to be an expositor of Scripture.[58] Again we find his teaching on the true Temple based on the fifty-fourth chapter of Isaiah; his interpretation of Psalm 118, "The stone which the builders rejected / has become the head of the corner" (v. 22); his teaching on the resurrection of the dead based on the third chapter of Exodus; his interpretation of the great and first commandment; and finally his interpretation of Psalm 110.

In Matthew 23 we have what appears to be a new construction, in which the sayings of Jesus are particularly vivid. As it now stands it might be considered the conclusion of the Sermon in the Temple, but more

---

56. For commentary on this material, see Hagner, *Matthew*, 2:607-81; Jeremias, *The Parables of Jesus*, pp. 120-39; Lohmeyer, *Lord of the Temple;* Alan Hugh M'Neile, *The Gospel according to Matthew* (London: Macmillan & Co., 1955), pp. 304-42; Schweizer, *Good News according to Matthew*, pp. 400-447.

57. Possibly this is the reason why the last half of Matthew 21 and the whole of 22 are not counted as one of the five sermons of Matthew. It was put together by one of Matthew's sources. Obviously the memory that Jesus had preached in the Temple had a strong place in the tradition. The Sermon in the Temple as we found it in Mark is repeated in Matthew and then quite a bit of additional material is added to it. Cf. Schweizer, *Good News according to Matthew*, pp. 401ff.

58. There is much work yet to be done on the subject of Jesus as interpreter of Scripture. See the introduction to Hagner's commentary on Matthew for his concise essay, "Matthew's Use of the Old Testament," pp. liii-lvii. See as well his defense of Gerhardsson's work on the oral tradition on p. xlix. Especially helpful are Hagner's biographies on pp. xlviii and liiiff.

probably it is to be understood as one of a number of sermons preached in the Temple, for we find in Matthew, just as we found in Mark, that Jesus reproached the Jews for not arresting him openly in the Temple where he had taught "day after day" (Matt. 26:55). As Matthew understands it, Jesus preached frequently in the Temple.

The sermon in chapter 23 is a prophetic denunciation of the scribes and Pharisees. It is a series of woes:

> "But woe to you, scribes and Pharisees, hypocrites! because you shut the kingdom of heaven against men; for you neither enter yourselves, nor allow those who would enter to go in. . . .
>
> "Woe to you, scribes and Pharisees, hypocrites! for you tithe mint and dill and cummin, and have neglected the weightier matters of the law, justice and mercy and faith; these you ought to have done, without neglecting the others. You blind guides, straining out a gnat and swallowing a camel! . . .
>
> "Woe to you, scribes and Pharisees, hypocrites! for you are like whitewashed tombs, which outwardly appear beautiful, but within they are full of dead men's bones and all uncleanness. So you also outwardly appear righteous to men, but within you are full of hypocrisy and iniquity." (23:13-14, 23-24, 27-28)

Amos had cast one of his prophetic sermons in a series of woes denouncing the people of God for their sins (Amos 5:18–6:7), and Jesus may well have borrowed this dramatic rhetorical device from this classic prophet of Israel in order to emphasize the continuity between his preaching and the preaching of the ancient prophets.[59] But there is more at play here than literary form. The message of Jesus when he preached in the Temple of Jerusalem was all the world like that of Amos when he preached against those who polluted the solemn assemblies of Israel, their feasts and their sacrifices, their festal songs and the melody of their harps. Jesus' whole sermon could have taken Amos 6:1 as its text, " 'Woe to those who are at ease in Zion.' "

Of particular interest among Matthew's additions to this material is the way he presents this sermon as the fulfillment of the whole preaching ministry of the Old Testament. We are told, for instance, that the Temple authorities would have liked to have arrested Jesus but dared not because

59. On Jesus' fulfilling the role of the prophets, see Cullmann, *Christology of the New Testament,* pp. 13-50.

the people "held him to be a prophet" (Matt. 21:46). Matthew incorporates several sayings already found in Mark which speak of the Temple authorities rejecting the messengers or prophets who had been sent to them. We hear of the scribes and Pharisees rejecting the authority of John the Baptist, whom the people accepted as a prophet. We hear the parable of the vineyard owner sending messengers to his tenants, clearly a reference to the prophets. We hear of the stone rejected by men but in God's sight chosen and precious, obviously a reference to Jesus himself who shared the rejection of the prophets. To this Matthew adds the woe against the scribes and Pharisees who built tombs for prophets whose blood they themselves had shed. Finally, Matthew concludes this sermon with the lament over Jerusalem, "'O Jerusalem, Jerusalem, killing the prophets and stoning those who are sent to you!'" (23:37). The obvious point is that Jesus as Matthew portrays him in this sermon is the culmination and fulfillment of the prophetic ministry.

This point is made even clearer by Matthew's introduction of a series of sayings which show Jesus to have fulfilled the magisterium of the Messiah. It is the Messiah who is the true teacher of Israel:

> Then said Jesus to the crowds and to his disciples, "The scribes and the Pharisees sit on Moses' seat; so practice and observe whatever they tell you, but not what they do; for they preach, but do not practice. . . . But you are not to be called rabbi, for you have one teacher, and you are all brethren. And call no man your father on earth, for you have one Father, who is in heaven. Neither be called masters, for you have one master, the Christ." (23:1-10)

That this is preeminently a text about preaching becomes clear from the phrase "seat of Moses." This phrase was an honorific or perhaps a term of endearment for the pulpit of the synagogue. The very existence of the term shows how highly preaching was regarded. It was the apostolic succession of the synagogue. To sit in the seat of Moses was to preach, and to maintain the succession of preaching was to maintain the succession of authority. What Matthew shows is that it is Jesus, preaching in the courts of the Temple, who really maintains the succession. The teaching ministry of Jesus in the Temple, as Matthew presents it to us, shows Jesus cleansing the Temple, and then filling it with the proclamation of the gospel. By this Jesus fulfills the Temple. When Jesus teaches in the courts of the Temple it becomes what it was always intended to be, the sanctuary of holy wisdom.

5. Sermon on Last Things

The last collection of homiletical material which Matthew arranges for us follows immediately after the Sermon in the Temple (Matt. 24:1–25:46).[60] This sermon might be called the Sermon on Last Things. Sometimes it is called the Little Apocalypse. Again it is presented as a teaching not to the crowd but to a more intimate group of disciples.[61]

The sermon begins in a way reminiscent of the Sermon on the Mount: "As [Jesus] sat on the Mount of Olives, the disciples came to him." (Compare Matt. 24:3 and Matt. 5:1.) From this we gather that Matthew intends us to understand that what follows is a formal sermon. In it we find an extended interpretation of the prophecies of Daniel.

Jesus warns his disciples against those who will come with false claims about the second coming. The disciples will hear of wars and rumors of wars (24:6), nation will rise against nation, and there will be all kinds of disasters, earthquakes, and famines, but this will only be the beginning (24:8). On top of this there will be persecutions of the faithful and a falling away, but those who endure to the end will be saved (24:13). Yet, in spite of all this, the gospel must be preached to all nations. Only then will the end come (24:14).

Again Jesus warns his disciples that when they see the desolating sacrilege spoken of by the prophet Daniel, they are to flee — let no one turn back to rescue precious possessions. There will be great tribulation in the last days (24:21). Do not be fooled; when the end finally comes, it will be as clear as day. "'For as the lightning comes from the east and shines as far as the west, so will be the coming of the Son of man'" (24:27). Just as Daniel promised, the Son of Man will come on the clouds of heaven with power and glory (24:30). "'But of that day and hour no one knows'" (24:36). To make his point Jesus reminds his congregation of how it was in the days of Noah. The common people ignored the warning and suddenly judgment was upon them. Here we see Jesus using that classic principle of explaining Scripture by Scripture. The story of the flood is used as a biblical illustration of the significance of the prophecies of Daniel.

---

60. Hagner, *Matthew*, 2:682-747; and M'Neile, *The Gospel according to Matthew*, pp. 342-72. On the structure of this discourse see especially pp. 343ff. See also Schweizer, *Good News according to Matthew*, pp. 450-82.

61. On Matthew's arrangement of this material, see Schweizer, *Good News according to Matthew*, pp. 448ff.

The sermon continues with a number of parables. The parable of the wise and foolish virgins makes much the same point as the biblical illustration (25:1-13). This is followed by the parable of the talents (25:14-30) and the parable of the sheep and the goats (25:31-46). This latter parable is interesting because it is a reinterpretation of the image of the divine shepherd which appears and reappears throughout Scripture. As we have said, Jesus often interpreted and reinterpreted this fundamental biblical image.

The sermon as a whole makes a strong impression. For our purposes two things should be noticed: first, that this sermon gives sustained attention to the interpretation of Scripture. It is particularly concerned with the interpretation of the apocalyptic material in Daniel. Once again we see Jesus as an interpreter of Scripture. The second is that this collection of homiletical material suggests that preaching about last things must have been a major concern of the preaching ministry of Jesus. Here also we have material which Jesus must have used again and again in his preaching.

6. The Great Commission

The final scene of the Gospel of Matthew has left a strong impression on the Church.[62] It is often spoken of as the Great Commission, by which is usually meant that this is where Jesus sent out the apostles to evangelize all peoples. The most Jewish of the Gospels makes the strongest possible point that the final words of Jesus laid firmly upon the shoulders of the Church that the kingdom of God was now open to the Gentiles. The apostles were to go out to every land and nation and make disciples of Christ. They were to make disciples by baptizing them and teaching them. That is, they were to be ministers of Word and sacrament.

It is interesting to look carefully at Matthew's choice of words. Matthew reports that Jesus sent the disciples out to teach the commandments of Christ. Again we see evidence that in the Synoptic Gospels at least, the words "preaching" and "teaching" can be used synonymously. We might expect to read that the apostles were to go to all peoples and κηρύξατε τὸ εὐαγγέλιον, proclaim the gospel, but instead we read they are to go διδάσκοντες αὐτός, teaching them to observe everything Jesus

---

62. See the article by Günter Bornkamm, "Die Auferstandene und der Irdische, Mt. 28:16-20," in Bornkamm et al., *Überlieferung und Auslegung*, pp. 289-310.

had commanded them. In the light of a text like this it is rather hard to drive a wedge between preaching the gospel of salvation and teaching the Christian way of life. Obviously according to this text Christian preaching is to do both. At times the Church has understood this passage as the charter of evangelistic preaching, and at other times as the charter of catechetical preaching. The least we can say is that in regard to the apostolic ministry it puts a high priority on preaching.

Those who have tried to de-emphasize the place of preaching in worship have made a great mistake. If anything is clear from the Gospel of Matthew it is that Jesus laid great stress on the centrality of preaching in the apostolic ministry of the Church. Jesus gave much time to preaching himself, but he also gave much time to preparing the Twelve to go out and preach. Then, finally, as the crowning act of his earthly ministry, he sent his apostles out to preach.

II. The Ministry of Preaching in the Gospel of John

The Gospel of John presents Jesus as the Word of God. He is the eternal Word who from all eternity was with God and actually is God. Jesus is the Word of God full of life and light. He is the Word become flesh, full of grace and truth, foreshadowed in the Law of Moses, to be sure, but now present in all fullness to those who receive him by faith. The Gospel of John comes to its grand conclusion in the Upper Room when Thomas kneels before the risen Jesus and confesses, "My Lord and my God." In the fullest sense, as we find it in the Gospel of John, Jesus is God. In Jesus God's Word is fully revealed. Jesus is the Word of God become flesh. He is the Word of God dwelling among us — heard, understood, and received by the people of God. In light, then, of John's strong affirmation of Jesus as the Word of God, the question becomes: What does John have to say about the *preaching* of the Word of God? Indeed, as we shall see, the high logos Christology of the Gospel of John leads to an equally high theology of proclamation.

Before getting into the heart of this subject, we have to be clear about one thing. For generations commentators have remarked about the way the Gospel of John makes its witness to Christ by means of a vocabulary which was very familiar to the popular philosophy of the Hellenistic world.[63] More

63. For a study of the different ways the word *logos* was understood in biblical times, see C. H. Dodd, *The Interpretation of the Fourth Gospel* (Cambridge: At the University

recently New Testament scholars have begun to discover that John was much more solidly grounded in the thought world of Palestinian Judaism than in that of Hellenism.[64] John's debt to Jewish Wisdom theology is beginning to be appreciated.[65] It is in terms of this newer approach that we are able to understand what the Gospel of John has to say about preaching. John's high theology of proclamation is a development of Jewish Wisdom theology. What we said in the last chapter about the piety of the Wisdom school and the sapiential approach to the ministry of the Word has to be appreciated before one can grasp what the Gospel of John has to say about the preaching of the Word.

A. Jesus as the Word

The prologue to the Gospel of John explains Jesus in terms of the Word of God. It is in terms of the Word of God as it had been read and preached in Israel ever since the time of Moses that John would have us understand the coming of the long-awaited Messiah. It is in a very profound sense that John speaks of Jesus being the Word.

> In the beginning was the Word, and the Word was with God, and the Word was God. He was in the beginning with God; all things were made through him, and without him was not anything made that was made. In him was life, and the life was the light of men. The light shines in the darkness, and the darkness has not overcome it. (John 1:1-5)

Our concern in looking at this passage is to learn what it might have to say about preaching. Christianity, like Judaism and Islam, is a religion of the book. It is not surprising that the Son of God, the Savior of the world, should be identified as the Word. Nor is it surprising that when

---

Press, 1958), pp. 263-85. Cf. also H. Kleinknecht, "λέγω B," *Theological Dictionary of the New Testament*, 4:77-91.

64. See the essay of Leon Morris on the meaning of *logos* in the Gospel of John, *The Gospel according to John,* The New International Commentary on the New Testament, vols. 29 and 29A (Grand Rapids: Wm. B. Eerdmans Publishing Co., 1971), pp. 115-26. Cf. also O. Procksch, "λέγω C," *Theological Dictionary of the New Testament*, 4:91-100.

65. Again the essay of Leon Morris is most helpful on this point. See as well Raymond E. Brown, *The Gospel according to John,* 2 vols., The Anchor Bible (Garden City, N.Y.: Doubleday & Co., 1966), pp. lii-lxiv. See also G. Kittel, "λέγω D," *Theological Dictionary of the New Testament*, 4:127-36.

the long-promised Messiah came he would be identified as the fulfillment of the Word of God which had been read and preached in the synagogue for centuries. And it is not at all surprising that the God who had never been seen as an idol but had been heard through his Word would come to dwell among us as the Word of God.

There has been much speculation, as we have said, as to what the word "Word" really means as found in the Gospel of John. That the Gospel should use the Greek word λόγος has often led interpreters to search for the meaning in various schools of Greek philosophy, as the Greeks often used λόγος as a philosophical term. The Jewish philosopher Philo of Alexandria, who lived shortly before Jesus, had popularized the term among Greek-speaking Jews. It was imagined by many that the author of the Gospel of John had in mind some highly philosophical speculations when he spoke of Christ being the Word of God.[66] By the word λόγος the Greeks meant the meaningful structure of existence, the understandable framework of things. To say to the Greeks, then, that Jesus was the Word meant that Jesus was the key to understanding life.

If more recently it has been recognized that John is speaking out of a more thoroughly Palestinian Judaism, it needs to be further recognized that he is speaking out of that sector of Jewish thought which had come under the influence of the Wisdom school.[67] The more philosophical Alexandrian Judaism probably had little influence on John. On the other hand, the Wisdom theology, which had a strong influence on Palestinian Jewish thought, seems to have had a much stronger influence on the author of the Fourth Gospel. He may well have chosen to use the term λόγος because it communicated a positive impression to the Greek-speaking world, but he himself had developed his idea out of the speculation of the more Jewish Wisdom school. Jewish theology tended to understand the Hebrew word חכמה to mean that quality of mind which was characteristic of good rulers such as Solomon. It was "a quality apart from men, above and beyond man, existing ideally with God."[68] That the prologue to the Gospel of John should go so far as to say that the Word was God was an important theological development.[69] Proverbs had said that Wisdom was with God at the time of

---

66. Dodd, *Interpretation of the Fourth Gospel,* pp. 263-85.

67. Brown, *The Gospel according to John,* pp. lix-lxiv.

68. S. H. Blank, "Wisdom," *Interpreter's Dictionary of the Bible,* 4:852-61.

69. On the significance of the term in the way the New Testament Church understood Jesus, see Cullmann, *Christology of the New Testament,* pp. 249-69.

creation, but it had not said that Wisdom was God from the beginning (Prov. 8:22-31). Even at that the Wisdom school had prepared the way for the affirmation of the Gospel of John that Jesus is the Word of God who was in the beginning with God and who was God himself in human flesh. One might have expected that the author of the Fourth Gospel would have translated חכמה with the Greek word σοφία, but that would not have conveyed those close connections which the Wisdom school made between the transcendent Wisdom of God and the revealed Word of God, as it was read and preached in the worship and devotion of Israel.[70] The Greek verb λέγειν is the verb used ordinarily for speaking. λόγος means first of all something said. It is John's preference for λόγος rather than σοφία in this very important passage which makes it profoundly evident how he regarded the reading and preaching of Scripture in the worship of the Christian Church. For the Gospel of John the ministry of the Word is central to our worship. The incarnation, as John understood it, implied a strong emphasis on the reading and preaching of Scripture. If the Law was given through Moses as the Word of God, so grace has been given to us in Jesus Christ, as the Word of God.

One might even go so far as to say that according to the prologue of the Gospel of John, Jesus is God's sermon to us preached in the living out of a human life. It is to this sermon, then, that all our sermons witness; it is this sermon that all our preaching unfolds and interprets. If God's ultimate revelation is a word, then we can serve God in no higher way than to be ministers of that Word. Furthermore, it must be to God's Word that our word responds. Our sermons only have authority to the extent that they reflect his sermon. When they do reflect his sermon then they have tremendous authority.

B. John the Baptist as Minister of the Word

The way the Gospel of John understands the ministry of the Word is evident also from what it says about the ministry of John the Baptist. We read:

---

70. On the use of σοφία in the New Testament, see U. Wilckens, "σοφία κτλ," *Theological Dictionary of the New Testament*, 7:514-26. Interestingly enough, σοφία does not appear in the Gospel of John.

> There was a man sent from God, whose name was John. He came for testimony, to bear witness to the light, that all might believe through him. He was not the light, but came to bear witness to the light. (John 1:6-8)

John's ministry was to witness to Christ; his testimony was that Jesus is the Christ, the long-awaited Savior. It is clear from the rest of the first chapter that John's witness is essentially the Christian gospel. This is especially the case when John points out Jesus and says, " 'Behold, the Lamb of God, who takes away the sin of the world!' " (1:29). After the author of the Gospel of John has finished writing his Gospel, which no doubt was the summary of Jesus' whole preaching ministry, we are told, "This is the disciple who is bearing witness to these things, and who has written these things; and we know that his testimony is true" (21:24). The Greek word here, μαρτυρεῖν, is a theologically significant word.[71] We usually translate the verb μαρτυρεῖν with the English verb "to witness" and the noun μαρτυρία as "testimony" — a word used in court and other legal procedures to indicate a statement assuring others that what someone else has said is true.[72] While the Synoptic Gospels emphasize preaching as the proclamation of the gospel, the Gospel of John speaks more frequently of preaching as witnessing to the truth. What John seems to have in mind is that the Christian preacher should be like John the Baptist, who confessed quite openly that he was not the Christ, that he was not the savior of the world, but that he had come to bear witness to the Christ. It is Christ who is the Lamb of God who takes away the sin of the world. John the Baptist pointed to him, not to himself. We should do the same. The preacher is a minister of Christ. He bears witness that Christ should increase and the preacher should decrease.

C. The Feast of Holy Wisdom

In John 2 we find in the story of the wedding feast at Cana another indication of how fundamental the Wisdom theology is to the gospel.[73]

---

71. On the theological use of this word in the Johannine literature, see H. Strathmann, "μάρτυς κτλ," *Theological Dictionary of the New Testament*, 4:499-502.

72. Strathmann, "μάρτυς κτλ," *Theological Dictionary of the New Testament*, 4:502-4.

73. The interpretation of this story offered by more recent commentators takes several very different directions. Rudolf Bultmann in *Das Evangelium des Johannes,* Meyers

The story makes a point of indicating that this was the first sign Jesus performed and that in this sign he manifested his glory and therefore his disciples believed in him. It was a sign the meaning of which the disciples recognized. This may mean that the miraculous nature of the sign convinced the disciples of his divine power, but it may also mean that the disciples recognized that here was the Wisdom of God, the Word of God become flesh, the holy Wisdom from above.

This latter interpretation would make sense if in fact the prologue of the Gospel of John does intend to identify Jesus as the Wisdom of God. As anyone well versed in the Hebrew Scriptures would easily recognize, the divine Wisdom is a feast. The figure was put very beautifully in the ninth chapter of Proverbs.

> Wisdom has built her house,
>   she has set up her seven pillars.
> She has slaughtered her beasts, she has mixed her wine,
>   she has also set her table.
> She has sent out her maids to call
>   from the highest places in the town,
> "Whoever is simple, let him turn in here!"
>   To him who is without sense he says,
> "Come, eat of my bread
>   and drink of the wine I have mixed.
> Leave simpleness, and live,
>   and walk in the way of insight."
>
> (Prov. 9:1-6)

This figure was developed at some length in the Song of Solomon. There the feast is a wedding feast, or at least that is how many devout Jews at the time

---

Kritisch-exegetischer Kommentar über das neue Testament (Göttingen: Vandenhoeck & Ruprecht, 1964), pp. 83ff., understands the story as a Christian reworking of the Dionysus myth. Oscar Cullmann in *Early Christian Worship,* trans. A. Stewart Todd and James B. Torrance (London: SCM Press, 1954), pp. 66-71, sees in it the first allusions to the Lord's Supper. Charles Kingsley Barrett, *The Gospel according to St. John* (New York: Macmillan, 1956), pp. 156-58, finds it hard to deny that this story may go back to Greek myths about Dionysus. Dodd, *Interpretation of the Fourth Gospel,* pp. 297-300, finds the story explained by similar passages in Philo of Alexandria. Brown, *The Gospel according to John,* pp. 101-11, recognizes the Wisdom motifs in the story, while Morris, *The Gospel According to John,* pp. 174-88, insisting on the genuineness of the account, sees only the contrast between law and gospel.

understood it. The subject was hotly debated, but apparently enough Jews were convinced of this interpretation to allow for the book to be canonized.[74] The Wisdom school had long taught that devotion to sacred wisdom was a holy passion and the erotic poetry of the Song of Solomon was understood to speak of this passion, this sacred love. It was the son of David, Solomon, who manifested this holy love. His wisdom was legendary. It was Solomon who was the bridegroom in the Song of Solomon.

When Jesus came to the wedding feast at Cana and the wine failed, Jesus showed himself to be the true bridegroom by doing what the earthly bridegroom had failed to do. He provided a wine that was better than any that had been served up to that time. He was the Son of David, of which Solomon was only a foreshadow, the bridegroom of whom Solomon was only a type, the Wisdom of which the wisdom of Solomon was but a foretaste.

We have spoken several times of the importance of prophetic signs in sealing and confirming the Word. The Gospel of John gives much attention to these signs; in fact, the first part of the Gospel is organized around a series of seven such signs.[75] The changing of the water into wine at the wedding of Cana is carefully recognized as the first of these signs. What is interesting at this point is how in a Gospel so devoted to presenting Jesus as the Word of God we find at the same time a considerable interest in the signs with which Jesus accompanied his ministry of preaching and teaching. Like the parables, sometimes the signs are explained at length; sometimes no explanation is reported. But whether explained or not, they bear much of the meaning of the gospel and invite the reader to meditate on them and give the preacher an opportunity to explain them. They are there to support and confirm the Word.

D. The Sermon on the Bread of Life

Perhaps the best way to get to the heart of the Johannine concept of the ministry of the Word is to study Jesus' sermon on the Bread of Life found in the sixth chapter of the Gospel. It would be very tempting at this point to analyze a number of the discourses in the Gospel of John to see what they tell us about the preaching of Jesus. A careful study of the Upper

74. The debate has left its mark in the Mishnah in the tractate *Megilloth*.
75. Cf. Dodd, *Interpretation of the Fourth Gospel*, pp. 289-91.

Room Discourse would be a most fruitful field for our study. We have just done this sort of thing with the discourses in the Gospel of Matthew. In the Gospel of John, however, something else captures our attention. Many of the things we have found in the other Gospels we would find in John as well, but there is something special in the Gospel of John, namely, the logos Christology and what it says about preaching. We therefore concentrate on just one of these discourses.

As was true of Jesus' sermon in the synagogue of Nazareth, the Sermon on the Bread of Life is a sermon on sermons. But it is also a sermon on how the incarnate Word of God is the food which nourishes us to eternal life. It is particularly appropriate therefore that John is careful to put this sermon in the literary form of a rabbinical sermon. We suspect that John has carefully preserved the homiletical form used by Jesus and other early Christian preachers in his reporting of this sermon. The Sermon on the Bread of Life is a condensed version of a sermon, to be sure, but even condensed it preserves the form of a perfect four-point sermon worked out on a text from the Law and developed by means of a second text from the prophets. In terms of homiletical form this is a traditional rabbinical sermon.[76]

The text from the Law is Exodus 16:4, "He gave them bread from heaven to eat." That is at least the way John reports it. In fact, the text is a conflation of Exodus 16:4, "Then the LORD said to Moses, 'Behold, I will rain bread from heaven for you,'" and Exodus 16:15, "And Moses said to them, 'It is the bread which the LORD has given you to eat.'" We also find traces of other Old Testament texts here such as Psalm 78:24 and Psalm 105:40. This was a typical procedure of rabbinical preachers. The base text was often elaborated by other texts of Scripture so that parallel texts speaking of the same thing were set together. In this way all the relevant information in Scripture was collected together. When a preacher elaborated a text in this way he would have spent some time putting it all together for the congregation even if the condensed form of the sermon does not give us all this information. The secondary text taken from the prophets is Isaiah 54:13, "'All your sons shall be taught by the LORD.'" The sermon now goes over each phrase of the primary text, explaining each in turn.

The first phrase is, "He gave them." Jesus explains, "'Truly, truly, I say to you, it was not Moses who gave you the bread from heaven; my Father gives you the true bread from heaven'" (John 6:32). Jesus immediately moves the text from the merely historical to the contemporary.

76. See above, chapter 1, on the homiletical form of the rabbinical sermon.

That is, it was not Moses back then and there but, rather, the Father here and now. This was significant because of the sign of the feeding of the multitude which Jesus had just performed. Just as in the days of Moses it was God who fed Israel with manna, so even now it is God who feeds us.

Then Jesus moves on to the next word, "bread." He tells his congregation, "'I am the bread of life'" (6:35), and goes on to explain that he himself is the nourishment which God provides his people that they might come to eternal life. God's people receive eternal life by believing in Christ. "'Every one who sees the Son and believes in him should have eternal life'" (6:40). What seems to be intended here is that eating the bread is a prophetic sign of hearing the Word and believing it. Eating is more than hearing; it is believing, accepting, and appropriating it in one's life.

Next Jesus moves on to the third phrase in the text, "from heaven." He tells his congregation, "'I am the bread which came down from heaven'" (6:41). His listeners wonder how it is possible for him to have come down from heaven if it is known by everyone that Mary and Joseph are his parents. At this point Jesus assures us of his divine origin by quoting the secondary text from Isaiah 54: "'and your sons shall be taught by the LORD.'" The point is that in the messianic age God himself will teach his people. In fact the Messiah is none other than God himself, among his people, teaching his people. When God himself teaches his own people, they are nourished unto eternal life. But just as the teacher in the messianic age is God himself, so is the teaching God himself. Jesus is the incarnation of the divine Wisdom. It is natural, then, that he is both teacher and teaching. He himself is the bread of life. "'I am the living bread which came down from heaven; if any one eats of this bread, he will live for ever; and the bread which I shall give for the life of the world is my flesh'" (John 6:51).

These last words, of course, put a sudden and surprising turn to the whole sermon, bringing into it the theme of the divine sacrifice, the broken body and the poured-out blood. The divine teaching presence who in Christ dwells among his people is a suffering presence who has suffered all the way through tribulation to victory. The divine teaching presence is a presence of one who is crucified and risen, who has given his flesh for the life of the world. He is far more than Moses or any of the prophets; he is the Lamb of God. At the very beginning of the Gospel John the Baptist identified Jesus as the Lamb of God, and here with the feast of Passover at hand we discover him again as the Lamb of God, the Passover

Lamb. Only the Passover Lamb who is slain and lives evermore can be the very Word of God in human flesh, the divine teaching dwelling among us, the food that nourishes unto eternal life.

Finally Jesus takes up the fourth phrase, "to eat." Jesus explained, " 'Truly, truly, I say to you, unless you eat the flesh of the Son of man and drink his blood, you have no life in you; he who eats my flesh and drinks my blood has eternal life, and I will raise him up at the last day' " (6:53-54). Obviously for the Gospel of John it is no mere hearing of sermons which will give us eternal life. It is a matter of believing them and living them, to be sure, but more needs to be said.

Since the Word of God is a matter of presence, one must have fellowship with the Word. " 'He who eats my flesh and drinks my blood abides in me, and I in him' " (6:56). Here we are talking about communion, fellowship between divinity and humanity, or, put more powerfully, between God and man. We abide in Christ, the Son of God, and Christ abides in us, human beings of flesh and blood. It is a very intense sort of fellowship, the sort which is had in the covenant bond. We are talking here neither about cannibalism nor about what is often called mystical union. We are not talking about any kind of mixing of identities. This is not the sort of mystical union where I become Christ and Christ becomes me. It is not, at least as Reformed theology understands it, any kind of theosis or divinification. It is a covenantal union, the sort of union of which the covenantal meals of the Old Testament were the sacrament. In fact, the whole sixth chapter of the Gospel of John needs to be read while remembering that this miraculous feeding of the multitude took place when "the Passover, the feast of the Jews, was at hand."[77] One could simply regard the whole story of the feeding of the multitude, the crossing of the sea, and the Bread of Life Discourse as a Christian interpretation of Passover.

But we also need to recognize that there were three covenantal meals which were types or foreshadowings of John's version of the feeding of the multitude, namely, the Passover meal, the manna, and the meal on the mountain. The text specifically tells us that this meal took place about the time Passover was celebrated (6:4). That we are supposed to have the story of the manna in mind when hearing this story is clear because the Bread of Life Discourse mentions it several times. Less obvious is the most cultic of all three meals, the story of Moses and the elders of Israel going up

---

77. Cf. Bertil Gärtner, *John 6 and the Jewish Passover* (Lund: C. W. K. Gleerup, 1959).

Mount Sinai and there eating and drinking and beholding God (Exod. 24:9-11). That this story is important to this sermon should be clear from the setting. We read, "Jesus went up on the mountain, and there sat down with his disciples" (John 6:3). When we grasp the relation of the Bread of Life Sermon to the three covenantal meals of the Exodus story, we discover the nature of this fellowship which the Christian has with the Word of God. It is covenant fellowship. Through hearing the Word and participating in the sacraments we enter into a covenantal union with Christ. It is our fellowship with the Word of God which gives us eternal life. "'As the living Father sent me, and I live because of the Father, so he who eats me will live because of me'" (6:57). What we understand by this is that those who hear the Word, believe the Word, and live out the Word thereby have fellowship with the Word, and to have fellowship with the Word is to have eternal life.

While we are first of all interested in what this sermon says about the ministry of the Word, we are, to be sure, aware that something is also said here about the ministry of the sacrament of Communion.[78] While we cannot go into that subject at length, it is important to see that John 6, in its canonical form, is speaking of both sacrament and sermon. It is through both the preached Word and the Lord's Supper that we have covenant fellowship with the incarnate Word. It is in both together that Christ is truly present. One might say that this chapter speaks both of the eucharistic presence and the kerygmatic presence, but one might better speak of the two together. Just as in Exodus 24 Israel came before God in

---

78. The Church Fathers were surprisingly slow to hear a reference to the sacrament in the Bread of Life Discourse. Augustine is a case in point, *Sermons on the Gospel of John.* In more recent times Bultmann claims that the passage has nothing to do with the Eucharist. *Das Evangelium des Johannes,* pp. 154-77 and 340-46. Cullmann is certainly more convincing when he tells us that the Evangelist intends us to understand both. *Early Christian Worship,* pp. 93ff. Several attempts have been made to explain the sacramental references as the work of a redactor. Cf. Brown, *The Gospel according to John,* 1:260-304. For another evaluation of the discussion see Morris, *The Gospel according to John,* pp. 351ff. It seems to me that what we are dealing with in the Bread of Life Discourse is the keen sense of typology which was an important facet of the theological reflection of Jesus and his contemporaries. It has long been recognized that this is the case with the Gospel of Matthew, but it is also the case in John. John finds typological significance in the feeding of the multitude. Furthermore, it was from the preaching of Jesus that John had learned the eucharistic typology. The sacraments Jesus instituted had from the beginning a strong typological basis. Without an understanding of their typology it is hard to understand how they functioned as signs.

their solemn assembly and Moses as minister of the Word read and preached the Scriptures of the covenant and then the elders went up on the mountain and ate and drank and beheld God, so when the Christian assembly hears the reading and preaching of the Word and shares in the Lord's Supper the gospel is sealed. The covenant assembly is united in communion with Christ. By partaking of the cup of the New Covenant all the responsibilities and the blessings of Christ and his cross are made ours. If there was ever a classic passage of Scripture on the unity of Word and sacrament, here it is. Here we see in the clearest terms the relation of the reading and preaching of the Word to Communion. Here we see how important preaching is to the covenantal assembly. Our fellowship with God is through the Word. Because we have fellowship with the Word of God we have fellowship with God.

The Gospel of John teaches us that in the preaching of Jesus the Word of God, that is, the divine Wisdom which was with God from the beginning, which was God and by which all things were created, that Word, is truly present among his people. This presence is full of grace and truth, begetting children of God and giving them eternal life. The sermon was perplexing to the disciples, and we are told that "After this many of his disciples drew back and no longer went about with him" (6:66). Jesus asked the Twelve if they too wanted to leave, and Peter answered, " 'Lord, to whom shall we go? You have the words of eternal life; and we have believed, and have come to know, that you are the Holy One of God' " (6:68-69). Not only is Jesus the Word of Life, but even his words are the words of eternal life. He is the Word of God and therefore his words are the Word of God.

But what about the preaching of the apostles? Is it different? Is it, too, the Word of God? To this question the Gospel of John gives a very clear answer. We read in the High Priestly Prayer of Jesus, " 'I have given them the words which thou gavest me' " (17:8). Obviously as John sees it the apostolic preaching which has been preached down through the centuries is also to be understood as the Word of God. We read on in this prayer, " 'I do not pray for these only, but also for those who believe in me through their word, that they may all be one; even as thou, Father, art in me, and I in thee . . .' " (17:20-21). The apostolic word has the same authority and power as the dominical word; it brings about saving faith and life eternal. Yes, the high Johannine Christology leads to a high theology of proclamation. We find it put very clearly in the prologue to the First Epistle of John.

> That which was from the beginning, which we have heard, which we have seen with our eyes, which we have looked upon and touched with our hands, concerning the word of life — the life was made manifest, and we saw it, and testify to it, and proclaim to you the eternal life which was with the Father and was made manifest to us — that which we have seen and heard we proclaim also to you, so that you may have fellowship with us; and our fellowship is with the Father and with his Son Jesus Christ. And we are writing this that our joy may be complete. (I John 1:1-4)

It is when we see this as parallel to the prologue of the Gospel of John that it becomes interesting. The incarnation of the Word leads to the proclamation of the Word, and this proclamation is in the end the establishing of communion both with God and with the worshiping congregation. To put it succinctly, the apostolic proclamation of the Word is the basis of worship. It is, for us who cannot see but yet do believe, the presentation of the presence of him with whom we have communion.

III. The Ministry of Preaching in the Acts of the Apostles

The Acts of the Apostles is most generous in giving us information about the preaching of the apostles. In addition to between eight and a dozen reports of sermons, some quite lengthy, we have numerous indications of how preaching fit into the worship of the earliest Christians.[79] At the end of chapter 2, for instance, we read a sort of summary of the life of the church of Jerusalem in those early days, "And they devoted themselves to the apostles' teaching and fellowship, to the breaking of bread and the prayers" (2:42). The apostolic teaching ministry was a primary feature of the life of the earliest Christian community.[80] We have a similar statement at the end of chapter 4: "Now the company of those who believed were of one heart and soul. . . . And with great power the apostles gave their testimony to the resurrection of the Lord Jesus, and great grace was upon

---

79. On the place of preaching in the worship of the earliest Christians, see David Peterson, *Engaging with God: A Biblical Theology of Worship* (Grand Rapids: Wm. B. Eerdmans Publishing Co., 1993), pp. 144 and 152ff.

80. For C. F. D. Moule the preaching of the earliest Church had a more restrained role. *Worship in the New Testament* (Richmond: John Knox Press, 1967), pp. 43ff.

them all" (4:32-33). From this we gather that the central emphasis of the preaching was kerygmatic; it was proclaiming the good news of the resurrection; it was giving the apostolic witness that indeed Jesus was risen from the dead. From chapter 5 we gather that it became the practice during a certain period, at least, for the apostles to teach daily at a particular place in the Temple (5:12). This was done in spite of the disapproval of the Temple authorities. Yet God commanded them to continue to preach in the Temple (5:20), and the people held them in high honor. Even the great Gamaliel counseled against restraining them. Finally we read, "And every day in the temple and at home they did not cease teaching and preaching Jesus as the Christ" (5:42).[81]

The picture we get is that the apostles maintained a strong ministry of preaching and teaching. In the sixth chapter of Acts we find that as the Church grew, it became necessary to appoint deacons to carry out certain administrative functions in order that the apostles might devote themselves to prayer and to the ministry of the Word (6:4). There was more to the ministry of the Word than just preaching; there were the daily study sessions like those held in the rabbinical schools. At these sessions one codified, interpreted, and applied the teachings of Jesus. All this, however, fed the preaching. In fact, the preaching had its source in this kind of community study. The preaching of the Word of God was central in the life of the Church (6:2). In the eighth chapter we read of how persecution arose and how the Christians were scattered and, being scattered, "went about preaching the word" (8:4). We hear further of the preaching of Philip in Samaria and then along the coast from Azotus to Caesarea (8:5-40). In chapter 11 we hear of some disciples of Cyprus and Cyrene

---

81. A generation or two ago a number of the pupils of Rudolf Bultmann accused Luke of being under the influence of incipient catholic presuppositions. Such New Testament scholars as Ernst Haenchen and Ernst Käsemann cast considerable doubt on the reliability of Luke's account of Christian origins. Ernst Käsemann, "Paulus und der Frühkatholizismus," in *Exegetische Versuche und Besinnungen,* 2nd ed., 2 vols. (Göttingen: Vandenhoeck & Ruprecht, 1965), 2:239-52; and Ernst Haenchen, *Die Apostelgeschichte,* 5th ed., Meyers Kritisch-exegetischer Kommentar über das neue Testament (Göttingen: Vandenhoeck & Ruprecht, 1965). While taking a different line, Martin Dibelius found it very difficult to accept the historical reliability of Acts. Martin Dibelius, *Studies in the Acts of the Apostles* (London: SCM Press, 1956). English-speaking scholars have been slow to follow this line of thought. The commentary of F. F. Bruce very convincingly shows the Acts of the Apostles to be quite dependable. For a concise discussion of the problem, cf. W. C. Robinson, Jr., "Acts of the Apostles," in the supplementary volume of the *Interpreter's Dictionary of the Bible,* pp. 7-9.

who, fleeing the persecution in Jerusalem, went to Antioch and began to preach to the Greeks about the Christ (11:20).

With chapter 13 the story begins to center on the missionary journeys of the apostle Paul, and preaching appears to be central to his mission. Typically he would enter a town, go to the synagogue on the Sabbath, and preach (17:2). In larger synagogues where there were daily study sessions, he would teach daily (17:11). We are told very specifically that this teaching consisted of explaining the Scriptures and showing "that it was necessary for the Christ to suffer and to rise from the dead" (17:3). In Ephesus it was possible for Paul to maintain this kind of preaching ministry in the synagogue for three months before there was a rupture. Paul withdrew and rented a lecture hall and there continued his daily teaching ministry for another two years (19:9-10). Even under house arrest in Rome Paul seems to have maintained a regular ministry of preaching and teaching.

The overall impression given by Acts is that much attention was given to the ministry of the Word.[82] While one hesitates to go so far as to call it the one central activity of the apostolic ministry, clearly it was far more than simply one ministerial function among many.

That preaching is understood as among the cardinal acts of the Acts of the Apostles is demonstrated by Luke's emphasis on recounting sermons. While an older school of New Testament scholars looked at these sermons as literary inventions of Luke, more recent scholars have found them to be a most reliable account of the apostolic preaching.[83] The study of C. H. Dodd in particular has bolstered the confidence of the modern scholar in Luke's reports of early Christian preaching.[84] Let us look at some of these sermons.

---

82. On Luke's understanding of early Christian preaching, see Conzelmann, *The Theology of St. Luke*, pp. 218-25.

83. Frederick J. Foakes-Jackson and Kirsopp Lake, eds., *The Beginnings of Christianity*, 5 vols. (London: Macmillan, 1920-33). The work of Henry Cadbury still maintained that these speeches were the inventions of Luke, but he insists they are a most admirable work. *The Book of Acts in Historical Perspective* (London: A. & C. Clark, 1955), and *The Making of Luke-Acts*, 1st ed. (New York: Macmillan, 1927). For a recent discussion of the problem, cf. F. F. Bruce, *The Acts of the Apostles: The Greek Text with Introduction and Commentary*, 3rd rev. ed. (Grand Rapids: Wm. B. Eerdmans Publishing Co, 1990), pp. 34-40 (hereafter referred to as *Acts of the Apostles: Greek Text*).

84. Dodd, *Apostolic Preaching and Its Developments*.

A. *The Proclamation of Peter*

We begin with Peter's sermons in Jerusalem, the first of which occurred on the feast of Pentecost. The text is rather vague as to where this sermon was preached.[85] We are told that the disciples were all gathered together in one place, possibly for worship. The sign itself (the outpouring of the Holy Spirit) took place in a house or building, and yet the sign gathered such a crowd that by the time Peter had finished preaching three thousand people were added to the Church. An informal prayer meeting of Galileans, gathered no doubt behind closed doors somewhere, detonated by the pouring out of the Holy Spirit, exploded into a great congregation of men and women from all corners of the earth. Perhaps the Day of Pentecost began in the Upper Room and then moved to the courts of the Temple. The sign reversed the tide of Babel. Whereas once the peoples of the earth were all divided from each other by different languages, now they were brought together by the pouring out of the Holy Spirit and the proclamation of the gospel of the resurrection of Christ. This was the first public assembly of worship celebrated by the Church, and Peter's sermon is the first Christian sermon. Up until this time the resurrection of Christ had been the experience of a few of Christ's disciples. With this sermon it was publicly announced.

As in so many of the sermons of the prophets, the prophetic sign is the occasion for the sermon. The sign was that the Holy Spirit had been poured out on the disciples as they were gathered together. This outpouring of the Holy Spirit was made visible in tongues of fire and was manifested by the worship of the faithful in an ecstatic language, understood by peoples from all over the earth. Anointed by the Holy Spirit, the Church proclaimed the mighty works of God.

Peter begins his sermon by explaining that this sign is the fulfillment of the prophecy of Joel.

> "'And in the last days it shall be, God declares,
> that I will pour out my Spirit upon all flesh,
> and your sons and your daughters shall prophesy,

---

85. For the sermon at Pentecost, see Adolf Schlatter, *The Church in the New Testament Period* (London: SPCK, 1955), pp. 15-24; F. F. Bruce, *The Book of the Acts: The English Text with Introduction, Exposition, and Notes*, rev. ed. (Grand Rapids: Wm. B. Eerdmans Publishing Co., 1988), pp. 59-72 (hereafter referred to as *The Book of the Acts*); Peterson, *Engaging with God*, pp. 142ff.

and your young men shall see visions,
and your old men shall dream dreams;
yea, and on my menservants and my maidservants in those days
I will pour out my Spirit; and they shall prophesy.'"

(Acts 2:17-18)

This passage from Joel, which Luke quotes at length, is the text of which Peter's sermon is the exposition. Peter's point is that the inhabitants of Jerusalem have just witnessed the outpouring of the Holy Spirit prophesied by Joel. Furthermore, this joyful recounting of the mighty acts of God is the manifestation of this outpouring. The prophetic ministry, which in the days of Jesus was recognized to have ended with Malachi, would, according to Joel, be reestablished, and this was what was happening before their very eyes.

But the text from Joel, as this sermon evidently understood it, speaks also of great wonders and signs which would herald the establishment of the kingdom. This gives the preacher his second point. "'Jesus of Nazareth'" was "'attested to you by God with mighty works and wonders and signs'" (Acts 2:22). Peter then speaks of the sign which God performed in the death and resurrection of Jesus. "'This Jesus, delivered up according to the definite plan and foreknowledge of God, you crucified and killed by the hands of lawless men. But God raised him up, having loosed the pangs of death, because it was not possible for him to be held by it'" (Acts 2:23). This point is then supported by the exposition of a passage from Psalm 16. David, being a prophet and knowing God had promised him an heir who would be the Messiah, foresaw the resurrection of this Messiah. It is in this way that the sermon presents the text from Psalm 16, "'"For thou wilt not abandon my soul to Hades, / nor let thy Holy One see corruption"'" (Acts 2:27). It is this risen and glorified Christ who has poured out the Holy Spirit who is so obviously manifest before you. Peter gives an exposition of Psalm 110, which he understands as Jesus himself had interpreted it, namely, that the Messiah was not only David's son but also David's Lord and as such was seated at God's right hand in heaven.[86] The sermon now comes to its central affirmation, "'Let all the house of

86. As we have already shown, the interpretation of this psalm was important to the preaching of Jesus, as was illustrated by the Synoptic reports of the preaching of Jesus in the Temple. As a reference to Nestle-Aland, *Novum Testamentum Graece*, p. 754, shows, it is one of the most frequently cited Old Testament texts found in the New Testament.

Israel therefore know assuredly that God has made him both Lord and Christ, this Jesus whom you crucified'" (Acts 2:36). With this the proclamation of the resurrection of Christ is publicly made to Israel.

The congregation responds. "Now when they heard this they were cut to the heart, and said to Peter and the rest of the apostles, 'Brethren, what shall we do?'" (Acts 2:37). Peter resumes his sermon with a third point: an admonition to repentance and faith, and an offer of baptism. This point is also a development of the text from Joel, which, as quoted in Acts 2, ends with the line, "'"And it shall be that whoever calls on the name of the Lord shall be saved"'" (Acts 2:21). Peter assures his hearers that if they repent and are baptized they will receive the gift of the Holy Spirit. The promise of the prophet Joel is made to them and to their children, to their sons and to their daughters. This last point is enlarged upon with the aid of Isaiah 57:19, which makes clear that the promise is not only to Israel and the children of Israel but also to those who are far off, that is, the Gentiles.

This sermon, even in the brief form that is reported to us, is a very weighty piece of exegesis. In fact, one does not even suspect the beauty of the sermon until one sees it as exposition of Scripture. Three points are taken from this passage of Joel, and, according to Luke's report, the second and third are supported by parallel passages of Scripture. Scripture is explained by Scripture. The sign of tongues opened the ears of the congregation, and by an exposition of a passage from the prophet Joel the resurrection was proclaimed.

Peter's second Jerusalem sermon is found in Acts 3:12-26.[87] It is occasioned by the healing of the lame beggar Peter and John found at the Beautiful Gate as they were going to the Temple for the afternoon service of prayer. The sermon was given in a very specific area of the Temple, Solomon's Portico, a place where the disciples regularly met to hear the preaching of the apostles. Given the occasion, it is not at all surprising that the sermon is on the subject of the healing power of Jesus. For our purposes, however, it is even more interesting that it is an exposition of a passage from the prophet Isaiah, the Song of the Suffering Servant, Isaiah 52:13–53:12.[88] This passage

---

87. For an analysis of this sermon, see Bruce, *The Book of the Acts*, pp. 87-94; Adolf Schlatter, *Die Apostelgeschichte* (Stuttgart: Calwer Verlag, 1948), pp. 42-47.

88. On the importance of the servant Christology in the thinking of the early Church, see Bruce, *The Book of the Acts*, pp. 81 and 87. See also Joachim Jeremias, "παῖς θεοῦ C, D," *Theological Dictionary of the New Testament*, 5:677-717; and George, *Études sur L'oeuvre de Luc*, pp. 193ff.

was fundamental to Jesus in teaching his disciples to understand that the Messiah must suffer. This is no proof text discovered by the disciples years later. It is no after-the-fact interpretation of the prophets. It is rather a cornerstone of the teaching of Jesus. When Jesus taught his disciples the interpretation of the Scriptures, this was one of the passages that was given greatest attention. Jesus' interpretation of this passage is found in all strata of New Testament tradition. It explains both why the Christ had to suffer and only then was exalted, and that by his suffering therefore we are healed.[89]

Peter begins his sermon, "'Men of Israel, why do you wonder at this, or why do you stare at us, as though by our own power or piety we had made him walk?'" (Acts 3:12). It was the Suffering Servant spoken of by Isaiah, by whose wounds we are healed, who healed this man. This Suffering Servant has been highly exalted. "'The God of our fathers . . . glorified his servant Jesus'" (Acts 3:13), and it is by faith in him that this man has been healed. The Song of the Suffering Servant begins:

> Behold, my servant shall prosper,
>> he shall be exalted and lifted up,
>> and shall be very high.
>
> (Isa. 52:13)

And it is here that Peter begins, saying God "glorified his servant." But then Isaiah goes on to speak of the suffering of the servant:

> He was despised and rejected by men;
>> a man of sorrows, and acquainted with grief.
>
> (Isa. 53:3)

Peter's sermon takes the same turn and speaks of how Jesus was despised and rejected. It was Jesus "'whom you delivered up and denied in the presence of Pilate, when he had decided to release him'" (Acts 3:13). Although even Pilate found him innocent, "'you denied the Holy and Righteous One, and asked for a murderer to be granted to you'" (Acts 3:14). Here, too, our sermon continues to follow the Song of the Suffering Servant, whose suffering is innocent suffering.

---

89. Cf. I Peter 2:21-24; Matthew 8:17; Romans 4:25; and John 1:29. For further references, see Nestle-Aland, *Novum Testamentum Graece,* p. 761.

> He was oppressed, and he was afflicted,
>> yet he opened not his mouth;
> like a lamb that is led to the slaughter, . . .
> although he had done no violence,
>> and there was no deceit in his mouth.
>
> (Isa. 53:7, 9)

Isaiah makes it very clear that the Suffering Servant is indeed the righteous one (Isa. 53:11). In fact, the servant of the Lord, the Holy One, and the Righteous One are titles characteristic of Deutero-Isaiah, so that when Peter says in his sermon "you killed the Holy and Righteous One," it is abundantly clear that he is still commenting on Isaiah 53. He is charging the people of Israel with having rejected and put to death the Suffering Servant whom God sent to be their savior. Yet in the marvelous providence of God, this suffering has been turned to our healing: "Upon him was the chastisement that made us whole, / and with his stripes we are healed" (Isa. 53:5). Again Peter's sermon follows the turn of the Song of the Suffering Servant:

> Therefore I will divide him a portion with the great,
>> and he shall divide the spoil with the strong;
> because he poured out his soul to death,
>> and was numbered with the transgressors;
> yet he bore the sin of many,
>> and made intercession for the transgressors.
>
> (Isa. 53:12)

Once again the apostle returns to the exaltation of the Servant of the Lord. Through his exegesis of Isaiah the apostle shows that the role of the Suffering Servant was fulfilled by Jesus. Next the apostle begins to interpret the spiritual riches which God has bestowed on the Servant. His portion, the spoil of his spiritual conquest, is the power of healing. The chastisement which the Servant suffered has borne fruit in bringing health and wholeness to the many. It is a strong doctrine of vicarious atonement that is taught by Isaiah, and by Peter as well: "'And his name, by faith in his name, has made this man strong whom you see and know; and the faith which is through Jesus has given the man this perfect health in the presence of you all'" (Acts 3:16). In spite of the condensed form in which this sermon is reported, it is in fact a very full exposition of the fifty-third chapter of Isaiah.[90]

90. Cf. the chapter of Oscar Cullmann, "Jesus the Suffering Servant of God," in

This full exposition is followed, as was so often the case in the apostolic preaching, by a call for repentance and faith. The sermon then presents Jesus as the prophet about whom Moses spoke and admonished Israel to hear (Deut. 18:15-19). Jesus fulfilled the Law as well as the prophets. Deuteronomy 18:15-19 was a favorite passage for the earliest Christian preachers,[91] and we can imagine that the sermon Luke is summarizing explained the Christian understanding of it at length. Peter urges his listeners to repent of their rejection of the promised Messiah. In following the Messiah whom God has surely sent, they will enter into the covenant blessings promised to Abraham. Here there was, no doubt, an exposition of the Abrahamic covenant which showed Jesus to be the seed promised to Abraham, much as Paul explained it in Galatians 3:16.

Again we find in this sermon a wealth of expository material, which suggests that when Peter taught daily in the Temple, it was in this manner that he preached. He showed from the Scriptures that it was necessary for the Christ to suffer and so enter into his glory. He proclaimed that the promises of God found in the Law and prophets had been fulfilled in the death and resurrection of Jesus.

B. The Sermon of Stephen

One could argue that Stephen's sermon before the Council[92] is not so much a sermon as a defense in court, but then evangelistic preaching often uses the most diverse situations to present the gospel. The apostle Paul, for example, used any opportunity that presented itself for preaching. Apparently Stephen had carried out a ministry of teaching in the Greek-speaking synagogues of Jerusalem. It is not too clear whether this ministry was exercised at worship on the Sabbath or at the less formal teaching sessions held on weekday mornings. Be that as it may, one gets the impression that Stephen was regarded as one of the more accomplished

---

Christology of the New Testament, pp. 51-82; and George, *Études sur L'oeuvre de Luc,* pp. 192-96.

91. Cf. Cullmann's chapter, "Jesus the Prophet," in *Christology of the New Testament,* pp. 13-50, especially, pp. 16ff., 37, and 40.

92. Cf. William Manson, *The Epistle to the Hebrews* (London: Hodder & Stoughton, 1951), pp. 25ff.; Bruce, *The Book of the Acts,* pp. 129-51; Schlatter, *Die Apostelgeschichte,* pp. 83-89; Peterson, *Engaging with God,* pp. 139-42.

among the early Christian preachers. Several features about his sermon, which Luke reports at considerable length, deserve our attention.

First we notice that it is a defense against charges brought against him, namely, that he preached against the Temple and against the customs of Moses. This sermon therefore gives considerable attention to the ministry of Moses and Israel's rejection of it, as well as to the question of the true Temple and its ultimate role in the kingdom of God. In each case, Stephen followed the line of Christian interpretation which even at this early date had become standard for the infant Church. As had Peter before him, Stephen spoke of the prophet like unto Moses in the eighteenth chapter of Deuteronomy. In the same way he followed the Christian understanding of the Temple which Jesus had evidently preached in the courts of the Temple after he had purified it. Stephen interpreted the Scriptures as Jesus had taught his disciples to interpret them. His defense in this religious court was an interpretation of Scripture, which was, after all, what was expected.

Second, we find in this sermon a recounting of holy history. To recount the whole story of the mighty acts of redemption was, and would continue to be, a standard element of missionary preaching. He begins with Abraham; goes on to Joseph, Moses, David, and Solomon; and is embarking upon the prophets when his hearers erupt in anger and stone him. No doubt he would have gone on to speak of God's mighty works of redemption in Christ, but as he died his martyr's death he caught sight of the glorified Christ enthroned in heaven and witnessed to that transcendent reality.

Third, we note that Stephen's sermon is polemic, and this, too, as we shall see, is a constant element in the missionary preaching of the Church. This sermon is an attack on the perversity of Israel, a theme found in both the sermons of Peter we examined above. Peter accused his hearers of having crucified the Messiah. Indeed, Jesus himself had accused Israel of " 'killing the prophets and stoning those who are sent to you!' " (Matt. 23:37). In the preaching of Stephen the polemic sticks out in a much starker way; he does little to win over his hearers. This can perhaps be explained by the fact that the sermon was interrupted. Yet even at that, it seems as though the words of Stephen were calculated to harden the hearts of those who listened. One might say that Stephen was using poor missionary strategy if it were not for the fact that one of Stephen's hearers was Saul of Tarsus, destined to be the greatest of missionaries. For that one hearer, Stephen's sermon would long be remembered.

One could argue that all the sermons in the book of Acts are evangelistic sermons or missionary sermons. Yet this is not altogether true. Peter's sermons are a proclamation of the gospel to Israel. Even his sermon in the house of Cornelius is to people one would expect to hear the good news and receive it with joy; this sermon is in many ways very similar to the sort he preached in Jerusalem, even though he is preaching to those who are clearly Gentiles. Peter's sermons are sermons preached to the household of faith. They are preached in the synagogue, in the courts of the Temple, or in the homes of the faithful in a context of worship or at least of reverence. They were preached in the literary form of sermons.

From this point on, however, things begin to change. The missionary sermon begins to become a distinct genre of sermon. With Stephen's preaching as with that of Philip, about which we know considerably less, there is a turning out toward the broader world. Stephen preached to the Hellenized Greek-speaking Jews of Jerusalem; Philip to the Samaritans and to an Ethiopian who had come up to Jerusalem to worship; Peter to Cornelius and his household even though they were out-and-out Gentiles. The missionary or evangelistic sermon begins to develop as a genre as Christian preachers begin more and more to preach to those who know less and less about Scripture. Increasingly they find themselves preaching outside the community of faith.

C. Paul's Sermon in a Synagogue of the Diaspora

When Paul preaches in the synagogue at Pisidian Antioch, while still within the context of organized worship, he preaches a classic rabbinical sermon; nevertheless it is also the classic apostolic proclamation of the gospel that in the death and resurrection of Jesus the Law and the prophets have been fulfilled.[93] We are told that "On the sabbath day they went into the synagogue and sat down. After the reading of the law and the prophets," Paul was asked to preach (Acts 13:14-15).[94] Nothing

93. On Paul's sermon at Pisidian Antioch, see Bruce, *Acts of the Apostles: Greek Text,* pp. 299-316.

94. This along with Luke's report of the sermon in the synagogue at Nazareth is one of the earliest records which have survived of the synagogue liturgy. In this case the record is of a synagogue in the Diaspora. For further literature, see Bruce, *Acts of the Apostles: Greek Text,* p. 303. Also see Ned B. Stonehouse, *The Witness of Luke to Christ* (Grand Rapids and London: Wm. B. Eerdmans Publishing Co., 1951), pp. 68-92. Here at least the implication is that the invitation was spontaneous and that Paul was not given an opportunity to prepare.

is said about what the lessons from the Law and the prophets might have been or how the apostle might have drawn his sermon out of those lessons. Possibly he gave little or no attention to the lessons; however, he would have been aware that to have preached on the lessons would have lent authority to his preaching in a most important way.[95] Whatever the case, Paul preached his way through the whole history of salvation from Moses to Christ.[96] Perhaps he found this necessary because there were those among the God-fearing Gentiles who were not too well acquainted with the basic progression of salvation history, or perhaps he did it in order to make more dramatic the culmination of salvation history in the death and resurrection of Christ. Again we notice that in telling the story of God's mighty acts in Christ, he makes clear that all this happened in fulfillment of Scripture.[97] Having recounted the story of redemption, the apostle gives an exposition of several of the classic messianic passages of the Old Testament, namely, Psalm 2, Isaiah 55, and Psalm 16. Finally, Paul ends his sermon with a call to repentance. All this is familiar material to us. Paul, like Peter and the other apostles, must have preached this sort of sermon frequently.

The congregation of the synagogue at Antioch in Pisidia was favorably impressed, and Paul was invited to come back the Sabbath following. Unfortunately things did not go as well the next week. The same sort of opposition met Paul that had met Peter and the other apostles in Jerusalem. On the other hand, the Gentiles who were at the edge of the synagogue community were very interested. As Luke tells the story, this experience at Antioch in Pisidia brought about a turning point in the ministry of Paul and Barnabas. Up to that time, their missionary work had been to the Jews of the Diaspora, not to the Greeks. This had been a matter of conviction. The gospel first had to be preached in the synagogue to the Jews, but since they rejected it, Paul and Barnabas turned to the Gentiles.

---

95. Possibly the sermon was based on Deuteronomy 4:25-46 for the lesson from the Law and II Samuel 7:6-16 for the lesson from the prophets. J. W. Doeve, *Jewish Hermeneutics in the Synoptic Gospels and Acts* (Assen: Van Gorcum, 1954); and J. W. Bowker, "Speeches in Acts: A Study in Proem and Yelammedenu Form," *New Testament Studies* 14 (1967-68): 96-111.

96. Several scholars have suggested that this sermon is a standard one, which Paul would often use when he had the opportunity to preach in a synagogue. Cf. Bruce, *Acts of the Apostles: Greek Text,* p. 303.

D. Paul's Sermon to the Philosophers of Athens

The next sermon we find is a pure example of a missionary sermon.[98] It is not preached in the courts of the Temple or in the synagogue, nor in the context of the worship of the faithful, but in Athens, the cultural capital of classical antiquity. It was preached on the Areopagus, which was a sort of forum for philosophers.[99] It is far removed from the rabbinical homiletic tradition.

The sermon on the Areopagus is classic oratory.[100] The apostle opens with the most polite and diplomatic sort of apologetic, speaking to his audience of their own experience and affirming the sincerity of their inquiry into things divine: "'Men of Athens, I perceive that in every way you are very religious'" (Acts 17:22). No text of Scripture is given or expounded; instead, Paul speaks of seeing a statue erected to an unknown god,[101] a point he uses to drive home that their religious culture, as well intentioned as it may be, has not gotten beyond seeking God. It does not have the firm foundation of God's self-revelation. "'What therefore you worship as unknown, this I proclaim to you'" (17:23). With this Paul takes up the standard Jewish polemic against paganism. It must be said, however, that it is the polemic of Hellenistic Judaism. It leans in the direction of the spiritualization of Alexandria.

---

97. C. H. Dodd, *According to the Scriptures* (London: Nisbet & Co., 1952), p. 29.

98. See Peterson, *Engaging with God*, pp. 144-47.

99. On the nature of "the court of the Areopagus," see W. M. Ramsay, *St. Paul the Traveller*, 14th ed. (London: n.p., 1920), p. 247; Cadbury, *Book of Acts*, pp. 51-57; J. Finegan, "Areopagus," *Interpreter's Dictionary of the Bible*, 1:216ff.; and E. Vanderpool, "Areopagus," *Interpreter's Dictionary of the Bible*, supp. vol., p. 52.

100. The story of Paul preaching in Athens has inspired an extensive literature. It became even in patristic times a favorite text for meditating on the relation of Greek philosophy and Christian faith. See the bibliography in Bruce, *Acts of the Apostles: Greek Text*, pp. 379ff. Of special interest for our purposes are: Hans Conzelmann, "The Address of Paul on the Areopagus," in *Studies in Luke-Acts*, ed. L. E. Keck and J. L. Martin (Nashville and New York: Abingdon, 1958), pp. 217-30; Bertil Gärtner, *The Areopagus Speech and Natural Revelation* (Lund: C. W. K. Gleerup, 1955); Ned B. Stonehouse, *Paul before the Areopagus and Other New Testament Studies* (Grand Rapids: Wm. B. Eerdmans Publishing Co., 1957), pp. 1-40.

101. On the religious situation in Athens at the time Paul preached there, see Foakes-Jackson and Lake, *The Beginnings of Christianity*, vol. 5, the two chapters entitled, "The Unknown God" and "Your Own Poets," pp. 241ff.; and O. Broneer, "Athens, City of Idol Worship," *Biblical Archaeologist* 21 (1958).

> "The God who made the world and everything in it, . . . does not live in shrines made by man, nor is he served by human hands, as though he needed anything, since he himself gives to all men life and breath and everything. And he made from one every nation of men to live on all the face of the earth, having determined allotted periods and the boundaries of their habitation, that they should seek God, in the hope that they might feel after him and find him." (17:24-27)

There is, to be sure, much in this that is standard biblical teaching, yet there is also much that the enlightened, philosophically inclined pagan would find quite compatible.[102]

At this point the apostle Paul's apologetic goes even so far as to quote the sacred writings of the Greeks. Indeed, the poets were for the Greeks what the Scriptures were for the Jews. One would hesitate to say that Paul preached the sermon on a text from the Greek philosophers, but one might say that he borrows a couple of proof texts from them:

> "Yet he is not far from each one of us, for
>   'In him we live and move and have our being';
> as even some of your poets have said,
>   'For we are indeed his offspring.'

> Being then God's offspring, we ought not to think that the Deity is like gold, or silver, or stone, a representation by the art and imagination of man." (17:27-29)

Here the polemic against idolatry becomes specific. This sermon is an attack on paganism. It is not at its core a proclamation of God's redemptive work in the death and resurrection of Christ, although it opens the way to such a proclamation.

The sermon concludes with a call to repentance. "'The times of ignorance God overlooked, but now he commands all men everywhere to repent, because he has fixed a day on which he will judge the world in righteousness by a man whom he has appointed, and of this he has given assurance to all men by raising him from the dead'" (17:30-31). Polite apologetic has been put aside here. There was nothing diplomatic about telling the Athenians, of all people, that they were ignorant. To threaten the day of judgment was to reveal oneself as being hopelessly beyond the

---

102. F. F. Bruce puts it very well: "Paul's ability to adapt his tone and his approach to his audience must not be underestimated." *Acts of the Apostles: Greek Text*, p. 379.

pale of polite humanism, and to affirm the resurrection was to kiss enlightenment a fond farewell. Be that as it may, essential to the missionary sermon has always been the call to repentance. No matter how disguised it may be, a call to repentance can never really be diplomatic or polite; it is always an affront to our self-sufficiency. The missionary sermon aims at baptism, even if baptism is not specifically mentioned, and baptism is the sacrament of mortification.

When the apostle Paul's ministry became more settled as it did from time to time in places such as Corinth, Ephesus, and Rome, he preached daily. In such situations, we can imagine that his preaching and teaching was much more like that of the rabbi, that it was more biblical and in some way more systematic. We can imagine that it was related to the regular service of daily prayer during the week and the celebration of the sacraments on the Lord's Day. We catch a brief glimpse of this in the story of the raising of Eutychus (20:7-12). The congregation at Troas was gathered on the Lord's Day to break bread. On this occasion the apostle was preaching to them and we are told that he prolonged his speech until midnight. Sermons on such occasions, when there was an established congregation, were probably not oriented toward the missionary task. They would have been aimed at the edification of the congregation through the exposition of Scripture, just as the traditional sermon in the synagogue was.

E. Paul's Witness

Finally, in our look at the preaching of the apostles in Acts we come upon two missionary sermons preached by Paul completely outside the context of worship, in the most unusual of circumstances. One is preached to a mob from the steps of the military garrison next to the Temple in Jerusalem, a mob which would gladly have torn the Missionary to the Gentiles apart if the Roman authorities had not rescued him (Acts 22:1-21).[103] The other is Paul's defense before Agrippa (26:1-29).[104] One might well question whether they are to be regarded as sermons at all, because formally

103. For commentary on this passage, see Bruce, *The Book of the Acts,* pp. 414-23; and Schlatter, *Die Apostelgeschichte,* pp. 267-71.
104. For commentary on the passage, see Bruce, *The Book of the Acts,* pp. 461-71; and Schlatter, *Die Apostelgeschichte,* pp. 295-304.

each is the defense of one who is on trial.[105] Paul tells us more about himself than he does about Jesus. About this we would say, much as we said about Stephen's sermon, that the early Christian preachers were happy to present their message in any situation or in any form which presented itself.[106]

Both sermons present an element of missionary preaching which recurs frequently in the history of Christian homiletics, namely, the recounting of the missionaries' own conversion experience. In both Paul begins with a personal witness, telling those before him how thoroughly he was trained in the most accepted religious institutions of Judaism and of his zeal against the Christians. He presents his experience on the Damascus road in great detail, his conversion, baptism, and commission to take the gospel to the Gentiles. At this point the first of the two sermons is interrupted, but the train of thought is continued in the sermon at the court of Agrippa. The apostle tells of his activities as a preacher in Damascus, Jerusalem, Judea, and finally throughout the Gentile world. It was because of his preaching to the Gentiles that the mob was stirred up against him in the Temple that day. He was falsely accused of bringing Gentiles into the Temple. Having dealt with the charge leveled against him, Paul then comes to the classic witness, " 'And so I stand here testifying both to small and great, saying nothing but what the prophets and Moses said would come to pass: that the Christ must suffer, and that, by being the first to rise from the dead, he would proclaim light both to the people and to the Gentiles' " (26:22-23). Paul of course realized that the royal court to which he was preaching had heard rumors of the resurrection of the prophet Jesus of Nazareth whom Pilate had crucified, and so this sermon comes down solidly on affirming that it is indeed true, this story about Jesus. " 'I am speaking the sober truth. For the king knows about these things, and to him I speak freely; for I am persuaded that none of these things has escaped his notice' " (26:25-26).

The sermon as reported by Luke does not include a call for repentance and an offer of baptism. The preacher evidently considered it suffi-

---

105. On "Roman Law and the Trial of Paul," see the essay of H. J. Cadbury in Foakes-Jackson and Lake, *The Beginnings of Christianity,* 5:297-338.

106. On the significance of these speeches as Christian witnesses to the truth of the gospel before both the secular and religious powers of Judaism, see Schlatter, *Church in the New Testament,* pp. 206-17.

cient to testify to the truth of the resurrection. One wonders why. It may have to do with the personal nature of this sermon. Paul begins by talking about his own experience, and as the sermon comes to its climax he seems particularly sensitive to the spiritual temper of the king. One almost detects in Paul a sympathy for the rascal wearing the crown.[107] It's hard to say exactly what is going on here even though we are probably about as close to eyewitness reporting at this point as we are anywhere in Scripture. But quite possibly what we have here is a great missionary at his best, one sinner witnessing to another that God is indeed gracious.[108]

It is at this point that we want to bring up one of the major questions of these volumes. How is this kind of preaching — missionary or evangelistic preaching — related to worship? We have noted how many of the sermons reported at length in Acts are not part of what could be called a service of worship. The point we want to make is that the missionary sermon, no matter where it is preached, no matter how secular its literary form, whether it be a philosophical polemic in Athens or a defense in a court of law — the missionary sermon always implies a call to repentance and baptism. Missionary preaching is part of the sacrament of baptism. The missionary sermon belongs to the substance of a true celebration of baptism, as do the penitential sermon and the catechetical sermon. Such preaching may be at the gate of the Temple, as it were, before the faithful enter, but it is essential to true worship. Jeremiah's Temple sermon was certainly true worship, and so were its counterparts in the New Testament. That is abundantly clear from the Acts of the Apostles. When Jesus commissioned his apostles to make disciples of all nations by baptizing them and teaching them to observe all things which he had commanded them, it was exactly this that Jesus had in mind.

IV. The Ministry of the Word as Understood by the Pauline Writings

Another mine of information on the preaching ministry of the earliest Christians is the epistles of the apostle Paul. It is a very different kind of

---

107. As Schlatter points out, Paul regarded it of the utmost importance to give his witness before the rulers of the Jews. Schlatter, *Church in the New Testament,* p. 217.

108. On Agrippa as a Jewish king, see Cadbury, in *The Beginnings of Christianity,* 5:487ff.

source than the Acts of the Apostles. While Luke gives us a valuable collection of reports of early Christian sermons and a certain amount of historical material about how the ministry of the Word was carried out in the early Church, the Pauline writings reflect on the inner meaning of this ministry. The two taken together give valuable perspective to each other.

The biggest problem with treating Paul's understanding of the reading and preaching of Scripture is an embarrassment of riches. Paul has always had the reputation for being the great preacher of the apostolic age, and Christian preachers have again and again taken him as their model, be it John Chrysostom or Charles Haddon Spurgeon. In his *De doctrina christiana* Augustine looks to Paul as the stellar example of Christian preaching. But if Paul is that, he is also the stellar example of what an apostle is. In fact, sometimes he is simply referred to as the apostle. In Paul we find a demonstration of how central the ministry of the Word is to the apostolic ministry. Just as preaching was a cardinal ministry of the Christ, so it was a cardinal ministry of his apostle. All through the epistles of Paul there are rich passages on the nature of preaching. There are constant allusions to preaching which give us marvelous flashes of insight. In the treatment which follows we cannot pretend to be exhaustive. It will be enough if we can be suggestive.

A. Romans 10:14-17: Faith Comes by Hearing

This well-known passage tells us that preaching, like prayer and the sacraments, is a means of grace. Romans is the systematic theology of the New Testament,[109] a work which in logical progression thinks through the gospel Paul preached. Here in the book of Romans, the Pauline epistle which gives us such a thorough exposition of the doctrine of justification by faith, we find a passage on the relation of preaching to faith:

> But how are men to call upon him in whom they have not believed? And how are they to believe in him of whom they have never heard? And how are they to hear without a preacher? And how can men preach

109. The caveat of James S. Stewart is to be taken as well. In the opening chapter of his study of the life and thought of the apostle Paul, Stewart insists that Paul's religion is not to be systematized. *A Man in Christ: The Vital Elements of Paul's Religion* (New York and London: Harper & Brothers, 1955), pp. 3-31. See as well Charles A. Anderson Scott, *Christianity according to St. Paul* (Cambridge: University Press, 1927).

unless they are sent? As it is written, "How beautiful are the feet of those who preach good news!" . . . So faith comes from what is heard, and what is heard comes by the preaching of Christ. (Rom. 10:14-15, 17)

It is preaching which engenders faith, according to this passage. Preaching is the instrument God uses to produce faith in the human heart. Just how preaching engenders faith is spoken of here in a most concise form. Here we get to the heart of what Paul says about preaching. Calvin calls this "a noteworthy passage on the efficacy of preaching." It is not preaching in and of itself that engenders faith, but when God is pleased to use it for that purpose. Calvin puts it in a rather startling way: "Certainly the human voice cannot by its own power penetrate into the soul." God can and does use human agents, and it is that, in the final analysis, which makes them effective.[110] We should be careful to note that it is what God does in preaching which counts. It is because in the preacher's word we hear Christ's word that it produces faith; it is not because the preacher is clever or the listener is wise that the word is effective.[111] It is because the Word is true; it is because the Word is God's Word. Faith comes about by hearing that God is gracious to us in spite of all that we are and even all that we are not. It comes through hearing the story of how the Father offered up his Son to atone for our sins that we might have eternal life. It is through hearing this story and realizing that it proves God's profound love for us that faith comes. When we hear this and believe it, our whole relationship to God changes. Now we realize God can be trusted. Now fellowship with God is really possible.

The classical Protestant theology of Luther and Calvin has had much to say on *fides ex auditu.* That faith comes by hearing is a well-known principle.[112] To understand it is to realize that we become Christians not by some sort of ceremonial magic but by hearing God's Word and somehow

---

110. John Calvin, *The Epistle of the Apostle Paul to the Romans,* trans. Ross Mackenzie (Grand Rapids: Wm. B. Eerdmans Publishing Co., 1960), p. 233.

111. Otto Michel makes the point that the logic of what Paul says here is that we become Christians because of the Word of Christ. *Der Brief an die Römer,* Meyers Kritisch-exegetischer Kommentar über das neue Testament (Göttingen: Vandenhoeck & Ruprecht, 1966), p. 262.

112. The RSV translates, "So faith comes from what is heard, and what is heard comes by the preaching of Christ." The KJV reads, "So then faith cometh by hearing, and hearing by the word of God." The Vulgate gives, "Ergo fides ex auditu, auditus autem per verbum Christi." It is from the Vulgate that the theological term *fides ex auditu* comes.

knowing it is true. That, at least, is what it meant in the context of the Reformation. The insight of the Reformers into the significance of this text for our worship is something we want to keep carefully in mind. We are not saved by religious rites but by hearing the Word of God and believing it.

For Old School Presbyterians in the last century *fides ex auditu* meant that evangelism was not a matter of a dynamic pulpiteer being able to cast a spell on a great crowd. It was rather an intelligent exposition of biblical truth. Charles Hodge in 1835, the same year in which Finney's lectures on revivals appeared, published his commentary on Romans. By that time American revivalism had shifted into high gear. Commenting on this passage, Hodge insisted on the necessity of knowledge to faith. The Word of God is the foundation of faith because it is true. It is because faith is built on the truth, the truth of God, that it is effective for salvation.[113]

Today the principle that faith comes by hearing counters the idea that church growth is just a matter of sociology or demographics or something programmed by church administrators. Evangelism is not a matter of psychology and especially not mass psychology. Neither is it a matter of communication techniques or how to win friends and influence people. It is rather a matter of truly preaching the Word and rightly administering the sacraments. *Fides ex auditu,* properly understood, is a defense against all those who would advocate hot-box conversion techniques and brainwashing. It is our reason for deploring all kinds of rhetorical manipulation, political pressure, or economic incentives to bring about conversions.

Fides ex auditu is a corollary to a strong Augustinian theology which believes that it is essentially God himself who reaches out to his people in the preaching of the Word, and therefore it is what God does in and through these means of grace which makes them effective. That faith comes by hearing follows naturally from the doctrine of grace. It is by the grace of God that we are saved. God saves us because he loves us; therefore he has spoken to us and in his speaking has revealed himself to us. By giving us his Word God opens up communion with himself. Faith comes about when the Word is preached and the people of God hear it and know it is true. Faith is not making a decision that something is true but rather knowing something is true because it is true. The Word is true because the Word is God's Word, and that is what makes the difference. The Word

113. Charles Hodge, *A Commentary on Romans* (London: Banner of Truth Trust, 1972), p. 348.

has in itself the power to produce faith, as Jesus put it in more than one parable. The Word is like the leaven put in the dough. It is the Word which is the active ingredient. The Word has in itself a divinely given power to accomplish that which it proclaims. It is the seed which in spite of the soil produces a miraculous harvest (Matt. 13:18-33 and par.).

A second thing we notice in this text is that a preacher is one who is sent. He goes not on his own initiative but rather is called by God, set apart, consecrated, and then sent out to preach. Because it is God who calls the preacher, it is God who equips the preacher. The apostle Paul always understood himself as an ἀπόστολος, that is, as one who is sent.[114] We find Paul using this term in the very first verse of the Epistle to the Romans: "Paul, a servant of Jesus Christ, called to be an apostle, set apart for the gospel of God" (1:1). That one is sent is of the essence of the apostolate.

That one is sent to preach makes clear the ministerial nature of preaching.[115] Paul often emphasizes this point, and develops it particularly well in the Second Epistle to the Corinthians. There he speaks of his work of preaching and teaching as a ministry and of himself and his fellow workers as "ministers of a new covenant" (II Cor. 3:6). He tells us that they have their ministry by the mercy of God (4:1). Then a bit further on he makes the same point, "All this is from God, who through Christ reconciled us to himself and gave us the ministry of reconciliation" (5:18). What he wants to get across is, "For what we preach is not ourselves, but Jesus Christ as Lord, with ourselves as your servants for Jesus' sake" (4:5). We have already spoken of how John the Baptist understood the ministerial nature of preaching. John made it very clear that he was not the light but that he came to bear witness to the light. The preacher is an ambassador of Christ, a servant of Christ, even a slave of Christ. Whatever term might be used, the point is that the minister of the Word is subservient to the Word. God has chosen to present the treasures of the gospel to us in earthenware vessels (4:7). It is this ministerial nature of preaching which is behind the old American custom of calling our preachers "ministers." As preachers we are ministers of the Word of God.

114. Cf. Rengstorf, "The Classical Form of the Apostolate in the Person of Paul," *Theological Dictionary of the New Testament*, 1:437-43.

115. On the ministerial nature of church office in general, see Philippe-H. Menoud, *L'Église et les ministères selon le Nouveau Testament* (Neuchâtel and Paris: Delachaux & Niestlé, 1949), pp. 35-40.

A third thing this passage makes clear is that the preacher proclaims good news. Here again we find those words which Jesus and the early Church took from Isaiah, κηρύσσειν and εὐαγγελίζεσθαι, that is, to proclaim the Gospel, to announce the good news of salvation.[116] These are the words that the earliest Christians used to distinguish their preaching from the preaching of the synagogue. There was, of course, a continuity between the preaching of the synagogue and the preaching of the Church, but there was also a discontinuity, something unique about Christian preaching. Christian preachers were distinguished by the fact that they proclaimed the gospel. The allusion in Romans 10:15 to Isaiah 52 is of the greatest possible importance:

> How beautiful upon the mountains
>> are the feet of him who brings good tidings,
> who publishes peace, who brings good tidings of good,
>> who publishes salvation,
>> who says to Zion, "Your God reigns."
> Hark, your watchmen lift up their voice,
>> together they sing for joy;
> for eye to eye they see
>> the return of the LORD to Zion.
> Break forth together into singing,
>> you waste places of Jerusalem;
> for the LORD has comforted his people,
>> he has redeemed Jerusalem.
>
> (Isa. 52:7-9)

That Christian preaching is the proclamation of good news seems to be a consistent affirmation of the early Church. Today, speaking of preaching in these terms seems a matter of course; we are so accustomed to hearing it spoken of as such. In New Testament times the terminology was used because it conveyed a new approach to preaching. This vocabulary is evangelistic; it is kerygmatic. What is being preached here is a revival for the Jews, but a revival which goes hand in hand with the conversion of the Gentiles. This is something we find again and again throughout the New Testament. Of the essence of preaching the gospel is its universalism — it is to be preached to all peoples. This becomes clear a bit further on

116. Cf. John Murray, *The Epistle to the Romans*, two volumes reprinted in one (Grand Rapids: Wm. B. Eerdmans Publishing Co., 1993), 2:58-59.

in Isaiah. The revival of Zion is achieved when all nations come up to Jerusalem to acknowledge the reign of God. In Isaiah 60 we find in the clearest terms the evangelistic imperative of the preaching of the age to come:

> Arise, shine; for your light has come,
>   and the glory of the LORD has risen upon you.
> For behold, darkness shall cover the earth,
>   and thick darkness the peoples;
> but the LORD will arise upon you,
>   and his glory will be seen upon you.
> And nations shall come to your light,
>   and kings to the brightness of your rising.
>
> (Isa. 60:1-3)

The glory of Zion is revealed with the gathering in of all the nations of the earth and the homage of even the Gentile kings. For Paul Christian preaching is nothing less than the proclamation that this age has come. The Scriptures have been fulfilled.[117] Nothing makes our worship quite so profound as when we recognize that God has been faithful to his promises. When all peoples recognize the wisdom of God's eternal purposes, then God is glorified and his glory resounds throughout the whole earth.

In Luke's account of Jesus' sermon in Nazareth Jesus took as his text a very similar passage from the sixty-first chapter of Isaiah (Luke 4:16ff.). There, too, this same vocabulary is used. Isaiah again speaks of the joyful proclamation of the good news. Here in Romans Paul alludes to this passage from Isaiah 52, where we read of the proclamation of the good news of salvation. It is in these evangelistic terms that Paul understands Christian preaching.

Finally, a fourth point we find in Romans 10:14-17 is a sense in which by hearing the gospel we experience the presence of Christ. Several passages in the New Testament have spoken of what we have called the kerygmatic presence. Basically what this means is that when the word of Christ is truly preached, then Christ is present. John Murray brings this

---

117. On the apostle Paul's uses of the Old Testament, see Joseph Bonsirven, *Exégèse rabbinique et exégèse paulinienne* (Paris: Beauchesne, 1939); W. D. Davies, *Paul and Rabbinic Judaism*, 2nd ed. (London: SPCK, 1965); Dodd, *According to the Scriptures;* E. Earle Ellis, *Paul's Use of the Old Testament* (Edinburgh: Oliver & Boyd, 1957); Otto Michel, *Paulus und seine Bibel* (Gütersloh: Bertelsmann, 1929).

out in his commentary with a literal translation of the Greek text. He translates, "How shall they believe him whom they have not heard," and then comments, "A striking feature of this clause is that Christ is represented as being heard in the Gospel when proclaimed by the sent messengers. The implication is that Christ speaks in the gospel proclamation."[118] This insight has the greatest possible implications for our understanding of worship. In listening to the Word of Christ we enter into his presence, and in believing his Word and living according to his Word we serve his glory.

B. Romans 15:15-16: Preaching as Sacrifice

A second passage which gives us insight into the apostle Paul's understanding of the ministry of the Word is found at the end of the Epistle to the Romans.[119] The beauty of the passage is found in the poetry of its typology:

> But on some points I have written to you very boldly by way of reminder, because of the grace given me by God to be a minister of Christ Jesus to the Gentiles in the priestly service of the gospel of God, so that the offering of the Gentiles may be acceptable, sanctified by the Holy Spirit. (Rom. 15:15-16)

Several things stand out in these lines. In the first place we once again discover that Paul understands his being a minister as an act of grace in some way distinct or over and beyond the act of grace by which he became a Christian. For him there is a particular grace of apostleship which has set him apart to be a minister of Christ.[120] We have already mentioned that in the

---

118. Murray, *The Epistle to the Romans*, 2:58.

119. For a particularly good interpretation of this passage, see Menoud, *L'Église et les ministères selon le Nouveau Testament*, especially p. 23. More recently David Peterson has investigated the implications of this passage for a biblical theology of worship in his *Engaging with God*, pp. 179-82.

120. Otto Michel makes the point in commenting on Romans 1:5 that what the Greek actually means is "the grace of apostleship." As Michel sees it, apostleship is a special gift of God's grace. He goes on to say that whenever Paul speaks of his ministry he always makes clear that this ministry is a gift of grace. That God should have made him, a persecutor of his Son, an apostle, was always for Paul an act of grace marvelous beyond words. *Der Brief an die Römer*, p. 41. Calvin, interestingly enough, interprets the text the same way.

first verse of Romans Paul claims that he had been "set apart" for the gospel. As some of us translate it, Paul goes on in that opening paragraph to claim that he has received the grace of apostleship.[121] One could mention a number of other passages where Paul is obviously speaking of the grace of apostleship (I Cor. 3:10; Gal. 2:9; Eph. 3:2; and so forth). All this, of course, has to do with the doctrine of ordination, and that is outside the immediate scope of our study. Still, for our interest it is important to be clear that preaching, from beginning to end, is a work of God's grace.

The second thing we notice is that the gospel ministry is in some sort of continuity with the Levitical priesthood of the Old Testament. The New Testament speaks of a continuity between the ministry of the Old Covenant and the ministry of the New Covenant. This is especially clear in II Corinthians when Paul speaks of himself and Timothy as "ministers of a new covenant" (II Cor. 3:6). There is also a discontinuity. When Christ offered himself up on the cross as a full, complete, and perfect sacrifice for the sins of the world, the sacrifices of the Law were thereby completed and the priestly service of the Temple was ended. It was no longer necessary to have a priesthood to serve the altar. All that had been put away, as is made so clear in the Epistle to the Hebrews. The Church did not need a priesthood to offer sacrifices and so the priesthood of the Old Covenant came to an end. And yet, as we have said, for Paul there is clearly a New Covenant ministry (II Cor. 3:6). Paul would have undoubtedly agreed with Luke's report in Acts that the ministry of the New Covenant was dedicated to prayer and to the ministry of the Word (Acts 6:4). As Paul understands it, the ministry of the New Covenant performs its sacred function in proclaiming the sacrifice of Christ, in witnessing to the completeness of the redemption purchased by the Lamb of God, and in announcing that the Lamb who was slain lives forevermore. The sacrifice of the ministry of the New Covenant is a ministry of reconciliation because it publishes the good news that the sacrifice of Christ has atoned for all sin.

Thirdly, we notice that the apostle says that in his preaching he is offering up the Gentiles as a sacrifice. In the Greek text the vocabulary is especially suggestive. When Paul speaks of himself as a "minister" of Christ

---

121. RSV translates, "We have received grace and apostleship." See Walter Bauer, *A Greek-English Lexicon of the New Testament,* trans. and ed. W. F. Arndt and F. W. Gingrich (Chicago: University of Chicago Press; Cambridge: University Press, 1957), p. 886, paragraph 4.

Jesus to the Gentiles, he uses the Greek word λειτουργός. This word suggests the Old Testament ministry of the Levitical priesthood. When Paul speaks of "the priestly service" of the gospel, he uses the word ἱερουργέω, which means to act as a priest, to perform priestly service.[122] We obviously have a figure of speech here. What does it mean? Does preaching offer up the hearers of that preaching? Is it a typological metaphor suggesting that the preaching of the gospel is in succession to and fulfillment of the Temple cultus? Surely this is part of it, but let us draw out the figure, which is of course permitted and encouraged when an author uses a figure of speech like this. Perhaps Paul has in mind that it is through preaching that God ignites our hearts in sacrifice to himself. Perhaps he means that it is through preaching that the way of life is opened up for the Gentiles that they might make the passage from this world to the Father.

Many such attractive ideas suggest themselves, but what the apostle appears to be driving at here is more sober, more simple. The preaching and the hearing of the Word of God is in the last analysis worship, worship in its most profound sense. Preaching is not an auxiliary activity to worship, nor is it some kind of preparation for worship which one hopes will follow. To be sure, missionary preaching, catechetical preaching, and penitential preaching prepare the congregation for worship, but it is at the same time worship because it is part of baptism. That is all quite true and elsewhere we have tried to make that point, but it is even more true that the proclaiming of the Word of God, simply in itself, is high service to God. The solemn reading and preaching of Scripture in the midst of the congregation is a cultic act, if we may use that term, in continuity with the sacrifices of the Old Testament. Even more it fulfills these ancient cultic acts. The Old Testament sacrifices were but the type, the foreshadow, of something far greater, the proclamation of the gospel. The reading and preaching of Scripture is worship of an even greater intensity, an even greater depth, and an even greater magnificence than were ever the sacrifices of the Temple.

C. I Corinthians 1 and 2: On Pulpit Eloquence

In Paul's first epistle to the Corinthians we find several practical discussions of the nature of preaching. Unlike Romans, which seems to entail a

---

122. Cf. Michel, *Der Brief an die Römer*, pp. 364ff.; and Murray, *The Epistle to the Romans*, 2:210ff.

reasonably complete and systematic unrolling of the gospel, some of Paul's other epistles, and I Corinthians in particular, seem to be directed to certain specific problems not necessarily related to each other. In this epistle Paul tells us what he means by preaching the gospel, not in the general, theological terms we find in Romans but in terms of very particular questions.

The Corinthian Christians had been stirred up by a group of people who understood themselves to have a great love for wisdom and felt Paul did not really teach them the highest sort of wisdom. Hellenistic society made a big issue of wisdom, admiring its philosophers such as Plato and Aristotle because they taught wisdom. This σοφία was one of the four virtues of classical philosophy. The philosophers of classical antiquity often wore a special garb and spoke with a special lingo. Paul never adopted these affectations, and some therefore did not take him as seriously as they might otherwise have done. At the beginning of I Corinthians Paul has to address himself to criticism of his plain style of preaching; some in Corinth were much too impressed with the high rhetoric of Apollos, the preacher Paul had left in Corinth.[123] This may well have been to the embarrassment of Apollos himself, but be that as it may, Paul found it necessary to put the matter in perspective. Arguments between the supporters of Apollos and the supporters of Paul and his more pragmatic approach to preaching were disturbing the peace and unity of the Church. There were other matters at issue, but this is the first one Paul takes up in this epistle.

Those who know something of classical antiquity are aware of how the Greeks and Romans loved the art of oratory. Well before the time of Christ and the apostles it reached a zenith in the speeches of Demosthenes and then, closer to the time of Christ, in the orations of Cicero. Even at that the art was rather well known for degenerating into artificiality. Plato had scolded the rhetoricians for this in his famous dialogue *Gorgias*. What Paul has to say about the relative importance of a cultivated literary style in the opening chapters of I Corinthians might well be read against the background of Plato in this respect. The cultivated rhetoric of Hellenistic society was notorious for grabbing center stage, as it were, and losing sight of the primary concern of the message. That this should not happen in

---

123. It has often been suggested that Apollos was the author of the Epistle to the Hebrews. If this is indeed the case, then we know what the rhetoric of Apollos was like. As we find it in Hebrews, it is of the most admirable sort.

Christian preaching was Paul's main concern in the opening chapters of his first epistle to the Corinthians. In fact, the greatest of Christian preachers, whether Augustine in the dying gasp of Hellenistic civilization or the Puritans at the height of the baroque age in Europe, have often had to make this point.

Let us look at several particular points in this rather long passage, beginning with verse 17:

> For Christ did not send me to baptize but to preach the gospel, and not with eloquent wisdom, lest the cross of Christ be emptied of its power. (I Cor. 1:17)

It would be a mistake to make too much of Paul's statement that baptism was not a primary concern of his ministry.[124] Surely he is not overlooking the importance of baptism. What interests us here, rather, is the apostle's positive affirmation that Christ sent him "to preach the gospel," and to preach it not with "eloquent wisdom." This is the way the Revised Standard Version translates it. The Greek text simply has the verb εὐαγγελίζε-σθαι, to evangelize, and the phrase οὐκ ἐν σοφίᾳ λόγου, which might be translated very literally "not in a wisdom of the word." What Paul means is plainly that Christ sent him to change human hearts through the preaching of the gospel, not to impress them with his literary eloquence.[125] Skill in rhetoric is not what changes our hearts; it is the message of the Cross. The Word of God has its own power; it bears within itself the power of God, for it is God's Word. Paul said the same thing in Romans. As Paul understands it, faithful preaching must never let the art of oratory call attention to itself "lest the cross of Christ be emptied of its power."

With this the apostle takes up at some length his understanding of the preaching of the Cross. Paul constantly makes clear the objective nature of our salvation. It is the redemptive act of Christ in offering himself up

---

124. Just how we are to explain this text is not clear. See the explanation of Gordon D. Fee, *The First Epistle to the Corinthians,* The New International Commentary on the New Testament (Grand Rapids: Wm. B. Eerdmans Publishing Co., 1993), p. 63; Hans Conzelmann, *Der erste Brief an die Korinther,* Meyers Kritisch-exegetischer Kommentar über das neue Testament (Göttingen: Vandenhoeck & Ruprecht, 1969), p. 51; and Hans Lietzmann, *An die Korinther I/II,* 4th ed. (Tübingen: J. C. B. Mohr, 1949), pp. 9 and 168.

125. Charles Kingsley Barrett translates "rhetorical skill." *The First Epistle to the Corinthians* (New York: Harper & Row, 1968), p. 49.

in atonement for our sin which saves a sinful humanity, not great preaching. The preaching of the gospel is the means of our salvation, but it is the death and resurrection of Christ which has saved us. Just as we are saved by grace through faith, so we are saved by Christ's atoning sacrifice through the preaching of God's saving work. Grace has its means, and preaching is one of them. The preacher must be careful to distinguish between the mighty acts of God's grace and the means by which they are communicated.

The point Paul seems to be making is this: It is a matter of reverence to observe a sort of simplicity or humility in regard to the means of grace so that the glory of God's grace itself may be emphasized. This has always been the intention of plain-style preaching. As the apostle puts it elsewhere, God has chosen to give us the riches of his grace in earthen vessels in order that it might be clear that the transcendent glory belongs to God:

> For the word of the cross is folly to those who are perishing, but to us who are being saved it is the power of God. For it is written,
>
> "I will destroy the wisdom of the wise,
> and the cleverness of the clever I will thwart."
>
> Where is the wise man? Where is the scribe? Where is the debater of this age? Has not God made foolish the wisdom of the world? (I Cor. 1:18-20)

It has always been a temptation to turn the gospel into a philosophy, but the Christian preacher is not a Greek philosopher and should not attempt to appear as one. High literary form has often exerted the same kind of temptation. Some might have felt that the way to win the Greeks was to affect the learning and culture of the Greeks, but that is not what the apostle would have the Christian preacher do. It belongs to the preaching of repentance to recognize the foolishness of the wisdom of this world that we might turn away from it and receive in faith the wisdom of God. There is the power to change human life; there is the wisdom of God. Paul sums it up in the famous line: "Christ [is] the power of God and the wisdom of God" (I Cor. 1:24). The preacher should never try to assume the glory which is rightfully Christ's. Christian preaching should never call attention to itself, to its splendid literary style, its brilliant reasoning or powerful argumentation. This, to be sure, is why the Reformed preacher has traditionally worn the simple black preaching gown without decoration or jewelry, rather than the richly brocaded vestments popular in some traditions. The splendor is reserved for Christ. *Soli Deo gloria:* to God alone be the glory!

This thought was very dear to the apostle Paul. He begins the second chapter by telling us:

> When I came to you, brethren, I did not come proclaiming to you the testimony of God in lofty words or wisdom. For I decided to know nothing among you except Jesus Christ and him crucified. And I was with you in weakness and in much fear and trembling; and my speech and my message were not in plausible words of wisdom, but in demonstration of the Spirit and of power, that your faith might not rest in the wisdom of men but in the power of God. (I Cor. 2:1-5)

It has been suggested that after preaching to the philosophers of Athens, Paul, going on to Corinth, was especially conscious of the futility of human philosophy.[126] His preaching in Corinth was therefore consciously not a philosophical appeal. Quite purposely he did not preach the mystery of God in lofty words of wisdom; that is, he did not adopt the idiom of philosophical discussion.

When Paul tells us that, going to Corinth, he left philosophical argument aside and "decided to know nothing among you except Jesus Christ and him crucified" (I Cor. 2:2), he apparently meant that the gospel is best presented in its own terms. The story of Jesus and his redemptive work has to be understood in the biblical context, not in the context of Greek philosophy or any other philosophy for that matter, be it Hindu philosophy or the philosophies of our own day such as existentialism.

Although Paul resolved not to try to prove the faith either by rhetorical ingenuity or philosophical argument, he did rely on spiritual means. What Paul meant by "demonstration of the Spirit and power" is probably what theologians have called the inner testimony of the Holy Spirit. Paul depended not on his eloquence but rather on the power of the Word itself to convey its authority. The self-authenticating power of the Word was what won Paul's hearers.[127] Even more Paul saw that in the long run the truth that one recognized in the flash of spiritual insight which came from

126. Archibald Robertson and Alfred Plummer, *A Critical and Exegetical Commentary on the First Epistle of St. Paul to the Corinthians,* 2nd ed., International Critical Commentary (Edinburgh: T. & T. Clark, 1914), p. 31.

127. Barrett, *First Epistle to the Corinthians,* pp. 65ff.

God's Holy Spirit was confirmed by the demonstration of the power of the Spirit to change people's lives.[128]

One thing should be clear in the two opening chapters of I Corinthians. The Hellenistic world had one way of looking at wisdom, while those educated in the biblical tradition had another.[129] The two crash head-on in this passage. Paul was clearly a student of biblical wisdom. It, too, was a system of learning, but it is based on a completely different perception of what reality is all about. Paul is very realistic about the opposition between the humanistic worldview of Greek philosophy and the theistic worldview of biblical wisdom theology. It is not simply a matter of the Greeks being enlightened and the Jews being benighted, as some have tried to make it out:

> Yet among the mature we do impart wisdom, although it is not a wisdom of this age or of the rulers of this age, who are doomed to pass away. But we impart a secret and hidden wisdom of God, which God decreed before the ages for our glorification. . . . And we impart this in words not taught by human wisdom but taught by the Spirit, interpreting spiritual truths to those who possess the Spirit. (I Cor. 2:6-7, 13)

For Paul it is the work of the Holy Spirit both in the preacher and in the congregation which gives preaching its power. This is not some stuffy arcane wisdom, not some legalistic tradition, but rather a living, enlightening power that imparts life even to the old, the jaded, and the academic. The Holy Spirit has a way of guarding the integrity of the Word, reforming it when it becomes corrupt, invigorating it when it becomes feeble, and even refreshening it when it becomes sour. The Holy Spirit has a way of guarding the riches of God's grace from all our attempts to package it and promote it. We have a human propensity to divert the grace of God to our own purposes; we would glorify ourselves rather than let God glorify us. Yet when the Holy Spirit takes over, all our attempts appear vain and tawdry. The Holy Spirit can do with our preaching what we never dreamed possible:

---

128. Cf. Fee, *First Epistle to the Corinthians*, pp. 95-97.

129. On the theological aspects of this whole passage (I Cor. 1:18–3:23), cf. Conzelmann, *Der erste Brief an die Korinther*, pp. 53-100. Conzelmann is particularly helpful in bringing out the distinction Paul makes between the wisdom of God and the wisdom of this world.

But, as it is written,

> "What no eye has seen, nor ear heard,
> nor the heart of man conceived,
> what God has prepared for those who love him,"

God has revealed to us through the Spirit. (I Cor. 2:9-10)

The graciousness of God is filled with wonderful surprises.

D. I Corinthians 12–14:
Various Forms of the Ministry of the Word

The apostle Paul discusses the ministry of the Word in chapters 12–14 of I Corinthians as well.[130] The three chapters as a whole speak about the variety of gifts of ministry with which God has endowed the Church; while not all of these gifts of ministry have to do with the ministry of the Word, a good many do.[131] The utterance of wisdom, the utterance of knowledge, the gift of prophecy, and the gift of tongues are mentioned at the beginning of the chapter, while at the end a variety of ministries are further elaborated. There are apostles, prophets, teachers, workers of miracles, healers, helpers, administrators, and speakers in various kinds of tongues.[132] Beside these two lists we should put several others found elsewhere in the Pauline literature. In Romans 12:6-8 we read of the gifts of prophecy, teaching, and exhortation, and in Ephesians 4:11 of apostles, prophets, evangelists, pastors, and teachers. Obviously the ministry of the Word could take a number of different forms.[133]

---

130. On the significance of these three chapters for the Christian understanding of worship, see Peterson, *Engaging with God*, pp. 194-226.

131. Hans Lietzmann with his wide knowledge of Hellenistic religions makes the point that those who were troubling the Corinthian church were influenced not so much by the philosophical strain of Greek religion as by the mystical, gnostic strain of the mystery religions. This strain of Greek religion stressed ecstatic experiences rather than the intellectual dimension of religion. When Paul gives a priority to the ministry of the apostles, prophets, and teachers, he is insisting that Christianity is an intellectual and moral religion based on the Word of God rather than a cultic religion based on ecstatic spiritual experiences. *An die Korinther I/II*, pp. 60-65.

132. Perhaps the best interpretation of what Paul says here about the ministry of the Word is that of Menoud, *L'Église et les ministères selon le Nouveau Testament*, pp. 40-42.

133. Hans Lietzmann makes the point that apostles, prophets, and teachers were

While the major point we gather from the different lists is the great variety of ways the ministry of the Word can be exercised, we need to savor the full richness of this variety by studying several of these terms. Not all these terms are to be clearly distinguished from one another; many appear to be used as synonyms at least some of the time.

1. The ministry of the apostle appears with a certain priority in two of these lists.[134] Paul understood this gift to have been given to him (I Cor. 1:17). In Galatians, as we shall see, he defends his right to be regarded as an apostle just as Peter, James, John, and the original Twelve were (Gal. 2:9). His argument was based not only on his having seen the risen Christ in an ecstatic experience on the road to Damascus, but also on the fact that he had done the work of an evangelist and that God had prospered that work. He understood his apostolic ministry as one of planting the Church by means of the proclamation of the gospel. It was a ministry of evangelism (Rom. 15:19). It was also both proclamation (κήρυγμα) and exhortation (παράκλησις). Evangelistic preaching both proclaims the message of salvation and exhorts those who hear it to receive it.

2. Prophecy likewise appears prominently in these lists.[135] As Paul uses the term, it appears to be synonymous with preaching. This is particularly the case in I Corinthians 14:3, where we are told that "He who

---

for Paul the leading ministers of the Church. They clearly have a place above "workers of miracles, healers, helpers, administrators, speakers in various kinds of tongues." The triad apostles, prophets, and teachers makes up the "charismatic offices" *(die charismatischen Ämter)*. The apostles were the wandering missionaries; the prophets were the divinely inspired preachers of the local congregation; the teachers were, perhaps, the expositors of the Old Testament Scriptures. *An die Korinther I/II,* p. 63.

134. On the New Testament understanding of the ministry of the apostle, see Hans von Campenhausen, "Der urchristliche Apostelbegriff," *Studia Theologica* 1 (1947): 96-130; Thomas W. Manson, *The Church's Ministry* (Philadelphia: Westminster Press, 1948); Menoud, *L'Église et les ministères selon le Nouveau Testament;* H. Mosbech, "Apostolos in the New Testament," *Studia Theologica* 2 (1948): 166-200; and K. H. Rengstorf, "ἀπό-στολος," *Theological Dictionary of the New Testament,* 1:420-50.

135. On the ministry of the prophets in the New Testament Church, see G. Friedrich, "προφήτης κτλ," *Theological Dictionary of the New Testament,* 6:848-56; H. Greeven, "Propheten, Lehrer, Vorsteher bei Paulus," *Zeitschrift für die neutestamentliche Wissenschaft* 44 (1952/1953): 3-15; W. A. Grudem, *The Gift of Prophecy in I Corinthians* (Lanham, Md., New York, and London: University Press of America, 1982); and Menoud, *L'Église et les ministères selon le Nouveau Testament,* pp. 40-42.

prophesies speaks to men for their upbuilding (οἰκοδομή) and encouragement (παράκλησις) and consolation (παραμύθιον)." The Greek words παράκλησις and οἰκοδομή are often used to explain what preaching is in the New Testament (e.g., Rom. 12:8; I Tim. 4:13; and II Tim. 3:14–4:5). On the other hand, prophecy was probably understood to include not only preaching but also the special revelation of truth from God in a manner similar to the way the prophets of the Old Testament were given special revelations. It is in this way that we understand Acts 21:9-11 and I Timothy 1:18. Some passages suggest that prophecy was a mere private or personal ecstatic speech which rejoiced in the gospel of Christ but did not have the authoritative nature of the apostolic proclamation of the gospel or the teaching of the elders of the church. While this ecstatic element is no doubt to be included in the gift of prophecy, it does not seem to be primary. Preaching seems to be the primary activity of the New Testament prophets. One wonders, then, why Paul uses the word "prophecy," if it is preaching he really has in mind. Perhaps it is because the word implies that in the preaching of the Church the preaching ministry of the Old Testament prophets has been not only restored but fulfilled. These lists of gifts which include the word "prophecy" do not include the word "preaching." Very specifically, none includes *kerygma* (κήρυγμα) or *paraclesis* (παράκλησις), a fact which encourages us to think that this is what Paul has chiefly in mind when he uses the word "prophecy." He understands it as an inclusive term for the preaching ministry.

3. Teaching also appears prominently in these lists.[136] While in many New Testament passages there is a clear distinction between teaching and preaching,[137] the distinction between the two words does not

---

136. On the ministry of the teacher in the New Testament Church, see Dodd, "Jesus as Teacher and Prophet"; Floyd V. Filson, "The Christian Teacher in the First Century," *Journal of Biblical Literature* 60 (1941): 317-28; Greeven, "Propheten, Lehrer, Vorsteher bei Paulus"; Menoud, *L'Église et les ministères selon le Nouveau Testament*, pp. 40-42; Moore, *Judaism*, 1:308ff.; and Rengstorf, "διδάσκαλος," *Theological Dictionary of the New Testament*, 2:161-63.

137. On the distinction between preaching and teaching, see Philippe-H. Menoud, "Preaching," *Interpreter's Dictionary of the Bible*, 3:868-69. Dodd, *Apostolic Preaching and Its Development*, has had a great influence on our understanding of preaching in the last fifty years. Surely it is one of the classics of modern New Testament scholarship. One should be careful not to take it to extremes, and to approach it with a *sic et non* attitude. The criticisms of Robert Mounce are not to be overlooked, *The Essential Nature of New Testament Preaching* (Grand Rapids: Wm. B. Eerdmans Publishing Co., 1960).

always hold true. When the distinction is clear, then preaching is the proclamation or announcing of God's mighty acts of redemption in Christ, while teaching is the interpreting of the Scriptures, admonition to faith and faithful living, and training in righteousness. Philippe Menoud used to make the point that while the New Testament uses the word κηρύσσειν to speak of preaching the gospel to those who have not yet heard it, it uses the word διδάσκειν to speak of instructing an established Christian congregation on various aspects of Christian life and thought. Teaching is a primary function of the elders of the Church, as Paul makes clear in I Timothy 5:17. Again it is Philippe Menoud who points out that it was through the teaching of Christian wisdom (Col. 1:28) that Paul expected to bring Christians to maturity.

4. Evangelism is mentioned as a specific ministry in Ephesians 4:11. From the derivation of the term we would gather that an evangelist is one whose primary concern was to preach the message of salvation. The implication is that an evangelist would differ from a teacher in that while a teacher would teach the Scriptures and the Christian way of life in a settled and systematic context, an evangelist would move about constantly introducing new groups of people to the central Christian message. Timothy is exhorted to do the work of an evangelist (II Tim. 4:5); Paul himself speaks of his work as evangelism (Rom. 15:19-20). While the apostolic ministry includes evangelism, the two are evidently not synonymous. One imagines that evangelists such as Philip carried on much the same ministry as Peter, John, or Paul, but somehow they are not thought of as having the apostolic authority to plant churches (Acts 8:4-17).

Finally something needs to be said about the gift of tongues. From time to time in the history of the Church tongues has been a cherished spiritual gift. From Acts we learn that speaking in tongues was experienced by many early Christians, and from I Corinthians it is evident that some in the Corinthian church prized this gift. The significance of this gift seems to be that it gives a sort of ecstatic enlightenment to those who experience it that raises one above ordinary rational knowledge or wisdom. It provides a dimension of speech which is quite different from the utterance of wisdom and knowledge. Its particular value is that it can edify the Church when for one reason or another the ordinary conduits of rational communication are not open, have become clogged, or have broken down. The gift of tongues as the gift of prophecy, that is, the ecstatic aspect of the gift of prophecy, seems to have been most active in the Church at periods when the Church did not have the Scriptures in its own language, or when for some reason it was deprived of the Scriptures, or even at times when the legitimate ministry ceased to teach the Word. The ancient Church enjoyed speaking in tongues with greatest profit before the New Testament had been committed to writing, just as Nabiism seems to have been strongest and most valuable in the days of Samuel and Elijah. It was in the mid–eighteenth century when the French Huguenots were deprived of a regular ministry and regular worship that "prophetism" appeared in the Reformed tradition. On the mission field it is often observed to have been of service to the first generation of Christians, but after the Scriptures have become available in the language of the new church the gift seems to disappear. In our own time the gift seems to have appeared in the American church at times when the legitimate ministry of the Word was suffocated by a rather totalitarian kind of secular learning. When the children of God were silenced, the stones themselves cried out.

A proper understanding of the gift of tongues helps us put the ministry of the Word in perspective. It shows us that God can speak over and above all human failures and inabilities to understand. God can even use the tongues of stammerers and the lips of the dumb. This is the point of that strange quotation from Isaiah 28:11-12 which Paul introduces into I Corinthians 14:21: "'By men of strange tongues and by the lips of foreigners will I speak to this people, and even then they will not listen to me, says the Lord.'" It is when the priest and the prophet "err in vision" and "stumble in giving judgment" (Isa. 28:7) that God uses strange tongues. If the legitimate ministry is unfaithful, God will still be heard. This, it seems to me, is just what we have seen in the last few years. The ordinary channels of hearing the Word of God have been clogged up by every kind of infidelity, but God's Word has been heard in some of the strangest ways and some of the strangest places. Even more than that, the Word has been confirmed by signs and wonders.

Having spoken at some length now about variety, we must necessarily say that Paul establishes a priority among those possessing the charismata of the ministry of the Word. "God has appointed in the church first apostles, second prophets, third teachers . . ." (I Cor. 12:28). We find something quite similar in I Timothy 5:17, "Let the elders who rule well be considered worthy of double honor, especially those who labor in preaching and teaching." The reason for this is that the ministry of the Word is constitutive of the Church. Luther was right; the true Church is where the Word is truly preached and the sacraments rightly administered. There may be other valuable ministries in the Church from time to time such as speaking in tongues, healing, charitable works, political effectiveness, and social relevance, but none of these has anything like the centrality of the ministry of the Word.

Finally, one notices from these three chapters of I Corinthians, which taken as a whole have so much to say on the nature of Christian worship, that preaching is a charisma, χάρισμα; it is a spiritual gift. Surely there is much in preaching which is human skill or literary art, but none of it is nearly as central as the fact that preaching is a charisma. The apostle Paul was a great theologian trained in all the intellectual rigors of academic rabbinical science. He was an accomplished intellectual, and yet he strove to make his ministry dependent on that which God had given. He realized that what made his ministry real was not his intelligence, nor even his training, but the fact that God had anointed him, that God blessed his work. He submitted himself entirely to God. Somehow this is possible with truly great minds. They seem to be able as the consummate stroke of genius to arrive at great simplicity. The divinely given flash of light gives to such accomplished intellects an amazing clarity, simplicity, and humility. It can be explained in no other way than to say that it is charisma, χάρισμα, an anointing of the Holy Spirit.

E. I Corinthians 15: Preaching as the Proclamation of the Resurrection

With the fifteenth chapter of I Corinthians Paul takes up a new subject — the resurrection from the dead.[138] Evidently there were those who had

138. Aside from the standard commentaries there is a wealth of special studies on this chapter. Among the more recent, see the following: Hans Conzelmann, "On the Analysis of the Confessional Formula in I Corinthians 15:3-5," *Interpretation* 20 (1966): 15-25; J. Kloppenborg, "An Analysis of the Pre-Pauline Formula in I Cor. 15:3b-5 in Light of Some Recent Literature," *Catholic Biblical Quarterly* 40 (1978): 351-67; Bruce M. Metzger, "A Suggestion concerning the Meaning of I Cor. XV,4b," *Journal of Theological Studies* 8 (1957): 118-23; K. A. Plank, "Resurrection Theology: The Corinthian Controversy Reexamined," *Perspectives in Religious Studies* 8 (1981): 41-54; H. Ridderbos, "The Earliest Confession of the Atonement in Paul," in *Reconciliation and Hope,* ed. Robert Banks (Grand Rapids:

troubled the church of Corinth by denying the Christian hope of the resurrection of the body. The denial of the resurrection had been characteristic of the Sadducees. There must have been Sadducees who were attracted to Jesus and who had even gone so far as to be baptized but who nevertheless had trouble accepting the Christian teaching on the subject of the resurrection. The miracle of Christ's resurrection they accepted, but the implication that all Christians will likewise be raised they found difficult.[139]

Paul's first argument in defense of the doctrine is that the proclamation of Christ's resurrection is central to the apostolic ministry as Paul and the other apostles had exercised it. The passage says much about preaching and its essential nature:

> Now I would remind you, brethren, in what terms I preached to you the gospel, which you received, in which you stand, by which you are saved, if you hold it fast — unless you believed in vain.
>
> For I delivered to you as of first importance what I also received, that Christ died for our sins in accordance with the scriptures, that he was buried, that he was raised on the third day in accordance with the scriptures, and that he appeared to Cephas, then to the twelve. Then he appeared to more than five hundred brethren at one time, most of whom are still alive, though some have fallen asleep. Then he appeared to James, then to all the apostles. Last of all, as to one untimely born, he appeared also to me. For I am the least of the apostles, unfit to be called an apostle, because I persecuted the church of God. But by the grace of God I am what I am, and his grace toward me was not in vain. (I Cor. 15:1-10)

There is much here about which we have already spoken. Again we see that Paul understands the ministry to be a work of God's grace which in sovereign disregard of Paul's worthiness or unworthiness set him apart for the gospel ministry. Again we see that preaching is the proclamation of the gospel. Again

---

Wm. B. Eerdmans Publishing Co., 1974), pp. 78-89; R. J. Sider, "St. Paul's Understanding of the Nature and Significance of the Resurrection in I Corinthians XV,1-19," *Novum Testamentum* 19 (1977): 124-41; B. Spörlein, *Die Leugnung der Auferstehung: eine historisch-kritische Untersuchung zu I Kor 15* (Regensburg: F. Pustet, 1971); A. J. M. Wedderburn, "The Problem of the Denial of the Resurrection in I Corinthians XV," *Novum Testamentum* 23 (1981): 229-41; and J. H. Wilson, "The Corinthians Who Say There Is No Resurrection of the Dead," *Zeitschrift für die neutestamentliche Wissenschaft* 59 (1968): 90-107.

139. On the precise nature of this disagreement and the possibility of Sadducean influence, see Fee, *First Epistle to the Corinthians*, p. 715, especially n. 6.

we see that the proclamation of the gospel of Christ's death and resurrection is emphatically "in accordance with the scriptures." The phrase is used twice. The proclamation of the Christian gospel had taken place in preaching, preaching not unlike the preaching of the synagogue, the sort of preaching which is an interpretation of Scripture. One does not proclaim the resurrection simply in general terms but rather very specifically in terms of Scripture. One preaches the gospel as the fulfillment of the promises of Scripture. New Testament preaching is not to be cut off from the Old Testament. Naturally the Old Testament Scriptures continued to be read in Christian worship, as Paul made clear to Timothy (I Tim. 4:13); they were the basis of Christian preaching. It was of the greatest possible importance to the early Church that the death of Christ was to be proclaimed as being according to Scripture and the resurrection of Christ as being according to Scripture.

What we find new in this passage is that the proclamation is also the passing on of a living tradition. Paul delivered the tradition he had received from the other apostles. He uses the formula which rabbis were accustomed to using when they passed on the oral tradition of how the rabbis of the past had interpreted Scripture, "I delivered to you . . . what I also received." Paul preached to the Corinthians an interpretation of Scripture which he received from the apostles who were eyewitnesses of the crucifixion, the burial, the empty tomb, and one or more of the various encounters and appearances of the risen Christ which followed.

There are two things to be observed here: first, the importance of the continuity of the living witness to the resurrection of Christ; and second, the immediacy of Paul's experience of the exalted Christ who appointed him and sent him to the Gentiles to bear witness. Paul's apostleship rested on his being a witness to the exalted Christ, as the other apostles had been, and his being sent by Christ to proclaim what he had witnessed.[140] It was the risen and exalted Christ who sent those who experienced him as risen and exalted to proclaim his resurrection glory. Not only that, but the proclamation that Jesus is the risen and exalted Christ was constitutive of the Church. It planted it; it brought it into being. It was the essence of the apostolic ministry. The highest and holiest office of the apostle is to proclaim that Christ has risen. The proclamation of the resurrection is the heart and center of all Christian preaching.

140. Ernst Fuchs, "Die Auferstehung Jesu Christi und der Anfang der Kirche," in *Glaube und Erfahrung* (Tübingen: J. C. B. Mohr [Paul Siebeck], 1965), pp. 49-69; and Floyd V. Filson, *Jesus Christ, the Risen Lord* (New York and Nashville: Abingdon, 1956).

F. Galatians and the Charismatic Authority of the Preacher

Some of the most important insights we have into the apostle Paul's understanding of the ministry of the Word are occasioned by the objections of certain Galatians who insisted that Paul did not have the authority to preach what he was preaching. There were evidently in the region of Galatia a number of Jews who had accepted Jesus as the Messiah but who had strong reservations about accepting Gentiles into the kingdom of God. Perhaps if Gentiles were willing to be circumcised and converted to Judaism and agreed to observe all its laws and traditions, they might be accepted; but essentially these Galatians believed one first had to become a Jew before one could become a Christian. Not following Paul's teaching on justification by faith, they introduced a new legalism.[141] They argued against the preaching of Paul and claimed that he did not have the authority to preach as he did. Faith in Christ was not really enough, they insisted. Certain ceremonial requirements such as circumcision needed to be observed as well. Looking at it realistically, what these Galatians were doing was making Christianity into one more Jewish sect. They were trying to turn the gospel into a rather narrow sort of sectarian teaching. Furthermore, they assumed they had the backing of the original apostles. In fact, they claimed Paul did not have apostolic authority at all. They figured that Paul did not have the same authority as James, the Lord's brother; Peter, and the other apostles back in Jerusalem.

Paul's epistle to the Galatians is his response to this challenge. Basically his answer was that when he had been called to the ministry of the Word, the gospel that he was to preach was revealed to him by none other than Christ. This fact made him an apostle with the same authority as the original Twelve. In Galatians we find a strong statement of the authority of the ministry of the Word.

The Epistle to the Galatians is very direct. Paul gets to his argument rather quickly.

> For I would have you know, brethren, that the gospel which was preached by me is not man's gospel. For I did not receive it from man,

---

141. Recent New Testament scholars have tried to draw more precisely the picture of these Galatians who had opposed Paul. For a thorough discussion of the problem, see Hans Dieter Betz, *Galatians* (Philadelphia: Fortress Press, 1979); Günther Bornkamm, *Paulus* (Stuttgart: W. Kohlhammer, 1969); and Walter Schmithals, *Paulus und die Gnostiker Untersuchungen zu den kleinen Paulusbriefen* (Hamburg-Bergstedt: Reich, 1965).

nor was I taught it, but it came through a revelation of Jesus Christ. (Gal. 1:11-12)

We notice the emphatic term used for Paul's preaching, τὸ εὐαγγέλιον τὸ εὐαγγελισθέν, "the gospel preached to you," or, more literally translated, "the gospel with which I evangelized you." Paul is more apt to say something like we find in Galatians 2:2, τὸ εὐαγγέλιον ὅ κηρύσσω, that is, "the gospel which I proclaimed." Paul is talking about evangelistic preaching. To preach the gospel is to proclaim the message of salvation. It is a saving message which is preached, the message which brings about our salvation "by hearing with faith" (Gal. 3:2 and 6). Once again we find Paul's doctrine of *fides ex auditu*. This doctrine is a corollary to the doctrine of justification by faith. In Galatians we find it perhaps clearer than anywhere else in Paul's writings. If salvation is through faith, then faith is through the preaching of the gospel. This certainly is a theme we find elsewhere in the New Testament, although it is especially strong here where Paul has to defend his preaching. This is essential to the Christian understanding of preaching. It had been for Jesus and it was for Paul.

A phrase like τὸ εὐαγγέλιον τὸ εὐαγγελισθέν certainly would appear to set the preaching of the saving message apart from the teaching of the Christian way of life. One gathers from this phrase that the proclamation of the gospel is a distinct dimension of Christian preaching.[142] There is no question but that, for Paul, preaching is above all the preaching of the gospel. Paul understood himself especially as an evangelistic preacher. His call was to preach the gospel to the heathen, that is, to the Gentiles, those who were outside the household of faith. To be sure, others had been called to preach the gospel to the Jews, but in Galatians it is Paul's evangelizing of the Gentiles which is at issue. When Paul talks about preaching, that is his central concern.

One notices further: This gospel which Paul preached is not merely a human teaching. It is not simply the message the Church put together as a way of explaining the unique religious experience the disciples enjoyed in sharing the company of Jesus. This gospel was the message of salvation. Paul claims that this was the message Jesus gave him at the time he called

---

142. See the following commentaries: F. F. Bruce, *The Epistle to the Galatians*, The New International Commentary on the New Testament (Grand Rapids: Wm. B. Eerdmans Publishing Co., 1982), p. 88; Richard Longenecker, *Galatians*, Word Biblical Commentary (Waco, Tex.: Word, 1990), p. 22.

him to be a preacher. This gospel was revealed to him, he insists.[143] It was not simply his explanation of an experience of religious ecstasy he had had outside Damascus. The apostle goes so far as to use the phrase δι' ἀποκαλύψεως, that is, by revelation. It was not handed down to him by tradition nor was it taught to him as some teacher's teaching, but rather it came to him by revelation. As we have mentioned, Paul could speak of receiving important elements of the tradition such as the Words of Institution of the Lord's Supper and the list of witnesses to the resurrection by tradition (I Cor. 11:23 and 15:3-6). Paul learned of these things in the way the Jews had passed on oral tradition for centuries. What Paul tells us here, however, is something very different. The gospel itself, which the ascended and glorified Christ called Paul to preach, Paul received directly from Christ himself.

Three times in Acts we have the story of Paul's call to preach the gospel.[144] In chapter 9 we have the Damascus road experience (Acts 9:1-31). The report of the original vision (9:3-9) says nothing about a call to preach the gospel to the Gentiles; nevertheless, a few verses later the passage implies that there was another vision later on in which Paul saw a man named Ananias restoring his sight (9:12). Furthermore, the passage tells us Ananias also had a vision in which God told him of the mission to which Paul was to be called (22:17ff.). A second version of the story is found in Acts 22 where Paul defends himself after his arrest in Jerusalem. He tells of his conversion on the Damascus road and also of how Ananias told him of the call he was to be given to preach the gospel to the Gentiles. Then a few verses later we read of Paul's having yet another vision granted to him while worshiping in the Temple at Jerusalem. How long after his conversion Paul was granted his vision is not clear.[145] In the report of this vision we find that Paul was told he was to be sent to the Gentiles (22:21).

---

143. On Paul's claim that the gospel he preached was given to him by revelation, cf. Heinrich Schlier, *Der Brief an die Galater,* Meyers Kritisch-exegetischer Kommentar über das neue Testament (Göttingen: Vandenhoeck & Ruprecht, 1971), pp. 43-48; Ronald Y. K. Fung, *Galatians,* The New International Commentary on the New Testament (Grand Rapids: Wm. B. Eerdmans Publishing Co., 1988), pp. 53ff.

144. On the vocation of the apostle Paul, cf. Lucien Cerfaux, *Le chrétien dans la théologie paulinienne* (Paris: Les Éditions du Cerf, 1962), pp. 69-97.

145. Biblical scholars have tried to harmonize the account Luke gives us in chapter 9 of Acts and the account Paul gives us of his visions in Galatians. Cf. the excursus on the problem in Schlier, *Der Brief an die Galater,* pp. 105-17. See as well Longenecker, *Galatians,* p. 32.

Finally, we find a third report of Paul's conversion in his defense before Agrippa (26:12-18) which goes into greater detail about Paul's being commissioned to preach the gospel to the Gentiles. There we read that when Jesus appeared to Paul on the Damascus road he said to him:

> " 'I have appeared to you for this purpose, to appoint you to serve and bear witness to the things in which you have seen me and to those in which I will appear to you, delivering you from the people and from the Gentiles — to whom I send you to open their eyes, that they may turn from darkness to light and from the power of Satan to God, that they may receive forgiveness of sins and a place among those who are sanctified by faith in me.' " (26:16-18)

It is not difficult to harmonize the three reports we have in Acts. To harmonize them with what we learn from Paul himself in Galatians might be a bit more difficult, although certainly not impossible.[146]

Surely what we learn from these reports tallies well with what we read of other occasions when God has appeared in a vision and called someone to the ministry of the Word.[147] The vision Paul experienced in the Temple is reminiscent of the call of Isaiah (Acts 22 and Isaiah 6). That Paul went off into Arabia after his conversion is reminiscent of Jesus' going into the wilderness to pray about the call he received at the time of his baptism. When one thinks about it, what Paul tells us about his call to preach the gospel to the Gentiles is very similar to what Matthew tells us about the way the risen Jesus appeared to the Eleven and appointed them to make disciples of all nations (Matt. 28:19). This resurrection appearance had as its purpose the sending of the apostles to preach to the Gentiles. Paul tells us that he had the same sort of experience of call as the other apostles and therefore understands himself to have apostolic authority. God himself sent him to do what he was doing.[148]

Even at that one wonders how Paul got the full story about Jesus.

---

146. The harmonizing of these different accounts is far removed from our concern here. Those interested might consult Longenecker, *Galatians,* pp. lxxiiff., for a recent discussion of the problem.

147. On the prophetic vocation of the apostle Paul, cf. Cerfaux, *Le chrétien dans la théologie paulinienne,* pp. 77-88.

148. One should not overlook the fact that the apostles in Jerusalem did confirm the gospel that Paul had preached. On this subject, cf. Schlier, *Der Brief an die Galater,* pp. 64-81.

One could understandably ask if it was really possible for Paul to have learned all the teachings of Jesus and all the stories of his mighty acts and the signs he performed as thoroughly as did the apostles, who had been with Jesus throughout his three-year ministry. It is a legitimate question.[149] Two different answers suggest themselves, and quite possibly they are complementary rather than exclusive. In Galatians Paul insists that he received the fundamental message from Christ himself. In Acts we are told of a series of visions. The reference in Galatians to a trip to Arabia may be taken as a hint of a more prolonged period of divine instruction similar to that of Moses on Mount Sinai, which, we remember, Paul understood to be in Arabia (Gal. 4:25). This might imply that Paul learned a good amount of material from Jesus, just as Moses was supposed to have been taught not only the Law but the tradition of interpretation while he was with God on Mount Sinai. On the other hand, one might argue that Paul is only insisting that Jesus himself taught Paul his gospel, that is, the essentials of his preaching, especially his message of justification by faith, as Paul preached it to the Gentiles.[150] One could argue that beyond the essentials of the gospel, Paul learned a good amount of oral tradition from Ananias. The ninth chapter of Acts tells us that very soon after he received his sight again he began to preach in the synagogue, proclaiming Jesus as the Son of God (Acts 9:19-20). The same chapter also tells us that Paul remained in Damascus "many days" (9:23). This would have given Paul plenty of time to have learned the oral tradition from Ananias or any other Christian who happened to be part of the Christian community in Damascus at the time. He might have learned this oral tradition the way the disciples of rabbis had always learned the oral tradition, that is, by memory. This would not seem to contradict what Paul tells the Galatians. The main point is that Paul in Galatians is making a very strong claim that his message did not depend on those who had been apostles before him. This does not rule out, however, his having learned a good amount of oral tradition from those who had actually known Jesus and had accompanied him during his ministry.

When all has been said we still have to recognize that the apostolic tradition which the primitive Church did maintain was important for the

149. On Paul's knowledge of the historical Jesus, cf. Stewart, *A Man in Christ*, pp. 273-98.

150. Philippe-H. Menoud, "Revelation and Tradition: The Influence of Paul's Conversion on His Theology," *Interpretation* 7 (1953): 131-41.

apostle Paul. Galatians comes out strongly for a sort of charismatic authority, but charismatic authority by itself is not enough to maintain the health of the Church. This is clear from the Pastoral Epistles.[151] Even more it is clear from I Corinthians, where Paul has to restrain the charismatics.[152] The Church needs its exciting young charismatics and the Church needs solid elders and learned scholars. The amazing thing about Paul is that he was all of these together.

Paul in Galatians claims he was an apostle in much the same sense that the prophets were prophets.[153] God had directly given him authority:

> But when he who had set me apart before I was born, and had called me through his grace, was pleased to reveal his Son to me, in order that I might preach him among the Gentiles, I did not confer with flesh and blood, nor did I go up to Jerusalem to those who were apostles before me, but I went away into Arabia; and again I returned to Damascus.
>
> Then after three years I went up to Jerusalem to visit Cephas, and remained with him fifteen days. (Gal. 1:15-18)

The passage reminds us of the story of the call of Jeremiah (Jer. 1:5).[154] God had set Paul apart before he was born to exercise this ministry. What has always stuck out is the statement that he did not confer with flesh and blood and that he did not go up to Jerusalem to those who were apostles before him. In the first place this seems to contradict what we read in Acts.[155] Even more than that it gives the impression that Paul saw himself as a sort of freelance apostle. To put it in terms of contemporary discussion, it sounds like Paul had not yet heard of collegiality, let alone apostolic succession.[156]

Is this the way we are to understand Paul? What Paul seems to be

---

151. E. Earle Ellis, *Pauline Theology: Ministry and Society* (Grand Rapids: Wm. B. Eerdmans Publishing Co., 1989), pp. 102-11.

152. Ellis, *Pauline Theology,* pp. 112-17.

153. Some scholars have tried to explain Paul's sense of immediate experience as "Paul's mysticism." They explain his strong sense of authority as something mystical. For a discussion of Paul's mysticism, cf. Davies, *Paul and Rabbinic Judaism,* pp. 86-110; Scott, *Christianity according to St. Paul,* pp. 122-34, 150-51, and 191; and Stewart, *A Man in Christ,* pp. 147-203.

154. Cf. Fung, *Galatians,* pp. 63ff.

155. Cf. Fung, *Galatians,* pp. 62-72.

156. Bruce, *The Epistle to the Galatians,* pp. 97-99; and Longenecker, *Galatians,* p. 42.

saying here is that in the appearance of the risen Christ on the Damascus road were both a conversion and a call, as there had been with both Jeremiah and Isaiah. Having received this call, he went off into the Arabian wilderness to pray and meditate. This follows the pattern of so many before him whom God had called to preach his Word.[157] Then much later he went to Jerusalem and there met Peter and James. The Judean church only rejoiced at his preaching ministry. Then again, many years later he laid before the leaders of the Jerusalem church his ministry to the Gentiles which was expressly confirmed. They recognized the real thing when they saw it. Paul had had a unique calling. Christ himself had appointed him to preach to the Gentiles. Surely when Paul met Peter he was full of questions about the historical Jesus, about the tradition.[158] Paul knew Christ as the Word of God by personal experience and also by having received the historical witness, the apostolic tradition.[159]

Surely one of the most important things we learn from this passage is that to exercise the ministry of the Word one must receive a particular gift of God's grace, a special anointing of the Holy Spirit. Paul tells us that when the other apostles "perceived the grace that was given to me," they gave Paul the right hand of fellowship. The epistles of Paul make it clear in a number of places that there is a particular grace of ministry.[160] We have already spoken of the important passage in the fifteenth chapter of Romans in which Paul makes very clear the idea that the ministry of the Word is a gift of God's grace. He tells the Romans that he is bold to write to them "because of the grace given me by God to be a minister of Christ Jesus to the Gentiles in the priestly service of the gospel" (Rom. 15:15-16). A bit further on we will speak of the passage in Ephesians where Paul says that he was made a minister of the gospel "according to the gift of God's grace which was given to me by the working of his power" (Eph. 3:7). When understood in the context of these other passages, it should be evident that a distinct ministerial grace sets ministers apart to perform the ministry to which they have been called. Paul is speaking of a gift of grace

157. On the other hand, see Bruce, *The Epistle to the Galatians,* p. 96.

158. Bruce, *The Epistle to the Galatians,* p. 98.

159. Very helpful on this subject is the article of Menoud, "Revelation and Tradition." Especially perceptive on the subject of charism and order is Ellis, *Pauline Theology,* pp. 87-121.

160. Among the clearest passages Walter Bauer lists in his lexicon are Romans 1:5; 12:3; 15:15; I Corinthians 3:10; 15:10; II Corinthians 12:9; Galatians 2:9; and Ephesians 3:7.

that not everyone had received. It meant being set apart and empowered to perform a ministry not everyone had been called to perform.

What Paul has to say in the Epistle to the Galatians about the ministry of the Word may be a bit hard to swallow for today's highly institutionalized clergy. Even more the ideology of our day finds it hard to deal with ministers who have a high sense of authority. Paul would not fit very well into the organization. Yet much of the power of his ministry came from his overwhelming sense of mission, which came from his consciousness of being called to that ministry by Christ himself. He was an apostle because Christ appeared to him and personally sent him to preach the message Christ himself had given him. So much of what makes for great preaching is just exactly that.

This has been a continuing problem in the Church. So often the creative geniuses in the Church, the outstanding preachers who have a sense of knowing the Word of Truth on a personal basis, make for problems with the more humdrum and less inspired officeholders. Either they become schismatic or they get stifled by the institution and its politics. Any kind of personal authority is looked at with suspicion by the more up-to-date clergy of our day. We are told that the authority is in the institution rather than in the person. The more stodgy sort of ecclesiastical politicians may not be able to inspire their congregations, but they do, on the other hand, have a way of keeping things in their control. Paul obviously had charisma, and great preaching needs charisma even if the less gifted have a way of feeling threatened by it. Charisma by its very nature cannot be institutionalized, and no one should try! It cannot be induced. Yet, things have a way of going rather flat without it. When we sense it is missing there is no way of faking it. The Holy Spirit has a way of working when and where and how he pleases. Charisma is a gift of God. It is a blessing for which we can only be thankful when it comes, but when it does not, we can only wait for it with patience and prayer.

G. Ephesians and the Proclamation of the Mystery

Paul's epistle to the Ephesians sets preaching in a whole theology of worship.[161] The first three chapters unfold as a great doxology in which

161. Much recent scholarship denies the Pauline authorship of the Epistle to the Ephesians. For a survey of the discussion, see G. Johnson, "Ephesians, Letter to the,"

the message of salvation is recounted as a hymnic gospel.[162] In fact, the apostle frames his gospel in the language of prayer, as it was framed in the synagogue service and, no doubt, the church service of the time as well.[163]

> Blessed be the God and Father of our Lord Jesus Christ, who has blessed us in Christ with every spiritual blessing in the heavenly places, even as he chose us in him before the foundation of the world, that we should be holy and blameless before him. He destined us in love to be his sons through Jesus Christ, according to the purpose of his will, to the praise of his glorious grace. . . . (Eph. 1:3-6)

The language is exalted and compact, as it often is in prayer. It exalts in the eternal purposes of God and proclaims man's chief end as living to the praise of God's glory. Through the preaching of the gospel God has made known to us in all wisdom and insight the mystery of his will. It is

---

Interpreter's Dictionary of the Bible, 2:108-14. After a full survey of the discussion of Pauline authorship Markus Barth concludes, "The burden of truth lies with those who question the tradition. The evidence produced by them is neither strong nor harmonious enough to invalidate the judgment of tradition." Markus Barth, *Ephesians,* The Anchor Bible, vols. 34 and 34A (New York, London, Toronto, Sydney, and Auckland: Doubleday, 1974), 2:41; and Lucien Cerfaux, "En faveur de l'authenticité des épîtres de la captivité. Homogénéité doctrinale entre Éphésiens et les grandes épîtres," in *Littérature et Théologie pauliniennes,* Recherches bibliques, vol. 5 (Bruges: Desclée de Brouwer, 1960), pp. 59-71. On the other hand, see Andrew T. Lincoln, *Ephesians,* Word Biblical Commentary (Dallas: Word Books, 1990), pp. lix-lxxiii. On the whole question of pseudepigrapha in the Bible, cf. Bruce M. Metzger, "Literary Forgeries and Canonical Pseudepigrapha," *Journal of Biblical Literature* 91 (1972): 3-24.

162. There have been a number of special studies of the benediction or prayer of thanksgiving with which Ephesians begins. H. W. Beyer, "εὐλογεω," *Theological Dictionary of the New Testament,* 2:754ff.; J. Cambier, "La Bénédiction d'Éphésiens 1,3-14," *Zeitschrift für die neutestamentliche Wissenschaft* 54 (1963): 58-104; Ernst Lohmeyer, "Das Proömium des Epheserbriefs," *Theologische Blätter* 5 (1926): 120-25; C. Maurer, "Der hymnus von Epheser 1 als Schlüssel zum ganzen Brief," *Evangelische Theologie* 11 (1951-52): 151-72; J. T. Sanders, "Hymnic Elements in Ephesians 1-3," *Zeitschrift für die neutestamentliche Wissenschaft* 56 (1965): 214-32.

163. The relation of the doxology which opens the Epistle to the Ephesians to the prayers of the synagogue liturgy has often been noticed. Barth, *Ephesians,* 1:97-98; N. A. Dahl, "Adresse und Proömium des Epheserbriefs," *Theologische Zeitschrift* 7 (1951): 241-64; R. Deichgräber, *Gotteshymnus und Christushymnus in der frühen Christenheit* (Göttingen: Vandenhoeck & Ruprecht, 1967), pp. 65-76. For more on the doxologies of the early Church and the synagogue, see Eric Werner, *The Sacred Bridge: Liturgical Parallels in Synagogue and Early Church* (New York: Schocken Books, 1970), pp. 273-312.

according to God's eternal purposes, according to the counsel of his will, that we who first hoped in Christ have been appointed to live for the praise of his glory. We have heard the preaching of the Word of truth, the gospel of our salvation, and have believed in Christ. We have been sealed with the promised Holy Spirit until the time when we enter into the fullness of our salvation to the praise of his glory. Finally, these three doxological chapters are brought to a close with an ascription of praise:[164]

> Now to him who by the power at work within us is able to do far more abundantly than all that we ask or think, to him be glory in the church and in Christ Jesus to all generations, for ever and ever. Amen. (Eph. 3:20-21)

Taken as a whole, these three chapters make very clear that our salvation glorifies God. This is the root of the theology of worship found in Ephesians. If this is the fundamental insight, then the next insight comes quite naturally. Making known God's gracious purposes and announcing the accomplishing of these purposes in his mighty acts of redemption glorifies God as well. When preaching unfolds the eternal counsels of God's will and the glorious destiny he has appointed for his creation, God is worshiped. Even more, when preaching becomes a means of bringing about these purposes, then it is doxological. It serves the glory of God.

As Christians we worship when we are confronted by the revelation of the mystery of God's grace. A true hearing of the gospel generates within us the awe and wonder that is the substance of worship, and we can do nothing but bow in wonder and confess God's glory. One of the concepts characteristic of the apostle Paul is that the gospel is the revelation of the mystery of our salvation. For Paul the wisdom of God is a mystery which, although hidden for ages, is now revealed in the preaching of the gospel. There are three Greek words here which we find in various combinations, μυστήριον, ἀποκαλύψις, and σοφία. It is in the preaching of the gospel that God has made known in all wisdom and insight the mystery of his will (Eph. 1:9). It is all a matter of grace. God gives to those who hear this preaching "a spirit of wisdom and of revelation in the knowledge of him" (Eph. 1:17). This is done so that the eyes of our hearts might be enlightened, that we might know what is the hope to which we have been called (Eph. 1:18). In a rather remarkable way Paul has taken these three

---

164. Markus Barth points out that the prayer begun at Ephesians 1:3 is not really concluded until 3:21. *Ephesians,* 1:162.

Greek words and related them to each other to express a very profound and uniquely Christian concept. The preaching of the gospel is the revelation of the wisdom of God.[165] Until the fullness of time when God sent his Son to redeem a lost humanity, this wisdom of God was a mystery hidden in the secret counsels of God. Now, however, with the performing of Christ's redemptive work, this mystery is revealed. It is revealed that the heavenly hosts might glorify God and that we, hearing of God's grace, might receive it in faith and so live to the praise of his glory. This is what God had destined us to do from all eternity.

In the second chapter of Ephesians Paul continues his hymn to the grace of God revealed in Christ. To speak about the grace of God is to praise God, and one is amazed how Paul apparently cannot speak about this subject in anything but a hymnic style.

> And you he made alive, when you were dead through the trespasses and sins in which you once walked, following the course of this world, following the prince of the power of the air, the spirit that is now at work in the sons of disobedience. . . . But God, who is rich in mercy, out of the great love with which he loved us, even when we were dead through our trespasses, made us alive together with Christ (by grace you have been saved), and raised us up with him, and made us sit with him in the heavenly places in Christ Jesus, that in the coming ages he might show the immeasurable riches of his grace in kindness toward us in Christ Jesus. (Eph. 2:1-2, 4-7)

One of the things which gives these three chapters such a strong doxological flavor is the way the purposes of God are put in a cosmic context.[166]

---

165. On the relation of wisdom, mystery, and revelation in Ephesians, see Günther Bornkamm, "Glaube und Vernunft bei Paulus," in *Studien zu Antike und Urchristentum, Gesammelte Aufsätze* (Munich: Chr. Kaiser, 1963), 2:119-37; Lucien Cerfaux, *Le Christ dans la théologie de St. Paul* (Paris: Les Éditions du Cerf, 1954), pp. 189-208; N. A. Dahl, "Cosmic Dimensions and Religious Knowledge (Ephesians 3:18)," in *Jesus and Paul,* ed. E. E. Ellis and E. Grässer (Göttingen: Vandenhoeck & Ruprecht, 1975), pp. 57-75; Davies, *Paul and Rabbinic Judaism,* pp. 147-76; Jacques Dupont, *Gnosis: La connaissance religieuse dans les Épîtres de Saint Paul* (Paris: J. Gabalda, 1949); André Feuillet, *Le Christ, Sagesse de Dieu* (Paris: J. Gabalda, 1966); Heinrich Schlier, "Kerygma und Sophia," *Die Zeit der Kirche* (1956): 206-32; Ulrich Wilckens, "σοφία κτλ," *Theological Dictionary of the New Testament,* 7:517-24.

166. The cosmic Christology of Ephesians has been one of the points of issue between Ernst Käsemann and Heinrich Schlier. For Schlier this has led to a strong Catholic ecclesiology. His commentary on Ephesians, *Der Brief an die Epheser,* 2nd ed. (Dusseldorf: Patmos Verlag, 1958), has stimulated a vigorous discussion over what some have claimed

Our redemption, by which we are restored to our destined role as members of the household of God, is the fundamental fact of our existence. This is of eternal significance. To recount this history of redemption is at the center of Christian worship. It is the main feature in the theater of God's glory. And in this context Paul gives us that great text:

> For by grace you have been saved through faith; and this is not your own doing, it is the gift of God — not because of works, lest any man should boast. (Eph. 2:8-9)

When we understand life as the theater of God's glory rather than merely the marketplace of human values, then we can begin to grasp why salvation is by grace. Grace is ultimately wondrous; it amazes us as nothing else. God's power certainly impresses us, and his wisdom is impressive, too, as is his justice, but we expect all that from God. God's grace is another matter. His grace, as the old gospel song puts it, is amazing. If God is truly gracious, then all we can do is worship him. At the center of life is a marvelous surprise. God is more than powerful; he is more than just and wise; he is gracious. God is our Father, faithful and loving toward his sons and daughters. It is when we discover this that we can do nothing else but worship him. "Blessed be the God and Father of our Lord Jesus Christ, who has blessed us in Christ with every spiritual blessing" (Eph. 1:3). Preaching proclaims the mystery of God's graciousness. That is what Ephesians tells us about preaching as worship.

In the middle of the second chapter Paul turns to his Gentile converts and reminds them of how far they were from God and the blessings of the covenant before they heard the gospel which Paul had preached to them.

> But now in Christ Jesus you who once were far off have been brought near in the blood of Christ. For he is our peace, who has made us both one, and has broken down the dividing wall of hostility. . . . And he came and preached peace to you who were far off and peace to those

---

is an incipient catholicizing tendency in the "deutero-pauline" writings of the New Testament. Cf. Käsemann's article "Epheserbrief," *Die Religion in Geschichte und Gegenwart,* 6 vols., ed. Kurt Galling (Tübingen: J. C. B. Mohr [Paul Siebeck], 1957-65), 3rd ed., 2:517-20; and "Paulus und der Frühkatholizismus" and "Das Interpretationsproblem des Epheserbriefes," in *Exegetische Versuche und Besinnungen,* 2nd ed., vol. 2 (Göttingen: Vandenhoeck & Ruprecht, 1965), pp. 239-52 and 253-61. Much more to the point than either Schlier or Käsemann is John Alexander Mackay, *God's Order: The Ephesian Letter and This Present Time* (New York: Macmillan, 1956).

who were near; for through him we both have access in one Spirit to the Father. So then you are no longer strangers and sojourners, but you are fellow citizens with the saints and members of the household of God. (Eph. 2:13-14, 17-19)

One can hardly read through this passage without being struck by the phrase "He came and preached peace" (2:17), particularly since we are especially interested in how Jesus and his earliest disciples understood their preaching. It was so central to their work. We have heard that John the Baptist and even Jesus himself preached repentance, and also that the apostles "preached repentance and the forgiveness of sins," but here we have "He came and preached peace." The phrase may not appear frequently in the New Testament, but it gives us a significant insight into how the earliest Christians understood their preaching. It was because they understood that "we have peace with God through our Lord Jesus Christ" (Rom. 5:1) that they preached peace. There was peace with God, and even in the midst of the hostilities of the world they experienced peace with each other. That was the gospel preached by the heavenly host when Christ was born:

"Glory to God in the highest,
and on earth peace among men with whom he is pleased!"
(Luke 2:14)

Even the angels worshiped God by proclaiming peace. They glorified God in the highest by singing peace on earth. The incarnation itself was the preaching of peace. What Paul had preached was nothing new; it was a hymn from eternity. Paul had preached the gospel of peace to the Ephesians, but the ultimate preacher of the gospel of peace is none other than Christ himself. "He came and preached peace" (Eph. 2:17). It was because Christ was a preacher, in fact, the preeminent preacher, that Paul was a preacher. The same was true for all the apostles, and even now it is true of us as Christian preachers.[167] We preach because Christ preached, and it is in our preaching that we serve him.

At the beginning of the third chapter Paul comes back to speaking of his preaching ministry as the revelation of the mystery of God's wisdom:

167. On the significance of this passage for Christian worship, see the comment of Barth, *Ephesians*, 2:311-14.

215

The mystery was made known to me by revelation, as I have written briefly. When you read this you can perceive my insight into the mystery of Christ, which was not made known to the sons of men in other generations as it has now been revealed to his holy apostles and prophets by the Spirit; that is, how the Gentiles are fellow heirs, members of the same body, and partakers of the promise in Christ Jesus through the gospel. (Eph. 3:3-6)

Here the words μυστήριον and ἀποκάλυψις are used together in such a way that they help define one another. A long time before Paul the word μυστήριον had loosed itself from its association with the mystery religions and came to have a more general meaning. Whereas originally it had meant the rites and ceremonies of the mystery religions, it had come to have a more philosophical meaning, that is, the doctrines of a particular school.[168] When Paul uses the word it has none of its pagan meaning. It simply means a truth which was previously unknown but which now has been revealed.[169]

In the New Testament the word μυστήριον is used primarily in the Pauline writings.[170] We find it in Matthew 13:11 and parallels, and then four times in the Revelation of John. The word is also especially characteristic of Ephesians, where it is used six times, three of which are especially informative about what this mystery is supposed to be. In Ephesians 1:9 the mystery which is finally revealed is the secret counsels of God, that is, the mystery of his will. In 3:4 it is ἐν τῷ μυστηρίῳ τοῦ Χριστοῦ — the mystery is Christ. Then further on in 6:19 it is the mystery of the gospel,

---

168. Cf. Brooke Foss Westcott, *Paul's Epistle to the Ephesians* (Grand Rapids: Wm. B. Eerdmans Publishing Co., 1952), p. 182: "Already in Plato . . . the word is used metaphorically, not, that is, of the actual, ceremonial mysteries or mystic implements, but of philosophical doctrines belonging to men of a particular School and expounded with authority by them alone, though the exposition may be subsequently by a hearer to others. Already the idea of secrecy is subordinate to that of special discovery or possession."

169. Cf. Westcott's quotation of Lightfoot: "But when adopted into the Christian vocabulary by St. Paul, the word signifies simply 'a truth which was once hidden, but now is revealed,' 'a truth which without special revelation would have been unknown.' Hence μυστήριον is almost universally found with words denoting revelation or publication." Westcott, *Ephesians*, p. 182.

170. Cf. Günther Bornkamm, "μυστήριον," *Theological Dictionary of the New Testament*, 4:819-24; and Edward Schillebeeckx, *Le Christ, Sacrament de la rencontre de Dieu* (Paris: Éditions du Cerf, 1960).

τὸ μυστήριον τοῦ εὐαγγελίου. Other passages could be mentioned, but these are sufficient to show how the word can be used to speak of the essentials of the Christian faith which have been made known in Christian preaching but were not preached previously.

To understand the preaching of the apostle Paul we must look at what he means when he says that the mystery was made known to him by revelation, ἀποκάλυψις. Unlike the word μυστήριον, it has no particular cultic origins and is a very neutral sort of word in the Greek language that simply means the act of taking away a veil, an unveiling. In the New Testament, however, it becomes a distinct theological term.[171] This revelation of the mystery must first of all refer to the vision he experienced on the Damascus road. In that vision Jesus, the messianic Son of God, veiled in human flesh, was suddenly unveiled so that Paul understood that the Jesus whom he had persecuted was none other than the Christ. That was not the only such revelation Paul had experienced — in II Corinthians he confesses to an abundance of visions and revelations (12:1-7). As had the ancient prophets, Paul too experienced frequent revelations. In fact, these revelations were an important basis of his preaching, as we find in Romans 16:25-27:

> Now to him who is able to strengthen you according to my gospel and the preaching of Jesus Christ, according to the revelation of the mystery which was kept secret for long ages but is now disclosed and through the prophetic writings is made known to all nations, according to the command of the eternal God, to bring about the obedience of faith — to the only wise God be glory for evermore through Jesus Christ! Amen.

Paul never suggested that he therefore had an access to truth which the other apostles, who had merely known Christ in person, did not have. If anything his revelations were only a substitute for their personal knowledge and experience. Yet one notices in this passage from Romans how these phrases are in apposition, "according to my gospel and the preaching of Jesus Christ, according to the revelation of the mystery which was kept secret for long ages but is now disclosed." Paul's preaching of the gospel and the preaching of the gospel of Jesus Christ as it was taking place all over the Church were the same thing as the revelation of the mystery. As Paul understood it, his preaching

---

171. George Hendry, "Revelation," in *Theological Word Book of the Bible*, ed. A. Richardson (New York: Macmillan Company, 1951), pp. 195-200; and Westcott, *Ephesians*, pp. 178ff. See as well A. Oepke, "ἀποκαλύπτω," *Theological Dictionary of the New Testament*, 3:580-91.

of the gospel is the revelation of the mystery. This revelation was the all-engrossing experience of the early Church. It was at the center of the worship experience of the first Christians. The mystery of our redemption in Christ was revealed in the preaching of the Church. What else could one do but worship when in the preaching of the Church one was confronted with the revelation of the mysteries of God.

Paul makes this clear in Ephesians 3, where we find an important statement of how Paul understood his preaching:

> Of this gospel I was made a minister according to the gift of God's grace which was given me by the working of his power. To me, though I am the very least of all the saints, this grace was given, to preach to the Gentiles the unsearchable riches of Christ, and to make all men see what is the plan of the mystery hidden for ages in God who created all things; that through the church the manifold wisdom of God might now be made known to the principalities and powers in the heavenly places. (Eph. 3:7-10)

That Paul understood himself as a minister of the gospel has had a prolonged effect on English-speaking Protestantism. We commonly speak of those who have been ordained to preach the gospel as ministers of the Word. Only recently has the unfortunate corruption of this tradition appeared in the phrase "the professional ministry," or even worse, as we have often seen it on church signboards:

First Presbyterian Church
Ministers: All the members of the Church
Pastor: Rev. John Smith, M.Div.

What a flagrant abuse of the biblical vocabulary! Notice how this text reads, "I was made a minister according to the gift of God's grace." Again Paul makes it quite clear that the exercising of the ministry of the gospel is only possible by a special empowering, a special "gift of God's grace." This empowering is, of course, the work of the Holy Spirit. It is for this reason that we ordain ministers with prayer and the laying on of hands. Ordination recognizes that preaching is a gift of God's grace. As we have pointed out elsewhere, the New Testament offers a strong sense that preachers have been sent to perform this ministry.[172] Being divinely sent, they are divinely empowered as well.

---

172. On Paul's ministry as a service of worship, cf. Peterson, *Engaging with God*, pp. 179-88.

Paul himself, when the exalted Christ was revealed to him on the Damascus road, fell down in worship. Here is the very essence of worship — to be confronted with the mystery of God's glory and to fall down before him in awe. Someone has referred to this as the "oh wow!" experience. Although this not a particularly elegant expression, it does get the point across. Worship is the experience of being so overwhelmed by God's glory that we fall down on our faces and, like Isaiah, confess, " 'Woe is me! For I am lost' " (Isa. 6:5). And ever after when Paul perceived the mystery he could do nothing less than bow in prayer:

> For this reason I bow my knees before the Father, from whom every family in heaven and on earth is named, that according to the riches of his glory he may grant you to be strengthened with might through his Spirit in the inner man, and that Christ may dwell in your hearts through faith; that you, being rooted and grounded in love, may have power to comprehend with all the saints what is the breadth and length and height and depth, and to know the love of Christ which surpasses knowledge, that you may be filled with all the fulness of God. (Eph. 3:14-19)

On the Damascus road the revelation of the mystery brought him to fall down in prayer — a prayer of confession and repentance. Now the revelation of the mystery brings him to prayer again, but this time to prayers of intercession, the intercessions which naturally follow the preaching of the gospel. These intercessions are essential to the service of worship.

One could make the point that the first three chapters of Ephesians follow the order of the early Christian service of worship. Ephesians begins with hymns of praise, with invocations and prayers of adoration, continues with the proclamation of the gospel and the revelation of the mystery of our salvation, moves on to prayers of intercession, and concludes with that admirable doxology:

> Now to him who by the power at work within us is able to do far more abundantly than all that we ask or think, to him be glory in the church and in Christ Jesus to all generations, for ever and ever. Amen. (Eph. 3:20-21)

When Paul speaks of the ministry of the Word in the Epistle to the Ephesians he speaks of it in terms of its cosmic dimension, its place in the eternal purposes of God. Preaching is the revelation of the mystery of our redemption. When this mystery is revealed, then God is worshiped. The reason is simple. The mystery is the Wisdom of God, the Logos, the eternal Word of God. The divine nature by its very nature is glorious. It is by its own glory that it is glorified. This is all part of the inner communication of the persons of the Trinity. The Son by his very nature glorifies the Father. It is in light of this that we would define worship as the work of the Holy Spirit in the body of Christ to the glory of the Father.

V. The Ministry of the Word as the Teaching of Wisdom in the Epistle of James

The Epistle of James has often been a problem to commentators. Luther's difficulties with the epistle are well known, while Calvin's sympathy for it, on the other hand, is usually ignored. We hear nothing of it until almost the end of the second century; little attention was given to it during the patristic age, and not much more during the Middle Ages.[173] There were few commentaries on James until the Christian humanists and their students began to give it the attention it deserves. Erasmus and Vatable commented on it before Calvin. The seventeenth century produced a number of notable studies of James, the most important of which being that of the English Puritan Thomas Manton, but by the beginning of the twentieth century its popularity had again waned. The idea that the work might actually come from James, the brother of Jesus, seemed too clearly legendary to be taken seriously by the biblical criticism of a generation or two ago. Gradually, however, more recent scholarship is beginning to suspect that its peculiarities are indeed evidence of its high antiquity. It may very well come from James, the brother of Jesus, who presided over the church of Jerusalem in its earliest days.[174]

---

173. Augustine was an exception. His commentary on James has been lost, which is only one more piece of evidence for the general lack of interest in the work. For an evaluation of the patristic and medieval commentaries on James, see James H. Ropes, *A Critical and Exegetical Commentary on the Epistle of James,* International Critical Commentary (Edinburgh: T. & T. Clark, 1911), pp. 110-13.

174. Several of the most recent commentators come to similar conclusions, e.g., James Adamson, *The Epistle of James,* The New International Commentary on the New Testament (Grand Rapids: Wm. B. Eerdmans Publishing Co., 1974), p. 21. On the other hand, Martin Dibelius, one of the pioneers of form criticism, is convinced that James is the work of an unknown Christian teacher of the second if not the third generation. *Der Brief des Jakobus,* originally 1921, enlarged and reedited by Heinrich Greeven, Meyers Kritisch-exegetischer Kommentar über das neue Testament (Göttingen: Vandenhoeck & Ruprecht, 1964), pp. 23-35.

Commentators have often noticed the similarity of the "Epistle" of James to the Sermon on the Mount.[175] Quite possibly James is, like the Sermon on the Mount, an epitome of many sermons. In the same way the Sermon on the Mount represents the attempt of the primitive Church to condense the preaching of Jesus into a capsulized form that could easily be memorized, we suggest that the book of James is a condensed form of the preaching of James in the Jerusalem church.

One sometimes notices a strong relationship between James and the Wisdom tradition of Israel.[176] This is not exactly a new insight — Calvin called attention to it back in the sixteenth century. One can also speak of the Gospel of John being strongly influenced by the Wisdom tradition, although the influence showed up in a different way. In fact, this Wisdom tradition has shown up in a still different way in the epistles of Paul. What we find in James is an emphasis on Wisdom as it is found in Christian character and behavior. One could sum it up with the text found in the third chapter:

> Who is wise and understanding among you? By his good life let him show his works in the meekness of wisdom. But if you have bitter jealousy and selfish ambition in your hearts, do not boast and be false to the truth. This wisdom is not such as comes down from above, but is earthly, unspiritual, devilish. For where jealousy and selfish ambition exist, there will be disorder and every vile practice. But the wisdom from above is first pure, then peaceable, gentle, open to reason, full of mercy and good fruits, without uncertainty or insincerity. And the harvest of righteousness is sown in peace by those who make peace. (James 3:13-18)

The Wisdom that is from above is pure, peaceable, gentle, open to reason, full of mercy and good fruits. That seems to be the major concern of James. No doubt it was the major concern of his preaching as well. James was not ministering to the newly converted but to those who had been Christians for some time. Many of his congregation would have living memory of Jesus. They had responded positively to his preaching and may have been amazed at his works. Most of them would have been brought up in the best traditions of Jewish devotion. What they wanted was not introductory instruction but guidance for the deepening of the spiritual life. They had seen in Jesus the fulfillment of the piety of the Law and the prophets. In Jesus they had caught

175. Adamson, *The Epistle of James,* pp. 21ff.
176. Ropes, *Epistle of James,* pp. 18-19.

sight of true holiness, and they wanted to follow in the direction in which he had led. They wanted to mature in the Christian life.

As we have shown elsewhere, the Wisdom school produced in Judaism a distinct approach not only to theology but to worship as well. The doxology of the Wisdom school gives to teaching and to learning a major place in worship. Moral instruction, particularly the sort which leads to holiness, plays a major role in worship. Christians wanted to mature in the Christian life so that their worship would be "in spirit and truth," as we find it in the Gospel of John (John 4:24). Christians influenced by the Wisdom school understood the living of a holy life as essential to the "spiritual sacrifices" of Christian worship. We will find this subject treated more fully in the following pages on the First Epistle of Peter.

Much Christian preaching down through the centuries has been devoted to this same end. A phrase sometimes used to designate this type of preaching is "spiritual catechism." Frequently we find this kind of preaching in monastic communities. Gregory the Great's series of sermons, *Morals on Job,* and the *Spiritual Catechisms* of Symeon the New Theologian would be examples of this. The Puritans gave abundant attention to spiritual catechism, although it was often cast in the form of expository preaching. One thinks here of the sermons of Richard Sibbes or John Preston, and the long series of expository sermons preached at Stokes-Newington on the Epistle of James by Thomas Manton. In the first generation of American preachers spiritual catechism was offered by Thomas Shepard in his sermons on the wise and foolish virgins.

A thoughtful reading through of the Epistle of James, if our hypothesis is correct, should give us a good idea of what sort of things James preached. He must have delivered sermons on faith and steadfastness (James 1:3), on asking God for spiritual gifts such as wisdom and understanding, and on how to achieve faith that was beyond doubting (1:5-8). Surely he preached on the spiritual gift of humility (1:9-11); humility seems to be a favorite theme of James. He warned his congregation against the dangers and temptations of wealth and consoled those who had to endure poverty (1:10-11; 2:1-7). How the Christian is to meet trials and temptations is a theme to which our preacher often returned (1:2, 12-15). The importance of good works is another theme which must have frequently appeared in the teaching and preaching of our Lord's brother. "Be doers of the word, and not hearers only" (1:22) is one of the texts most frequently quoted from this epistle. The relation of faith and works is taken up again in the middle of the second chapter where we find the famous dictum, "Faith apart from works is dead" (2:26). Those of us who have taken the time to preach through James have discovered that it is filled with great texts for preaching, and no doubt the reason for this is that the whole book is a compendium of the preaching ministry of a man who understood profoundly what Jesus had to say.

One is tempted to speculate on just how James might have exercised the ministry of the Word in the church of Jerusalem in that first generation after Pentecost. Luke tells us in Acts that the disciples continued in the teaching and fellowship of the apostles. Presumably James was one of those apostles whose teaching brought together the earliest disciples. Another general impressions we gather from Luke is that there were several homes in Jerusalem in which the Christians met for prayers, for teaching, and for the sharing of the Lord's Supper. James does not tell us much about the worship services of the church of Jerusalem, yet he makes a few remarks which probably shed some light on how the ministry of the Word was carried out in those days.

The first remark which gives us a clue about early Christian worship is found at the beginning of chapter 2. There we hear of two men, one richly dressed and the other poorly dressed, coming "into your assembly," as the RSV has it.[177] The Greek reads εἰς συναγωγὴν ὑμῶν. Translating literally, we might read "into your synagogue." A good number of scholars find in this the suggestion that in Jerusalem during the thirty or forty years between Pentecost and their expulsion from the city the Christians had their own synagogues and maintained the synagogue liturgy much as other synagogues in the city.[178]

If that is indeed the case, then the earliest Christian services of worship might have gone something like this: On the Lord's Day morning there would be the reading of the Law and the prophets.[179] At least one

---

177. See Adamson, *The Epistle of James,* pp. 105ff.

178. Luke tells us that at first the disciples of Jesus continued to attend worship in both the Temple and the synagogue (Acts 3:1; 6:9; 17:2). How it was that they developed their own synagogues we do not know. The meetings in the Upper Room with their observance of the Supper must have continued. They probably gathered for morning prayer and study sessions afterward. We find evidence of this in Acts 4:32 and Acts 12:12. When they were expelled from the synagogues these meetings became their Christian synagogues.

179. Just when the Church began to hold its principal service on the Lord's Day morning is not clear. The meeting in the Upper Room on the evening of the first Easter Sunday may have included the sharing of the Supper. One might regard that meeting as the first Lord's Day service. More than likely the first Lord's Day morning services would not have been held until after the Christians had been expelled from the synagogue.

sermon would be preached on these readings, but there might be more. Psalms would be sung, the Shema would be recited, and prayers would be spoken, especially the *Amidah,* the long prayer of petition and intercession with its eighteen benedictions. It would have been in addition to these regular Lord's Day morning services that the Supper would have been observed. The Supper, which in those days was apparently held on the evening of the first day of the week, began with the singing of psalms and prayer, followed by devout discussion at the table. This had been the custom at the Jewish *chabburah,* the fellowship meals of Jewish sacred brotherhoods. Again psalms would be sung and there would be prayers of thanksgiving over the food. After the meal the discussion would continue, often going far into the night. The discussion would have been like the Upper Room Discourse we find in the Gospel of John. Practically speaking, these discussions would have been sermons, although perhaps in dialogue form or allowing for several speakers. Such services apparently became increasingly characteristic of the Christian community. Then, in the same way as in the synagogue, there would be the day-to-day study sessions held in most synagogues after morning prayers. The daily prayer services would have been an important part of the worship of the early Church just as they had been a major feature of the synagogue. As best we can reconstruct it, there must have been much preaching and teaching in the church of Jerusalem in the middle of the first Christian century, just as there was in the Jewish synagogues of the same period.[180]

James's little remark about Christian synagogues suggests that the Christians of Jerusalem started out by following the worship patterns of the Jewish synagogue, with its strong emphasis on preaching and teaching. Furthermore, we imagine that the didactic aspects and the doxological aspects of worship would have been tightly woven together.

Something else gives us a hint about the ministry of the Word in those days — and again, it is only a hint. Twice James uses the phrase "the law of liberty," ὁ νόμος τῆς ἐλευθερίας (James 1:25; 2:12). Once he uses the phrase "the royal law," ὁ νόμος βασιλικός (2:8), and another time "the perfect law," ὁ νόμος τέλειος. These phrases seem to refer to the Christian gospel and, in context, to the Word one hears in the worship

---

180. From Acts 6:1-7 we get the impression that the ministry of preaching and teaching took the full time of a number of men in the Jerusalem church. This would suggest that there was daily teaching and perhaps preaching at a number of different locations in the city. We get the same impression from James 3:1.

of the Church (1:22-25). Could this imply that already a primitive form of the Gospels was read in worship as a complement to the reading of the Law? One often speaks of the sources of the Gospels, collections of sayings or stories either oral or written which the writers of our four Gospels used. Could these sources have been read as the law of Christ which complemented and fulfilled the Law of Moses? Perhaps James means nothing more by the law of liberty, the royal law, or the perfect law than the recounting of stories of Jesus which some who were present were able to remember. Perhaps he has in mind the reciting and expounding of the teachings of Jesus by the apostles, who had heard Jesus so often. But one wonders. How long after Pentecost would it have been before the Church had a collection of the sayings of Jesus? Whenever this step was made, this reasoning must have been behind it; namely, that the words and works of Jesus were the Christian law, the perfect law, the law of liberty, the royal law.

We can only guess how these synagogue services became church services. At a very early date the disciples would probably have remembered to recite the words of Jesus at the Supper. (The sharing of the Supper must have been the earliest specifically Christian service of worship.) Likewise it was probably very early that the disciples recited, during their prayers, the prayer Jesus had taught them. Reciting the Shema must have come about in the same way. Jesus had taught about the summary of the Law. He, too, was convinced that Deuteronomy 6:5, " 'You shall love the LORD your God with all your heart . . . ,' " was the essence of the Law, but he wanted it clear that there was a second commandment like it. One can well imagine that the Christian synagogues of Jerusalem had a version of the Shema which reflected the teaching of Jesus. Something similar must have happened with the reading and preaching of Scripture. One can well imagine that when the Law and the prophets were read some in attendance remembered how Jesus interpreted those passages. When such people shared this with the congregation it was Christian preaching. This was the case whether it was done in synagogues hostile to the disciples of Jesus or those friendly.

If in James's time there was as yet no reading of the Christian Scriptures in the Christian synagogues, the first steps toward it had already been made. The words of Jesus which the disciples of Jerusalem remembered and recounted, the stories of God's mighty acts of redemption when Jesus fulfilled the Passover and passed from this world to the Father, were already thought of as the revelation of God's Word, just as the stories of Exodus were. The recounting of the teaching and the saving works of Jesus were already thought

225

of as the perfect law, the law of Christ which fulfilled the Law of Moses. That the gospel of Christ is the fulfillment of the Law of Moses implied that it was appropriate to recount the gospel in worship. To read the record of the words and works of Jesus as the "royal law" was the obvious next step.

At the least one can say that these phrases indicate this step had quite possibly already been made. In any event, the recounting of the words and works of Jesus must have had a place in the earliest Christian worship services. James already has in mind that the words and works of Jesus are the fulfilled law, the law of liberty, the royal law. Perhaps for James this law was already Christian Scripture. The gospel of Christ had its place in worship just as the Law of Moses did.

VI. The Service of the Word in I Peter

Although very short, the First Epistle of Peter represents a distinct tradition in the literature of the New Testament. We should probably understand the salutation at the beginning of the letter quite straightforwardly, "Peter, an apostle of Jesus Christ, To the exiles of the Dispersion in Pontus, Galatia, Cappadocia, Asia, and Bithynia . . ." (I Pet. 1:1). The epistle represents the teaching of the apostle Peter. It was written toward the end of the apostle's ministry while he was in Rome, the spiritual Babylon, and is addressed to Christians, probably those of Jewish origin, in Asia Minor. Even after a number of attempts to show that the epistle is pseudepigraphic, the Petrine authorship seems to be fairly generally accepted. Increasingly recent scholarship affirms that the work is in fact what it claims to be. The least one can say is that there is no compelling reason not to take the epistle at face value.[181]

---

181. The valediction of the epistle suggests that Sylvanus served as Peter's secretary. The excellent style of the work is no doubt due to him, but basic insights of the apostle show through very clearly. Among the more recent commentaries, see Peter H. Davids's very plausible hypothesis. Peter H. Davids, *The First Epistle of Peter*, The New International Commentary on the New Testament (Grand Rapids: Wm. B. Eerdmans Publishing Co., 1990), pp. 3-8. On the other hand, see Leonhard Goppelt, *Der erste Petrusbrief*, Meyers Kritisch-exegetischer Kommentar über das neue Testament (Göttingen: Vandenhoeck & Ruprecht, 1978); Eng. trans., *A Commentary on I Peter*, ed. Ferdinand Hahn, trans. John E. Alsup (Grand Rapids: Wm. B. Eerdmans Publishing Co., 1993). The commentaries of Edward Gordon Selwyn, *The First Epistle of St. Peter*, 2nd ed. (London: Macmillan & Co., 1955), and J. N. D. Kelly, *A Commentary on the Epistles of Peter and Jude* (London: Adam and Charles Black, 1969), both basically accept Petrine authorship.

First Peter witnesses to the way the earliest Christians understood the ministry of the Word. The Synoptic Gospels, the Gospel of John, Luke's report of the preaching of the apostles, the epistles of Paul, and James have all given us distinct soundings into the depths of New Testament Christianity, and now in I Peter we have still another.[182] Much of what we find in I Peter is the same, which gives resonance to what has already been said, but two insights call for special attention. To begin with, we find in I Peter 1:23-25 the development of a theme which might be called the vitality of the Word. This is an important theme, and we will find it appearing and reappearing in the history of preaching. Then we find in I Peter 2:4-8 an important statement on the reading and preaching of the Word as the spiritual sacrifice of the royal priesthood.

Let us look at this first passage, which speaks so poetically of the vitality of the Word:

> You have been born anew, not of perishable seed but of imperishable, through the living and abiding word of God; for
>
> > "All flesh is like grass
> > and all its glory like the flower of grass.
> > The grass withers, and the flower falls,
> > but the word of the Lord abides for ever."
>
> That word is the good news which was preached to you. (I Pet. 1:23-25)

The Word has a vivifying power all its own, quite apart from who preaches it. It has this power from the fact that it is God's Word. It is God's Word about God's saving works, and therefore it is a saving Word. What is said here about our being born anew on account of the preaching of the Word is said a few verses earlier about the resurrection of Christ: "By his great mercy we have been born anew to a living hope through the resurrection of Jesus Christ from the dead" (I Pet. 1:3). Ultimately the cause of our salvation is the love of God, or, as Peter puts it, God's "great mercy." It is the love of the Father which sent the Son to redeem us from the power of sin through his atoning death and life-giving resurrection. Through the preaching of his saving works we

182. See the introductory studies in the commentary of J. Ramsey Michaels, *1 Peter*, Word Biblical Commentary (Waco, Tex.: Word Books, 1988), where this point is made with particular clarity.

have come to believe in Christ. We have believed this Word because this Word, being God's Word, has the power of God's Spirit within it. Because God's Word is inspired, it has the power to inspire. God's Word inspires life. Nothing demonstrates the inspiration of Scripture more than its ability to bring the Church to life. Nothing demonstrates the truth of Scripture more than its ability to reform a ruined human life. Because it is God's Word it is a Word of truth. As we have seen elsewhere, it is a self-authenticating Word. Because it is truth it shows us the truth. As the psalmist puts it, "In thy light do we see light" (Ps. 36:9).

The Word of truth is also a Word of life. When Peter understands that the preaching of the gospel has the power to give us new and eternal life, he is only drawing on a fundamental biblical insight. In the beginning God created everything out of nothing by the Word of his power. "God said 'let there be light,' and there was light." The Word has the power within itself to bring about what it says. As we find it in Isaiah:

> "For as the rain and the snow come down from heaven,
>   and return not thither but water the earth,
> making it bring forth and sprout,
>   giving seed to the sower and bread to the eater,
> so shall my word be that goes forth from my mouth;
>   it shall not return to me empty,
> but it shall accomplish that which I purpose,
>   and prosper in the thing for which I sent it."
>
> (Isa. 55:10-11)

The Word that is creative is also redemptive. You were born anew, ἀναγεγεννημένοι, Peter tells us. Quite literally this means you have been begotten again. The kingdom of God is a new creation, and the new creation, as the old creation, has its beginning in the Word of God.[183]

If the teaching in I Peter about the vivifying power of the Word comes quite naturally from the oldest biblical traditions, it also comes quite clearly from the teaching of Jesus. These words remind us of several

---

183. Davids comments, "In the beginning God generated life through his word, a theme repeatedly seen in Gen. 1 (cf. Ps. 33:6, 9; Rom. 4:17) and in John 1:3, but also significantly found in Isa. 40 (especially v. 26, although the whole chapter speaks of the creative and re-creative power of God). Now he regenerates through his word (as in Jas. 1:18), which is here described as 'living,' that is, 'life-giving,' 'creative,' or 'effective.'" *The First Epistle of Peter,* p. 78.

parables of Jesus: the parable of the sower, the parable of the seed growing secretly, and the parable of the wheat and the tares.[184] In all three the preaching of the Word is compared to the sowing of seed.[185] The parable of the mustard seed makes the same point. The mustard seed is the smallest of seeds and yet it produces the greatest of trees. Even more obviously the parable of the leaven in the lump of dough makes the point that it is the hidden, secret power of God which gives growth to the kingdom of God.

This passage tells us that the Word which has been preached to us is "the living and abiding Word of God."[186] The Greek could be translated "the Word of the living and eternal God," as we find it in the Jerusalem Bible, which, not surprisingly, follows the tradition of the Vulgate.[187] The chances are that Jerome just did not catch the depth of thought in the original text. Jerome, brilliant as his translation was, sometimes missed obscure facets of the Hebrew rhetoric. Peter, on the other hand, is much closer to the biblical worldview. Again it is the Wisdom theology which is at play here. The wisdom of God has its own power. In fact, that is one of the remarkable things about it — it is a powerful wisdom. It is not that wisdom needs to be supported by power; it is power. As we find it in the Epistle to the Hebrews, "For the word of God is living and active, sharper than any two-edged sword" (Heb. 4:12). Peter, as the primitive Church generally, did understand the preached Word to have a vitality which the merely human word, in and of itself, does not have. The preaching of the gospel is the Word of life.

The second passage of which we must take special note follows close on the heels of the first. It tells of the spiritual worship of the royal priesthood (I Pet. 2:4-10),[188] and is of the greatest possible importance for the understanding of Christian worship:

---

184. Michaels, *1 Peter*, p. 76. On the interpretation of the different parables about seeds, see most recently Guelich, *Mark*, 1:186-253.

185. Jeremias, *The Parables of Jesus*, pp. 89-92, presents a somewhat different approach.

186. Goppelt comments, "Das Wort Gottes ist 'unvergänglicher Same'; den es ist 'lebendig' . . . d. h. schöpferisch wirksam, und 'bleibend'. . . ." *Der erste Petrusbrief,* p. 132.

187. Most of the commentators assure us that the Vulgate translation is possible, but that the meaning probably is that it is the word which is living and abiding. Cf. Selwyn, *First Epistle of St. Peter*, p. 151. See also E. A. la Verdière, "A Grammatical Ambiguity in I Peter 1:23," *Catholic Biblical Quarterly* 36 (1974): 89-94.

188. See the essay of Dean Selwyn, "The 'Spiritual House,' Its Priesthood and Sacrifices in ii.4, 5," in the appendix of *First Epistle of St. Peter,* pp. 285-97.

Come to him, to that living stone, rejected by men but in God's sight chosen and precious; and like living stones be yourselves built into a spiritual house, to be a holy priesthood, to offer spiritual sacrifices acceptable to God through Jesus Christ. For it stands in scripture:

"Behold, I am laying in Zion a stone,
   a cornerstone chosen and precious,
and he who believes in him will not
   be put to shame."

To you therefore who believe, he is precious, but for those who do not believe,

"The very stone which the builders rejected
has become the head of the corner,"

and

"A stone that will make men stumble,
a rock that will make them fall";

for they will stumble because they disobey the word, as they were destined to do.

But you are a chosen race, a royal priesthood, a holy nation, God's own people, that you may declare the wonderful deeds of him who called you out of darkness into his marvelous light. Once you were no people but now you are God's people; once you had not received mercy but now you have received mercy. (I Pet. 2:4-10)

In all probability these ideas about the "spiritual" nature of Christian worship go back to Jesus himself, who must have done a considerable amount of preaching on the worship of the temple not built with human hands.[189] The discourse with the woman of Samaria where Jesus exclaimed that the true worshiper must worship God in spirit and in truth was a development of the same theme. These ideas seem to have come from his interpretation of the Passover Psalm, Psalm 118, which spoke of the stone which was rejected by men but chosen and precious in God's sight. Psalm 118 was always sung at Passover, and the Gospels tell us it was sung by the children as Jesus rode into Jerusalem; it is the same psalm which acclaims the coming Messiah with the festal shout, "Hosanna." Jesus also preached on this psalm in the courts of

---

189. Cf. Yves Congar, *Le mystère du Temple,* 2nd ed. (Paris: Éditions du Cerf, 1963), pp. 140-47. On the other hand, see Goppelt, *Der erste Petrusbrief,* pp. 145ff.

the Temple at his last Passover in which he warned the Jews that if they destroyed the temple of his body, in three days it would be raised up. Psalm 118 had a rich meaning for the primitive Church.

Jesus was not the only one who pressed for "spiritual worship."[190] We find the idea beginning to appear in the Old Testament.[191] Psalm 50 shows us that faithful Jews even before New Testament times were beginning to raise questions about the value of the sacrifices of the Temple:

> "If I were hungry, I would not tell you;
>   for the world and all that is in it is mine.
> Do I eat the flesh of bulls,
>   or drink the blood of goats?
> Offer to God a sacrifice of thanksgiving,
>   and pay your vows to the Most High;
> and call upon me in the day of trouble;
>   I will deliver you, and you shall glorify me."
>
> (Ps. 50:12-15)

Devout Jews had begun to think that the real sacrifice is maintaining the disciplines of prayer and observing the statutes and ordinances of the covenant. It is love for God and the neighbor as stipulated in the Law that God will have as true worship. From Psalm 50 we learn first that "spiritual worship" is prayer. The prayers of lamentation and supplication, of thanksgiving and praise, are the true worship of the heart. The true worshiper comes to God in prayer when in need. It is to the one true God that we turn when the frailties of life threaten us. That in itself is a confession of faith in God's rich sufficiency. It is not that God needs our gifts, but rather that we need his bounty. From this psalm we also learn that the true worshiper "orders his way aright," and praises God for the constant supply of blessings which he pours out upon his own:

> "He who brings thanksgiving as his sacrifice honors me;
>   to him who orders his way aright
>   I will show the salvation of God!"
>
> (Ps. 50:23)

190. On Jesus' criticism of the temple cult and his advocacy of a spiritual worship, see Lohmeyer, *Lord of the Temple*, pp. 92-116.

191. André Feuillet, "Les 'sacrifices spirituelles' du sacerdoce royal des baptises (I Pierre 2:5) et leur préparation dans l'Ancient Testament," *Nouvelle Revue Theologique* 96 (1974): 704-28; Michel, *Der Brief an die Römer*, p. 364 n. 6; and Michaels, *1 Peter*, p. 101.

"Spiritual worship" is not just a matter of following the prescribed forms with sincerity, of practicing what one preaches or living what one prays. "Spiritual worship" implies a worship where the emphasis is on the ministry of prayer. One prayed to God in time of need. One recounted how God had heard the prayer of his people. One gave thanks to God by ordering one's way aright. Psalm 50 assumes a covenantal understanding of prayer. We call on God in our need, and God hears our prayer. Then in return we witness to God's mercy and recount his saving acts. This glorifies God, but even more we offer to God our thanksgiving by ordering our lives aright. By living a godly life our worship is perfected.

We find the same thing in the prophet Malachi, at least we do if we understand it as the earliest Christians did.[192] They understood Malachi to envision a day when Jews and Gentiles over the whole world would unite in the offering of spiritual sacrifices:

> "For from the rising of the sun to its setting my name is great among the nations, and in every place incense is offered to my name, and a pure offering; for my name is great among the nations, says the LORD of hosts." (Mal. 1:11)

Malachi goes on to lament the increasing inability of the priesthood to offer pure instruction in the Law. Malachi would call the priesthood back to a more vigorous and sincere ministry of the Word, " 'For the lips of a priest should guard knowledge, and men should seek instruction from his mouth, for he is the messenger of the LORD of hosts' " (2:7).[193] As the earliest Christians understood it, this more conscientious attention to the teaching ministry was of the essence of the "spiritual worship" of the royal priesthood.

It was common practice for many Jews to emphasize the "spiritual worship" of the synagogue with its psalms, its prayers, its reading of the Law and the prophets, and its sermons rather than the worship of the Temple with its animal sacrifices, its offerings of incense, its festal processions up to the altar, and its elaborate musical settings. At its best the

192. On the Christian understanding of Malachi, cf. Luke 13:29; John 4:21ff.; II Thessalonians 1:12; and Acts 15:4. See as well J. Behm, "θύω," *Theological Dictionary of the New Testament*, 3:180-90.

193. Cf. Robert C. Dentan, "The Book of Malachi: Introduction and Exegesis," *Interpreter's Bible*, 6:1132ff.

worship of the Temple had a vital ministry of the Word, but at other times, times when the spiritual intensity of the people ebbed, the ministry of the Word degenerated and became perfunctory. At such times the worship of the Temple became formalized and ceremonial. It was against this that one emphasized a spiritual worship,[194] and it was with those who emphasized this spiritual worship that Jesus and his disciples made common cause.[195] The early Christians did not mean by "spiritual worship" some sort of idealized philosophical worship which had no physical expressions or traditional order. That would have been "spiritualist worship." Very specifically they meant the sort of worship, maintained in the synagogue, that put the emphasis on prayer, the study of the Scriptures, and the service of praise.

One more thought: This passage from I Peter is the one to which appeal is always made when speaking of the priesthood of all believers. What we should particularly notice here is that this passage sees the ministry of the Word as being performed by the whole congregation. It is clear from the text that the whole congregation is the royal priesthood. "But you are . . . a royal priesthood . . . that you may declare the wonderful deeds of him who called you out of darkness into his marvelous light" (I Pet. 2:9). The public reading and preaching of the *Magnalia Dei*, the mighty acts of God, is a witness the Church as a whole lays before the world. The recounting of the mighty acts of God has always been a prominent feature of biblical worship, whether in the Old Testament or the New Testament. This is at the heart of the remembrance to be observed either on the Sabbath or on the Lord's Day. This is what is remembered on the Sabbath day to keep it holy (Exod. 20:8), and what we do on the Lord's Day in remembrance of him (I Cor. 11:25). It may be the preacher who gives voice to this recounting of God's saving acts in Christ, but it is the witness of the whole congregation nevertheless. When the preacher preaches, surrounded by the elders in the midst of the congregation, then the sacred memorial has been performed.

Alas! This seems to have been forgotten. It is not surprising that, because of the influence of "modern culture," the last few generations have

---

194. Bertil Gärtner, *The Temple and the Community in Qumran and the New Testament* (Cambridge: University Press, 1965).

195. Cf. Behm's study of the concept of spiritual sacrifices in both Hellenistic Judaism and early Christianity, "θύω," *Theological Dictionary of the New Testament*, 3:180-90. See as well the commentary of Michaels, *1 Peter*, pp. 101ff.

had an individualistic approach to preaching, to the neglect of the corporate nature of preaching. That has been the tendency of the Enlightenment; an individualistic understanding of the ministry of the Word seemed obvious. Did not the preacher get up there all alone and preach? How often have we heard this jibe? Actually that is not the way Christians had up until very recently understood it. What we should notice is that the earliest Christians had a much more corporate understanding of the ministry of the Word. The Reformers, as we shall see, understood this very well. Both preaching and listening to a true sermon is a liturgical act of the whole people of God.

Fundamental to this corporate approach to preaching is the conviction of the earliest Christians that the Church is a spiritual temple, the transcendent reality of which the Jerusalem Temple was but the type. The earliest Christians firmly believed the Church to be this spiritual temple built on Jesus Christ, the Rock of our Salvation. This is the temple not built with human hands; it is ἀχειροποίητος, to use that famous term. It is the temple to which we are to come that we might be built into it as living stones. It is through the prayer and praise, the reading and preaching of Scripture, and, to be sure, the living of the Word that is preached that we are built into this spiritual temple. It is through the spiritual service of this spiritual temple that the presence of God in this world is made known. When this is done God is worshiped.

VII. The Ministry of the Word as *Didache* in the New Testament: The Beginnings of Catechetical Preaching

We must now take a closer look at that genre of Christian preaching which is primarily concerned with teaching the Christian way of life. It has often been observed that many of the New Testament epistles are divided into two parts, the first containing the kerygma, that is, the proclamation of the Christian gospel, and the second containing the *didache,* the teaching of the Christian way of life. Most prominently one finds this in Romans, Ephesians, and I Peter. What seems to be behind this is that at times the earliest Christian Church saw its ministry of the Word in two distinctly different ways: as the preaching of the gospel and as the teaching of the Christian way of life. Sometimes the two are very closely related, but at other times they are quite distinct. As we continue through the whole history of preaching we will notice that sometimes the proclamation of the gospel is given preeminence and sometimes preaching seems to be completely preoccupied with moral instruction and admonitions to righteousness. For many of us Sunday worship has always been divided into Sunday school with its emphasis on teaching, and church with its preaching. The configuration of the problem was rather different in the first Christian century, but there are obvious similarities.

In all honesty one has to make clear that this distinction between preaching the gospel and teaching the Christian way of life is far from absolute in the New Testament. Sometimes the terms "kerygma" (κήρυγμα) and "didache" (διδαχή) seem to be used interchangeably, most notably in that prominent formulation of the Great Commission found at the end of the Gospel of Matthew: "Make disciples of all nations, . . . teaching them to observe all that I have commanded you." Obviously the teaching of the Christian way of life is intended in the Great Commission just as much as the preaching of the gospel. In fact, throughout the Gospel of Matthew preaching and teaching are held closely together. The Sermon on the Mount proclaims the gospel by showing Jesus as the divinely appointed interpreter of the Law. For the Gospel of Matthew the teaching of Jesus on the nature of the Christian life is gospel. We find the same thing in the Epistle of James. There the moral teaching offered is regarded as the law of liberty. To teach Christian morality is part of proclaiming the gospel.

There have always been those who have tried to put law and gospel in some kind of dialectic and have imagined that law only has significance as preparation for the gospel. There is a certain point to this, to be sure. One often thinks of Luther this way, but then we must not forget that Luther was a great catechist! In recent years antinomianism has led some to hold that too much attention to the disciplines of the Christian life is to defeat the Christian life. Yet it is clear that as the Gospel of Matthew presents it, Jesus taught a fulfilled law. The Pauline Epistles typically begin with the proclamation of the gospel and then teach the Christian way of life. That is, first the gospel is presented showing that there is deliverance from a sinful life in the atoning sacrifice of Christ, and then there is the beginning of a new life of righteousness in Christ. The preaching of the New Testament Church, just as the preaching of the Church ever since, always gave considerable attention to instruction in the Christian way of life. That teaching is an essential component of the ministry of the Word.

It was only natural that the Church should give generous attention

235

to the teaching of the Christian way of life, for the rabbis had taught daily in the courts of the Temple, and the larger synagogues both in Palestine and in the Diaspora gave time each day to the systematic teaching of the Law. It was a daily practice to go over the interpretation of the Law subject by subject, discussing the interpretations of the rabbis of the past. All this teaching has been collected for us, first in the Mishnah and then later in the Talmud. It is the same sort of thing we find in Ephesians 4:1–6:20, I Peter 2:11–5:11, I Timothy, and, outside the canon, in the *Didache*. In fact, I Timothy and the *Didache* are entirely devoted to this systematic teaching of the Christian way of life. German New Testament scholars like to call this the New Testament *Haustafeln*.[196] Among English-speaking scholars it is usually called the primitive Christian catechism, and one might even go so far as to label it a sort of Christian Talmud. Whatever it is called, it is clearly an important dimension of the ministry of the Word in the New Testament Church. Let us concentrate our attention for a few moments on three passages of Scripture which preserve for us parts of this primitive Christian catechism.[197]

A. *I Peter 2:11–5:11*

Again we must take up the First Epistle of Peter. We have already said that this book passes on to us a considerable amount of homiletical

---

196. On the other hand, see the objection of Goppelt, *Der erste Petrusbrief*, pp. 163-68. According to Peter Davids, the expression goes back to Luther. *The First Epistle of Peter*, p. 94.

197. There is an extensive literature on the primitive Christian catechism. Among the more important works the following should be noted: Jean Paul Audet, *La Didachè, instructions des Apôtres, Études Bibliques* (Paris: J. Gabalda, 1958); Philip Carrington, *The Primitive Christian Catechism* (Cambridge: University Press, 1940); F. L. Cross, *I Peter: A Paschal Liturgy* (London: A. R. Mowbray, 1954); Oscar Cullmann, *Les premières confessions de foi* (Paris: Presses Universitaires de France, 1948); Kurt Niederwimmer, *Die Didache, Kommentar zu den Apostolischen Vätern* (Göttingen: Vandenhoeck & Ruprecht, 1989); Willy Rordorf, "Un chapître d'éthique judéo-chrétienne: les deux voies," in *Liturgie, foi et vie des premiers Chrétiens, études patristiques* (Paris: Beauchesne, 1986), pp. 155-74; G. Schille, "Das Evangelium des Matthäus als Katechismus," *New Testament Studies* (1958): 101-14; G. Schille, "Katechese und Taufliturgie," *Zeitschrift für die Neutestamentliche Wissenschaft* (1960): 112-31; Selwyn, appendix in *First Epistle of St. Peter*, "Essay II, On the Inter-relation of I Peter and other N.T. Epistles," pp. 363-466; André Turck, *Évangélisation et catéchèse aux deux premiers siècles* (Paris: Les Éditions du Cerf, 1962).

material. In a way quite similar to the Old Testament book of Deuteronomy, the material contained in I Peter had been used in preaching time and time again over the years. First Peter may be presented to us in the literary form of a letter, but in fact it is an epitome of the apostle's preaching.[198] The first part of this work is an epitome of the gospel as Peter preached it. By the mercy of God the Father "we have been born anew to a living hope through the resurrection of Jesus Christ" (1:3). Just as at Pentecost, the primary theme of Peter's preaching was the resurrection. This epitome then makes clear that our salvation is the outcome of our faith in the risen Christ (1:9). Next we are presented with the theme of the fulfillment of prophecy in the death and resurrection of Jesus Christ (1:10-21). Several significant prophetic passages are commented upon (1:24-25; 2:6; and 2:7-10). The interpretation of Psalm 118 is particularly important here, just as it was in the preaching of Peter in Acts (Acts 4:11). Finally, the rest of the epistle (I Peter 2:11–5:11), by far the larger part, is devoted to an epitome of the moral teaching of the apostle Peter.[199]

This epitome of moral teachings begins very appropriately:

> Beloved, I beseech you as aliens and exiles to abstain from the passions of the flesh that wage war against your soul. Maintain good conduct among the Gentiles, so that in case they speak against you as wrongdoers, they may see your good deeds and glorify God on the day of visitation. (2:11-12)

In I Peter Christian conduct is motivated primarily by a concern to glorify God, "that the Gentiles . . . may see your good deeds and glorify God." One keeps the Law that God might be honored. The good behavior of Christians is worship. It is this which is the spiritual sacrifice of the royal priesthood mentioned at the beginning of chapter 2 (2:5, 9). The moral life is essential to the priestly service of all Christians. If this is indeed the case, then we can hardly be surprised if even the most didactic type of moral instruction is considered part of worship.

The moral instruction starts out with this basic principle: "Be subject for the Lord's sake to every human institution" (2:13). This is expanded

---

198. On questions of introduction to I Peter, see n. 181 above.

199. On the relation of the two major sections of I Peter, see Goppelt, *Der erste Petrusbrief*, pp. 155ff. Also Kelly, *Epistles of Peter and Jude*, pp. 102ff.; and Michaels, *1 Peter*, pp. 44-120.

with a considerable amount of material on being a good citizen. The purpose of civil government is explained. Civil disorder is understood as foolishness. There are some good thoughts on the subject of freedom and order in civic life. All this is given in summary statements which encapsulate whole sermons. Peter, like Jesus before him, worked as any rabbi would:[200] He boiled down his sermons into short and easy-to-remember statements. Then they were arranged in a topical order. Just as in the Talmud, there is a traditional succession of *loci*. First, submission to the emperor is taught, then servants are admonished to be submissive to their earthly master, then wives to their husbands. Again we find homiletical material which Peter was in the habit of going through when he taught on the subject of the moral responsibilities of Christian wives. Simplicity in dress and wifely virtues were surely treated at length. Apparently Sarah was the wifely paradigm, and one can imagine that a typical sermon thoroughly elaborated this. Husbands are admonished to live considerately with their wives (3:7). After these passages on different aspects of Christian submissiveness the subject of humility is taken up. One is to have a humble mind, not returning evil for evil (3:8-9). One must be prepared to suffer for righteousness (3:14). In fact, Christ set us an example of righteous suffering. It is good to suffer for righteousness but not good to be enflamed by human passion (4:1). All this, "licentiousness, passions, drunkenness, revels, carousing" (4:3), the Christian must leave behind. This is followed by an exhortation to Christian love and Christian stewardship (4:8-11). Here, too, we find homiletical material recorded in the most abbreviated fashion. Finally, there is a passage on submission to the elders of the Church (5:1-5), and a concluding summary on the subject of humility and submission.

The Epistle of First Peter, when understood as we have just presented it, gives us a good index of what the apostle taught in the way of catechetical instruction. As we shall see, it has an amazing similarity to several other documents which give us a synopsis of early Christian catechetical teaching.

---

200. Goppelt sees the moral precepts in I Peter as coming not in the context of rabbinical instruction, but in the context of Stoic moral principles. *Der erste Petrusbrief,* pp. 168ff. With this we find it hard to agree.

B. Ephesians 4:1–6:20

Let us now turn to one of several Pauline versions of the primitive Christian catechism. In Ephesians we find a clear presentation of the apostle Paul's message, formulated toward the end of his career[201] in the twofold division spoken of earlier. The first three chapters present the gospel of the mystery of redemption now revealed in the saving death and resurrection of Christ that by grace we have been saved through faith (2:8), and the last three chapters, 4–6, present the Christian way of life.

This final passage begins:

> I therefore, a prisoner for the Lord, beg you to lead a life worthy of the calling to which you have been called, with all lowliness and meekness, with patience, forbearing one another in love, eager to maintain the unity of the Spirit in the bond of peace. There is one body and one Spirit, just as you were called to the one hope that belongs to your call, one Lord, one faith, one baptism, one God and Father of us all, who is above all and through all and in all. (4:1-6)

Right away one is struck with the similarity of this transition to the central transition between the kerygmatic and didactic portions of Romans. The transition in Romans reads:

> I appeal to you therefore, brethren, by the mercies of God, to present your bodies as a living sacrifice, holy and acceptable to God, which is your spiritual worship. (Rom. 12:1)

Evidently Peter was not the only one who had gotten the message about the relation of the living of the Christian life to worship.[202] Paul understands that the "spiritual worship" of the Christian is above all the leading of a life worthy of the people of God. The Christian leads the Christian life not out of some legal requirement but out of a sense that it is the life which is fitting for the people of God. Again we are dealing with the third use of the Law. One follows the way of Christ because it is good, acceptable, and perfect.

The first subject taken up by Paul's version of the primitive Christian

---

201. On questions of introduction see above, n. 161.

202. Whether there is any literary dependence of one upon the other is beside the point if, as we believe, both are dependent on oral tradition. Cf. Michaels, *1 Peter*, p. 122.

catechism is the order of the Church in which the new Christian must take his or her place.[203] Every Christian is given spiritual gifts — to some it is given to be apostles, some prophets, some evangelists, some pastors and teachers (Eph. 4:11).[204] Paul went over this material frequently;[205] we find it mentioned again and again in his epistles. No doubt it appeared just as frequently in his regular teaching, particularly that part which presented the basic information on how one was to function in the Church, that is, the catechetical instruction of new converts. Here we get a clear picture of Paul doing catechetical instruction. It is clear here as in so many passages of the Pauline Epistles that the apostle not only did evangelistic preaching but also instructed those who had been converted.

Next we have a long section on how the Christian life differs from Gentile life (4:17). This is a frequent theme in the primitive Christian catechism. Gentile vices are enumerated: hardness of heart, licentiousness, greed, uncleanness (4:18-19); lying, untruthfulness, anger, idleness, slander, wrath, and malice (4:25-31). To each of these the contrasting Christian virtue is given. The whole passage is filled with homiletical material which gives us hints as to how the apostle in his sermons was accustomed to developing his teaching.[206]

Chapter 5 goes on in much the same vein. Here considerable attention is given to what is meant by Christian love: "Therefore be imitators of God, as beloved children. And walk in love, as Christ loved us and gave himself up for us, a fragrant offering and sacrifice to God" (5:1-2). In contrast to Christian love is the fornication, impurity, and covetousness of the children of darkness. Christians, Paul teaches us, are the children

203. On the place of church order in the primitive catechism, cf. Selwyn, *First Epistle of St. Peter*, pp. 415ff.

204. On the variety of ministries in the primitive Church, see the bibliographical notes above as well as most recently Lincoln, *Ephesians*, pp. 248-53, which gives a good discussion of the recent literature.

205. On the relationship of Ephesians 4:11, Romans 12, and I Corinthians 12–14, see above, but also see Menoud, *L'Église et les ministères selon le Nouveau Testament*. Markus Barth seems to miss the relation of this material to the primitive Christian catechism. In fact, he seems to miss the whole point of what Paul is saying about the ministry. An egalitarian political ideology does not explain the order of the Christian ministry any more than does a hierarchical ideology. Barth, "The Church without Laymen and Priests," in *Ephesians*, 2:472-84. Philippe Menoud, who was equally Swiss and equally republican, summed it up one time: The Church is not a democracy but a Christocracy.

206. On this whole section and its relation to the Christian catechism, cf. Barth, *Ephesians*, 2:550-53.

of light, and are therefore to walk as children of light and try to learn what is pleasing to the Lord.[207] Developing his moral discourse with the familiar imagery of light and darkness, Paul finally makes his point by quoting an early Christian hymn:

"Awake, O sleeper, and arise from the dead,
and Christ shall give you light."

(5:14)

All this homiletical material, which the apostle must have used again and again, helps us get a picture of Paul as a Christian interpreter of the Law, a rabbi who has found Christ to be his savior. Moral instruction is clearly as important to the Christian minister of the gospel as it was to the Jewish rabbi.[208]

With the middle of chapter 5 Paul's epistle turns to yet another familiar element of the primitive Christian catechism. Having treated the order of the Church, the comparison of the Gentile way and the Christian way, he now turns to the order of the Christian household, the mutual responsibilities of wives to husbands and husbands to wives, children to parents and parents to children, slaves to masters and masters to slaves.[209] To any reader of the New Testament this is all quite familiar because this sort of material appears so often, and is so similar even in authors so different as Peter and Paul and in books of such obviously different purpose as Ephesians and I Peter.

The passage begins with a summary statement which serves as the key to the order of the Christian household, "Be subject to one another out of reverence to Christ" (5:21). Just as in Peter's version, the word "submission" is basic to the order of the Christian household. Then in good rabbinical form we have the key phrase of the first subject, "Wives, be subject to your husbands" (5:22), a phrase found almost verbatim in all versions of the early Christian catechism. But now Paul brings in his own homiletical material: "For the husband is the head of the wife as Christ is the head of the church. . . . As the church is subject to Christ,

---

207. On the children of light and the children of darkness in the primitive Christian catechism as well as the theme of the two ways, cf. Selwyn, *First Epistle of St. Peter,* pp. 375-82; Turck, *Évangélisation et catéchèse aux deux premiers siècles,* pp. 23-46; and Rordorf, "Un chapître d'éthique judéo-chrétienne."

208. Cf. Davies, *Paul and Rabbinic Judaism,* pp. 122-30.

209. Cf. Selwyn, *First Epistle of St. Peter,* pp. 429-37; Barth, *Ephesians,* 2:754-58.

so let wives also be subject in everything to their husbands" (5:23-24). Paul now goes on to the responsibilities of husbands: "Husbands, love your wives, as Christ loved the church and gave himself up for her" (5:25). Again we have a combination of traditional material from the primitive Christian catechism expanded by homiletical material original with Paul. This is the sort of material which a preacher develops over the years, as anyone who has taught catechism classes knows.

An example from my own pastoral experience jumps to mind. It has to do with doctrinal catechism rather than moral catechism, but the same principle holds true. By tradition there is always at least one session on the Christian doctrine of the Trinity. When most of us teach that session we have our own favorite illustrations, stories, and diagrams for explaining it. I don't think I have ever taught a communicants' class about the Trinity without telling the story of Saint Patrick explaining to the Irish king about the three-leaf clover and how like the Trinity it is. There are three leaves and yet it is still but one clover. In the same way I will always draw the shield of the Trinity on the blackboard and explain it. That is my own personal expansion of the basic catechetical material.

After going through the mutual responsibilities of parents and children and masters and servants, Paul comes up with his superb figure for the Christian life, "Finally, be strong in the Lord and in the strength of his might. Put on the whole armor of God . . ." (6:10-11). What a clever sermonic device. The Christian virtues are compared to the different pieces of armor. The breastplate of righteousness, the helmet of salvation, and the sword of the Spirit must have served to make the apostle's point in many a lesson on the Christian life.

One more element in Paul's catechetical teaching appears here in the last half of Ephesians. It is found only very briefly, but it is clearly there, and it might be called liturgical catechism,[210] or the explaining of the service of worship. It gives instruction in prayer and praise, in the meaning of baptism and the Lord's Supper.[211] Two brief passages of liturgical catechism appear in Ephesians almost incidentally. Elsewhere in the Pauline writings liturgical catechism is more fully developed — in I Timothy,

---

210. On the liturgical dimension of the primitive Christian catechism, see Selwyn, *First Epistle of St. Peter,* pp. 389ff.; and Niederwimmer, *Die Didache,* pp. 158-209.

211. Tertullian's *On Prayer* as well as Cyprian's *On the Lord's Prayer* probably preserve for us the catechetical material used at the time in regard to prayer. The same could be said of Tertullian's *On Baptism.*

for example. As we shall see, liturgical catechism will become an important genre of preaching in following centuries.[212] In Ephesians 5:18-20 we read:

> Be filled with the Spirit, addressing one another in psalms and hymns and spiritual songs, singing and making melody to the Lord with all your heart, always and for everything giving thanks in the name of our Lord Jesus Christ to God the Father.

And then further on we find another admonition on the subject of prayer:

> Pray at all times in the Spirit, with all prayer and supplication. To that end keep alert with all perseverance, making supplication for all the saints, and also for me, that utterance may be given me in opening my mouth boldly to proclaim the mystery of the gospel. (6:18-19)

The fact that this material appears in such a similar form in Colossians would indicate that it was indeed part of the primitive Christian catechism. In fact, the Colossians material makes it much more obvious that it is indeed a separate topic in the catechism as Paul presents it.

One can make the same point about the long passage on prayer in the Sermon on the Mount (Matt. 6:1-21). In fact, many have made this point. This material in Matthew is basically catechetical material on prayer. We find in it not only the Lord's Prayer but a number of other materials on prayer, particularly the auxiliary disciplines of prayer, fasting, and almsgiving. For centuries this material, particularly the Lord's Prayer, was a prominent part of catechetical instruction. The earliest Christians felt there was something special about praying in the Spirit, or, as we find it in the Gospels, praying in the name of Jesus (John 14–17), and they preserved for us significant catechetical material on this subject.

It should be fairly obvious that this generous slice of catechetical material in Ephesians is but Paul's version of the same catechetical preaching we found in the First Epistle of Peter. Let us take up one further example.

---

212. See below the sections on liturgical catechism of Ambrose of Milan, Theodore of Mopsuestia, and Cyril of Jerusalem. Particularly helpful is the work of Suzanne Pogue, *Augustin d'Hippone, Sermons pour la Pâque* (Paris: Les Éditions du Cerf, 1966), pp. 65-69.

C. I Timothy

Paul's first epistle to Timothy is almost completely devoted to an epitome of Paul's teaching rather than his preaching.[213] Unlike I Peter and Ephesians, it does not devote its first half to kerygma. The whole epistle is devoted to presenting Paul's didache. Actually Paul uses the term διδαλκαλία more often than he does διδαχή, but, as we shall see, it amounts to the same thing. A particularly interesting feature of this version of Paul's catechetical teaching is that it is most obviously not elementary teaching. It is apparently directed to church leaders such as Timothy. It is instruction on the basic principles of church order. As we have seen in both I Peter and Ephesians, teachings on church order belonged to the basic instruction on the Christian way of life. Those who were entering the Church could go over the basic principles of church order at an elementary level, and those who had been entrusted with church leadership could go over the same material at a more advanced level.

We find the same situation in the Church today. When we have classes for new church members, particularly when we are receiving adults by transfer from other denominations, we go over the polity of our denomination. We explain how the Church is governed, the function of ministers, elders, and deacons, how they are elected, and what authority they have. We make clear our service of worship and our disciplines of devotion. We cover our approach to the sacraments and our traditions of prayer. When teaching new members we go over this material rather briefly, but then we go over much the same material at another level with newly elected elders and deacons. The same material is treated in greater detail. I Timothy, it would seem, is a more advanced recital of the material.

In this respect I Timothy is much like that very ancient document which today we simply call the *Didache*. The *Didache* is, quite straightforwardly, a very early church constitution. I Timothy is much the same thing, a recital of Pauline material on the subject of church order. Sometimes one

---

213. For introductory material on I Timothy, see the following: Joachim Jeremias, *Die Briefe an Timotheus und Titus,* 6th ed. (Göttingen: Vandenhoeck & Ruprecht, 1957); J. N. D. Kelly, *The Pastoral Epistles* (London: Adam and Charles Black, 1963); Bruce M. Metzger, "A Reconsideration of Certain Arguments against the Pauline Authorship of the Pastoral Epistles," *Expository Times* 70 (1958); C. Spicq, *Saint Paul: les Épîtres pastorales* (Paris: J. Gabalda, 1947).

gets the impression that catechetical material is limited to the elementary material taught to candidates for baptism. As we find it in the New Testament, especially in the Pauline literature, catechetical instruction seems to be the teaching of the fundamentals of the Christian faith.[214] Only later, it appears, was catechetical instruction thought of as introductory instruction. This is the case in Tertullian and frequently throughout the patristic era.[215] It was certainly the case in the fourth century.

At the time of the Reformation the Protestants reestablished catechetical instruction based on the catechetical disciplines of the fourth century. The obvious difference was that since the catechumens had been baptized as infants they went through their catechetical instruction at ten to twelve years old. Before too long this changed, of course. Preaching through the Heidelberg Catechism became a highly sophisticated kind of doctrinal preaching. It had not begun that way. Reformation catechetical instruction was originally introductory material just as the fourth-century catechetical material was. For historical reasons it is understandable that one assumes that catechetical material is introductory, elementary material.

There is, however, another aspect to didache which comes out so obviously in I Timothy, and that is the aspect it inherited from the synagogue. Didache could become quite advanced, just as the systematic study of the Law became quite advanced in the courts of the Temple and in the discussions of the schools of synagogues in larger Jewish communities. Christian didache could develop along the lines that produced the Talmud in the synagogue. It could develop in the line of a systematic discussion of church polity, discipline, and doctrine. And just like the synagogue, the Church recognized a distinction between the preaching of the kerygma and the teaching of the didache.

Several passages in I Timothy give us helpful insights into the way the catechetical teaching reviewed in the epistle fit into the life of the early Christian Church. One that particularly claims our interest is the following:

> Command and teach these things. Let no one despise your youth, but set the believers an example in speech and conduct, in love, in faith, in

214. H. W. Beyer, "κατηχέω," *Theological Dictionary of the New Testament*, 3:638-40.
215. Beyer, "κατηχέω," *Theological Dictionary of the New Testament*, 3:639; E. Lohse, "Paränese und Kerygma im I Petrusbrief," *Zeitschrift für die neutestamentliche Wissenschaft* 45 (1954): 68-89; and G. Schille, "Das Matthäus Evangelium als Katechismus," *New Testament Studies* 4 (1958): 101-14.

purity. Till I come, attend to the public reading of scripture, to preaching, to teaching. Do not neglect the gift you have, which was given you by prophetic utterance when the council of elders laid their hands upon you. Practice these duties, devote yourself to them, so that all may see your progress. Take heed to yourself and to your teaching; hold to that, for by so doing you will save both yourself and your hearers. (4:11-16)

What interests us here is that the apostle exhorts Timothy to occupy himself with three aspects of the ministry of the Word: the public reading of Scripture, preaching, and teaching.[216] Earlier in the epistle Paul used four very specific words to exhort Timothy to organize the prayers of the Church: supplications, prayers, intercessions, and thanksgiving. These four words speak to the breadth and variety of a full diet of prayer. In the same way the three words used by the apostle here, public reading of Scripture, preaching, and teaching, indicate the fullness of the ministry of the Word.

This is particularly the case if one regards the original Greek terms. ἀνάγνωσις is the liturgical reading of the Old Testament in the synagogue. The Law of Moses was read through on a *lectio continua* Sabbath by Sabbath; a passage of the prophets was read as well; and the passages which had been read were explained.[217] No doubt the practice of the synagogue was continued in the Church, and this passage from I Timothy is the strongest possible evidence of this.[218] At the center of Christian preaching from the very beginning was this exposition of the public reading of Scripture. But preaching was always more than a sort of objective explaining of the text. Paul mentions παράκλησις, which was using the explanation of Scripture as the basis of a message of exhortation or comfort.[219]

216. J. N. D. Kelly comments, "In the Greek the words translated *Scripture reading, exhortation,* and *teaching* are each preceded by the definite article; this shows they are recognized items in the congregational meeting for worship." *The Pastoral Epistles,* p. 105.

217. Bultmann, "ἀναγινώσκω," *Theological Dictionary of the New Testament,* 1:343-44.

218. Kelly tells us that Scripture reading "denotes, primarily, the public reading of the Old Testament which at this time was the Church's Bible. This was a feature of the synagogue service . . . and was immediately adopted by the Christian congregations. This is, in fact, the earliest reference to the use of Scripture in the Church's liturgy. . . . Public reading in the ancient world called for some technical accomplishment, for the words in the codex were not divided. From the middle of the second century at any rate the function was delegated to an official called *lector*. . . ." *The Pastoral Epistles,* p. 105.

219. O. Schmitz, "παρακαλέω, παπάκλησις F," *Theological Dictionary of the New Testament,* 5:793-99. Kelly comments, "By *exhortation* is meant the exposition and appli-

Perhaps the Scriptures would be opened up in such a way that the message of salvation was proclaimed to the heathen, or expounded in such a way as to offer encouragement to experienced Christians who had become weary or discouraged. Then again there were times when these exhortations were a challenge to stir up a somnolent congregation. Finally Paul mentions διδασκαλία, that is, teaching.[220] This word is a synonym of διδαχή; indeed, the two words seem interchangeable.[221]

Certainly one thing we get from this passage, especially when taken in context, is that early Christian preaching had a strong didactic flavor. Preachers were supposed to move the heart and will, but they were also supposed to teach. The two went hand in glove. In fact the three, ἀνάγνωσις, παράκλησις, and διδασκαλία, all worked together. The reading and exposition of Scripture, the admonishing of the congregation, and the teaching of the Christian way of life were all integral parts of the ministry of the Word.

This text probably also implies that the ministry of the Word took place at several different kinds of services. Not only was there the formal reading and preaching of Scripture in the service of worship on the Lord's Day, there would also have been the daily morning teaching sessions about which we have often spoken. This teaching was probably carried on at a more advanced level, and it was in this kind of setting that one would go over the teachings outlined in I Timothy. No doubt there would also have been very elementary teaching sessions at some other time and place for those who approached the Church without any knowledge of the Law and the prophets. It was not for the teaching of beginners that the material found in I Timothy is formulated; here we have a more advanced kind of teaching. It must have been for this more advanced teaching ministry that Paul rented the hall of Tyrannus in Ephesus (Acts 19:9).

One would like to know how this catechetical teaching was organized in the early days. One imagines it was organized in such a way that one regularly went through a series of subjects one after the other. That was the way the tradition of the rabbis was taught in the synagogue, and that is how

---

cation of scripture which followed its public reading, in other words, the sermon." *The Pastoral Epistles,* p. 105.

220. Again we find the comment of Kelly most helpful, that "*teaching* signifies catechetical instruction in Christian doctrine; this too had its place in meetings for worship from the earliest times, and it is evident that a great deal of catechetical material is embodied in the New Testament writings, including the Pauline letters." *The Pastoral Epistles,* p. 105.

221. Rengstorf, "διδασκαλία," *Theological Dictionary of the New Testament,* 2:160ff. and 163ff.

this material appears to be organized in an impressive amount of early Christian literature. There was a distinct contrast between the preaching of the Scriptures on the basis of a *lectio continua* and the systematic discussion of one doctrinal question or one ethical theme or one problem of church order after another. It seems, however, that the early Church, as the synagogue before it, had both. This systematic teaching was, to be sure, related to Scripture just as much as expository preaching was, but in a different way. Biblical quotations were brought in to establish the points that were being made, and, very significantly, biblical examples were used to illustrate these points. Job was used as an example of patience (James 5:11), Elijah as an example of perseverance in prayer (5:17), and Sarah of modest and reverent behavior (I Pet. 3:6). When the relationship between husbands and wives is discussed in Ephesians, a text from the creation story is quoted: "'and the two shall become one flesh'" (Eph. 5:31). A few traces of this are found in I Timothy. We notice, for example, that Deuteronomy 24:4 is quoted to support the paying of ministers of the Word: "'You shall not muzzle an ox when it is treading out the grain'" (I Tim. 5:18). Scripture was interpreted in catechetical teaching just as it was in formal preaching. This principle is formally enunciated in II Timothy: "All scripture is inspired by God and profitable for teaching, for reproof, for correction, and for training in righteousness, that the man of God may be complete, equipped for every good work" (II Tim. 3:16-17). There was a rich use of Scripture in the *didache* of the early church.

Not only was there the interpretation of the Old Testament Scriptures, there was also the apostolic tradition. Twice we find the phrase "The saying is sure" (I Tim. 1:15; 3:1), followed by a formulation of doctrine or polity.[222] The first of these is clearly doctrinal. "The saying is sure and worthy of full acceptance, that Christ Jesus came into the world to save sinners." The second, "The saying is sure: If anyone aspires to the office of bishop, he desires a noble task." One easily gets the impression that Paul is quoting the catechetical material he had taught the Ephesians, and Timothy was now continuing to teach in his place. Many commentators on I Timothy have noticed several passages which seem to be memorized material that would be recognized by early Christians. For example:

---

222. Again we find the comment of Kelly particularly to the point: "Paul now interjects a striking formula, 'It is a trustworthy saying,' which is found . . . in four other contexts in the Pastorals. . . . It has a solemn ring, and in each case is used to introduce, or follow, a citation, probably drawn from early catechetical or liturgical material." *The Pastoral Epistles*, p. 54.

For there is one God,
And there is one mediator
  between God and man,
The man Christ Jesus,
Who gave himself as a ransom
  for all,
The testimony to which was
  borne at the proper time.
                (I Tim. 2:5-6, RSV, but arranged as in Metzger)

This appears to be a doctrinal formulation of the sort catechetical instructors love to teach their students. Another example is found in chapter 3:

He was manifested in the flesh,
  vindicated in the Spirit,
Seen by angels,
  preached among the nations,
Believed on in the world,
  taken up in glory.
                (I Tim. 3:16, RSV, but arranged as in Metzger)

These statements are almost creedal in nature and would obviously have belonged to the doctrinal instruction which was carried on in the Ephesian church. While we do not find in I Timothy the beautiful long discussions of doctrine we find in Romans or Ephesians, we do find a number of little gems like these which are prized for their brief and precise formulation of doctrine. Even in the earliest Christian Church much attention was given to the teaching of doctrinal theology. Certainly these short catechetical formulations would bear this out.

In chapter 6 we find two passages which would appear to have their place in the ethical or moral part of that instruction:

There is great gain in godliness with
  contentment;
for we brought nothing into the world,
  and we cannot take anything out
  of the world;
but if we have food and clothing,
  with these we shall be content.
                (I Tim. 6:6-8, RSV, but arranged as in Metzger)

249

And a few verses later:

> But as for you, man of God, shun all this; aim at righteousness, godliness, faith, love, steadfastness, gentleness. Fight the good fight of the faith; take hold of the eternal life to which you were called when you made the good confession in the presence of many witnesses. (I Tim. 6:11-12)

It would appear that there is much teaching of this sort in I Timothy. It was apostolic tradition that Paul was in the practice of passing on in his teaching, even if he had not formulated it himself. This was the way Jewish rabbis had taught for centuries. Paul passed on to his pupils that which he had himself received.

From another passage in I Timothy we get an impression of how important this catechetical teaching was in the life of the early Church:

> Let elders who rule well be considered worthy of double honor, especially those who labor in preaching and teaching. (I Tim. 5:17)

The Greek reads very literally, "especially those who labor in the word and in teaching." "Teaching" in this passage translates διδασκαλία. Again we seem to have a comprehensive statement of the ministry of the Word. The ministry of the Word includes the proclaiming of the message of salvation and the teaching of the Christian way of life. Again and again in I Timothy teaching is mentioned as an important ministerial function. At the very beginning of the epistle we learn that Paul had left Timothy in Ephesus that he might correct false teachers (1:3). Finally at the end of the epistle the apostle directs his young assistant to "teach and urge these duties." Good teaching, Paul assures Timothy, agrees with the sound words of our Lord Jesus Christ and is in accordance with godliness (6:3). The Epistle of First Timothy makes it abundantly clear that the teaching of Christian doctrine and instruction in piety and even the principles of church order have their place in the ministry of the Word.

Not only from I Timothy but from Ephesians and I Peter as well, it should be clear that the early Christian Church could be both didactic and doxological at the same time.

250

CHAPTER III

The Second and Third Centuries

For those who received the preaching of the apostles that Jesus is the risen Lord and the Savior of the world, worship broke into a new and deeper reality. Two veils had fallen away: The veil of the Temple had been torn from top to bottom, but, even more, a veil was lifted from the reading of Moses in the synagogue. When Christians met together to worship God they continued to read the Law and the prophets, as many who had belonged to the synagogue had done before that veil had been removed. The same Scriptures were read and preached, much as faithful Jews had done for centuries, but the difference was that now the Law and the prophets were understood in a different sense. It was the responsibility of the ministry of the Word to make this new understanding clear. The Christian understanding of the Scriptures went back to the teaching ministry of Jesus. It was Jesus himself, as summed up in the story of the Emmaus road, who opened to his disciples the Scriptures (Luke 24:32). It was Jesus who established the Christian interpretation of the Scriptures, and it was from Jesus that the apostles learned this interpretation. We have already seen how much of the preaching of the New Testament Church was devoted to presenting Christ as the fulfillment of the Scriptures. As the apostle Paul put it so succinctly, Christ died according to the Scriptures and on the third day he was raised according to the Scriptures (I Cor. 15:3-4). As we shall see, it was the primary task of the Christian preachers of the second and third centuries to pass on this witness, that in Christ is the fulfillment of the Law, that in him the visions of the prophets have been realized. This was the heart of the earliest Christian preaching.

251

As Jaroslav Pelikan has observed, those who have written about the worship of the second and third centuries have tended to put all the emphasis on the sacraments and neglected the role of preaching as a means of grace.[1] We admit that the Church of the second and third centuries has not left us a great amount of material about its worship, especially in regard to actual sermons, so other kinds of sources must be consulted in this chapter. What material has come down to us is, however, quite revealing. Even though it does not allow us to answer all the questions we would like to ask, it does provide us with enough to reconstruct a picture of how the Scriptures were read and preached in that period between the close of the New Testament and the era of the Christian empire. Let us look briefly at these sources.

First we have two early church orders, the *Didache,* which comes very early, possibly before the end of the first century, and the *Apostolic Tradition* of Hippolytus. While much of the information in the *Didache* is indirect, as we shall see, a careful reading yields up much. The *Apostolic Tradition* of Hippolytus dates from the beginning of the third century. Hippolytus was not a very profound observer of church life of his day, but nonetheless he provides us with some useful information.

Two apologists, Justin Martyr in the middle of the second century and Tertullian at the end of the second century, give us brief descriptions of Christian worship addressed to the non-Christian world. From the same period we have three sermons: one from Melito of Sardis; another, the so-called *Second Epistle of Clement,* from an unknown author; and a third from Clement of Alexandria. Taken together this is a rather small collection of sources on which to base a study of the preaching of two centuries. Happily we have another very rich source on which to base our study.

Origen, one of the giants of Christian preaching, one of the most seminal of Christian thinkers, and even more one of the most saintly of Christian scholars, has left us a wealth of preaching material. Over a period of several years early in the third century his sermons were taken down by stenographers, and while many of these have been lost, a good number have survived. He also left us an essay on the interpretation of Scripture as well as some carefully written commentaries. Origen was a controversial preacher, and succeeding centuries have argued over the value of his work.

---

1. Jaroslav Pelikan, *The Christian Tradition: A History of the Development of Doctrine,* 5 vols. (Chicago: University of Chicago Press, 1971-89), 1:162.

He had a tremendous influence on Christian preaching for more than a thousand years. In much he was undoubtedly an innovator, but, as we would like to show, in much else he was a faithful witness to the best of Christian preaching in this very early period of Christian history. From the time of Origen until the emergence of the great preachers of the last half of the fourth century, a period of well over a century, we have nothing. As Ronald Heine has put it, Origen is the great oak standing alone in the pasture of the ante-Nicene Church.[2] We will therefore give special attention to him in the study that follows.

There are several questions on which we will focus in this chapter. First we will ask how the Church moved from an emphasis on what we might call missionary preaching to what we might call liturgical preaching. What we read about preaching in the Acts of the Apostles assumes a proclamation of the gospel to those who had not heard. It was frequently done in the Jewish synagogue or before a hostile crowd. The preaching we read about in the second and third centuries was to a Christian audience. The preaching of Origen was aimed at the nurture of Christians. Does this mean that the evangelistic thrust of preaching disappeared? Does it mean that the Church of this period ceased to use preaching as an evangelistic method? Does it mean that liturgy monopolized preaching or that preaching became the captive of cultic interests?

A second question we will ask is how the writings of the New Testament came to find a place beside the Law and the prophets in the worship of the earliest Church. When the apostle Paul directed Timothy to give attention to the public reading of the Scriptures in worship, it was the Old Testament Scriptures he had in mind, but by the middle of the second century New Testament writings had found a place in Christian worship. As we have seen, the Epistle of James gives us a hint of how this came about. As we will see, the reading of the New Testament was laid beside the reading of the Old Testament. In this early period, at least, the New Testament Scriptures did not replace the Old Testament. How was it that the New Testament Scriptures came to be read in the worship of the Church?

A third matter which will claim our attention is the prodigious labor given during this period to the question of how the Old Testament was to be interpreted. While not so pressing to the Church in our day, this

---

2. Cf. the introduction to his edition of the sermons of Origen, *Homilies on Genesis and Exodus,* trans. Ronald E. Heine (Washington, D.C.: Catholic University of America Press, 1982), p. 1.

question was of the greatest possible importance to the early Church. Surely one of the most commendable liturgical reforms of the Second Vatican Council has been the recovery of regular Old Testament reading in the liturgy. Indeed, there is high value in the regular reading and preaching of the Old Testament, as the preachers of classical Protestantism demonstrated at the time of the Reformation. As we will see, this was a regular feature of Christian worship in the second and third centuries as well. Origen was not the only one who was concerned with it. It was no doubt because Origen gave such an impressive answer to it that he was so prized as a preacher. The question is whether there is any value in the Old Testament interpretation of the earliest Christians. Was their interpretation of the Old Testament simply eccentric?

Fourth, we will note the major role preaching and teaching played in the life of the Church of the second and third centuries. Even in the earliest documents which have come down to us it is evident that preaching and teaching occupied a primary place in the life of the earliest Christians. The *Didache* presents preaching and teaching as obviously the first concern of the leaders of the Church, as does Justin Martyr. The one who presided at the assemblies of the Church was the one who preached. The earliest documents show that daily preaching was a cardinal feature of the life of the ante-Nicene Church.

Fifth, we want to ask, as we will again and again through the whole history of the Church, how the reading and preaching of Scripture was understood as worship. This question is most relevant to the contemporary discussion of the renewal of worship. In many quarters the liturgical renewal has aimed at de-emphasizing the role of preaching in worship. Preaching is thought of as preparation for worship, a sort of ancillary activity that brings us to the central concerns of worship rather than being worship in itself. The High Church movement ever since Queen Elizabeth I has pretended that preaching and teaching was a secondary concern of the Church. What we want to know is whether this squares with what we find in the practice of the ancient Church. Today many regard the function of preaching as a sort of pep talk designed to get people to think positively and make them feel good. Perhaps put better, the sermon is used as a word of encouragement designed to build fellowship. We want to ask whether this kind of preaching was what nourished the Church through the second and third centuries, those times of such fierce persecution and solid growth.

I. The Historical Documents

A. *The* Didache *(ca. 80–ca. 110)*

Having raised these questions, let us look at the sources which are available. We begin with the *Didache*.[3] It is only a little more than a hundred years ago that the *Didache* was rediscovered after centuries of obscurity. While some dismissed the document as the work of some eccentric schismatic or heretical group, church historians have gradually come to realize that it gives us a valuable look into the church life of Palestine or Syria toward the end of the first Christian century. The *Didache* contains material which goes back to the earliest Jewish Christian communities. The title of the work, *The Teaching of the Twelve Apostles,* is in certain respects quite justified. Surely some of the material it contains does reflect the age of the apostles, but then the material has been edited by the hand of someone who came later and was concerned to guard the tradition of the apostles. This is of the greatest possible interest, for here we find information of how the Church moved from being a fellowship of the disciples of Jesus to being an organized religious institution.

The first thing we notice is that the Church which produced the *Didache* must have given much time to preaching and teaching. In the *Didache* there is no description of a regular preaching service. This is a rather striking omission, especially in regard to the preaching services which were undoubtedly held the morning of the Lord's Day. We do hear about the Lord's Supper services, which in all probability were still held on the evening of the Lord's Day.[4] We even hear of daily preaching services, although only in the most cursory fashion. Surely the early Church had something similar to the Sabbath morning service of the synagogue, except, of course, that it would have been held on the Lord's Day morning. It is just that the *Didache* does not discuss it. So it often is with things that an author and his readers took for granted. Still, there is solid evidence that

---

3. For the text of the *Didache,* see *The Apostolic Fathers,* ed. and trans. Kirsopp Lake, 2 vols., Loeb Classical Library (Cambridge: Harvard University Press, 1965), 1:309-33. Among the more recent studies of this document are the following: Jean Paul Audet, *La Didachè, Instructions des apôtres* (Paris: J. Gabalda, 1958); Kurt Niederwimmer, *Die Didache* (Göttingen: Vandenhoeck & Ruprecht, 1989); and Willy Rordorf and A. Tuilier, *La Doctrine des douze apôtres (Didachè), Introduction, Texte, Traduction, Notes* (Paris: Éditions du Cerf, 1978).

4. *Didache* 14.

the ministry of preaching and teaching was of paramount importance to the Church which produced the *Didache.* Somewhat indirectly, yet nevertheless quite clearly, the *Didache* gives us a picture of a vigorous and varied ministry of the Word.

While nothing is said about how preaching fit into the liturgy, the *Didache* does indicate that the Church provided a daily preaching ministry. This we gather first from the instructions given to catechumens. Catechumens are admonished to pray for those who teach them the Word of God and honor them as they would honor the Lord, and furthermore to seek daily the presence of the saints so as to find rest in their words.[5] It is not simply daily catechetical instruction presided over by a catechist that the *Didache* has in mind, but rather a daily assembly of the saints, at which the Word was preached for the glory of God and the spiritual strengthening of the congregation. What seems to be intended here is that the catechumens should attend the daily preaching services, where they will hear the Christian interpretation of the Scriptures and learn how Jesus fulfilled the Law and the prophets in his death and resurrection. While the Eucharist was held on the Lord's Day,[6] preaching services were held daily.

There is a second reason for believing the *Didache* reflects the life of a Church which conducted daily preaching for the whole congregation, not merely for catechumens. This daily preaching was directed toward the mature members of the congregation; it was not simply elementary instruction designed for catechumens. This is made clear not only from what is said to the catechumens but even more from the fact that the *Didache* assumes a rather large body of prophets, teachers, bishops, and deacons who devote full time to their preaching and teaching.[7] The *Didache* seems to have in mind a group of professional preachers who devote their lives to their ministry rather than lay preachers, if we may use the modern terms.

The *Didache* assumes that the main function of the various ministries it mentions is teaching.[8] This is clear at several points. Chapters 11–13 are devoted to traveling apostles and prophets. They are specifically called teachers, and teaching apparently was their main function although they

---

5. *Didache* 4.1-2.

6. *Didache* 14.1.

7. On the paying of prophets, cf. Niederwimmer, *Die Didache*, pp. 225-26.

8. *Didache* 11.1; 11.10; and 15.1. On the functions of the apostles, prophets, and teachers mentioned in the *Didache*, see Rordorf and Tuilier, *La Doctrine*, pp. 51-80.

might also perform signs or even lead in prayer at the Eucharist. Prophets may settle in a church, and if they do are to be paid on the principle that a true teacher is worthy of his support.[9] A bit later on churches are told to appoint bishops and deacons, for they also perform the ministry of prophets and teachers.[10] The picture one gets is of a church with a number of teachers, which would hardly be a necessity were there but a single sermon each week. In fact, if there were but a single sermon each week one could well imagine that all these prophets, teachers, and bishops might get into considerable competition for the pulpit. On the other hand, if there was daily preaching one might be glad to welcome a traveling evangelist from time to time.

Even if what the *Didache* tells us about the regular preaching services comes by way of inference, the *Didache* gives us a very good look at the beginnings of catechetical preaching.[11] In the *Didache* it is not yet clear whether catechetical instruction has developed to where it can be called preaching. In time it would develop into a distinct genre of Christian preaching, the roots of which go back to the words of Jesus recorded in the last chapter of the Gospel of Matthew, " 'Make disciples of all nations, baptizing them . . . , teaching them to observe all that I have commanded you' " (Matt. 28:19-20). It has often been pointed out that the *Didache* has its own peculiar affinities to Matthew, and here we find a clear example.[12] The catechism outlined in the *Didache* seems to be a good example of what the Gospel of Matthew has in mind. It is what Christ commanded his disciples — that is, it is not a summary of the gospel but rather a summary of the Law as Christ interpreted it, particularly in such places as the Sermon on the Mount as recorded in Matthew.[13] The earliest Christian catechetical material was moral instruction;[14] it was teaching

9. *Didache* 13.2.

10. *Didache* 15.1-2.

11. On the catechetical instruction in the *Didache*, see Willy Rordorf, "Un chapitre d'éthique judéo-chrétienne: les Deux Voies," *Recherches de Science Religieuse* 60 (1972): 109-28; also found in Willy Rordorf, *Liturgie, foi et vie des premiers chrétiens*, Études patristiques (Paris: Beauchesne, 1986), pp. 155-74.

12. Rordorf and Tuilier, *La Doctrine*, pp. 85-88. For a more detailed study, see Willy Rordorf, "Le problème de la transmission textuelle de *Didachè* 1,3b–2,1," *Überlieferungsgeschichtliche Untersuchungen* (*Texte und Untersuchungen* 125) (Berlin, 1981): 499-513. Also found in Rordorf, *Liturgie*, pp. 139-53.

13. Cf. Niederwimmer on what the *Didache* had in mind by the term "gospel." *Die Didache*, p. 246 n. 8.

14. On the Jewish sources of the catechetical material found in the *Didache*, see Audet, *La Didachè*, pp. 189 and 255-81.

converts how to live the Christian life. The *Didache* puts as an introductory title at the head of its catechetical material that this teaching is what the Lord gave the apostles to teach to the "nations," that is, to those coming over from paganism. This catechetical material is then followed by a chapter on baptism, which at least in the final redaction of the *Didache* begins by telling us that candidates are to receive this instruction before being baptized.

Unfortunately the *Didache* tells us nothing about how this catechetical instruction took place. The very fact that a manual for the instruction of candidates for baptism is provided in the *Didache* suggests that something more than private lessons is intended. On the other hand, the amount of material to be conveyed is not so great that one would need to hear a catechetical sermon every week, let alone every day, for a year or more. The *Didache* does give evidence for a catechumenate but not for the three-year catechumenate of later times. As we have said, the existence of daily preaching services is hardly explained by the need to instruct the catechumens. No doubt the material could be covered in a few weeks even allowing for the memorizing of much of the material by the candidates for baptism. One or more of the teachers were probably assigned to lecture or preach to the catechumens on a daily basis until the material was covered, after which the candidates would be baptized. There is no suggestion that baptism was reserved for any particular season of the year or even any particular day of the week. The only thing the *Didache* seems to be interested in is what material needs to be covered.

It is at this point that the *Didache* is most helpful to the historian of Christian worship. The *Didache* makes very clear that whatever may have been preached in the way of gospel or done in the way of the exposition of Scripture, considerable attention was given to moral instruction. As we mentioned in the previous chapter, a number of scholars in the last generation studied the origins of the primitive Christian catechism and showed that even during the lifetime of the apostles a Christian catechism had begun to evolve. Parts of it are found in I Peter, Ephesians, Colossians, and I Timothy as well as in the postapostolic literature. This primitive Christian catechism was for the most part introductory instruction on the Christian life. It was particularly interested in the responsibilities of Christian husbands and wives, and the duties of parents to their children and children to their parents. Sometimes it included more advanced material on such subjects as the qualifications and responsibilities of church officers, but for the most part it treated such elementary subjects as the relation of students to their teachers and subjects to their rulers. It exhorted against unchastity, sodomy, and abortion and extolled the virtues of generosity, almsgiving, and acts of personal kindness. It advised the convert on how to keep oneself from entanglement with idols and pagan culture. The instructions of this catechism were practical and down-to-earth.

Catechetical instruction as we find it in the earliest documents did not open up the mysteries of eternal reality, nor try to speak of the nature of God or of the salvation of the world. It did not even go over the significance of the death and resurrection of Christ. As we shall see, the catechetical preaching of Cyril of Jerusalem, more than two hundred years later, will have a very different character. Cyril and a number of other preachers of the fourth and fifth centuries give much more attention to doctrinal instruction. One wonders, then, what happened to the preaching of the kerygma, the gospel, the central message of the Church. Did it disappear like the ministry of the apostles? The ministry of the "apostles" as we find it in the *Didache* seems to be in decay. Apparently no one was doing the sort of evangelistic preaching the apostle Paul did. There were still a few "apostles" going about, but the ministry seems to have degenerated. They do not seem to be planting churches by the proclamation of the gospel. What happened to evangelistic preaching? Although the *Didache* does not really tell us, what probably happened was that the central affirmations of the gospel were more and more preached in the Lord's Day service and in the daily weekday services, and one went there to hear the preaching of the gospel and the Christian interpretation of Scripture. In Palestine especially, where such a large portion of the population was Jewish, the unrolling of the Christian interpretation of Scripture was crucial to evangelism. With the martyrdom of many of the leading apostles the Church more and more confined its evangelistic preaching to its churches, which by this time had been planted throughout the Mediterranean world. As we have already pointed out, the *Didache* tells us nothing explicitly about the regular preaching services which the Church undoubtedly held. When we come to the sermons which have been preserved from the second and third centuries, we will see that, indeed, worship and evangelism went hand in hand. Sunday by Sunday, even day by day, the Scriptures were expounded as they had been in the synagogue. The gospel was presented as the fulfillment of the Scriptures, and this was to the glory of God. This was the service of worship which the earliest Christians offered to God, the witness to God's grace in Christ.

259

Let us turn to another very important question. Had the Church whose worship is reflected in this document found a place for the reading of the New Testament Scriptures in its services? No doubt the Law and the prophets were read each Lord's Day just as they had been each Sabbath in the synagogue, but had the step been taken of reading the writings of the New Testament as sacred Scripture? Had the Gospels and Epistles been added to the Law and the prophets? There is no simple answer to this question. At the present we do not have the evidence needed for certainty, but an hypothesis might be advanced.

It seems to me that the *Didache* comes to us from that time in which this step was being taken. The *Didache* reflects the situation which gave rise to the establishment of New Testament Scripture lessons; it reflects the problems, the attitudes, and the convictions which made it possible to take this important step in the development of Christian worship. The living witness of the apostles was no longer there to confirm the faith of the Church, and the Church found itself in the position of having to choose new leaders to take the place of the apostles and prophets of earlier times. That is the situation we find in the *Didache*. When we set the *Didache* beside the Gospel of Matthew and the Epistle of James, we can get an idea of what happened.

At a very important juncture in the *Didache* there is an appeal to the authority of the gospel.[15] We are specifically told that in matters having to do with discipline, polity, works of charity, and worship, the Church is to do all this as it is found "in the Gospel," ἐν τῷ εὐαγγελίῳ. It is not at all clear just exactly what is meant by "in the Gospel." Is it a general reference to the teachings of Christ or a reference to one of the canonical Gospels, such as the Gospel of Matthew?

The question has often been asked if the Church which produced the *Didache* had a New Testament at all.[16] While there are in the *Didache* a good number of allusions to the sayings found in the Synoptic Gospels, there are no clear indications that the author is familiar with either the Gospel of John or the Pauline Epistles. It is sometimes said that the *Didache* had access to many of the traditions recorded in Matthew, and that both writings came from the same circle.

While it is not completely clear just exactly what is meant by ὡς

---

15. *Didache* 15.3-4. See *Didache* 8.2 and 11.1.

16. On the question of whether the *Didache* had a New Testament which was recognized as sacred Scripture, or whether it was still largely dependent on oral tradition for its knowledge of the words and works of Jesus, see Rordorf and Tuilier, *La Doctrine*, pp. 83-91.

ἔχετε ἐν τῷ εὐαγγελίῳ τοῦ κυρίου ἡμῶν, "as you have it in the Gospel of our Lord,"[17] it is quite clear that the phrase is an expression of the principle that the discipline, polity, and worship of the Church are to be according to Scripture, and that this includes the New Testament Scriptures even if they had not yet achieved the written form implied in the word "Scriptures." The apostles who knew the Lord and the prophets who spoke by the Spirit were being replaced by bishops and deacons whose authority, unlike that of the apostles and prophets, was based on "the Gospel of our Lord."[18] The passage speaks for itself:

> 1. Appoint therefore for yourselves bishops and deacons worthy of the Lord, meek men, and not lovers of money, and truthful and approved, for they also minister to you the ministry of the prophets and teachers. 2. Therefore do not despise them, for they are your honourable men together with the prophets and teachers.
>
> 3. And reprove one another not in wrath but in peace as you find in the Gospel, and let none speak with any who has done a wrong to his neighbour, nor let him hear a word from you until he repents. 4. But your prayers and alms and all your acts perform as ye find in the Gospel of our Lord.[19]

The authority of the apostles came directly from the Lord, but the authority of the bishops and deacons which the Church chose for itself was to be the Gospel of our Lord. It was at this point that it was recognized that the gospel had to be put in written form. Up to this time traditions of the words and works of Jesus had circulated orally, but as more and more Church leaders had no living memory of Jesus or even of the apostles and

17. It is hard to decide whether the phrase "the Gospel" means a written Gospel or an oral Gospel or both. Rordorf and Tuilier are inclined toward a written Gospel, *La Doctrine*, p. 194 n. 4.

18. This phrase, "bishops and deacons," has evoked a number of questions. Are we dealing with a period in the history of the Church which knew only bishops and deacons? Why are elders not mentioned? Does the term "bishop" include elders? While there are a great number of opinions on this subject, certain things seem to be clear. The monarchical episcopate as we find it in Ignatius of Antioch had not yet appeared in the Church which produced the *Didache*. More than likely in this Church the word "bishop" was used to refer to those who in the Christian community fulfilled the function of elders in the Jewish community. In other words, the two terms were synonymous. See Rordorf and Tuilier, *La Doctrine*, pp. 73-78.

19. *Didache* 15.1-4, using the translation of Lake, *The Apostolic Fathers*, 1:331.

fewer and fewer preachers seemed to be inspired directly by the Holy Spirit, the authority of a written gospel was needed to succeed to and fulfill the authority of the Law of Moses.

The Gospel of Matthew gives every indication of being written to fulfill this need. Jesus is presented as the one who came to fulfill the Law. Furthermore, Matthew is written in such a way that the books of the Law are a type of the ministry of Jesus. Matthew makes a strong use of typology. Biblical scholars have shown again and again that, for example, the sojourn in Egypt, the baptism in the Jordan, and the Sermon on the Mount all fulfill types found in the books of Moses. Jesus is clearly the Moses of the new and eternal covenant and the Gospel of Matthew is the book of the new and eternal covenant. In fact, one wonders if "the School of Matthew," that is, those who put together the Gospel of Matthew as we know it today, did not have the intention of producing for their Church a Christian Torah. They realized that liturgically they needed a written Gospel to succeed to the written Law.

Already in the writings of the New Testament we find that the gospel is being understood as the law of Christ. In fact, this is clearly stated in no less a place than Galatians, where Paul exhorts us to bear one other's burdens and in so doing fulfill the law of Christ (6:2). We have already spoken of the way the Epistle of James speaks of the gospel as the law of liberty and the royal law. And as we said at that point, these phrases opened the way for setting the reading of the Gospels and Epistles next to the Law and the prophets in Christian worship.[20]

It did not take the Church very long to understand the gospel as the law of Christ, the Christian Torah. As we find this phrase "the Gospel of our Lord" in chapter 15 of the *Didache,* it seems basically to mean the gospel as preached by Jesus and the apostles, and yet it probably means more. The point has often been made that the Church was realizing that

---

20. To be sure it would be some time before the term "epistles" would come to have the meaning it has for liturgists today. We begin to see the term "gospel" being used in a way very similar to its liturgical meaning already here in the *Didache,* but the term "epistle" is no way near in sight. It was, however, this same process which would lead to a twofold division of the New Testament Scriptures into Gospels and Epistles. The liturgical necessity of balancing the Law and the prophets with the Gospels and Epistles would lead the Church to divide the New Testament Scriptures into the Gospels and Epistles. For a brief account of the origin of the liturgical Gospels and Epistles, see Josef Andreas Jungmann, *Missarum sollemnia,* 5th ed., 2 vols. (Wien, Freiburg, and Basel: Herder, 1962), 1:501-16.

this oral gospel had to be written down just as the Law of Moses had been written down. The point we would make is that the reading of the law of Christ was a liturgical necessity. Furthermore, we would suggest that the Gospel of Matthew and perhaps the Epistle of James were written to fill that need. If the gospel of Christ had indeed a greater authority than the Law of Moses, then the gospel of Christ had to be solemnly read in worship just as the Law of Moses was, in such a way that the Law and the prophets prepared the way for the gospel of Christ and the witness of the apostles. When one thinks of the liturgical necessity involved, one can well imagine that the Gospels could have been written quite intentionally to serve as Scripture. It was all in accordance with the gospel that there should be a reading of the Gospel to fulfill the reading of the Law.[21]

Theologians, especially liberal theologians, may find this hard to imagine. The Enlightenment envisioned that those who produced the writings of the New Testament never thought of themselves as writing Holy Scripture, but that in time it was recognized as divinely inspired. This explanation seemed quite obvious, especially in relation to the epistles of Paul. For the Enlightenment what could be more reasonable! The writings of the New Testament, it was maintained, were produced by perfectly natural causes, but later they were endowed with supernatural authority. Today, however, we might well ask whether this was really the way it happened, or at least whether it was always the case. Could not the Gospel of Matthew as well as some of the other New Testament books have been written quite intentionally to fill the liturgical need of the worshiping Christian community?

Surely we do not want to suggest that the Word of God came "by the will of man" (II Pet. 1:21, KJV). Surely we would want to insist that in the end it was God who inspired Matthew to pick up his pen and write out what he knew of the words and works of Jesus. Surely we would want to affirm that the Holy Spirit guided the thoughts of Matthew and any who worked with him in producing the Gospel that bears his name. That all goes without saying. All we would suggest is that the Church which produced the *Didache* saw that in accordance with the gospel they were accustomed to hear preached, the Law had now been superseded by the gospel and therefore it was appropriate in the service of the Word to follow

---

21. As Norbert Lohfink has suggested, Deuteronomy was written to be read as Scripture, so it may well be that Matthew came to us in much the same way. See the section on Deuteronomy above.

the solemn reading of the Law with the solemn reading of the gospel. Certainly one reason the gospel was written out was that it might be read in worship.

In what the *Didache* tells us about the reading and preaching of Scripture in the ancient Christian Church, we are given a rather remarkable theology of preaching. We indicated earlier that the *Didache* has a very high regard for the ministry of the Word. In fact, according to the *Didache,* the bishops and deacons are to be honored because of their sacred service to the Church. This service is the same as that of the prophets and teachers.[22] Certainly this would indicate that the essential service or ministry of the bishops and even the deacons was preaching and teaching.[23] The Greek word for service or ministry at this point is λειτουργία, which is the word used for the priestly service of the Levitical priesthood. Here we find the same idea we found in Paul's letter to the Romans (Rom. 15:16), that the ministry of the New Testament is the ministry of the gospel. Again we find the same idea when the *Didache* speaks of the prophets and teachers as being the high priests of the Church.[24] Here the Greek word ἀρχιερύς is used, which in the New Testament is used for the Zadokite priesthood.[25] Clearly the *Didache* understands the ministry as above all the ministry of preaching and teaching. For the *Didache* it is by means of the ministry of the Word that Christ is present in the congregation. Apostles and prophets are to be received as the Lord.[26] This is in accordance with the words of Jesus in the Gospel, " 'He who receives you receives me'" (Matt. 10:40).[27] This is made even more explicit when the catechumens are told to honor their teachers as the Lord, because where the things of the Lord are spoken, there the Lord is present, γὰρ ἡ κυριότες λαλεῖται ἐκεῖ κυριός ἐστιν.[28] This is a very strong statement,

---

22. *Didache* 15.1.

23. That the deacons are thought of as preachers and teachers may be a bit surprising to us. The *Didache* may have had nothing more in mind than that the deacons read the Scripture lessons and perhaps teach catechumens. On the other hand, we find in Acts that two deacons, Philip and Stephen, did some significant preaching, especially to those outside the Church. One might well expect a Jewish Christian congregation to charge the deacons with the spiritual care of strangers.

24. *Didache* 13.3.

25. Niederwimmer, *Die Didache,* p. 231.

26. *Didache* 11.2.

27. *Didache* 11.1-3.

28. *Didache* 4.1.

but apparently Christ's presence in the worshiping congregation is understood to be by means of the teaching and preaching of the Word of God.[29] While in later centuries the Church came to think of Christ as being present by means of the consecration of the bread and wine of the Eucharist, the *Didache* understands that presence in terms of the preaching of the Word of God. If we may put it succinctly, the *Didache* teaches a doctrine of the real presence which is kerygmatic rather than eucharistic.

B. Justin Martyr's Apology (ca. 100–ca. 165)

Justin Martyr is the first Christian to give us a description of a service of Christian worship which makes clear the actual order of service.[30] Coming from the middle of the second century, his description, while brief, helps us see how the reading and preaching of the Scriptures fit into the actual service of worship.

Justin Martyr is supposed to have been born in Samaria sometime in the early second century. He was raised in paganism, however, and as a young man studied the different schools of pagan philosophy. At last he embraced Christianity as the true philosophy. As it was done in that day he set himself up as a private teacher of philosophy, yet it was Christian philosophy that he taught. As Justin saw it, Christianity fulfilled the aspirations of classical philosophy. For a number of years he lived and taught in Ephesus, where he held his famous disputation with Trypho the Jew. About 150 he appeared in Rome, where he wrote two apologies, one to the Roman emperor and another to the Roman Senate. He also wrote his *Dialogue with Trypho,* which, based on the disputation in Ephesus,

---

29. Rordorf and Tuilier translate, ". . . car, à l'endoit d'où sa souveraineté est annoncée, là est le Seigneur." *La Doctrine,* pp. 157-59.

30. For the English text, see *The Ante-Nicene Fathers* (Grand Rapids: Wm. B. Eerdmans Publishing Co., 1969), 1:186. See also Bard Thompson, *Liturgies of the Western Church* (Cleveland and New York: The World Publishing Company, 1961), pp. 3-10. Among the more important studies of the document, see Jungmann, *Missarum sollemnia,* 1:29ff.; Othmar Perler, "Logos und Eucharistie nach Justinus I Apol. c. 66," *Divus Thomas* 18 (Freiburg, 1940): 296-316; and Johannes Quasten et al., *Patrology,* 4 vols. (Utrecht and Antwerp: Spectrum Publishers; Westminster, Md.: The Newman Press and Christian Classics, 1966-94), 1:196-219. For the original Greek text, see Anton Hängi and Irmgard Pahl, *Prex eucharistica, textus e variis liturgiis, antiquioribus selecti* (Fribourg: Éditions universitaires, 1968), pp. 68-74.

discusses the differences between Christianity and Judaism. The two apologies and the dialogue balance each other, the one thinking out the essence of Christianity over against Judaism, the other over against paganism.

Rather than winning the tolerance of the pagans, Justin's *Apology* seems to have been sufficiently provocative that the Cynic philosopher Crescens denounced Justin to the state. Refusing to sacrifice to the pagan gods, Justin was executed, sealing his witness in martyrdom.

Justin is of special interest for the history of Christian worship because at the end of his first apology he describes the service of worship for us. The part which has to do with the ministry of the Word goes as follows:

> And on the day called Sunday, all who live in cities or in the country gather together to one place, and the memoirs of the apostles and the writings of the prophets are read, as long as time permits: then when the reader has ceased, the president verbally instructs, and exhorts to the imitation of these good things.[31]

Although brief, this text is most informative. We notice that "The memoirs of the apostles and the writings of the prophets are read, as long as time permits." Scholars have discussed at great length just what can be deduced from this. Are we to infer that there are two lessons, one from the Gospels and another from the prophets? Perhaps, but then we may be more prudent to understand the sentence generally, and draw from it that a number of lessons were read from both the Old Testament and New Testament Scriptures. The word "prophets" may simply mean the writers of the Old Testament books as it obviously does in Hebrews 1:1, and the phrase "memoirs of the apostles" probably refers to the writings of the New Testament as a whole. The practice, which we find sometime later, of reading a lesson from the Law, a lesson from the prophets, a lesson from the New Testament Epistles, and finally a lesson from the Gospels may already have been in practice. Surely we are not to press out of these words that neither the Law of Moses nor the New Testament Epistles were read at worship. The suggestion that the Church replaced the reading of the Law with the reading of the Gospels, especially on the Lord's Day, and that they retained the reading of the prophets because they so clearly spoke

---

31. Justin Martyr, *Apology* 1.67. The translation is quoted from *The Ante-Nicene Fathers,* 1:186. This text will serve as the basis for the discussion in the following paragraphs.

of Christ does not hold up because early Christians understood the Law to speak of Christ just as clearly. As we shall see, many of the sermons which have come down to us from the early days assume a lesson from the Law of Moses.

We can probably infer from Justin's phrase "as long as time permits" that a considerable amount of time was devoted to reading these lessons. This would, of course, be necessary because not many Christians could afford handwritten copies of the Scriptures. If people were going to hear the Scriptures, they would have to hear them in the service of worship. But there was more to it than that. The reading of God's Word was no doubt thought of as honoring God. It was of the essence of the service of worship. To listen to God's Word served God's glory. We will find this idea again and again through the history of Christian worship, just as we found it in the worship of the synagogue. One thing at least is clear from this brief sentence: By the middle of the second century the writings of both the Old Testament and the New Testament were read in worship side by side as Holy Scripture.

As regards preaching, Justin is equally brief. He tells us simply that after the reading of Scripture, the one presiding instructs and exhorts the congregation to the imitation of these excellent things. From this we gather first that the sermon was based on the lessons, and second, that it was primarily a discourse on the virtuous life. In view of our other sources, this appears to be a rather one-sided view of the sermon. Nothing is said about proclaiming Christ as savior or about his being the fulfillment of the Law and the prophets. This is probably because Justin, who is after all writing this apology to the pagan world of his day, figures that discourses on the moral life would win the approval of his audience. It is probably the case that Christian preachers, who more and more addressed themselves to Greeks and Romans who at their best were interested in the cultivation of virtue, began to give greater and greater attention to this subject because that was what their congregations were interested in. Wise preachers in any age know how to speak to the issues of the time. On the other hand, Justin's dialogue with Trypho the Jew shows much more interest in showing Jesus as the fulfillment of the Old Testament Scriptures. It would be a mistake therefore to imagine that in Justin's day the apostolic proclamation of the gospel had degenerated into nothing more than a discourse on virtue.

We also notice from Justin's very brief description of Christian worship that a reader reads the Scriptures and the one who presides at the service then gives a sermon on the readings. Unlike the service of worship in the synagogue where several different people take turns reading the Scriptures, only one reader reads the lessons, after which only one preacher, a different person from the reader, preaches. It is not specifically stated that the preacher is the bishop; in fact, even though the word "deacon" is used, the word "bishop" seems to be avoided. Nevertheless, one gets the impression that the preacher is the leader of the Church, the authority figure. From several larger churches we have evidence that in the second century the leadership of the Church was collegial and that the worship assembly was presided over by a group of elders, some of whom took turns preaching. We even hear that at a single service there were different sermons on different lessons. This practice of having a variety of preachers in a single church would follow more naturally from the synagogue practice, but the Church was moving in a different direction. It was moving toward investing the preaching office in a single figure who would eventually be called the bishop. It must be noted, however, that this tendency, however strong it may have become, never became an invariable law. As we shall see, only one of the four preachers whose sermons have been preserved from the second and third centuries was clearly a bishop, namely, Melito.

One wonders what might have given rise to this tendency to invest the preaching office in those who presided over the Church. Why is it that Church leadership and the ministry of preaching are so closely bound up together? Was it the idea that God rules over his kingdom through his Word? This is fundamentally a christological insight and typical of a logos theology; the Father invests the power and authority to rule the kingdom in the person of the Son. It is the Word of God as revealed in Christ which both calls the Church into existence and shapes its direction. Those who exercise leadership in the Church must therefore be ministers of the Word. A minister of the Word rules best when interpreting and applying the Word.

Also of interest is why one person reads the Scriptures and another preaches the interpretation. The ancient Church retained this from the liturgical practice of the synagogue. It can probably be explained by the great care the synagogue took to preserve the accuracy of the written text. The rabbis had such a high regard for the authority of the written Word of God that they wanted to make clear the distinction between what was Scripture and what was interpretation of Scripture. The reader read Scripture; the preacher interpreted it. This is a very wise precaution even today. It too often happens when the reading of Scripture is left to the preacher that the Scripture lessons get swallowed by the sermon. The dynamic between the Word and the interpretation of the Word gets lost.

Another remarkable feature of this short description of Christian worship is that preaching is closely linked with Sunday worship. "And on the day which is called Sunday, all who live in the cities or in the country gather together to one place. . . ." The assumption seems to be that the reading and preaching of Scripture is essential to the observance of the Lord's Day. It has often been noticed that in so many of the earliest records of Christian worship the point is prominently made that Christian worship is held on the Lord's Day. This was not a minor feature but a primary feature.[32] Just as the reading and preaching of the book of the covenant was essential to the solemn assembly at Sinai, so the reading and preaching of the Word of God was essential to the solemn assemblies of the Christian Church. This solemn assembly, this coming together in one place, was what sanctified the Christian Sabbath.

Justin's description of Christian worship is very short and tells us much, but there is also much that it does not tell us. Even at that one thing is very clear: the reading and preaching of Scripture was central to Christian worship. There were prayers. The sacraments were celebrated as well. The reading and preaching of Scripture, however, were given plenty of time and plenty of attention.

C. Tertullian (ca. 150–ca. 225)

A generation or so later another apologist, Tertullian, gives us a brief description of Christian worship.[33] The actual order of service is not reported, but several indications are given as to what happened in the typical worship service.[34] In speaking about the reading and preaching of the Scriptures Tertullian tells us, "We come together for the solemn

---

32. Willy Rordorf, "Origine et signification de la célébration du dimanche dans le Christianisme primitif. Etat actuel de la recherche," *La Maison-Dieu* 148 (Paris, 1981): 103-22. Also found in Rordorf, *Liturgie, foi et vie des premiers chrétiens,* pp. 29-48.

33. For a more general survey of the work of Tertullian, see Timothy D. Barnes, *Tertullian: A Historical and Literary Study* (Oxford: Clarendon Press, 1971); Quasten, *Patrology,* 2:246-383; Robert D. Sider, *Ancient Rhetoric and the Art of Tertullian* (London: Oxford University Press, 1971).

34. Quite consistent with Tertullian's epigrammatic style we have a number of short remarks about the service of worship scattered through his many works. For a comprehensive study of these, see Eligius Dekkers, *Tertullianus en der Geschiedenis der Liturgie* (Brussels: De Kinkhoren, 1947).

recounting of the divine words to consider what might be intimated or learned about the quality of the present time. To be sure, by these sacred words we nurture faith, we inspire hope, we establish piety, we make discipline more intense by the teaching of definite moral principles."[35] This is a very rich description of Christian preaching, and no translation will do it justice. Tertullian was a master of Latin prose, and part of his art was using words in very imaginative ways so that in a few words many things are suggested. Consequently, when he speaks about coming together for the solemn recounting of the divine words, more is meant than simply the reading of sacred Scripture. Of the very essence of the coming together of the Christian assembly of worship as Tertullian presents it is the concern to be taught by the divine Word. This is a clear indication that Tertullian, typical of Christians during the second and third centuries, understands worship from the standpoint of a logos Christology. Central to the way we relate to Christ, according to this approach, is the relation of student to teacher. Christ is the divine Word; therefore, we must be his disciples, sit at his feet, and learn from him. We must learn both how to live here on earth and how to relate to the mysteries of eternity. The logos Christology is firmly based on the Wisdom theology of the Old Testament; it is committed to a strong bond between piety and learning. The logos Christology implies a very distinct approach to the theology of worship.

One gets the idea from Tertullian's brief statement that in the reading and preaching of the Scriptures there is a sacred memorial of the divine revelation.[36] It is a memorial, however, in which the eternal Word of God speaks to the present day. Liturgical scholars have often made the point that commemoration is more than merely remembering. This is particularly evident in those two fundamental passages of Scripture which speak of worship, namely, the fourth commandment, "'Remember the sabbath day, to keep it holy'" (Exod. 20:8), and the words of Jesus at the Last Supper, "'Do this in remembrance of me'" (I Cor 11:24). That worship is a sacred memorial is a basic biblical concept. What is so very significant

35. "Coimus ad litterarum divinarum commemorationem, si quid praesentium temporum qualitas aut praemonere cogit aut recognoscere. Certe fidem sanctis uocibus pascimus, spem erigimus, fiduciam figimus, disciplinam praeceptorum nihilominus inculcationibus densamus." *Apology* 34.3. For the Latin text of Tertullian's *Apology*, see *Tertullien, Apologétique, texte établi et traduit*, ed. Jean-Pierre Waltzing, 10th ed. (Paris: "Les Belles Lettres," 1961).

36. "Coimus ad litterarum divinarum commemorationem."

is that here Tertullian speaks of Christian worship as a commemoration or memorial of the divine Word.

What a powerful idea! It is not just the mighty acts of God for our salvation, the *mirabilia Dei,* which are recounted and celebrated in worship. Worship is also recounting and remembering the Word of God, and celebrating the statutes and ordinances of the covenant as well. We will often have occasion to speak of Tertullian's covenantal theology of worship. Here is a very distinct expression of that theology. Fundamental to Christian worship is coming together *ad litterarum divinarum commemorationem,* the solemn remembering of the Word of God.

Furthermore, one gets the impression that this festive hearing of the eternal gospel is an act of the whole congregation, not merely something performed by lectors and preachers. The repeated use of verbs in the first person plural, "we come together, . . . we nurture faith, we inspire hope," indicates that the reading and preaching of the Scriptures is a community event. Much contemporary criticism of the importance of preaching in worship overlooks just this point. Preaching does not have to be an individualistic sort of activity. In fact, great preaching well understands this. The true preacher is not over against the Christian congregation but rather is an expression of the congregation. The true Christian preacher affirms the faith of the congregation, and raises up the hope of the congregation. Much of the genius of great preachers is their ability to express the faith of the people to whom they are preaching.

For Tertullian the recounting of sacred history clearly speaks to the present day. The biblical history is studied to see "what might be intimated or learned about the quality of the present time." Here is another basic biblical principle which has tremendous implications for the way Christian worship is shaped. Because God reveals himself in history, the recounting of that sacred history as it is found in the Bible enlightens the present time. In Deuteronomy and in both the former prophets and the later prophets we find the same thing. In the biblical tradition sacred history is an indispensable teacher. The prophetic dimension of the ancient traditions is understood very well by Tertullian.

The reading and preaching of Scripture, which Tertullian's carefully chosen words never allow to be separated, has a pastoral function. "By these sacred words we nurture faith." Literally the text reads "we pasture faith." For Tertullian the sermon is far more than a discourse on virtue! It is a means of grace and yet, "we make discipline more intense by the teaching of moral principles."

271

Tertullian gives another description of Christian worship, even briefer than the one in the *Apology,* in which he tells us that among the sacred services of the Lord's Day the Scriptures are read, the psalms are sung, sermons are preached, and prayers are offered.[37] We do not read from this that this was all that took place; a careful reading of Tertullian teaches us about many of the elements of early Christian worship, including the celebration of baptism and the conduct of public prayer.[38] All we would want to draw from these brief words is that at the end of the second century the reading and preaching of Scripture had a prominent place in the worship of Christian churches.

What always impresses one about Tertullian is his vitality. Sometimes this vitality is expressed in a moral rigorism which is hard for the mainline American Protestant to appreciate, but it also expresses itself in flashes of genius which illumine the profundity of early Christianity. Tertullian was a puritan in the same sense that John Chrysostom, or John Calvin, was a puritan; he was very moral and very literate, and the two seem to have a relationship.

Tertullian is the first Latin Christian writer from whom we have a significant amount of material. He is a brilliant writer whose most distinctive, fascinating style gives him a place in the history of Latin literature quite apart from his interest for the Christian historian. Although some find his style a bit too clever — it is often hard to read and almost impossible to translate — in his day that was what passed for literate Latin. He was a great writer, but we have no idea if he ever preached. Apparently he had an impressive career as a lawyer, which would indicate that he could have preached if that had been what God had called him to do. Perhaps church authorities hesitated to ask him. Perhaps the leadership of the church of Carthage could not deal with the presence of a man of such obvious gifts. Then again, it may have been that his style was considered too intricate or obscure. On the other hand, perhaps he did preach frequently. We really don't know.

What Tertullian does demonstrate, though, is that even at the end

37. "Inter dominica sollemnia . . . prout scriptura legentur aut psalmi canuntur aut allocutiones proferuntur aut petitiones delegantur . . ." *De anima* 9. Tertullian is actually speaking about the worship of a Montanist congregation, but we can no doubt assume that what he says would go for an orthodox congregation as well.

38. See Tertullian's treatises *De baptismo* and *De oratione dominica.* In addition see the frequently discussed third chapter of *De corona.* An especially good edition of the *De corona* with helpful notes on the liturgical passages is the one edited by Jacques Fontaine: *Q. Septimi Florentis Tertulliani, De corona* (Paris: Presses universitaires de France, 1966).

of the second century Christians were giving attention to the cultivation of the literary arts. How often this accompanies a healthy preaching ministry! Tertullian was hardly an isolated phenomenon. From a literary standpoint he was not unlike his Greek-speaking contemporary, Clement of Alexandria. He, too, cultivated the literary arts in his famous school. Tertullian is the founder of Latin Christian literature, a literature which would be a major vehicle for the reading and preaching of the Scriptures century after century. The Latin Christian literature Tertullian did so much to bring into existence would produce an outstanding Bible, and an outstanding idiom for preaching. Tertullian's great sensitivity to language began to make it possible for Christian preachers to preach effectively in a new language. The Christian Latin we begin to meet in the writings of Tertullian was destined to become one of the most important vehicles the ministry of the Word has ever had.

D. Hippolytus (ca. 170–ca. 236)

Hippolytus had quite another kind of personality. Whereas Tertullian is brilliant and sparkling, Hippolytus, who comes almost a generation later, is just plain stodgy. He is not so much a rigorist as a stickler for details, often putting the emphasis on matters of tertiary interest. Fine points of theology escaped him; he simply was not very perceptive as a thinker. He sallied forth to attack one heresy and yet unwittingly fell into the opposite heresy. He was forever at odds with his colleagues in the church of Rome, finally setting himself up as a rival to the legitimate bishop of the city and for a number of years presiding over his own sect. He must have inspired an intense personal devotion among his partisans, however, for his followers had a life-size statue made of him which has survived into our time. Today we would probably call him a divisive personality. Yet somehow Hippolytus managed to continue to regard himself as the true guardian of apostolic tradition.[39]

39. For more information on Hippolytus, see Dom Bernard Botte, ed., *La tradition apostolique de saint Hippolyte, essai de reconstruction* (Münster in Westphalia: Aschendorf, 1963); Bernard Capelle, "Hippolyte de Rome," originally in *Recherches de théologie ancienne et médiévale* 17 (1950): 145-74, reprinted in the collected works of Capelle, *Travaux liturgiques,* 3 vols. (Louvain: Centre liturgique, 1962), 2:31-70; Richard Hugh Connolly, "The Eucharistic Prayer of Hippolytus," *Journal of Theological Studies* 31:350-69; Richard Hugh Connolly, *The So-Called Egyptian Church Order* (Cambridge: University Press, 1916);

More than likely Hippolytus was born in the East. He wrote in Greek rather than in Latin. Possibly he studied in Alexandria, although he claimed to have been a student of Irenaeus. Sometime after the year 200 he appears as a leader of the Roman church. While visiting there about 212 Origen is supposed to have heard Hippolytus preach. Hippolytus liked to think he had the last word on correct doctrine, but unfortunately he pressed this to the point of attacking Pope Zephyrinus for the heresy of Modalism. Disappointed when Callistus rather than he was chosen to succeed Zephyrinus, he claimed that he was the rightful bishop of Rome. Sometime after this he published a church order which he called the *Apostolic Tradition*. One gets the impression that the work was intended to make clear that Pope Callistus was negligent in the performance of certain liturgical rites and, even worse, careless in matters of hierarchical order. The contentious spirit of Hippolytus took him even further, however, for in time he accused his rival of Sabellianism when it came to theology and laxity when it came to the penitential disciplines of the Church. Hippolytus continued his schism during the tenure of the next two bishops. Finally, the Roman state arrested both Hippolytus and Pontian, who by this time had been chosen the legitimate bishop of Rome, and sent them to the mines of Sardinia. Happily the two were reconciled about the year 235 before they joined each other in martyrdom.

The church order Hippolytus composed and gave out under the title *Apostolic Tradition* reflects the kind of churchmanship that is overly concerned with how cheese, olives, and oil are to be blessed at the Eucharist and how the evening lamps are to be lit at vespers. He goes into great detail, for example, on what kind of people can be admitted to the catechumenate — are they respectable? The ruling principle for Hippolytus seems to be propriety. And to read his remarks on baptism is to get the feeling that baptism is a series of exorcisms for chasing out the devil.

Gregory Dix, *The Treatise on the Apostolic Tradition of St. Hippolytus of Rome* (London: Alban Press, 1937); Heinrich Elfers, *Die Kirchenordnung Hippolyts von Rom* (Paderborn: Bonifacius Druckerei, 1938); Jean Michel Hanssens, *La Liturgie d'Hippolyte: Ses documents, son titulaire, ses origines et son caractère* (Rome: Pontifical Institute for Oriental Studies, 1959); M. R. P. McGuire, "Hippolytus of Rome, St.," *New Catholic Encyclopedia*, 17 vols. (Washington, D.C.: The Catholic University of America, 1967), 6:1139-41; Pierre Nautin, *Hippolyte et Josipe: Contribution à l'histoire de la litterature chrétienne au IIIe siècle* (Paris: Éditions du Cerf, 1947); Pierre Nautin, *Lettres et écrivains au IIe et IIIe siècles* (Paris: Éditions du Cerf, 1961); Quasten, *Patrology*, 2:163-207; C. C. Richardson, "The Date and Setting of the Apostolic Tradition of Hippolytus," *Anglican Theological Review* 30 (1948): 38-44; and Thompson, *Liturgies of the Western Church*, pp. 13-24.

About many of the more substantial matters of the service of worship, however, nothing is said. About the Prayer of Intercession, the major prayer of the service, about what should be included and who should lead it, Hippolytus is silent. The Eucharistic Prayer, on the other hand, he turns into a formula of consecration which begins to sound almost magical. We hear practically nothing about how the reading of Scripture is to be done, what books are to be read in worship, or what principles are to be used in interpreting them. Nothing is said about the preaching responsibilities of bishops, presbyters, or deacons. Perhaps all that was self-evident and did not need to be put down, whereas there were those who didn't bother to recite the *sursum corda* or include the Words of Institution in the Eucharistic Prayer. Hippolytus wanted to make the point that these things were all very, very important and should be done in correct order. The intellectual temper of Hippolytus was such that all these minute details were essential. He was, sad to say, a ceremonialist.

While Hippolytus does not speak of how the Scriptures are to be read and preached at the dominical service, he does give us some indications of the preaching ministry which was maintained at daily morning prayer. He admonishes the faithful to pray each day after rising and before beginning their daily work. To say morning prayers at home was acceptable by long tradition for both Christians and Jews, but Hippolytus makes the point that if there is teaching of the Word at the church, it is really better to go to the church for the refreshing of one's soul, for it is there that the Spirit flourishes.[40] What this probably means, sad to say, is that Hippolytus figures some sort of supernatural powers are connected with sacred buildings or sacred places, that when one prays in a consecrated sanctuary one avails oneself of numinous powers. A bit further on we read that the deacons and presbyters are to gather each day at the place their bishop appoints. When all are gathered together, they are to teach those who are found at the church.[41] This information is elaborated in some manuscripts by explaining why it is important to attend these daily services. In the first place it helps one avoid any evils which might fall upon one during the day. Besides that, those who speak are given something to say which is useful for each one, one learns things one does not know, and one profits from what the Holy Spirit gives through those who instruct.[42]

---

40. Hippolytus, *Apostolic Tradition* 35.
41. Hippolytus, *Apostolic Tradition* 39.
42. Hippolytus, *Apostolic Tradition* 41.

From these passages one gathers that morning prayer was held regularly at the church and normally included the reading of the Word, some sort of preaching and teaching of the Word, and the saying of prayers. In some churches, evidently, preaching was not offered every day. Village churches may not have had daily preaching or may have had it only twice or three times a week. The same was probably true for smaller neighborhood churches in the city. About this we can only make conjectures. What is clear is that there was a tradition of daily prayer services at the church, especially in the larger churches, which included the preaching of the Word. It is often argued that these were primarily catechetical services, but this does not appear to be the case. A careful reading of the text shows that it is the faithful, that is, the baptized members of the Church, who are admonished to attend.[43] The presbyters and deacons are also supposed to attend.[44] Their attendance would hardly be required if it were only catechetical instruction. Besides, Hippolytus does say the particularly fervent were there regularly.[45]

Aside from this issue, Hippolytus does inform us about the way catechetical preaching fit into the regular worship of the Church. Earlier in the document Hippolytus speaks of catechumens hearing the Word for three years before being baptized, but this evidently means they are to attend the regular preaching services of the Church, which the faithful attend as well. There were, on the other hand, special times for the instruction of the catechumens when, presumably, they were given the introductory instruction, but Hippolytus is not too clear about this. From the description given of how converts were admitted to the catechumenate we learn that they met with their teachers before the usual congregation arrived. At the first meeting they were questioned as to why they wanted to become Christians.[46] Presumably the actual catechetical instruction could be held at this time on other days. A bit further on we read of the prayers for the catechumens. There we are told that the teacher of the catechumens, whether he be a minister of the Church or not, after he has finished the instruction, is to lay hands on the catechumens, pray for them, and dismiss them.[47]

---

43. Hippolytus, *Apostolic Tradition* 35, 41.
44. Hippolytus, *Apostolic Tradition* 39.
45. Hippolytus, *Apostolic Tradition* 41.
46. Hippolytus, *Apostolic Tradition* 15.
47. Hippolytus, *Apostolic Tradition* 18, 19.

One gets the impression that Hippolytus has in mind that catechetical instruction was held before the regular preaching service, and that when this instruction was finished prayers were said for the catechumens and each one presented himself or herself to the teacher for the laying on of hands and a blessing. These blessings were probably given as the faithful were gathering in the church for the regular service, after which the catechumens retired to that section of the church reserved for them and remained for the first part of the regular service, that is, for the reading and preaching of the Scriptures, but then were dismissed before the prayers of the faithful and the celebration of the Eucharist. Most of the time, the catechumens, as it would appear from Hippolytus, got no special instruction. They heard the regular sermon and that was considered sufficient.

From Hippolytus, then, we can gather both that there was regular daily preaching for the faithful and also special daily preaching for the catechumens, for a limited period of time and at certain seasons of the year.

There is one more point. We have already touched on it, but there is more to say, because it is an important point for understanding the character of this whole document. The reasons Hippolytus gives for encouraging the faithful to attend the regular service are for the most part simply superficial. One of his reasons, however, is rather disturbing: Saying one's prayers at church helps one avoid the evils of the day. Does this mean that going to church at the beginning of each day helps keep the devil at bay? Judging by all the attention Hippolytus gives to exorcising candidates for baptism, one is tempted to imagine this to be the case. But however scandalized one may or may not be, this is not the point. The point is that Hippolytus sees attending sermons as one of those religious acts which ingratiate one with divine power. This is a rather disappointing viewpoint. To be sure those who first read this work may have found this a convincing argument, especially if they were still influenced by the sorcery and superstition of the paganism which prevailed at the time. But for others of us it sounds like nothing less than magic.

Ever since Gregory Dix published his interpretation of the history of Christian worship, *The Shape of the Liturgy*, it has been fervently believed that Hippolytus should be the starting point for the ecumenical discussion of liturgical reform. At this point in our study such an assumption seems more than questionable.

II. The First Christian Sermons

One of the principles which has guided this study from the very beginning is that the proper source literature for our study should be sermons. In the last few pages we have departed from this because the four documents we studied were so important for the period. Few sermons have come down from those early days, and those four documents give us the context we need to help us understand the few sermons which have survived. Now let us turn our attention to those sermons: a sermon from Corinth preached less than a century after the preaching ministry of Jesus, an Easter sermon of Melito of Sardis preached a generation later, a sermon of Clement of Alexandria preached at the end of the second century, and, of course, the large collection of sermons from Origen, preached early in the third century. These are very rich sources. They show considerable variety and are most interesting in themselves, but when looked at together they give us a recognizable picture.

A. A Sermon from the Church of Corinth (ca. 125)

We begin with what is commonly called the *Second Epistle of Clement.*[48] It is generally agreed that it is neither a work of Clement of Rome nor a letter. It is rather a sermon; in fact, it is frequently claimed as the first Christian sermon to have come down to us.[49] The fact that it is a real sermon is very clear at one point where the preacher tells his congregation that, having read the word of truth to them, he would now exhort them to take this word to heart and so attain salvation.[50] In other words, they have heard the Scripture lesson; now they will hear a sermon on that lesson.[51] While nothing in the

---

48. For the Greek text and English translation of *II Clement*, see Lake, *The Apostolic Fathers*, 1:128-63.

49. For a very thorough discussion of these questions, see the recent work of Ernst Baasland, "Der 2. Klemensbrief, und frühchristliche Rhetorik: 'Die erste christliche Predigt im Licht der neueren Forschung,'" in *Aufstieg und Niedergang der Römischen Welt*, ed. W. Haase and H. Temporini (Berlin: Walter de Gruyter, 1993), 27:79-157.

50. *II Clement* 19.1.

51. The Greek text runs as follows: Ὥστε, ἀδελφοὶ καὶ ἀδελφαί, μετὰ τὸν θεὸν τῆς τοῖς ἀληθείας γεγραμμένοις, ἵνα καὶ ἑαυτοὺς σώοητε καὶ τὸν ἀναγινώσκοντα ἐν ὑμῖν. Surely ἀναγινώσκω in this context means to go over again, enlarge upon, or exhort, rather than read aloud a sermon which he had previously written.

document allows us to date it precisely, the general opinion is that it must have been written in the first half of the second century. As for the authorship, the suggestion most frequently made is that it was preached by one of the elders of the church at Corinth. This would explain why it was preserved with the genuine Epistle of Clement, which had been addressed to the church of Corinth at the close of the first century and was no doubt kept for a long time in the archives of that church. While the sermon offers little in the way of literary refinement, it is well organized and carefully thought out. It is a direct and clear presentation of the Christian faith and worthy of our most careful attention.

The introduction of the sermon is an exhortation to praise Jesus Christ as God and to have the highest regard for the salvation that he has conferred upon us.[52] Our preacher asks what praise then should we offer to him who has bestowed such mercy upon us. This introduces the text:

"Sing, O barren one, who did not bear;
 break forth into singing and cry aloud,
 you who have not been in travail!
For the children of the desolate one will be more
 than the children of her that is married, says the LORD."

              (Isa. 54:1)

The preacher follows this with an outline of the interpretation he intends to develop.[53] He explains that this is addressed to the Church, which had been barren before children were given to her. In being admonished to cry to God we are being encouraged to praise God with sincerity. In saying that the children of the desolate have increased, the Scriptures are speaking of the marvelous growth of the Church. Presumably the preacher understands the contrast to be between the Christian Church made up largely of Gentiles and the Jewish synagogue. One notices that an ethnic distinction is avoided. A second text, taken from the Gospels, is brought to the primary text: "'I came not to call the righteous, but sinners'" (Matt. 9:13 and par., Mark 2:17, and Luke 5:32).[54] This second text, or auxiliary text, is the key to the interpretation our preacher intends to make. Again we see the homiletical method of the synagogue at work.

52. *II Clement* 1.1.
53. *II Clement* 2.
54. *II Clement* 2.

The sermon is developed by a series of comments on how the Church is to rejoice before God.[55] First we are to confess Christ before men. Our preacher quotes the words of Jesus, " 'So every one who acknowledges me before men, I also will acknowledge before my Father' " (Matt. 10:32), and explains that we confess Christ not only with our lips but with our hearts and minds.[56] Jesus had said that not everyone who cries "Lord, Lord" will be saved, but rather the one that does righteousness (Matt. 7:21). We confess Christ by doing good, by loving one another, and by following the commandments. Again the preacher illuminates his text by a saying of Jesus, " 'You shall be lambs in the midst of wolves' " (Matt. 10:16). The rejoicing of Christians is not hindered by the tribulations of this world but consists rather in turning away from this world.[57] Still another saying of Jesus is recalled, " 'No man can serve two masters' " (Matt. 6:24). This, the preacher tells us, shows that the Christian must leave behind the things of the world and dwell in the world to come. To support this admonition two examples are given. These examples are rather stereotyped, the sort that were the stock-in-trade of Hellenistic oratory, whether in a Diaspora synagogue or the Roman forum.[58] First he speaks of the way those who enter sailing contests must persevere to the end in order to win the prize; second of how clay in the hands of a potter can be fashioned as long as it remains moist, but once the vessel has been put in the kiln, faults cannot be corrected. From this second example we learn that we must amend our lives while we live in this world, for after this life there will be no opportunity for repentance.[59] The Christian indeed praises God in this life by waiting for the second coming of Christ with patience and purity. This thought, as those before, is developed by several sayings of Jesus, one of which, very interestingly, comes from a source other than the canonical Gospels.

The sermon now begins to develop the Pauline interpretation of the primary text, Isaiah 54:1, which Paul quotes in Galatians 4, where he takes

---

55. Ernst Baasland has recently shown us that *II Clement* is basically a "synagogue homily," that is, a formal exposition of Scripture as it was done in the synagogue. It is, however, a loose constructionist interpretation of the synagogue tradition. "Der 2. Klemensbrief, und frühchristliche Rhetorik," pp. 99-108.

56. *II Clement* 3.

57. *II Clement* 5.

58. On rhetorical figures and literary style of *II Clement*, see Baasland, "Der 2. Klemensbrief, und frühchristliche Rhetorik," pp. 116ff.

59. *II Clement* 8.

up the subject of the spiritual Church, the heavenly Jerusalem, the mother of us all (4:25). It is this spiritual Church which conceives children according to the Spirit (4:29). Our preacher goes on about the preexistent Church, which existed before creation.[60] He reminds his congregation of the teaching of Paul's epistle to the Ephesians that the Church is the body of Christ and of the apostle's teaching in I Corinthians 6 that the body is the temple of the Holy Spirit. How great this gift of life and immortality is, and how marvelous that our human flesh can receive this gift! No mere human being can express or speak of the things which God has prepared for his elect!

Having spoken at length of how we are to praise God through the living of a righteous life, our preacher returns to his text and takes up another aspect of it. The spiritual Church is to rejoice before God in her service of worship.[61] He makes it clear that faith and love are the basis of all service of God. He commends prayer to his hearers and assures them that many great benefits come through prayer. Hearing the preaching of the elders of the Church is clearly one of these services of worship by which the Church praises God.[62] This is particularly the case when those who hear the sermon in church go home and practice what they have learned. Our preacher admonishes his congregation to gather more frequently so that they make progress in the commandments of the Lord. Coming together, as Paul admonishes, makes us all of the same mind (Rom. 12:16 and Phil. 2:2), and this glorifies God. This is even more the case because it is a witness to the heathen. The outreach of the witnessing congregation is obviously, to our preacher, an important service to God. To make the point that bearing witness to the Gentiles is a service to God he quotes Isaiah 66:18, " 'I am coming to gather all nations and tongues; and they shall come and see my glory.' "[63]

The sermon then concludes with the admonition to give thanks, to persevere in righteousness and good works, that in the end we might enjoy the immortal fruit of the resurrection.[64] He exhorts his Christian brothers and sisters in the congregation to contend in the contest of the living God, for in this life we are being trained that we may gain in the life to come

60. *II Clement* 14.
61. *II Clement* 15.
62. *II Clement* 17.
63. *II Clement* 17.
64. *II Clement* 18.

the victor's crown.[65] The sermon ends with a doxology based on I Timothy 1:17, "To the only God, the invisible, the Father of Truth, who sent forth to us the Savior and Prince of Immortality, through whom he manifested to us the truth and heavenly life, to him be glory for ever and ever. Amen."[66]

If we regret that not many sermons have come down to us from the second century, we rejoice that this sermon has. We would say about this sermon as we would about the hymns found in the *Odes of Solomon:* If other preachers in that day did as well, there must have been some excellent preaching in the second century. It is not, of course, that this sermon is such great oratory. It is rather sincere worship and solid teaching. It is a perceptive exposition of Scripture. The sermon is not only a good example of what a sermon should be in terms of structure, but even more it makes a powerful and profound point.

One of the most appealing things about this sermon is that even though we have no idea who the author was, the personal witness of the preacher comes through loud and clear. He, too, struggles against the temptations of the devil and yet he seems confident that by the grace of God he will come through it all and rejoice in eternal blessedness. As we have said, we do not know exactly who this preacher was, but one gets the impression that he was one of the college of elders of the Church of Corinth, who was well known to his congregation. We gather from both First Clement and Second Clement that the church of Corinth was still presided over by a college of elders rather than by a single bishop. Our preacher must have been one of these elders. The sermon seems to have been carefully thought out beforehand, although it probably was not written out until afterwards.[67] Our preacher has carefully worked out his interpretation. It shows a broad familiarity with the Scriptures of both the Old Testament and the New Testament. Obviously this elder gave a large portion of his time to the study of Scripture; he was not an amateur for whom the study and preaching of

---

65. *II Clement* 19.

66. *II Clement* 20.

67. Some have thought, on the basis of *II Clement* 19, that the sermon was first written and then read in the service of worship. If this were the meaning of the text, it would be the only case we know of in classical antiquity of a sermon being written out and then read to the congregation. Neither Jewish rabbis nor Greek orators worked that way. The Greek text is rather ambiguous. See note 51 above. What the preacher seems to be saying is that he is going over in his sermon the material which has just been read to them in the Scriptures and using this material as the basis for his exhortation.

the Word of God was a pious hobby. The sermon may well have been preserved in the archives of the church of Corinth out of respect for the man and out of a recognition that the message it contained was a good expression of the Christian faith at its best. One gets the impression that the life that stood behind the sermon was its greatest eloquence.

This sermon is also interesting because of what it tells us about how the second-century Church approached evangelism. It is preached to a Christian congregation and yet it is also a witness to non-Christians. That the sermon is to be understood as having an evangelistic purpose is clear from the auxiliary text chosen from the Gospels, "'I have come not to call the righteous, but sinners'" (Matt. 9:17 and par.). We see here that the Church of the second century did its evangelistic preaching in the midst of the worshiping congregation, and it was the worshiping congregation which did the evangelism. This is not an evangelism based on some sort of theology of decisional regeneration, nor one based on a theology of baptismal regeneration. It is rather an evangelism based solidly on justification by faith, on the confidence that faith comes by hearing and hearing by the Word of God. But this evangelism also puts a strong emphasis on sanctification. The Christian life is lived out of gratitude to God for the gracious gift of salvation. Non-Christians are present in the service of worship, both Jews and Gentiles, and non-Christians as well as Christians need repentance. Our sermon ends by calling all who are present to repentance. The preacher begs his listeners to repent from the bottom of their hearts that they might be saved.[68] Evangelism did not require a special message preached for the unconverted, different from the one for the converted, nor did it mandate that the faithful hear and enthusiastically support again and again evangelistic sermons that were not really directed to them. Rather, when Christ is proclaimed as Lord and Savior, when God's promises are proclaimed and a witness is given that God is faithful and that in Christ those promises have been fulfilled, and will yet be fulfilled, then evangelism is done. When this kind of preaching is done, God's people hear this witness and believe it, and believing it they praise God that this is indeed true. Whenever the way of life which Christ taught his disciples is shown to be the fulfillment of the Law and the prophets, then evangelism is done. Whenever the beauty and the power and the sheer joy of holiness are proclaimed and God's people see that this is something for them, evangelism is done. When Christian preaching is done the way it should be done, then it is evangelistic.

68. *II Clement* 19.1.

This sermon is an expository sermon in the classic sense of the term. It is an exposition and application of a passage of Scripture. It is the same sort of preaching that was done in the synagogue. One notices one significant variation. Instead of the primary text being taken from the Law, it is taken from the prophets, and instead of the secondary text being taken from the prophets, it is taken from the Gospels. As in many sermons reported in the New Testament, here is a sermon concerned with the specifically Christian interpretation of the Old Testament — which concern is also the case for many, if not the great majority, of the sermons which have come down to us from the second and third centuries. This sermon takes as its text a passage from the prophet Isaiah which is quoted and given a specifically Christian interpretation by the apostle Paul in his epistle to the Galatians. That is, the primitive Christian Church already understood it to speak of the experience of the Church. *Second Clement* passes on the tradition of the Christian interpretation of Scripture. What is particularly striking about the sermon is the way the sayings of Jesus are used again and again to interpret the Scriptures. It is Christ who teaches us what Scripture means.

This sermon gives us a very sound theology of worship and of the place of preaching in worship. If we were allowed but one document from the patristic period with which to develop a theology of worship, this document would do very well. We worship God out of gratitude for our salvation. At the beginning of the sermon the preacher asks what we are to return to God for his gracious gifts toward us. In terms of covenant theology, he tells us that we are to serve God by confessing Christ: first by living a holy life, and second by rendering to him the service of worship. The preacher first develops this in terms of praise and prayer and second in terms of preaching. The proclamation of the Word of God in the worship of the Church glorifies God, particularly when this proclamation is a witness to the heathen. We take this to mean that evangelism is worship because it proclaims the glory of God before all peoples. This is, of course, an idea frequently found in the Psalms. When the covenant people have received the gracious gifts of God, it is their covenant duty to confess before the congregation the obligation they therefore have to God, and to witness before the world the graciousness of God. From the standpoint of a covenantal theology, worship is thanksgiving for God's grace, confession of our obligation to God, and witness to God's mighty acts. This is done in prayer, in praise, and in preaching. *Second Clement* gives us a classic statement of a covenantal theology of worship. Preaching plays a major role in worship. It is of the essence of the thanksgiving we owe to God.

B. Melito of Sardis (ca. 130–ca. 190)

The second-oldest Christian sermon which has come down to us is an Easter sermon preached by Melito of Sardis about a generation later. Melito, who was bishop of Sardis in Asia Minor, was a well-known and greatly respected Christian leader at the end of the second century.[69] Although we know that he wrote a number of works, only this sermon has survived, and only very recently has it been identified.[70] In several ways it is quite different from the sermon we have just studied. It is a jubilant and festive celebration of the Christian Passover. Often appearing more like poetry than prose, it is an elaborate piece of rhetoric.

The sermon was apparently preached during the Quartodeciman celebration of Easter.[71] It follows a reading of the Passover account from the book of Exodus and possibly the Song of the Suffering Servant from Isaiah 52 and 53, adhering to the synagogue tradition of using a text from the prophets to interpret a passage from the Law. That this is the case is suggested by the fact that the first Scripture actually quoted is Isaiah 53:7, "He was as a lamb led to be sacrificed."[72] This is, to be sure, one of those key interpretations of Scripture which may very well go back to Jesus himself. It was in a very similar way, we remember, that Jesus preached on the same passage of the Law in the sixth chapter of the Gospel of John. That Jesus was the Lamb of God whose suffering atoned for the sins of the many is an idea found throughout the New Testament (Matt. 8:17; Luke 22:37; John 1:29; Acts 8:32-33; and I Pet. 2:22-25). The point that is made when Isaiah 53:7 interprets the Passover story is that it was the

---

69. For more information on Melito of Sardis, see Campbell Bonner, ed., *The Homily on the Passion* (Philadelphia: University of Pennsylvania Press, 1940); Othmar Perler, *Méliton de Sardes, Sur la pâques et Fragments*. Introduction, critical text, translation, and notes by Othmar Perler, Sources chrétiennes (Paris: Éditions du Cerf, 1966) (it is on this edition that the following study is based); and Quasten, *Patrology*, 1:242-46.

70. Campbell Bonner, who identified the sermon, renders the title, "Homily on the Passion," which is certainly justified in light of what Melito says about the meaning of Passover. On the other hand, ΠΕΡΙ ΠΑΣΧΑ, the title found most often, is probably better rendered, "On the Christian Passover." See Perler, *Sur la pâques*, pp. 16-17 and 607.

71. Wolfgang Huber, *Passa und Ostern: Untersuchungen zur Osterfeier der alten Kirche* (Berlin: Verlag Alfred Töpelmann, 1969), pp. 31-45, argues that Melito is not a supporter of the Quartodeciman position. On the other hand, see Willy Rordorf, "Zur Ursprung des Osterfestes am Sonntag," *Theologische Zeitschrift* 18 (1962): 167-89.

72. Melito, *The Christian Passover* 4.

suffering of the innocent lamb that redeemed Israel from Egypt and that here is the prophetic type of our redemption in Christ. For just as the blood of the lamb redeemed Israel from Egypt, so the suffering of Christ redeemed the Church from the sins of this world and made it possible for us to enter into the Promised Land.

The first part of the sermon is devoted to explaining the Easter typology.[73] Melito has a very particular approach to typology, at least in regard to this text. The story as it is recorded in Exodus is a sacred mystery, and it is the purpose of the sermon to explain the words of this mystery, as Melito puts it, how the lamb is sacrificed and the people are saved.[74] The mystery of the Passover is old in regard to the Law but new in regard to the Logos; temporal in regard to the type but eternal in regard to grace; corruptible in regard to the sacrifice of the lamb but incorruptible in regard to the life of the Lord.[75] After recalling at length the story of God's judgment on the Egyptians and his protection of Israel, the preacher again addresses the subject of typology. That which happened in ancient Egypt is of no significance, Melito tells us, except insofar as it prefigured an eternal reality which was then yet to be revealed.[76] All that happened and was said participate in the symbol — that which was said concerns the symbolic meaning; that which happened was by way of prefiguration.[77] With this Melito gives us an example: Just as a sculptor or an architect constructs a model in wax, wood, or clay so that one can see what is going to be constructed, so God gave the types of the Old Testament so that one could see what he was going to do. The model, of course, implies something of grander size, greater stability, more beautiful form, and richer material. But when the plans have been realized, then the model is destroyed because it is no longer of value.[78]

Once more we find ourselves facing the question of how the early Church preached the Old Testament Scriptures. Typology is obviously an important approach to this problem, and Melito's understanding of typology is distinctive. It is strongly influenced by the popular Platonism of his day. We read, for instance, that just as there are things corruptible, so

73. Melito, *The Christian Passover* 11-71.
74. Melito, *The Christian Passover* 1.
75. Melito, *The Christian Passover* 1-3.
76. Melito, *The Christian Passover* 42.
77. Melito, *The Christian Passover* 35.
78. Melito, *The Christian Passover* 35-37.

there are certainly things incorruptible, and just as there are things temporal, so there are certainly things celestial. Indeed, the salvation of our Savior, the very truth itself, has been prefigured in the nation of Israel, and the teachings of the gospel were proclaimed in advance by the Law. The nation of Israel was therefore the sketch of a plan and the Law was the words of a parable, but the gospel is the explanation of the parable and the realization of the plan.[79] Up to this point we follow Melito easily, but then he tells us that with the establishing of the Church and the proclamation of the gospel, the prefiguration has become vain and Israel has lost its reason for existence.[80] With this Melito has gone far astray from the biblical understanding of typology. We will say more about this subject.

Typology is not the only thing we find in Melito's sermon. We find another of the classical elements of Christian preaching, namely, the recital of the history of salvation. Melito tells his congregation that they have heard the explanation of the type; now he would like to speak to them of the structure of the mystery. He begins by speaking of the etymology of the name of the paschal feast.[81] The text of Exodus explains the word in terms of the angel of death passing over the children of Israel, but Melito explains the word by its similarity to the Greek word for suffering or passion. (This indeed is a most curious etymology, but it was very popular in the ancient Church.) The name of the feast, according to Melito, is not Passover but Passion.[82] With this the preacher begins his account of the story of redemption, recounting the story of the Garden of Eden, the fall of Adam and Eve, and the dreadful sufferings of the human race which followed. From among those who suffered God raised up the saints of the Old Testament as types of redemption. Isaac was bound; Joseph was sold; Moses was exposed; David was persecuted; and all the prophets suffered.

Again Melito interjects a few words on what typology is all about. The purpose of these types was to acquaint us with the pattern of the idea

---

79. Melito, *The Christian Passover* 39-40.

80. Melito, *The Christian Passover* 42-43.

81. Melito, *The Christian Passover* 46.

82. This etymology was often claimed by the ancient Church in spite of the fact that "Passover" was actually given in the text. Various attempts have been made to explain the meaning of the word. Joachim Jeremias, "πάσχα," *Theological Dictionary of the New Testament*, 5:896-904; J. C. Rylaarsdam, "Passover," *Interpreter's Dictionary of the Bible*, 3:663-68; Hans-Joachim Kraus, "Zur Geschichte des Passah-Massot-Festes im Alten Testament," *Evangelische Theologie* 18 (1958): 47-67.

so that when the full realization finally came, our understanding would have been prepared to receive it and we would accept it.[83] In each of these types one sees a part of the redemptive suffering of the Messiah who was to come. Besides these types were the prophecies which spoke of the paschal sufferings of the Messiah. Finally, these types and prophecies were realized and the Christ was born of a virgin, and, having accomplished the suffering that was prefigured, he rose from the dead and won for us liberty, light, and life.

The sermon then turns to Israel's refusal of the Savior that was sent to her.[84] Melito takes off on the ingratitude of Israel, developing it at some length. Today Christians are very sensitive about anti-Semitism. We more and more find common cause with devout Jews as we both find ourselves discriminated against by different forms of secular humanism. Whether under the neo-paganism of the Nazis or the militant atheism of the communists or the secularism of the modern liberal establishment, Christians and Jews have suffered together. Today we feel a camaraderie with faithful synagogue Jews who really do believe the Old Testament Scriptures. We are therefore embarrassed by Melito's polemic against the Jews, but something needs to be said about it nevertheless.

As we pointed out above, Melito figured that once the types of Israel had been fulfilled there was no reason for Israel to exist. The problem with that argument is that it can become an argument against the Christian use not only of Old Testament typology in Christian preaching but of the Old Testament in general. As liturgical historians are well aware, the time eventually came when the reading of the Old Testament Scriptures was largely curtailed in both the Byzantine and the Roman rites. This was a catastrophe for the life of the Church. The Church should value the continued existence of the synagogue in even the most committed of Christian communities because it is a living witness to the history of salvation. To understand fully the Christian faith one must understand the dialectic between promise and fulfillment, between the Old Testament and the New. When we drive away the synagogue we deform the Church; when we ignore the Old Testament we misunderstand the New. Right there is the problem of anti-Semitism for Christians. It simply deforms the Church. The same is true of what might be called liturgical anti-Semitism. When we ignore the text of the Old Testament, we mutilate the gospel.

83. Melito, *The Christian Passover* 57.
84. Melito, *The Christian Passover* 72ff.

All we have from Melito is this one sermon and a few fragments of other works, and in these we are not specifically told there was a New Testament reading in the service of worship. Most churches by this date had Scripture lessons from both Testaments, as we learned from Justin Martyr. What the situation in Sardis was in regard to New Testament lessons we cannot be sure; Old Testament lessons it clearly had.[85] The force of tradition in the middle of the second century was probably too strong to allow the Church simply to replace the Old Testament readings with New Testament readings. Then, too, Melito himself might well have objected to discontinuing the liturgical reading of the Old Testament. He may not have felt about all the types the way he felt about the typology implied with Passover.

There is a strange ambiguity in the sermon. It shows how essential the study of the Old Testament Scriptures is to Christian piety and that a place of great honor was given to the reading of the Old Testament in worship, and yet it seems to argue against the value of God's revelation to Israel once the gospel had been proclaimed. Here we have an approach to Scripture that ends up ignoring the Old Testament. Alas, this sort of sentiment will become stronger and stronger until the Old Testament lessons will all but disappear.

Melito's Easter sermon concludes with an offer of repentance and the forgiveness of sin. This is first made specifically to the Jews who delivered to death the one in whom there is resurrection from the dead.[86] The conclusion of the sermon is then developed into a hymnic declaration of Christ's resurrection and ascension. It is with this that the history of salvation comes to its climax. With the atoning death and victorious resurrection of Christ the purposes of God are fulfilled, and with the proclamation of these mighty acts of salvation the mystery is revealed. This is followed by an appeal to all the families of the earth to come to Christ for the remission of sin, and an elaborate concluding doxology.[87] Melito, as the apostle Paul before him, understands that first the gospel is to be offered to the Jews, and only when that has been done is it to be offered to the Gentiles. Even Melito recognizes that in the eternal councils of God a certain right of primogeniture has been given to the Jews. This the Christian who is faithful to Scripture must recognize.

85. Melito, *The Christian Passover* 1.
86. Melito, *The Christian Passover* 100.
87. Melito, *The Christian Passover* 103.

A couple comments are in order at this point. We notice first of all that even though this sermon comes at the end of the second century, it is not preached on the New Testament Scriptures. Although, as mentioned above, we cannot be sure the New Testament Scriptures were read during this service, it is clear that Melito and his congregation knew most of the New Testament. The whole sermon is permeated with Johannine theology. There are several clear allusions to I Corinthians 5:7, "Christ our Passover has been sacrificed," perhaps because it was also a traditional reading for the Christian celebration of Passover. Possibly there was a reading from the Law, the prophets, an epistle, and a Gospel as we find elsewhere.

More probably, however, we are dealing with a sermon preached at the paschal vigil where numerous Old Testament lessons were read. The opening lines of the sermon tell us that the story of the Passover has just been read from the book of Exodus and that now the preacher intends to explain the reading.[88] In the third and fourth centuries these Easter vigils were highly developed. Their main feature was the reading through of a whole series of Old Testament types. Melito's sermon would fit very well into this sort of service.

What we find most interesting of all, however, is that here we have what might be called the first Christian festal sermon. There is a real question as to whether the Christian Church of the first century observed any annual feast days at all. Again and again we find early Christians arguing that they did not observe yearly feasts but instead the weekly Lord's Day. Origen was still making this point at the beginning of the third century. And this may be why Melito argues that once the type is fulfilled it is set aside. Quite possibly the Christian observance of Passover originated in the second century rather than the first. Still, in the second and third centuries, with the emphasis on the weekly celebration of the Lord's Day, Easter and Pentecost were the only yearly feast days celebrated by the Church, and so festal preaching was limited. But here at the end of the second century we do have a festal sermon.

We know that during this period there was considerable disagreement as to the nature of the Easter celebration.[89] In Asia Minor it was the

---

88. See. G. Zuntz, "On the Opening Sentence of Melito's Paschal Homily," *Harvard Theological Review* 36 (1943): 299-315; Campbell Bonner, "A Supplementary Note on the Opening of Melito's Homily," *Harvard Theological Review* 36 (1943): 317-19.

89. On the Quartodeciman controversy, see in addition to Huber, *Passa und Ostern*, Bernhard Lohse, *Das Passafest der Quartadecimaner* (Gütersloh: C. Bertelsmann, 1953).

custom to celebrate Easter on the day after the Jewish Passover, no matter what day of the week it happened to fall on, while in other places it was celebrated on the Sunday after the Jewish Passover. Debate over this question continued for some time. Melito of Sardis, being bishop of a city in Asia Minor, would have preached his sermon according to the Quartodeciman system for reckoning Easter. We will not go into the Quartodeciman question at any length, but a few things need to be said.

Although Melito's sermon does not offer enough information to give a full explanation, it does offer a few hints on the beginnings of a Christian celebration of Passover. Before explaining this we need to note a few points about the origin of the Christian celebration of the Lord's Day. It was on the evening of the first day of the week, of the day of the resurrection of Christ, that the disciples met together in the Upper Room. On the very first Lord's Day Jesus came to them, and a week later he came to them again on the evening of the first day of the week. That apparently was the beginning of the Christian practice of Lord's Day worship, a practice that continued for the remainder of the first century. By the beginning of the second century the practice had changed so that the Lord's Day service was held on the morning of the first day of the week. We really do not know why. Possibly government regulations proscribed evening meetings of certain groups which at the time were thought of as politically dangerous. By the middle of the second century the change to morning worship was complete. Christians throughout the empire met for worship on Sunday morning. Lord's Day worship was a distinctive characteristic of Christian piety which set it off very clearly from Jewish worship. It was understood as one of the fundamental institutions of Jesus himself. This must be the case because only the authority of the Messiah himself could have changed one of the Ten Commandments. To change one of the Ten Commandments would have taken an authority greater than Moses. The establishment of the Lord's Day as the day of Christian worship seems, then, to go back to Jesus himself.[90] What about the Christian celebration of Passover?

The Christian celebration of Passover does not seem to have been

---

90. The origins of Lord's Day worship are outside our immediate subject of inquiry. It is, nevertheless, crucial to the whole subject of the beginning of Christian worship. The definitive work on the subject is that of Willy Rordorf, *Geschichte der Ruhe- und Gottesdienstages im ältesten Christentum* (Zurich: Zwingli Verlag, 1962); Eng. trans., *Sunday: The History of the Day of Rest and Worship in the Earliest Centuries of the Christian Church*, trans. A. A. K. Graham (Philadelphia: Westminster Press, 1968).

regarded as being of dominical institution. From what little we know of the earliest Christian celebrations of this feast, it seems to have developed from a pious recollection of how Jesus had kept Passover. He kept it in his Passion, and furthermore, his keeping of it had fulfilled it. We would like to know just what the apostles in Jerusalem did when the feast of Passover came around that first year after the death and resurrection of Jesus. Did they celebrate it as faithful Jews had always celebrated it? Probably not. What they probably did was come together and remember how Jesus had fulfilled the Passover, in much the same way as in Melito's sermon. One recounted the Passover story and showed how Jesus had fulfilled the feast. The first Easter sermon was a sort of Christian Passover Haggadah. Just how soon Christians made a practice of fasting during the Jewish Passover is not clear, but it was probably very early. While the Jews feasted on the evening of the fourteenth of Nisan, the Christians fasted and recounted the story of Passover and how Jesus had fulfilled it. This is the origin of the kind of Easter sermon Melito preached.

Possibly this explains Melito's very negative approach to typology. Perhaps the earliest Christians did not really think of themselves as keeping the feast of Passover. Once Passover had been fulfilled they figured it ought to be set aside; it ought to be discontinued. As we have just said, they fasted during the Passover, but while they fasted they recounted the Christian understanding of the Passover. Put simply, the earliest Christians did not celebrate Easter. Every Lord's Day they celebrated the resurrection of their crucified Lord, but a yearly feast of the resurrection they did not have.

It seems to have been somewhat later that another kind of Easter sermon appeared — an Easter sermon that proclaimed the resurrection of Christ. It had its origin in the Sunday morning services of the earliest Christians. Perhaps it was at the time when the Christians were thrown out of the synagogue that they began on the Lord's Day morning to hold a service very similar to the Sabbath morning service of the synagogue. This may have occurred a few months after Pentecost, especially in Jerusalem; in the Diaspora it may have been a few years thereafter. This Sabbath morning service had always been for Jesus and his disciples, as for all devout Jews, the principal service of worship. It was a service of praise, of prayer, and of the reading and preaching of the Scriptures. It was this sort of service which Christians regularly held on the morning of the Lord's Day. Within a very short time after Pentecost the Christians of Jerusalem had two Lord's Day services: a Sunday evening service, at which the Lord's Supper was celebrated, and a Sunday morning service, at which the Scriptures were read and preached.[91] We have echoes of both in the New Testament. First, there are the evening appearances reported in both Luke and John: at Emmaus Jesus made himself known in the breaking of bread (Luke 24:13-35); in Jerusalem he appeared to the disciples on the evening of the first day of the week (Luke 24:36-43; John 20:19-23); then he came to the disciples precisely a week later (John 20:26-29). Second, there are the morning appearances reported in Matthew, Mark, Luke, and John (Matt. 28:1-10; Mark 16:1-8; Luke 24:1-12; John 20:1-18). Jesus appeared to the women, to Peter, and to Mary Magdalene. Both in regard to the morning and the evening the Gospels make a point of telling us that it was on the first day of the week that Jesus took the initiative and met with the disciples. The implication seems to be that both the morning and the evening Lord's Day services were of dominical institution.

In those first few years in the church of Jerusalem the morning service on the first Lord's Day after the Jewish feast of Passover must have been the occasion for recounting the story of the resurrection, for it was the sign that Jesus had indeed made the passage from this world to the Father (John 13:1). When the Law and the prophets were read at the Lord's Day morning service on that Lord's Day, one would surely have made a point of showing that Christ had risen according to Scripture (I Cor. 15:4) because of its evangelistic value, if for no other reason. Every Lord's Day was a witness to the resurrection, but in Jerusalem in those early days the Lord's Day after the Jewish Passover would have been the best possible time to proclaim that Jesus had fulfilled the ancient rites. His resurrection was the sign that he had entered the kingdom, leading the way for the faithful to follow. It was then, in order to evangelize the Jews, that the earliest Christians began to make a special occasion of the Lord's Day after the Jewish Passover.

By the beginning of the second century there must have been two types of paschal services: the Christian celebration of Passover and the celebration of the resurrection on the Lord's Day. Each required its own sermon. The Christian celebration of Passover required a sermon on how Jesus fulfilled the sacred rite; the celebration of the resurrection required a sermon which celebrated the empty tomb and the resurrection appearances. While in Melito's sermon we have a very early example of a sermon for the Christian

91. It is the famous letter of Pliny to the emperor Trajan in the year 112 which most clearly indicates this twofold Sunday worship. For a full discussion of the meaning of Pliny's description, see Rordorf, *Sunday,* pp. 202ff. and 253ff.

celebration of Passover, we do not have an early example of an Easter sermon of the second type. We have to wait until the fourth century for that.

Let us notice one more thing. For Melito the Easter sermon was an occasion for proclaiming the essential core of the gospel that Christ suffered according to the Scriptures and rose according to the Scriptures, after which Melito then called the congregation to repentance and faith. We notice it is an evangelistic sermon addressed to Jew and Gentile alike, but we also notice it is to the Easter congregation that the evangelistic appeal is made. Again we point out what we pointed out in regard to *II Clement:* The proclamation of the gospel is made in the context of the worshiping congregation. If we had more examples we might be led to other conclusions, but given what we have, we are also struck by the fact that these early sermons frequently have an evangelistic thrust. The evangelistic appeal is not made in neutral territory, so to speak, but in the bosom of the Church. This had not been possible with the earliest proclamations of the gospel found in Acts, where all too often the gospel was proclaimed to a hostile crowd. At best the proclamation of the apostles was made in a synagogue. When, however, Christian congregations were established, it would appear that evangelistic preaching was done in the course of Christian worship. The gospel was not preached on the edge of the Church so much as in the center of the Church.

C. Clement of Alexandria (ca. 150-215)

Clement of Alexandria has been called the first Christian gentleman. His teaching was urbane, cultured, and devout. The literary estate he left behind is appreciable. Regrettably, however, there is but a single sermon in this rich legacy.[92] It is a very literate sermon that was probably actually preached. It has not attracted much attention among the usual sort of

92. For a concise discussion of Clement's literary legacy, see F. Prat, "Projet littéraires de Clément d'Alexandrie," *Recherches de Science Religieuse* 15 (1925): 234-57; and Quasten, *Patrology,* 2:5-36, with full bibliography. On the subject of Clement's theological legacy, see J. Champonier, "Naissance de l'humanisme chrétien," *Bulletin de l'Association G. Budé* 3 (1947): 58-96; C. Mondésert, *Clément d'Alexandrie* (Paris: Aubier, Editions Montaigne, 1944); Eric Francis Osborn, *The Philosophy of Clement of Alexandria* (Cambridge: University Press, 1957); M. Spanncut, *Le Stoïcisme des Pères de l'Église* (Paris: Éditions du Seuil, 1957); and W. Völker, *Der wahre Gnostiker nach Clemens Alexandrinus, Texte und Untersuchungen* 57 (Berlin: Akademie Verlag, 1952).

church historians, and yet for the history of Christian worship it is of the greatest possible importance. For one thing, it is one of the few sermons that have come down to us from such an early date. But it is also a very well-constructed sermon, showing considerable oratorical ability, and, even more importantly, it gives us a good picture of how a capable preacher and theologian at the end of the second century went about interpreting the Scriptures from the pulpit. We can say about this sermon as we did about the sermon commonly called *II Clement:* If not many sermons from the second and third centuries have survived, we are glad this one has.

Unlike the two sermons studied above, this sermon comes from a preacher whose personality is well known to us.[93] Clement of Alexandria is supposed to have been born and raised in Athens. His parents were evidently in sufficiently comfortable circumstances for him to study in the schools of Athens and then to travel to southern Italy, Sicily, Syria, and finally Egypt seeking out the best Christian teachers of the day. How early Clement was won to the Christian faith we do not know, although he apparently was not brought up in a Christian family, nor do we know if he had been initiated into any of the mysteries which were so popular at the time.

What is clear is that Clement had a thorough and intimate knowledge of the religious and philosophical currents — including the mystery religions — popular at the end of the second century. He was well read not only in the Greek philosophers and moralists but in the poets, dramatists, and historians as well. The fact that he used anthologies and epitomes does not detract at all from our impression of his mastery of Greek literature. In addition to biblical literature, his writings show that he had a thorough knowledge of the earliest Christian literature, much of which, unfortunately, is lost today. He knew some of the apocryphal gospels such as the Gospel to the Hebrews and the Gospel of Matthias. He had studied the early Christian apologists and some of the theological treatises which were available in those days but which regrettably have today disappeared. When it came to the literature of the Church he was, along with his contemporary Tertullian of Carthage, one of the best-read Christians of his day.

---

93. Gustave Bardy, "Aux origines de l'école d'Alexandrie," *Recherches de Science Religieuse* (1933): 430-50; John Patrick, *Clement of Alexandria* (Edinburgh: Wm. Blackwood, 1914); R. B. Tollington, *Clement of Alexandria: A Study in Christian Liberalism* (London, 1914). For a particularly concise picture of Clement of Alexandria, see Hans Lietzmann, *A History of the Early Church,* 4 vols. (Cleveland and New York: Meridian Books, 1963), 2:275-94.

We do not know exactly when Clement arrived in Alexandria, but it was in Alexandria that he found Pantaenus, the teacher for whom he had been looking. So he settled down in that center of Hellenistic culture and became the disciple of the master he so much admired. Pantaenus was the principal of the catechetical school of Alexandria. There is some discussion as to just what that meant. Some have imagined that it was a Christian theological academy somewhat on the model of the schools of Athens, but it could just as well have been a house of study following the example of the Jewish house of study as it was found in Palestine. In time Clement succeeded his teacher and became the director of the school. It was probably Clement who made this school the comprehensive educational institution it became. Not only did it teach the arts of grammar, rhetoric, and logic, but it also taught the interpretation of Scripture. It took up into Christian education the whole of the traditional *paedia* which had been developed in the Greek-speaking world. Much of Clement's writing is an apology for this kind of broad education, and we can assume that was the sort of education given in the school. Like Archibald Alexander and the founders of Princeton Theological Seminary at the beginning of the last century, Clement thoroughly believed that faith and knowledge should be cultivated together. But unlike the founders of Princeton, Clement believed that the study of Greek philosophy was a good preparation for Christian faith.

While Christian historians and theologians of succeeding centuries have tended to point out the weaknesses of Clement's thought, our evaluation of this father of the Church would do better to recognize the tremendous advances he made. No Christian thinker up to his time had done nearly as much to establish Christian education. Clement built well on the foundations Pantaenus had laid. Although we are not too sure how much of Clement's work is owed to his teachers, it was Clement who got it written down. In his three works — *Protrepticus,* or *Exhortation to the Greeks; Paedagogus,* or *The Teacher;* and *Stromata,* or *The Carpets* — we discover a reflection of his approach to Christian learning. Far from being a systematic philosophy of education, it is an eclectic work which demonstrates how Clement drew into his Christian learning the edifying thoughts of Stoicism, Neoplatonism, and a number of other philosophies of life popular at the time. For our purposes, of course, this is all very important because it was this kind of education which the Church gave more and more to her preachers.

The ministry of Clement was cut short by the persecutions of the emperor Septimus Severus beginning in the year 202. Clement fled to Cappadocia, where one of his pupils, Alexander, had become bishop of the city of Ancyra. Some ten years later this pupil was chosen to be bishop of Jerusalem, and Clement may have accompanied him to the Holy City and died there sometime before 215. In the meantime, Origen, still a very young man, succeeded Clement as director of the catechetical school of Alexandria. Origen developed still further the sort of Christian education that was to be the vehicle of Christian preaching down through the centuries.

The single sermon of Clement's which has come down to us is of interest primarily because it shows us what kind of sermon was produced by a Christian preacher who had the sort of broad education in the liberal arts which Clement advocated.[94] Let us take a look at this sermon.[95]

The sermon is well organized. It has an introduction and a conclusion. The body of the sermon has two parts: the exposition of the passage of Scripture to be treated, and the exhortation which follows from the exposition. This sermon is clearly an expository sermon following in the tradition of the expository sermons of the synagogue, and provides one more piece of evidence that the earliest Christian preachers followed the pattern of expository preaching which Jewish preachers had developed before them.

This sermon was probably an occasional sermon which Clement was asked to give at some time or other. Perhaps his pupil Alexander asked him to preach on this subject to his new congregation at Jerusalem, or perhaps when he had been sent on a mission to Antioch the bishop there asked Clement to preach on a subject Clement had a reputation for treating particularly well. We cannot be sure, but the introduction, which is artfully constructed and presents the problem the sermon intends to address, does suggest that although the sermon is carefully expository it is thematic as well. Even more it treats a subject particularly important to Clement. If

94. For a particularly important insight on this sermon, see Lietzmann, *History of the Early Church*, 2:286.

95. This study is based on the English translation by W. Wilson in *The Ante-Nicene Fathers*, 2:591-604. There are also translations by P. M. Barnard, *A Homily of Clement of Alexandria Entitled "Who Is the Rich Man That Is Being Saved?"* (London and New York: SPCK, 1901), and an edition of the Greek text with English translation in the Loeb Classical Library by George William Butterworth, *Exhortation to the Greeks, the Rich Man's Salvation and a Fragment of an Address Entitled "To the Newly Baptized"* (London: William Heinemann, 1919), pp. 270-367 (hereafter referred to as Clement of Alexandria, *Sermon*).

we had no other work from this Christian philosopher, we could deduce much of his thought from this one sermon. As has often been said, Clement gave much thought to just how a cultured, well-educated member of the upper class went about being a Christian gentleman. The problem to be addressed is this: Can the rich be saved? As we have said, the chances are that Clement himself was a man of personal wealth or at least came from a family of means. One was not apt to come by the sort of education Clement so obviously had if someone back home was not paying the bills. It also seems to be the case that the catechetical school of Alexandria drew its following from the leisure class. The theme of this sermon was personally significant to Clement as well as to a good slice of his listeners; it has come down to us with the title "Who Is the Rich Man Who Is to Be Saved?" In the introduction our preacher explains that very often the rich, hearing that it is easier for a camel to go through the eye of a needle than for them to enter the kingdom of heaven, despair of being saved. This despair surely is not necessary if one listens with care to the story of the rich young ruler found in the Gospel of Mark.[96] What Clement proposes to do in this sermon is to show that even the rich, if they believe in Christ and love God and follow in the ways of the kingdom of God, can attain salvation.[97]

With this our preacher retells the story of the rich young ruler from Mark 10:17-31. This is a retelling of the story, not a reading of the lesson, and Clement does not stick exactly to the wording of the text. This suggests that the sermon was indeed preached in a service of worship and taken down by a stenographer. If it had been only a tract written in the style of a sermon, surely the lesson would have been copied out of the Gospel exactly.

Even in the introduction there is an anticipation of the exhortation he intends to make. One often finds this in the sermon introductions of well-trained homileticians. Like the overture to an opera, a sermon introduction can sound the themes to be developed in greater detail in the body of the sermon. So even here Clement exhorts the rich who wish to be saved to put themselves under the discipline of the Christian faith like athletes desiring to win an athletic competition. Here, of course, we have an obvious example of Hellenistic literary art. The figure of the athlete training for a competition is frequently used by classical orators — in fact,

96. Clement of Alexandria, *Sermon* 2.
97. Clement of Alexandria, *Sermon* 3.

even the apostle Paul uses this figure. For the artful orator the trick was to vary the figure so that it did not sound trite, and this Clement does very well. Exhorting the rich man who would be saved, he says:

> But let him go and put himself under the Word as his trainer, and Christ the President of the contest; and for his prescribed food and drink let him have the New Testament of the Lord; and for exercises, the commandments; and for elegance and ornament, the fair dispositions, love, faith, hope, knowledge of the truth, gentleness, meekness, pity, gravity: so that, when by the last trumpet the signal shall be given for the race and departure hence, as from the stadium of life, he may with a good conscience present himself victorious before the Judge who confers the rewards, confessedly worthy of the Fatherland on high, to which he returns with crowns and the acclamations of angels.[98]

As we read through this sermon we find again and again these beautiful literary flourishes which come so naturally from one who had the advantage of a broad education in arts and letters which this native-born Athenian so obviously had.

Following this full introduction our preacher begins to go through his passage of Scripture verse by verse. This, to be sure, was not a procedure he had learned from the classics of Greek oratory — the Greeks had nothing like the expository sermon to serve as a literary model. And although the obvious literary model here is the rabbinical sermon, neither was there a set of exemplary pattern sermons which every fledgling Jewish preacher was supposed to study. The preachers of the synagogue simply heard so many of these sermons that they knew how they went, and it must have been the same way in the Christian Church by the end of the second century. Clement would have learned this homiletical form from nothing so much as hearing a good amount of Christian preaching.

Our preacher begins by discussing the way the rich young ruler approached Jesus. He came up to him very politely and put to him a question, a very appropriate question. Clement draws this out elaborately. "For our Lord and Saviour was asked very pleasantly a question most appropriate for Him, — the Life respecting life, the Saviour respecting salvation, the Teacher concerning the chief doctrines taught, the Truth respecting the true . . . , the Immortal respecting immortality."[99] Rhetor-

98. Clement of Alexandria, *Sermon* 3.
99. Clement of Alexandria, *Sermon* 6.

ical ornaments like this delighted the cultured congregation of classical antiquity. The writings of Tertullian, who was Clement's contemporary, are filled with figures like this, and it was this studied sort of rhetoric which made both Tertullian and Clement so popular in their day.

Clement goes on to tell us that because Christ was divine he understood very well what the young man's problem was. He regarded salvation as something that depended on human goodness, the goodness of the rich young ruler or the goodness of a man like Jesus. It was for this reason that our Lord took up the young man's courteous salutation, "Good Master," and reminded him that God alone is good.[100] Salvation comes as a gift from God. Clement develops at length the principle that salvation is by grace.[101] As we will find Clement doing repeatedly in this sermon, he draws in a parallel text, in this case John 1:17, "The law was given by Moses; grace and truth came through Jesus Christ." This young man already knows deep in his heart that righteousness as attained by observing the Law of Moses is not enough to obtain eternal life. Otherwise, he would not be asking Jesus what more he had to do. He was insecure in what he had and therefore he wanted more.[102]

Our preacher moves on to the next verse, "If thou wilt be perfect." Clement comments that this young man had the volition to be perfect, but the fact that he yearned for perfection indicates that he had not yet attained it.[103] This volition toward salvation Clement finds very important. Trained by the Greek philosophers, he is concerned to defend the freedom of the human will. "For God compels not (for compulsion is repugnant to God), but supplies to those who seek, and bestows on those who ask, and opens to those who knock."[104] This issue will, of course, become a matter of some contention between the Greek theologians in the East, especially those influenced by the Alexandrians, and the Latin theologians in the West influenced by Augustine.

Our preacher moves on to still another verse. Jesus advises the rich young ruler, "Sell thy possessions." The reason Jesus told this particular young man to sell his possessions was that he was overly concerned with his material wealth. It was the same problem Martha had. As we read the

---

100. Clement of Alexandria, *Sermon* 6.
101. Clement of Alexandria, *Sermon* 7.
102. Clement of Alexandria, *Sermon* 8.
103. Clement of Alexandria, *Sermon* 10.
104. Clement of Alexandria, *Sermon* 10.

story in Luke 10:41-42, the one sister, Mary, set her household duties aside and sat at the feet of Jesus and listened to him teach. Martha, on the other hand, was completely absorbed in her day-to-day business. As Luke tells us, she was troubled by many things. She did not have time to sit and listen to the Savior, and yet for the well-being of her soul that was what was needed. In the same way Jesus told the rich young ruler to sell his possessions, give to the poor, and follow Jesus. It was following Jesus which was important, and the young ruler would not be able to do that until he could let loose of his possessions.[105]

Jesus certainly does not tell the young man to throw away the substance which he possessed or abandon his property, but rather to banish his notions about wealth, what wealth really is, and what wealth can do. He needed to be freed from a fascination with it or a compulsion to increase it or an anxiety over losing it.[106] According to Clement, what Jesus wanted to teach the man was that he needed to strip off from his soul his passion for material things.[107]

As Clement sees it, spiritual benefits can come from the wise use of wealth,[108] and he supports his point with a whole quiver of quotations from sacred Writ. Once more we notice that Clement is faithful to the principle that Scripture is best interpreted by Scripture. Had not Jesus himself taught that we are to make friends by a wise use of unrighteous mammon (Luke 16:9)? How are we to give food to the hungry, drink to the poor, clothing to the naked, and shelter to the homeless if we have already disposed of our goods (Matt. 25:34ff.)? Both Matthew and Zacchaeus were wealthy tax collectors who after their conversions used their money very wisely.[109] Clement sums up his teaching in one of the short epigrams which so delighted the literati of antiquity: "For they are possessions, inasmuch as they are possessed, and goods, inasmuch as they are useful and provided by God for the use of men."[110]

Again our preacher moves on to the next phrase in his text, "Come follow me." In a very positive way our preacher begins to build up a doctrine of stewardship. Here we find a most interesting anticipation of

99. Clement of Alexandria, *Sermon* 6.
100. Clement of Alexandria, *Sermon* 6.
101. Clement of Alexandria, *Sermon* 7.
102. Clement of Alexandria, *Sermon* 8.
103. Clement of Alexandria, *Sermon* 10.
104. Clement of Alexandria, *Sermon* 10.

the understanding of the spiritual value of wealth which was so fully developed by Protestantism in the sixteenth and seventeenth centuries. As Clement puts it, those who are truly blessed of the Lord are those who can hold their possessions, their gold, their silver, their land, as gifts from God. They can use them in God's service to support the spread of the gospel and to alleviate the needs of their neighbors. The wise know that they possess an abundance of the material things of life for the sake of their brethren rather than for themselves. When one begins to realize this, one gains control of one's possessions rather than becoming enslaved by those same possessions.[111] Again our Alexandrian Christian philosopher uses the time-honored biblical method of explaining Scripture by Scripture to make his point very sharp. This, he tells us, is what Jesus meant when he taught the Beatitudes. It is not just the poor who are blessed but the poor in spirit. In the same way, it is not just the hungry and thirsty who are blessed but those who hunger and thirst after righteousness.[112]

Once more our preacher moves on to the next verse, taking up the questions posed by the disciples, "Who can be saved?" and the answer Jesus gave them, "What is impossible with man is possible with God." As Clement understands it, this text means:

> For a man by himself working and toiling at freedom from passion achieves nothing. But if he plainly shows himself very desirous and earnest about this, he attains it by the addition of the power of God. For God conspires with willing souls. But if they abandon their eagerness, the spirit which is bestowed by God is also restrained. For to save the unwilling is the part of one exercising compulsion; but to save the willing, that of one showing grace.[113]

For a Western theologian, especially after the controversy between Augustine and the Pelagians, this statement seems rather synergistic, but that question had not yet come up in the days of Clement of Alexandria.

Next our preacher comes to the words of Jesus, "Verily I say unto you, whosoever shall leave what is his own, parents, and children, and wealth, for My sake and the Gospel's, shall receive an hundredfold." Again we notice that Clement is quoting inexactly, as would be quite natural for a preacher who has no notes before him. We find a different version of

105. Clement of Alexandria, *Sermon* 10.
106. Clement of Alexandria, *Sermon* 11.
107. Clement of Alexandria, *Sermon* 12.

the same saying in Luke 14:26, " 'Whoso hateth not father, and mother, and children, and his own life besides, cannot be My disciple.' "[114] One can draw very foolish inferences out of these words, our preacher points out. We can't take this saying literally. We have to think it over a bit. What does it really mean? Surely the point of both these sayings is that we are to put the spiritual relationships above the relationships of flesh and blood. Surely we have the same principle at work when we come to understand that very problematic verse from this passage, "Sooner shall a camel enter through a needle's eye, than such a rich man reach the kingdom of God." Sayings like this point to the mystery of our salvation. They challenge us to think about these matters. It is so easy for the rich to assume that because they have everything else they will have salvation as well, when in fact they will have to seek after it with special diligence because of the special temptations of wealth.[115]

Having gone through his passage of Scripture verse by verse, Clement turns to exhorting his congregation. We have already noted that the sermon falls into the two major parts of exposition and exhortation based on the exposition. What is noteworthy is the way even the exhortation revolves around a number of parallel passages of Scripture. The parable of the good Samaritan is the basis for one point Clement draws from his exposition. Did not this exemplary man have an abundant supply of goods with him which made it possible for him to care for the man he found wounded? He had a beast of burden to take the injured man to an inn; he had the money to pay for his keep.[116] He could never have supplied such neighborly service had he been poor and destitute, lacking enough material goods to care for himself let alone someone else.

With the same purpose in mind Clement recounts the parable of the sheep and the goats, pointing out that it was not those who had no goods that Jesus commended, but rather those who shared their goods, feeding the hungry, refreshing the thirsty, clothing the naked, and housing the homeless.[117] The rich have the opportunity to serve God in ways the poor do not. Surely they should not despair of salvation. Much more they

108. Clement of Alexandria, *Sermon* 13.
109. Clement of Alexandria, *Sermon* 13.
110. Clement of Alexandria, *Sermon* 14.
111. Clement of Alexandria, *Sermon* 16.
112. Clement of Alexandria, *Sermon* 17.
113. Clement of Alexandria, *Sermon* 21.

should be diligent in performing the good works which because of their wealth they are capable of performing. Quite naturally this leads our preacher to remind his congregation again of the saying of Jesus about making friends by means of unrighteous mammon. To this he adds some reflections on the saying of the apostle Paul, "For the Lord loveth a cheerful giver."[118] Truly God is delighted by the giving of those who are generous from their hearts.

Still another parallel passage Clement brings to his congregation by way of exhortation is the thirteenth chapter of I Corinthians, in which the apostle speaks so eloquently about love. It is toward love that the Christian should aim. Like anyone else, the rich should not despair of salvation if they will but make love their aim.[119]

Finally, we come to the conclusion, a rather remarkable conclusion for a sermon of such antiquity. In order to assure his congregation that there is salvation for anyone who repents and turns to Christ, our preacher tells in ample detail a legend in which the apostle John won to the Christian faith a fine young man in the course of his evangelistic travels in the backcountry of Asia Minor.[120] The youth was of ardent faith and great promise, and John committed him to the care of one of the elders of the Church and went his way. In time the handsome youth fell into bad company and ended up a brigand notorious throughout the area. Years later the apostle returned to this town in another evangelistic journey and inquired what had happened to the youth in whom he had seen such promise. On hearing the sad story the apostle set out to find him and, strangely enough, was apprehended by this very group of brigands, which his former disciple was now leading. On seeing the aged apostle, the youth, now middle-aged and hardened in his wicked ways, was suddenly filled with remorse. He repented and the apostle brought him back to the Church with great joy.

This dramatic story has often been retold, but it is in Clement that we first find it. Scholars have often discussed where the story came from and how Clement might have learned of it. For us, however, what is much more interesting is the way this human interest story fits into one of the oldest Christian sermons that has come down to us. While human interest stories such as this abound in the sermons of our own day, this is the only example I know of a story of this sort being used in a sermon of such antiquity.

114. Scripture quotations throughout these volumes follow the text of the preacher as it is reported to us. Apparently Clement quoted the Greek New Testament in a rather free fashion.

Having studied the actual text of this sermon at some length, let us consider some questions it raises. First, what does it tell us about the ministry of Clement as a whole? Clement of Alexandria is usually thought of as a teacher, a catechetical teacher, rather than as a preacher, yet this sermon suggests that he was a preacher of ability and probably experience. The famous catechetical school of Alexandria was not an institution for teaching children their catechisms; it would be closer to the truth to call it the first Christian theological seminary. While during the week Clement may have lectured to his students, he was the sort of man whom the church of Alexandria would frequently call upon to preach. The picture we get of Clement as a preacher fits in well with what we learn elsewhere.[121] In addition to daily preaching during the week, in the second century the Sunday service often incorporated two or three sermons, each based on one of several readings from Scripture. For this abundance of preaching a church like that at Alexandria or Rome or Corinth or Caesarea would have a whole covey of preachers. The preaching ministry was collegial, and certainly not the monopoly of the bishop. The bishop would no doubt preach, but there would be other preachers as well. In short, a man of Clement's talents could hardly have avoided the pulpit.

Second, what does this sermon tell us about the relationship between preaching and teaching? Students of the history of Christian doctrine often speak of the logos Christology of Clement. The high development of the logos Christology was characteristic of Alexandrian theology. Teaching, therefore, had a legitimate place in the worship of the church of Alexandria. We would expect, therefore, that the line between the two would not be too distinct. We will certainly find this to be the case in the sermons of Origen only a few years after Clement, and we will find it to be the case in those of Cyril of Alexandria two centuries later. Didactic sermons were both expected and appreciated in a city of such high intellectual culture. Surely Alexandria was not unique in this. It must have been a fairly general expectation. Wherever there was a strong logos Christology there would have been a keen appreciation of the place of teaching in worship.

Third, what does this sermon tell us about the relationship of grammatical-historical exegesis to allegorical exegesis in the preaching of the Egyptian church at the end of the second century? We have here only one sermon, of course, but it certainly shows us that there were preachers

115. Clement of Alexandria, *Sermon* 27.
116. Clement of Alexandria, *Sermon* 28.
117. Clement of Alexandria, *Sermon* 30.

in this city, so famous for its allegorical interpretation of Scripture, who knew quite well how to preach a sermon without recourse to allegory. Ever since Philo the Bible had been interpreted allegorically in Alexandria. It was early in Origen's career that he wrote his famous treatise *On First Principles,* in which he outlined his approach to biblical hermeneutics. This would mean that his work and Clement's sermon might well be almost contemporary. Just possibly the latter could be an indication that there was a considerable amount of grammatical-historical exegesis even in Alexandria at the end of the second century.

We have gone over this sermon in great detail because, in the first place, we have few sermons from such an early date. In the second place, however, the sermon demonstrates that the art of preaching was highly developed in Clement's day. Sermons like this do not appear in isolation; they depend on a preaching culture developed over several generations. This sermon has profited both from the academies of the Greeks and the synagogues of the Hebrews. It has behind it solid thinking and skilled artistic craftsmanship. All in all this sermon would indicate that there was some very sound preaching in the Christian Church at the end of the second century.

III. Origen and Our First Comprehensive Picture of Christian Preaching

One could not sum up Origen much better than the late Cardinal Daniélou did when he called him the genius of the ancient Christian Church. He was, in truth, a genius, a saintly genius. He was an exciting intellect, a poet of theological insight, one of the most imaginative thinkers who ever lived — and his imagination was baptized: He was totally devoted to the cause of Christ. To be sure, he was something of a Neoplatonic philosopher, and yet he loved the Scriptures of the Old and New Testaments above all. The Bible was his strength and nourishment, his joy and his delight.[122] And still, even at all this, one has to admit he all too often Platonized the gospel.

118. Clement of Alexandria, *Sermon* 31.
119. Clement of Alexandria, *Sermon* 38.
120. Clement of Alexandria, *Sermon* 42.
121. See Lietzmann, *History of the Early Church,* 3:289ff.; Gustave Bardy, "Un prédicateur populaire au IIIe siècle," *Revue practique d'apologétique* 45 (1927): 513-26 and 679-98.
122. Among the more recent general works on Origen the following have been

Origen was born and brought up in Egypt. He was a child of the Nile. What a land of contrast Egypt is! There is the lush life on the banks of the Nile and the ascetic life of the wilderness. From the standpoint of geography, Egypt is an allegory of asceticism. From the standpoint of culture, it is a paradigm of otherworldliness. The pharaohs could pour fortunes into preparations for the afterlife. How much of the Nile has flowed into Western civilization, and yet we hardly ever speak of it. With Origen, at least we have to say something about it.

In the same way we have to speak of Alexandria, which too often we confuse with ancient Greece. Alexandria was one of the capitals of the ancient world, the center of a culture that was just as unique as the culture of Athens or Rome or Antioch. It was a city where all the mysticism and the outright magic of ancient Egypt, the philosophy of Greece, and the ethical monotheism of the Jews mixed. It was perhaps the greatest of the Hellenistic cultures, and as such it had a tendency toward syncretism. It was a melting pot culture.

Origen made it possible for the Church to speak the language of that culture, and he made Christianity understandable in terms of that culture. He was the first in a long line of Christian preachers who would make a bridge between the Christian faith and the prevailing culture of the day. After Origen would come a Gregory the Great, a Bossuet, a Schleiermacher, an Adolf von Harnack, and a Harry Emerson Fosdick, each of whom in one way or another built a bridge between the Christian faith and a very different culture. It was the glory of these saints to serve the Church not so much because they recovered the essence of Christianity for the faithful in the bosom of the Church as that they made the world outside the Church think about what this Christian faith might say to them. Each made certain compromises, some acceptable, some regrettable.

One of the most interesting things about Origen is the way he moved from Egypt to Palestine. That was after all the basic biblical typology, and strangely enough the typology was played out in his own life. He, too, left Egypt, setting out on a pilgrimage that took him to Rome, to Greece, and to Syria. Finally he settled in the Holy Land, in Caesarea, the city which in his day was the metropolis of Palestine.[123] In Caesarea he reestablished his academy and, as in Alexandria, gave to his students a broad education. Students were required to study the Greek philosophers, formal logic and

found particularly helpful: Henry Chadwick, *Christianity and the Classical Tradition* (Oxford: Clarendon Press, 1966); Jean Daniélou, *Origène* (Paris: La table ronde, 1948); Rolf

ethics, and, as the crown of all wisdom, the divinely inspired Scriptures of the Old and New Testaments. We know quite a bit about Origen's life because several of his devoted students wrote about him. Eusebius, renowned as the first church historian, was bishop of Caesarea in the following century. The memory of this famous biblical scholar and preacher would have been kept fresh there, if nowhere else. Besides, it was in the library of the church of Caesarea that the writings of Origen were preserved, that is, until they were destroyed four centuries later during the reign of the emperor Justinian.

A. Origen's Hermeneutic, On First Principles

Origen was a great preacher and it was to his preaching that he gave his most intense efforts, although it was inevitable that his prodigious vitality spilled out into all kinds of other activities. His central interest was the interpretation of Scripture, and early in life he found it necessary to explain his innovative approach to biblical interpretation. While still in Alexandria between 220 and 230 he wrote his *Peri Archon* or, translating rather freely, *On the Basic Principles of Christian Doctrine*.[124] The fourth and last book of this work treats at length Origen's theory of the interpretation of Scripture.

Origen begins by affirming that the Scriptures of the Old and New Testaments are divinely inspired.[125] This inspiration, which is the work of the Holy Spirit, makes the Scriptures different from writings produced in the usual human way.[126] The words contained therein are the words of God. The evidence Origen gives to support the divine inspiration of the Scriptures is that what the Scriptures have prophesied has come true.[127] Perhaps this argument is not very forceful to our ears, but it is indeed a

Gögler, *Zur Theologie des biblischen Wortes bei Origen* (Düsseldorf: Patmos Verlag, 1963); and Pierre Nautin, *Origène, sa vie et son oeuvre* (Paris: Beauchesne, 1977). However, a much older work, Charles Bigg, *The Christian Platonists of Alexandria* (Oxford: Clarendon Press, 1886), is a particularly fine work.

123. On the congregation to which Origen preached in Caesarea, see Adele Monaci Castagno, *Origene, predicatore e il suo pubblico* (Turin: Aranco Angeli, 1987), pp. 45-50.

124. The classic translation is that of G. W. Butterworth, *On First Principles, Being Koetschau's Text of the De Principiis*, trans. into English with notes (London: SPCK, 1936). There is an American edition of Butterworth's translation published by Peter Smith in Gloucester, Massachusetts, in 1973. F. Crombie translated the text found in *The Ante-*

most biblical answer and in the end much more solid than we might imagine. Jeremiah had suggested this argument a long time before. But strangely enough Origen does not develop it as far as he might. He apparently overlooked that the dynamic of promise and fulfillment is central to the biblical epistemology and at the core of the kerygma and instead goes on to speak of the divine condescension.[128] God hides the treasure of divine wisdom in the earthen vessel of words.[129] To be sure, this, too, is a very biblical argument. Our faith, Origen tells us, should not depend on words of human wisdom but on the power of God. Appealing to the first two chapters of I Corinthians, he tells us that Christian preaching has been successful not because of plausible words of wisdom but rather "in demonstration of the Spirit and of power (I Cor. 2:4)."[130] Somehow Origen sees the simplicity of Christian preaching as a witness to its divine authority. It convinces not because it is elegant, but because it is true. The preaching of the Word of God has power because it is divinely inspired, that is, because it is indeed the Word of God. One could hardly ask for a more solid argument!

Origen's approach to the interpretation of Scripture is based on a strong belief in its divine inspiration. Having laid this out, he then takes up the question of the spiritual interpretation of the Bible.[131] Many heresies have come about, Origen claims, because people have been too literalistic in their approach to Scripture.[132] One sees at this point that Origen is eager to defend the Church from the ideas of Marcion, who would have eliminated the Old Testament from the canon of Scripture. Marcion was one of those who did not understand the Scriptures spiritually. According to Origen, the Scriptures, being inspired by the Holy Spirit, were entrusted to us by the Father through the Son, our Lord Jesus Christ. The true understanding of the Scriptures has come down to us from the apostles through the succession of Christian teachers.[133] Here we see another important aspect of Origen's teaching. It is from the tradition of the Church that we know that we are to interpret the Scriptures spiritually.

Nicene Fathers, 4:237-382. There is also a modern American translation by Rowan Greer in the volume devoted to Origen in The Classics of Western Spirituality (New York, Ramsey, Toronto: Paulist Press, 1979).

125. Origen, *Principles* 4.1.1.
126. Origen, *Principles* 4.1.6.
127. Origen, *Principles* 4.1.2.
128. Origen, *Principles* 4.1.7.
129. Origen, *Principles* 4.1.7.

Having made this point, Origen goes on to speak of the nature of spiritual understanding. Scripture, like a human being, has a body, a soul, and a spirit. Therefore we should understand Scripture in a threefold way. There is the body of Scripture, that is, the simple historical, narrative sense. For the more advanced there is the more profound understanding, which corresponds to the soul. And for those who are perfect there is the higher wisdom, which corresponds to the spirit. At this point Origen is not too clear as to the distinction between the second and third levels, but in later years he would work this out more clearly and would finally develop his fourfold interpretation of Scripture. What one senses at this point is that for Origen the essential matter is the distinction between the literal meaning and the spiritual meaning. Yet strangely Origen does not distinguish between a simple literal meaning and a more sophisticated literal meaning of the text, informed by a study of rhetoric and a sensitivity to how the biblical writers used language. The door is wide open for him to go in this direction, but that is not, or so it seems, the door he wants to enter.

It is when Origen gets down to speaking of some very specific passages of Scripture which show us how we are to discover a spiritual interpretation that we get a clear picture of what he has in mind. The most significant examples he uses are, first, the typological interpretation of the passage through the Red Sea and the trials of the wilderness mentioned by the apostle Paul in I Corinthians 10, and second, the Jerusalem typology in Galatians 4.[134] In each case Origen has chosen well-established biblical types which go far back in the history of biblical interpretation. It is also true that in each case Origen gives to these traditional types a strong Alexandrian interpretation which probably was not what the New Testament author, who in both cases was Paul, originally intended. There is no question that Paul was often perfectly happy to use both traditional rabbinical exegesis and Alexandrian exegesis when it helped him elucidate the fundamentals of the gospel. It is also true that he used the vocabulary of Alexandrian exegesis. This does not mean that Paul had confused the biblical concept of typology with Platonic allegory. Paul always understands the types in terms of promise and fulfillment. He understands them as signs given to the earlier generations of God's people which taught them to set their hope on greater things yet to come.

Origen, on the other hand, does seem to confuse the two; he takes leave from these examples to develop a thoroughly Platonic allegorical

130. Origen, *Principles* 4.1.7.

approach to the interpretation of Scripture. It was God himself who inspired these Scriptures in such a way that the truth is hidden in histories and legal observances. God, deeming it unwise for just anyone to discover the truth, has revealed himself in such a way that only the pure, the studious, and the zealous can find the higher wisdom.[135] These allegories are often put in shocking or repulsive forms to alert the wise to their deeper meaning.[136] The true interpreter of Scripture understands the secrets of unraveling these mysteries.[137] Once one has those basic keys, then the Scriptures are filled with marvelous mysteries just waiting to be unlocked.

Having pointed to New Testament passages which show how the New Testament itself encourages us to interpret the Old Testament allegorically, Origen brings out a number of Scriptures he thinks Christians must treat the same way.[138] These passages come not only from the Old Testament but also from the Gospels.[139] For Origen it is not a matter of either an historical meaning or an allegorical meaning for most passages. The greatest number of passages have a valuable historical or literal meaning, and so in most cases that meaning needs to be preserved, but beyond this obvious meaning there is also a mystery.[140] One can be confident of this because these are not human words but the words of God, which have been sown into the holy books.[141]

At this point Origen begins to develop the idea that what is said in the Scriptures about Israel is to be understood of the individual soul and its ascent to God.[142] Here Origen, and in fact the whole Alexandrian school of allegorical exegesis, makes a significant departure from biblical typology. Both the servitude in Egypt and the captivity in Babylon are allegories of the soul's struggle against sin. All these truths are mysteries hidden in Scripture like the treasure the Gospel tells us is buried in a field. Only by the help of God — the illumination of the Holy Spirit — can one dig them out. Our speculation must always be consistent with the rule of piety. For Origen scholarship and piety always go hand in hand.

131. Of particular interest on the subject of Origen's approach to the exegesis of Scripture is the study of Karen Jo Torjesen, *Hermeneutical Procedure and Theological Method in Origen's Exegesis* (Berlin and New York: Walter de Gruyter, 1986).

132. Origen, *Principles* 4.2.1.

133. Origen, *Principles* 4.2.2.

134. Origen, *Principles* 4.2.6.

135. Origen, *Principles* 4.2.7.

136. Origen, *Principles* 4.2.9.

No human mind can completely understand the mysteries of God,[143] and one must strive continually to understand so that one rises from one level of understanding to another. Those who want to understand these mysteries need not be concerned with names and words, for different nations have different customs in regard to the use of words. Apparently for Origen the science of philology and arts of grammar and rhetoric are not what ultimately lead us to understanding. One should pay more attention to what is meant than to how it is expressed in words.[144] In the end one understands by pure intellectual apprehension, which is the gift of the Holy Spirit, who inspired the Holy Scriptures. Apparently in the last analysis Origen is an illuminist.

After writing this work, Origen left Alexandria, traveling to Palestine, Syria, and even to Rome. He became well known and more than a little controversial. In Rome he heard Hippolytus preach. Unfortunately we don't know how Origen was impressed with Hippolytus. It would be fascinating to know how the two regarded each other, for they were such opposites. Origen was such a broad creative spirit; Hippolytus was so narrow and pedantic. In Antioch Origen became the tutor of the emperor's mother, Julia Mamara, a high-minded lady who wanted to be better informed as to Christian teaching. One wonders if she valued the experience. In Palestine he had several influential friends: Alexander, bishop of Jerusalem, and Theoctistus, bishop of Caesarea. Here his lectures and above all his preaching were particularly welcome. It was in Caesarea that he finally settled.

While in Caesarea as well as on frequent visits to Jerusalem, he preached daily. Between the years 240 and 246, his sermons were taken down by stenographers. Unfortunately many of these sermons were lost in the sixth century when the emperor Justinian ordered the writings of Origen destroyed. Most of the surviving sermons have come down to us in translation, although at least one series, the twenty sermons on Jeremiah, has been preserved in the original Greek. Even with the enormous number of sermons which were lost, we still have a sizeable collection of Origen's sermons. For example, there are sixteen sermons on Genesis, thirteen on Exodus, sixteen on Leviticus, twenty-eight on Numbers, twenty-six on Joshua, nine on Judges, nine on Isaiah, twenty on Jeremiah, fourteen on

---

137. Origen, *Principles* 4.2.8.
138. Origen, *Principles* 4.3.1.

Ezekiel, and thirty-nine on Luke. We have a good sampling of Origen's preaching.

Although this collection of sermons is valuable because it elaborates for us the thought of one of the world's most creative thinkers, for our purposes it is much more valuable because it is the only extensive collection of sermons which has come down to us from the first three centuries of Christian history. We are, it must be confessed, much more interested in what these sermons tell us about the preaching of the ancient Christian Church than in what they say about Origen. We wish a few more collections of sermons from other preachers of the period had survived so that we could be a bit more precise as to the exact nature of Origen's novelty. If we just had a collection of genuine sermons from Clement of Rome, or Melito of Sardis! How much we could learn if we had a dozen or more sermons from Clement of Alexandria or even from Ignatius of Antioch. As we have indicated, we have only a few isolated sermons besides this collection of Origen's. The information we do have, however, indicates that not only was Origen the greatest preacher of the second and third centuries, but he was in many ways a typical preacher of the period. He was not the greatest preacher of the period because he was so unusual but because he was so representative. To be sure, certain aspects of his approach to the interpretation of Scripture and the lengths to which he carried them were not shared by most of his colleagues in that day, but his approach to the ministry of the Word was essentially that which had been used since the time of the apostles all along the way until the time of Constantine.

B. Sermons on Genesis

It is usually suggested that the sermons on Genesis[145] represent a systematic preaching through of Genesis based on the daily reading of the book at morning prayer. This is no doubt the case; however, this being so, a number of explanations are needed. Sixteen of these sermons have

---

139. Origen, *Principles* 4.3.3.
140. Origen, *Principles* 4.3.4.
141. Origen, *Principles* 4.3.5.
142. Origen, *Principles* 4.3.6.
143. Origen, *Principles* 4.3.11.

come down to us in the Latin translation of Rufinus. We find sermons on the following texts:

1.	Genesis 1:1-30	On the Creation
2.	Genesis 6:13-16	On the Ark
3.	Genesis 17:1-13	On Circumcision
4.	Genesis 18:1-21	God's Appearance to Abraham and to Lot
5.	Genesis 19:17-38	Lot and His Daughters
6.	Genesis 20:1-18	On Abimelech
7.	Genesis 21:1-19	The Birth of Isaac
8.	Genesis 22:1-14	Abraham's Sacrifice
9.	Genesis 22:15-17	The Renewal of the Covenant
10.	Genesis 24:1-67	On Rebecca
11.	Genesis 25:1-19	Abraham's Marriage to Keturah
12.	Genesis 25:19–26:19	Birth of Esau and Jacob
13.	Genesis 26:12-22	The Wells Isaac Dug
14.	Genesis 26:23-29	Isaac at the Well of Shibah
15.	Genesis 45:25–46:4	On Jacob's Learning That Joseph Was Alive
16.	Genesis 47:20-27	On the Egyptians Becoming the Slaves of Pharaoh

A study of this list raises several questions. First, one wonders if we have the complete series or only a portion of the series. One is tempted to suggest the latter because a number of major passages such as the stories of the Garden of Eden, Cain and Abel, and the Tower of Babel are omitted. Only one rather minor aspect of the story of the flood is treated, and Abraham's call is completely passed over. Then beginning with Genesis 17 the series begins to treat the text in a much more systematic manner, continuing on through chapter 26 and averaging better than one sermon per chapter for the next twelve sermons. Finally after skipping almost twenty chapters, we find two sermons on short passages found in the Joseph cycle. How are we to explain these omissions?

One possible explanation is that these sermons were indeed preached on the *lectio continua* reading of Genesis at morning prayer in the church of Caesarea, and that while Origen began the series as planned, either he was prevented from preaching for the next several days or his stenographer was prevented from recording the sermons. It could even be that the sermons were preached and recorded but that either Origen or someone else decided, for one reason or another, against publishing them. Perhaps what we have here is an indication of how the ministry of the Word was carried out in the church of Caesarea at the time. The *lectio continua* went on each day even if another preacher filled in, or if there was no preacher to comment on the lesson. On the other hand, perhaps all this indicates is that while Origen had preached something like sixty or seventy sermons on Genesis, someone selected for publication the more edifying, remarkable, or unusual sermons of the series.

Another question this list of passages raises is how long the daily lessons were and how their length was determined. Again we can only suggest. The books of the Bible were not yet divided into chapters, and it probably fell to the lector to determine the length of the lesson. The lector would no doubt have recognized that the bishop had the final say in such matters, but no doubt the bishop would have given him general instructions on the length of the lessons and the importance of retaining the natural flow of thought or continuity of the narrative. Those who were chosen as lectors were supposed to have at least a certain amount of talent for performing their ministry. Even at that one wonders, for example, what the actual Scripture lesson was on the morning Origen preached on Genesis 22:15-17.[146] Was the whole story of Abraham's sacrifice read over again and continued to the end of the chapter? Were only those three verses read? One cannot quite imagine that Genesis 22:15-17 would have been a normal Scripture lesson. Surely the preacher would have to request the lector to read it because that was the passage on which he intended to preach. The picture we get from Origen's sermons is that the *lectio continua* was practiced in a rather loose fashion. One read through the books in order, but there were no hard-and-fast rules about how much one read on any given morning. Both the lector and the preacher were supposed to use good judgment. Not everything had to be commented upon and perhaps not everything had to be read.

Looking now at the individual sermons, we find that Origen had a consistent manner of approach. He takes the passage which has been read and goes over it verse by verse. He does not take every verse but rather those he figures will be most edifying to the congregation. He takes several words or expressions and, having explained them or thrown light on them or interpreted them, makes an application and then goes on to the next

144. Origen, *Principles* 4.3.15.

verse or group of verses. The result is that each sermon consists of a series of often unrelated points rather than there being a single theme for the sermon as a whole.

We find this in the sermon on creation.[147] He starts by commenting on the first verse, "In the beginning God made the heavens and the earth." Then he takes up verses 3-5, "Let there be a firmament in the midst of the waters."[148] Next he comments on verses 10 and 11, "And God said, 'Let the earth bring forth vegetation.'"[149] Origen continues in this manner until he comes to the creation of man, where he goes into the matter of man being made in the image of God at some length. It is a long sermon. Very often Origen will draw from the text a literal meaning, a typological meaning, an allegorical meaning, or a moral meaning. Rarely does he find the need to draw out all four levels of meaning for a single text.

In the sermon on Noah's ark, for instance, Origen takes some time looking into the historical narrative to discover what the ark actually looked like.[150] He calls on tradition to fill in what is needed to give us a picture of the ark. One gathers he is talking about rabbinical tradition at this point. Then he develops the allegorical meaning. The flood is a figure of the last judgment, an idea he gathers from Luke 17:26-27. Finally, he speaks of the moral interpretation. We should build an ark of salvation in our own hearts.[151]

Origen's sermons are loosely organized. One never gets the feeling that each sermon is made to fit the same pattern or outline, but rather that the passage itself suggests the outline. Occasionally there is a clever introduction or conclusion, but they are never forced or contrived. In style the sermons are informal and conversational. Our preacher's main purpose is always to give his congregation the devotional treasures he has found hidden in the treasury of Scripture. This he does as simply and directly as possible.

Frequently Origen brings out from the passage of Scripture before him comments on the philosophical issues of his time. Sermon 14, on Isaac at the well of Shibah, becomes an occasion for Origen to discuss the relation of Christian faith to Greek philosophy.[152] Abimelech represents the learned

145. This study is based on the edition of H. de Lubac and L. Doutreleau, eds., *Homélies sur la Genèse,* Sources Chrétiennes, vol. 7 (Paris: Éditions du Cerf, 1972), as well as *Homilies on Genesis and Exodus,* trans. Ronald E. Heine (Washington, D.C.: Catholic University of America Press, 1982). English translations are quoted from the edition of Heine.

146. Origen, *Sermons on Genesis* 9.

and the wise of the world, while Isaac represents the Word of God. Abimelech comes to make peace with Isaac, because he recognized that he was blessed of God, but Isaac is apprehensive because Abimelech has not always been friendly. Sometimes the wise of this world agree with God's truth and sometimes they do not. Nevertheless, Isaac prepares a great feast for him and the two enter into a covenant with each other. It is a sermon the essential points of which many a modern university chaplain would have been proud to preach, even if the exegesis is not the sort we usually practice today. Somehow the imagery as Origen has worked it out has a tremendous power to suggest things that go far beyond the rather simple sermon which Origen gives. What George Buttrick could have done with this text in Harvard University chapel if he could have just allowed himself the sort of exegetical imagination Origen felt free to take!

Origen is forever defending the Christian faith against the charge of anthropomorphism which the philosophically inclined pagans of his day loved to direct indiscriminately at the Greek poets and Hebrew prophets. It was one of the theological issues of the day. In his sermon on God's appearance to Abraham and to Lot,[153] Origen feels called upon to make it clear that the Holy Spirit intended much more by the story than putting God into a spatial relationship with either Abraham or Lot. God is not degraded when Moses tells us that God appeared in the form of three men standing before Abraham, nor is God's omniscience impinged when we are told that God descended to Sodom to see if the cries against that city were justified. It is much more that these expressions show a spiritual relation of one kind between Abraham and God and of a very different kind between Lot and God.

Origen's methods of exposition are rather sparse. He put a strong emphasis on etymologies. The key to the spiritual meaning of any biblical character is the meaning of the name. In Sermon 2, on Noah's ark, we are told that Noah means "rest" or "just."[154] From this Origen is led to believe that Noah is a type of Christ. It is Christ who provides for us an ark in which we can pass through the storms of the last days. Origen comes up with an etymology for the name Pharaoh in the sixth sermon[155] wherein Pharaoh means "the destroyer." The meaning of the name makes clear why God's people cannot be at peace with Pharaoh. In Sermon 10 we are

147. Origen, *Sermons on Genesis* 1.
148. Origen, *Sermons on Genesis* 1.2.
149. Origen, *Sermons on Genesis* 1.3.

told that the name Rebecca means "patience," which is the key to understanding how that godly woman, who trusted so faithfully in the providence of God, became the mother of Israel.[156]

Modern research has given considerable attention to the sources of
Origen's etymologies. A good number seem to come from Philo, for whom
etymologies were important keys to the allegorical interpretation of Scripture, as they had been for the Greek philosophers before him. These
philosophers tried to make mythology a bit more morally edifying by
claiming that the myths were allegories. Long before Greek philosophers
took up the etymologies of names, the Hebrew Scriptures often found that
the secret to someone's life was to be found in his or her name. The chances
are that later in life Origen got his etymologies not so much from Philo
as from the rabbis of Caesarea.[157]

Origen, as many before and since, was convinced that great meaning
was to be found in the mystical signification of numbers. If Origen called
on the etymologies of names so very frequently, he was considerably more
reserved when it came to sacred numerology. One finds a certain amount
of it, nevertheless, in his sermon on the ark. The ark was to be three
hundred cubits long. One hundred is the perfect number of the rational
creation, a number that bespeaks the mystery of the full and complete
rational world. Three is the number of the Trinity, and so the dimensions
of the ark make clear that we are dealing not only with the whole of the
rational creation as it exists but also as it is completed by the grace of God,
who is Father, Son, and Holy Spirit. The breadth of the ark was to be fifty
cubits. Fifty is the number of forgiveness. It is because of God's forgiveness
of our sins in Christ, the spiritual Noah, that rational existence comes to
its perfection and that the width and breadth of the Church comes to
embrace all humanity. While such speculations may be more amusing to
us than edifying, for the contemplatively inclined intellectual of Hellenistic
society so fascinated by Pythagorean mathematical mysticism, it was fascinating. Such discussions in the sermons of Origen probably turned on his
congregation as much as if a preacher in Silicon Valley were to present the
gospel in computerese.

150. Origen, *Sermons on Genesis* 2.1.
151. Origen, *Sermons on Genesis* 2.6.
152. Origen, *Sermons on Genesis* 14.
153. Origen, *Sermons on Genesis* 4.
154. Origen, *Sermons on Genesis* 2.3.

Origen is rather chaste in his use of what we call illustrative material. One does not find the sort of human interest stories which modern homileticians commend so unreservedly.

The one method of exposition Origen uses most effectively is to explain Scripture with Scripture. In fact, this explaining a text by bringing to it a number of other texts is characteristic of the preaching of the ancient Church generally. Origen does this in a number of different ways. He often does it in a simple philological way, showing how a word or phrase is used elsewhere in the Bible. In Sermon 4, on God's appearance to Abraham and Lot, Origen wants to explain why the text says God wanted to know whether things said about Lot were true.[158] God, our preacher tells us, knows neither sin nor sinners. To make this point he quotes a series of passages which show that God knows the righteous but not sinners. Even Jesus says to the wicked, "'I never knew you; depart from me, you evildoers'" (Matt. 7:23). Sometimes Origen does it to show how other writings in the Scriptures have said the same thing, thus making his comparisons theological rather than philological. At other times he shows how a passage in Scripture has specifically interpreted an older passage. In his sermon on the circumcision of Abraham he shows how this rite given to Abraham in the book of Genesis is interpreted by the prophets Ezekiel (Ezek. 44:9) and Jeremiah (Jer. 6:10).[159] Even under the Law, Origen would show his listeners, circumcision is a matter of the commitment of the heart.

His greatest delight, particularly in his sermons on Old Testament texts, is in showing how a passage of the Law or the prophets foreshadows a passage in the New Testament. It was his ability to do this which fascinated the members of his congregation. They never grew tired of hearing about his imaginative discoveries of New Testament truths hidden away in the text of the Old Testament. In Sermon 15 he finds in the text, "'I will go down with you to Egypt, and I will also bring you up again'" (Gen. 46:4), a foreshadowing of the whole drama of Christ's mission to come to earth and return to heaven leading a triumphant nation of redeemed souls.[160] To make his point he brings to his text Ephesians 4:9-10, which speaks of Christ descending into the lower parts of the earth and then ascending far above all the heavens. Reading this sermon for the first time, one is struck with the way the two texts fit

155. Origen, *Sermons on Genesis* 6.2.
156. Origen, *Sermons on Genesis* 10.2.
157. On the existence of a Hebrew tradition of allegorical tradition quite indepen-

together. By modern standards it is an impossible typology and we struggle against what Origen would show us, but Origen's congregation had no such inhibitions and we can imagine that this sermon delighted those who heard it. After a flash of insight into the mysteries of God's redemptive plan like this, who needs a human interest story to keep the congregation awake!

Reading the sermons of Origen, one is constantly amazed at his vast knowledge of the Scriptures. This amazement increases when we realize that he was the first biblical scholar produced by the Church. There had been important Christian thinkers before Origen — one thinks of Irenaeus and Clement of Alexandria — but these thinkers were not primarily biblical scholars. There had been great Jewish biblical scholars, to be sure, and competent elders and teachers in the Church, but from the time of Christ and the apostles until the time of Origen there had been no specifically Christian biblical scholar of recognized authority. Origen was the pioneer in the field.

In his preparation of sermons he could not consult commentaries of those who had gone before, nor did he have a stack of lexical aids at his elbow. He had no concordances or Bible dictionaries. One asks, then, how did Origen prepare a sermon? How did he study his text? Several things should be noted about this. Origen's native language was Greek, and while he seems to have studied some Hebrew he does not seem to have mastered it. Although dependent on a Greek translation, he did seek out other Greek translations of the Old Testament and even published a column-by-column comparison of the Greek translations available in those days. Origen made wide use of the commentaries of Philo of Alexandria and, as one would expect, generally absorbed a great amount of the exegetical tradition of his native city. He was brought up on Christian preaching, and in an important Christian center such as Alexandria there was no doubt learned exposition of Scripture at daily morning prayer. If the Church was to survive in a city with such a sophisticated Jewish population, it would have had to develop some very clear ideas about the Christian interpretation of Scripture. From earliest childhood Origen must have heard such discussions. Origen was happy to learn whatever he could from Jewish exegetes of his day. Both in Alexandria and Caesarea he was in constant conversation with Jewish teachers as well as Greek philosophers.

Yet we have still not put our fingers on his most basic work of preparing sermons: his reading of the Bible. He studied the text itself — read it, copied it, memorized it, meditated on it. Having given himself so completely to listening to the text of the whole Bible, he then commented on one passage after another.

C. Sermons on the Gospel of Luke

Origen must have preached more than 150 sermons on the Gospel of Luke, starting with the nativity narrative and going all the way through to the stories of the resurrection and the ascension.[161] More than likely they were preached in Caesarea — in those days the cultural metropolis of Palestine, Jerusalem having not yet recovered from its destruction more than 150 years before. These sermons must have been preached between 230 and 240, although little in the way of either record or internal evidence would indicate this date. They give the impression of having been preached in a series of daily sermons at either morning prayer or evening prayer. Although no internal evidence supports this, there are good reasons for thinking it is the case. Such a long series is much easier to keep in focus if it can be done in six months rather than three years. The history of preaching indicates that these long series of expository sermons on individual books are usually given at daily preaching services. As we have mentioned, the sermons on Genesis were preached at daily morning services. Possibly there was preaching at evening services as well. Already in the New Testament we have evidence of evening services and evening preaching. For reasons of evangelistic strategy evening services might well have commended themselves to the ante-Nicene Church.[162]

For years the transcripts of these sermons were kept in the library of the church of Caesarea. Some copies must have been made, for we know that Ambrose used them in his series of sermons on the Gospel of Luke.[163] Sometime around the year 400, Jerome started a Latin translation of the

dent of Philo and the Alexandrian tradition, see R. P. C. Hanson, *Allegory and Event: A Study of the Sources and Significance of Origen's Interpretation of Scripture* (Richmond: John Knox Press, 1959), pp. 11-36 and 125.

158. Origen, *Sermons on Genesis* 4.

159. Origen, *Sermons on Genesis* 3.4-5.

160. Origen, *Sermons on Genesis* 15.5-6.

161. As far as I know, there is no English translation of these sermons. A French translation is given in Sources chrétiennes by François Fournier, *Origène, Homilies sur S. Luc* (Paris: Éditions du Cerf, 1962). A German translation is given by Herman Josef Sieben, *Origenes, Homilien zum Lukasevangelium,* 2 vols. (Freiburg: Herder, 1991-92).

series but only got through the fourth chapter.[164] When the emperor Justinian ordered the works of Origen destroyed, except for a few fragments, all that survived was the Latin translation of Jerome. If the whole series had been preserved it would have been monumental. To appreciate the grandeur of Origen's series of sermons on Luke we also have to remember that all we have is very abbreviated reports of these sermons. The sermons were apparently taken down in summary fashion by a stenographer and are typically much shorter than the reports we have of the sermons on Genesis, for instance. In reading these sermons one is constantly tempted to imagine what the sermon must originally have been like, how the sketches we find must have once been fleshed out. Like the ruins of many a classical monument, all we have is a few magnificent pieces, and yet what we can get from them is enough to suggest the grandeur of what once was and fire our imaginations as to what could again be.

Starting with the beginning of the Gospel of Luke and going through the fourth chapter we have thirty-three sermons. Since there are twenty-four chapters to the Gospel of Luke, we can imagine that we have something like one-sixth of the original series. It is interesting to notice the way Origen has divided up the text.

Sermon 1, Luke 1:1-3	The Prologue to the Gospel
Sermon 2, Luke 1:6	Zechariah and Elizabeth
Sermon 3, Luke 1:11	An Angel Appears to Zechariah
Sermon 4, Luke 1:13-17	The Angel's Message
Sermon 5, Luke 1:18-23	The Sign of Silence
Sermon 6, Luke 1:24-32	Gabriel Is Sent to Mary
Sermon 7, Luke 1:39-45	Mary Visits Elizabeth
Sermon 8, Luke 1:46-51	Mary's Hymn of Praise
Sermon 9, Luke 1:56-67	The Birth of John the Baptist
Sermon 10, Luke 1:67-76	Zechariah's Hymn of Praise
Sermon 11, Luke 1:80–2:2	Caesar and Quirinius
Sermon 12, Luke 2:8-12	The Shepherds in the Field
Sermon 13, Luke 2:13-16	The Praise of the Angels
Sermon 14, Luke 2:21-24	The Circumcision and the Purification

162. On the evidence for daily preaching services, see Pierre Nautin's introduction to his edition of Origen's sermons on Jeremiah, *Homélies sur Jérémie*, ed. P. Husson and

Sermon 15, Luke 2:25-29	The Ministry of Simeon
Sermon 16, Luke 2:33-34	The Prophecy of Simeon
Sermon 17, Luke 2:33-38	The Ministry of Anna
Sermon 18, Luke 2:40-49	The Boy Jesus in the Temple
Sermon 19, Luke 2:40-46	The Boy Jesus in the Temple
Sermon 20, Luke 2:49-51	The Youth of Jesus
Sermon 21, Luke 3:1-4	John the Baptist
Sermon 22, Luke 3:5-8	John's Ministry
Sermon 23, Luke 3:9-12	Response to the Baptist
Sermon 24, Luke 3:16	Baptism with Water and Spirit
Sermon 25, Luke 3:15	Was He the Messiah?
Sermon 26, Luke 3:17	The Work of the Messiah
Sermon 27, Luke 3:18-22	Jesus Is Baptized
Sermon 28, Luke 3:23-28	The Ancestry of Jesus
Sermon 29, Luke 4:1-4	The Temptation of Jesus
Sermon 30, Luke 4:5-8	The Temptation of Jesus
Sermon 31, Luke 4:9-13	The Temptation of Jesus
Sermon 32, Luke 4:14-20	The Teaching Ministry of Jesus
Sermon 33, Luke 4:23-27	Jesus in the Synagogue

These thirty-three sermons cover a very rich portion of Scripture. Simply going over the topics listed above, it is easy to understand how Origen and his congregation had no difficulty finding sufficient material for thirty-three sermons. For Origen it was an opportunity to delineate the mystery of the incarnation, and to do it on a big canvas. It takes a Giotto or a Michelangelo or a Rembrandt to paint a canvas as expansive as this one, and clearly Origen is up to it.[165]

Two centuries later when Jerome was translating these sermons, he got to the middle of the fourth chapter and decided the project was taking longer than he had expected, or perhaps he was distracted by another project[166] — we can't be sure what happened — and the systematic translation breaks off, although six more sermons are given from later in the

P. Nautin, 2 vols. (Paris: Éditions du Cerf, 1976 and 1977), and Sieben, *Origenes, Homilien zum Lukasevangelium,* 1:13-14.

163. On the tradition of the Greek text of Origen's sermons on Luke, see Sieben, *Origenes, Homilien zum Lukasevangelium,* 1:46ff.

164. On Jerome's Latin translation, see the edition published in Sources chrétiennes by Fournier, *Origène, Homilies sur S. Luc,* pp. 65-78.

165. Strangely enough, what should have been two of the central pieces of this

series. Why these particular sermons were translated and not others is not at all clear.[167] We find the following sermons:

Sermon 34, Luke 10:25-37	The Parable of the Good Samaritan	
Sermon 35, Luke 12:58-59	On the Text, "Settle with Your Accuser"	
Sermon 36, Luke 17:20-37	The Revelation of the Son of Man	
Sermon 37, Luke 19:29-40	The Triumphal Entry	
Sermon 38, Luke 19:41-45	The Things That Make for Peace	
Sermon 39, Luke 20:21-40	The Questions of Scribes and Pharisees	

Beyond this there are a number of fragments of the original Greek text of these sermons, some of which are a page or more long — enough fragments, at any rate, to assure us of the quality of Jerome's translation. There are a number of sizeable fragments of the sermons on the eighth to the twelfth chapters of the Gospel. All this would indicate that these sermons had been studied by other biblical scholars from a fairly wide segment of the Church for several centuries.

For Catholic scholars one of the most interesting things the surviving sermons show is how the early Church, a bit more than two hundred years after the birth of Christ, understood the role of the Virgin Mary in the history of salvation. For most of us Protestants this has never been of particular interest. However, some of the more sober reflections of the ancient Church on the spiritual value of virginity might be a salutary medicine to the moral confusions of our promiscuous culture.[168] Be that as it may, we will leave this very specialized subject to others.

For most of us an easier place to dig into this series of sermons is the three sermons on the temptations in the wilderness. These three sermons give us an interesting contrast to the sermons on Genesis. In the

work, the sermon on the annunciation (Luke 1:31-35) and the sermon on the birth (Luke 2:4-7), are missing.

166. One suggestion which we hesitate to accept is that Jerome's sole purpose in translating these sermons was to make evident that Ambrose had gotten his ideas for his sermons on Luke from Origen. Jerome is supposed to have made his point with the first thirty-three sermons.

167. See the discussions of this problem as well as the problem of the missing sermons on the annunciation and the sermon on the actual birth of Christ in the introductory material provided by both the edition of Fournier and the edition of Sieben.

first place they are on a New Testament book where the problem of allegory does not have the same significance — they give first importance to the literal sense of the texts they want to interpret. Even at that, however, a grammatical-historical interpretation of this passage has to deal with literary figures. One might say that the temptations in the wilderness constituted a sort of mystical experience which is reported in a very literal way.

The first sermon, as it has come down to us, begins rather abruptly. There is nothing by way of introduction. All we have is a commentary on the opening words of the passage, "And Jesus, full of the Holy Spirit, returned from the Jordan. . . ." When we read that Jesus was full of the Holy Spirit and later in Acts that Christians were full of the Holy Spirit, we should not imagine, Origen warns us, that they were equally full of the Holy Spirit.[169] As Origen understands it, even at Pentecost the apostles were not filled with the Holy Spirit to the same extent that Christ was. It was a matter of capacity, according to our preacher. Just what Origen was driving at here is not too clear. The stenographer may not have gotten it down or else Origen himself may not have followed it through. Most exegetes today would say that Luke was eager to make the point that the first Christians were filled with the same Holy Spirit as Jesus and that was why they could continue the ministry Jesus began. A good number of modern exegetes would want to insist that Origen did not have it quite straight. But we have to remember the context in which Origen was preaching. With the appearance of Marcion the empowering work of the Holy Spirit was so overemphasized that Origen feels the need to underline the uniqueness of the Spirit's anointing of Jesus. Around the year 200 there were all kinds of gnostics running around who imagined that because they had been filled with the Holy Spirit they could speak with divine authority on all kinds of subjects. Origen saw a danger in this. Here we see a good example of how a wise preacher can be sensitive to what a particular passage of Scripture might mean in a particular historical context and what it surely would not mean in that context. This, of course, is what hermeneutics is all about, and this sermon models it very well.

The next verse Origen takes up tells us that Jesus had been tempted in the wilderness for forty days by the devil.[170] This would become a

168. On the possibility of a more positive approach to the understanding of Mary in Protestant theology, see David Wright, ed., *Chosen by God: Mary in Evangelical Perspective*

particularly significant story for the Egyptian desert saints. It was not until well over a century after this that Christian asceticism really began to flourish, but in his day Origen had begun to move in that direction. We don't know to what extent he himself practiced the disciplines of the desert, but from the brief comments preserved in this sermon we gather that he was quite familiar with all this. No one, of course, can really interpret these passages who does not know something of the experience of the desert. The Bible has always been best understood by those who live the kind of life the Bible itself teaches. Faith witnesses to faith. Origen speculates as to what temptations Jesus experienced during those forty days which led up to the three temptations about which the Bible tells us. Our preacher seems to have in mind the sort of things we read about in *The Temptations of St. Anthony.* As Origen understands it, the whole point of the wilderness experience is to mortify the desires of the flesh.

Origen moves on to the third verse. After forty days of serious fasting Jesus was hungry, and the devil said that if he was indeed the Son of God he should command the stones to turn into bread. Origen raises the question of just which stones Jesus was supposed to turn to bread. Was it not the stones the devil had pointed out? With a deft exegetical sleight of hand, Origen brings out a striking parallel passage. Were not these the stones to which Jesus referred when he spoke of the good father who would never give his children stones when they asked for bread (Matt. 7:9; see also Luke 11:11)? The problem, Origen suggests, was that the devil wanted Jesus to turn the devil's stones — the wrong stones — into bread. The devil wanted Jesus to feed on the stone of error rather than the rock of truth. To put it another way, the devil put before Jesus the stone of stumbling rather than the rock of our salvation. One deduces even from this abbreviated report of Origen's sermon a very clever juxtaposition of biblical metaphors. This was not a short sermon. The train of thought is too intricate to allow the preacher to go over the material quickly. Scripture explains Scripture because Scripture has over the centuries built up a whole language, a whole system of metaphors, figures, and parables. In this sermon we discover Origen patiently mining this rich vein. Some might find this exegetical sleight of hand dishonest or at least opportunist, but it is not really. It is far more a shrewd insight into epistemology, an appreciation of how we understand.

Now Origen's sermon turns to application. Here, too, his thought is complex and diverse. It seems to him that Jesus went through these temptations to show us the way to resist temptations, so that we might be able to triumph through his triumph.[171] This is an important approach to hermeneutics. In the Gospels we read of the way Jesus lived life, and it is the job of the preacher to show Christian people how Jesus set the example of how we are to live the Christian life. But we are not dealing here with a simple moral-influence soteriology; there is a vicarious dimension to it as well. Christ's triumph over the temptations in the wilderness was *pro nobis,* that is, for us. We are able to triumph through his triumph. This is a more classically Christian message. Here the hermeneutic puts the emphasis on announcing the gospel. The job of the preacher is to proclaim the good news of what Christ has done for us.

As Origen continues, it becomes more and more clear that he has no intention of leaving this story of temptation to be understood in merely moralistic terms. He tells us that he realizes quite well his meaning might be a bit obscure, so he gives us an example. If today, Origen suggests, we hear heretics teaching doctrine which is supposed to be spiritually nourishing, we need to be warned that it is false doctrine.[172] It is supposed to be the bread of life but actually it is a lie. The discourses of the heretics are the stones the devil has shown them. Today the devil has a whole bunch of stones he wants people to try to turn into the bread of life. That is just what the gnostic teachers have done. Marcion, Valentinus, and Basilides have tried to pass off the stone which the father of evil has given them. As Origen sees it, one of the major temptations for the Christians in his day was the seductive teachings of gnosticism.[173]

There is another reason why this bread was the wrong bread for Jesus to eat. It was important for Jesus to live in dependence upon the Father rather than to try by his own power to fulfill his own needs, to wait upon the Father and what the Father would supply.[174] The sermon we have does not completely fill in this application, but the implication is clearly there: Origen implies that the same is true for the Christian today. We all must learn to wait upon the Lord. God will supply our need at the right time and in the right way.

Very interestingly it is at this point that Origen makes a few remarks about his hermeneutic. Surely there is a spiritual meaning here, our preacher insists. How would this have been a temptation and how a victory

(London: Marshall Pickering, 1989). On the place of Mary in the history of redemption, see the essay of Henri Crouzel, "La théologie mariale d'Origène," in the introduction to the Sources chrétiennes edition of Origen's sermons on the Gospel of Luke. See also Cipriano Vagaggini, *Maria nelle opere di Origene* (Rome: Pontifical Institute for Oriental Studies, 1942).

over temptation if one were to take it literally?[175] Origen is pointing to the fact that it was Jesus himself who was spiritualizing the text of Scripture. With this Origen addresses himself to the verse from Deuteronomy which, as we find it in the Gospel of Luke, Jesus quoted in his reply to the devil, "Man shall not live by bread alone but by every word which comes from God." Origen realizes that Jesus, and in fact the whole biblical tradition behind him, is using bread as a metaphor for spiritual teaching. What was at play in the Gospel story was not just physical hunger and physical food but spiritual hunger and spiritual food. The Gospel story gives Origen a perfect opportunity to demonstrate his approach to the spiritual interpretation of Scripture. It is a major point of concern for Origen and so he chooses to emphasize his point by using a very dramatic bit of oratory. Our preacher himself assumes the role of Christ in this confrontation and with biting irony addresses the devil. Go ahead, O devil, father of deception, be subtle and misleading. You seem to have no fear of tempting me, the Son of God. Are you not aware that there is another bread which is the Word of God, which gives life to man?[176]

Our preacher broaches one more subject. It would appear that he had been bothered by this story of the temptations of Christ for some time; he had long searched for the sense in which the story should be understood.[177] How could Jesus, if he was really the Son of God, be tempted? For someone living in a culture strongly influenced by Greek philosophy this would be a troubling question. For Greek philosophy, divinity had been understood in terms of absolutes. God was the omnipotent, the omniscient, and the omnipresent. God was above all feeling, all suffering, and all desire. How could one possibly tempt God? How could the devil even dare to tempt the divine Son of God? The irony Origen uses here would surely have been applauded by the more philosophically inclined members of Origen's congregation. No doubt in the sermon as it was preached Origen fleshed all this out, even if in the report we have it is transcribed in only the most abbreviated fashion. The solution to this problem of whether the Son of God can be tempted is not given to us in full. As Origen no doubt saw it, the divine nature was never really tempted. The human nature which the Son of God assumed could, on the other hand, be tempted. As evidence that this is the correct under-

169. Origen, *Sermons on Luke* 29.1.
170. Origen, *Sermons on Luke* 29.2.
171. Origen, *Sermons on Luke* 29.3.

standing our preacher points to the fact that all three Synoptic Gospels tell us about the temptations but the Gospel of John does not. This is because John tells about Jesus as God, whereas the other Gospels present Jesus as man. It was Jesus in his human nature who was tempted, and so we can expect to be tempted, too. That belongs to our humanity. If we imitate the man who withstood temptation and passed the test, then we can have the hope of him who rose from the dead.

The conclusion of the sermon as it is reported to us seems a bit abrupt. It may have been just this abrupt, of course. Our preacher may have been aware that his hour was up and very briefly sketched in the more inspiring conclusion he had planned but now realized he did not have time to finish. The experienced preacher will recognize the predicament. Even given an hour, which was the standard time allotted to the preacher in the ancient Church, the fertile mind of Origen never had trouble filling up the time.

The sermon on the second temptation begins with a dramatic introduction. Origen tells us that the Son of God and the Antichrist, the one just as the other, aspire to rule. This is a rather shocking statement. In this regard Christ and the Antichrist are just alike, but there are differences, our preacher continues. The Antichrist aspires to rule that he might destroy those whom he subjects to himself, while the Christ aspires to rule that he might save those who accept his rule. There are great blessings for those who accept the rule of Christ. For the faithful, Christ rules by being the Word, the divine wisdom, heavenly justice, and eternal truth. If, however, we prefer the pleasures of this world to the blessing of the world above, then we become the slaves of sin. It is against this that the apostle Paul warns, "Let not sin therefore reign in your mortal bodies" (Rom. 6:12). So it is that two kings face each other: the devil, the king of sin who reigns over sinners, and Christ, the king of justice who rules over the righteous.[178]

Taking up the text, our preacher selects the words "He showed him all the kingdoms of the world" (Luke 4:5). Origen suggests that this does not mean kingdoms such as Persia or India but rather the kingdoms of luxury, greed, the attraction of fame, and the seduction of beauty.[179] It was a matter of the devil showing Jesus how he was so successful in ruling the world: He enslaved people by pleasure, fortune, excitement, and celebrity. Wisdom, justice, and truth, according to the devil's logic, will never

172. Origen, *Sermons on Luke* 29.4.
173. Origen, *Sermons on Luke* 29.4.

be as effective in winning the devotion of mortals. The devil knows that if only he can get Jesus to use his methods rather than God's methods, he will successfully pervert the Son of God.

Origen goes on to the next verse, which tells of how the devil offered Jesus worldwide dominion if he would only worship him (Luke 4:6). The devil showed him the innumerable masses he holds in his power. To be truthful, our preacher observes, the devil is the ruler of almost the whole universe. When the devil asked Jesus if he saw the masses that had submitted to his diabolical power and showed them all to him in an instant, the Savior already knew all about it. He hardly needed to take more than a glance at all those who had been enslaved by their vices. That, Origen assures us, is what the Gospel of Luke means by saying that the devil showed him all this in an instant.[180]

Again we find Origen elaborating the text. Jesus, he tells us, well understood the pride of the devil. He understood that it was pride that made him want to submit so many to his empire. Putting words in the mouth of the devil, Origen has him asking Jesus if it is really against him that he wants to struggle. Is it from me that you want to free all these people? Why do you want to do that? Why bother? Why put yourself to the trouble? No doubt the stenographer's report only gives us a hint at the dramatic oratory of this master preacher. As Origen so colorfully imagines it, the devil warns Jesus: Don't expose yourself to that kind of danger! All you have to do is bow down at my feet and worship me and all this will be yours.

After this brilliant flight of imagination our preacher calmly returns to a more deliberative style, telling us that what the devil wanted Jesus to do was exactly what he could not do. Jesus aspired to reign over human hearts because he wanted justice to prevail; he wanted the truth to be revealed and all good virtues to be established. Jesus wanted justice to reign without being sullied with sin and entangled in obligations to the devil.[181]

Finally, our preacher takes up the reply Jesus gave to the devil's tempting words. It is written, Jesus said, you shall worship the Lord your God and none other than he. What does this mean? Origen asks. It means that the Christ wants to rule over human hearts in order that they worship the Lord and him alone. That is what is behind the Savior's desire to reign. This time our preacher takes the words of Christ into his own mouth and

174. Origen, *Sermons on Luke* 29.4.
175. Origen, *Sermons on Luke* 29.5.

imagines what further Jesus might have said to his tempter. And you, O devil, you want to make of me the beginning of sin, the sin I came to destroy, the sin from which I want to deliver all humanity. Know this, that I have come so that the Lord God and he alone is to be worshiped. With this our preacher turns to his congregation. And as for us, he says, let us rejoice that we are in the kingdom of Christ, and let us pray God that sin have no more reign in our bodies, and Christ and Christ alone reign in our hearts.[182]

The third sermon on the temptations of Christ opens with a remark about how one should approach the interpretation of Scripture. Let us read the Scriptures, Origen tells us, even the simplest passages, in such a way that we discover the mysteries of true grandeur hidden within them.[183] These passages may appear simple, but they contain great mysteries. It is with this in mind that we examine the text of the Gospel we have heard read today. We are told that the devil conducted Jesus to Jerusalem (Luke 4:9). Look at this! How unbelievable! The devil takes Jesus, the Son of God, and Jesus follows after him. How are we to understand this? We gather that here is one of those little signs which prompt Origen to look for deeper meanings — in this case a remark that has a sort of anthropomorphic ring to it. This bothers Origen's penchant for Platonic philosophy. How could anyone, especially the devil, lead the Son of God anywhere? Origen answers with a brilliant simile. Perhaps the way to understand this is that Jesus allowed himself to be led as an athlete allows himself to be conducted to the field of contest or to the stadium where he must prove himself.[184] He does not fear his tempter nor the attacks of his very devious enemy.

Again we find Origen elaborating the story by putting words in the mouth of one of the characters, in this case Jesus. Lead me where you wish; tempt me as you will, he has Jesus saying. I freely expose myself to your temptations, but I am determined to resist them, and you will find that I am stronger at resisting them than you had ever imagined. We notice the rhetoric here with great interest. This is not allegory, yet it does intimate a deeper meaning. What Origen does is expand and elaborate the text in order to explain it. It is a most imaginative method of exposition, and it is certainly effective.

176. Origen, *Sermons on Luke* 29.5.
177. Origen, *Sermons on Luke* 29.
178. Origen, *Sermons on Luke* 30.1.

Our preacher again picks up his text, this time at the point where the devil leads Jesus to the pinnacle of the Temple and bids him to throw himself down so that the angels will rescue him in an astounding play of circus magic. The crowds will love it! With such pious feats of entertainment surely Jesus will win the adoration of the common people. Origen tells us that this was pure hypocrisy on the part of the devil. He pretends he wants to reveal the glory of Christ, but that is not his intention at all. For Origen the interesting thing in this story is the way the devil uses Scripture to tempt Jesus. Again Origen brings out his most imaginative rhetoric, even to the point of lashing the devil with sarcasm. How is it that you, O devil, know that these things are written in Scripture? Have you read the prophets? Do you know the Word of God? You don't have to answer; I can answer for you. You have read the holy books, not because you want to learn from them how to live a holy life, but because you want to destroy those who seriously want to be holy. You want to justify yourself by proving that holiness is foolish. You want to use the Word of God to destroy the Word of God. You want to use the letter of the Law to kill the spirit of the Law.[185]

One never ceases to be amazed at Origen's overwhelming sense of the authority of Scripture. It may very well be that he lived in a world where that authority could unfold in some ways which to us seem quite fantastic, if not even ridiculous, but for Origen there is a vitality in the authority of Scripture which is so abundantly creative. It is a constantly gushing fountain of new ideas and fresh vision. Are we so sure that all that is really so naive? Maybe that ancient preacher understood things much better than we. From the mouth of Jesus Origen reproaches the devil: You quote the Scriptures because you know they have authority and you have none. You have to use their authority because you have none of your own, and so you use the Scriptures, but you misuse them. You twist them in a treacherous way so that you pervert their creative power and it becomes a destructive power.

As our preacher sees it, the same sort of temptation was facing the Church of his time. Heretics like Marcion, Valentinus, and Basilides perverted the Scriptures; they quoted them to say what they in fact do not say at all. For Christians approaching the third Christian millennium, we cannot help but ask what makes the difference between Marcion and Origen. Marcion totally rejected the Old Testament; Origen delighted in

179. Origen, *Sermons on Luke* 30.2.

it. What was the difference between gnostics like Valentinus and Basilides and Origen? Origen was condemned as a heretic just as the gnostics were. We ask ourselves how we can be sure that we are interpreting the Scriptures as we should. Which of us today can mount the pulpit without a certain hesitation? We cannot help but ask ourselves if we really have it straight. Surely one thing is clear. For Origen the authority of Scripture was an ever creative power that somehow gets through in spite of every mistake he may have made, every misunderstanding of the age in which he lived, even in spite of the opposition of most eminent theologians. The emperor Justinian ordered his works destroyed, but somehow they survived. Sometimes one finds the strangest interpretations of Scripture in Origen, but sometimes one finds the deepest mysteries of the faith. For age after age Christians have found that Origen really does throw light on the meaning of Scripture. The *sensus spiritualis* may be forgotten from time to time, but it keeps reappearing. Origen's intention was always to be faithful to the Word of God. For the leading of the Holy Spirit he always prayed, and quite obviously that prayer was often answered. Indeed, the Spirit moves when and where and how he pleases, and yet the Spirit is, as are the Father and the Son, ever faithful. On that we can depend. In the end authority is revealed by creativity. The fact that God's Word can create today just as it did in the beginning is about the best proof there is that God's Word has authority.

D. Allegory and Typology

When looked at as a whole, Origen's sermons help us understand why he was such a greatly beloved preacher. They have a vitality to them, at once spontaneous and natural, that comes from his constant reading and re-reading of Scripture on the one hand and his constant engagement with the Greek philosophers and Jewish rabbis of his day on the other. And yet, as much as we can admire these sermons, we cannot treat Scripture as Origen treated it.[186]

Even in Origen's own lifetime there were those who objected to the

180. Origen, *Sermons on Luke* 30.3.
181. Origen, *Sermons on Luke* 30.3.
182. Origen, *Sermons on Luke* 30.4.
183. Origen, *Sermons on Luke* 31.1.

great preacher's methods of interpretation. In the fourth century they were challenged by the school of Antioch and its two great preachers, John Chrysostom and Theodore of Mopsuestia. But even with this challenge, Origen had many disciples, particularly in the West where Ambrose of Milan, followed by Augustine, adopted Origen's methods. In the East Gregory of Nyssa made wide use of Origen's methods, but even such prestigious supporters did not silence the criticism. In the sixth century the methods were condemned by a church council, then by a decree of the emperor Justinian his writings were destroyed. This certainly did not end Origen's influence. He had planted seeds deeply in both the East and the West. The monastic preachers of the Middle Ages, strangely enough, completely ignored Origen's condemnation and made Origen's four levels of interpretation the bedrock of their preaching ministry.

Surely if there was something wrong about the exegesis of Origen, there was something right about it, too. In fact, we have to say much was right about it, but at this point we want to zero in on one thing in particular. Origen's exegesis preserved much of the tradition of the Christian interpretation of the Scriptures which went back to Jesus and the apostles. It elaborated this tradition, to be sure, and it even elaborated it floridly, but it did preserve it.

Origen quite correctly pointed to the fact that the apostle Paul had given great attention to the spiritual interpretation of the Old Testament. He was particularly fond of identifying Paul's spiritual interpretations of the Law and the prophets as he found them in his New Testament epistles. Origen had his finger on something. We spoke about this at considerable length in the previous chapter. Not only the New Testament but the Old Testament itself had begun a spiritual interpretation of Scripture that went far back into the history of God's self-revelation to his people.[187] When Hosea spoke of a redemption of Israel that would someday come (Hos. 2:14-15 et passim), he said it would be a redoing of the exodus from Egypt, the wandering in the wilderness, and the entry into the Promised Land. When Isaiah promised that God would send Israel a king like David who would bring justice and peace to the land (Isa. 9:6-7 et passim), the foundation of biblical typology had been set.

The basic idea was that God had given Israel in the past a glimpse of the destiny toward which he was moving his people. These glimpses were not just fantasies but actual experiences of a higher and future reality.

184. Origen, *Sermons on Luke* 31.1.

They were not so much a foreshadow of what was to come as a foretaste, not so much visions of what was to come as experiences of what was to come. And most importantly, these experiences of God's redemptive activity in their lives were a promise, a prophetic promise given by God himself that what God had begun he would bring to completion. Origen understood this, and that was what was so very right about his preaching. He kept before his congregation the promises of God. He assured Christians that God is faithful to his promises and that the destiny established before all creation and revealed in all its splendor in the death and resurrection of Christ is an open reality to all who would enter into it.

The major biblical types had all been well established long before Origen. The exodus typology goes far back into Scripture — at least as far as the prophet Hosea. When Jesus interpreted his death in terms of the Passover, it had a logic that was convincing to the good Jew. Everyone in Israel knew that the exodus was the prefiguration and promise of an even greater redemption yet to come. The David typology is deeply ingrained in Scripture; we find it all through the book of Psalms and the New Testament. The David typology and the exodus typology are the two central types of Scripture, but there are others which are hardly less important.

The Adam-Christ typology is found clearly outlined by the apostle Paul in the fifth chapter of Romans, where we are told that Adam was a type of the one who was to come. "Therefore as sin came into the world through one man and death through sin, . . . much more have the grace of God and the free gift in the grace of that one man Jesus Christ abounded for many" (Rom. 5:12-15). Today New Testament scholars are aware that this typology was far from an invention of Paul's, but that it went deep into the history of biblical thought.

It is the same way with the Sabbath typology, which is even older. Both in the Epistle to the Hebrews (4:1-10) and in the Revelation (1:10 et passim) the Sabbath typology plays an important role. The weekly Sabbath is a sacrament, a sign and a promise of eternal rest. It is each week a foretaste of a higher coming reality, and yet, even more, the Old Testament Sabbath is a type of the Lord's Day, the day of the Lord, the day of judgment and consummation.

That Jerusalem is a type and sacrament of the holy city above is basic to biblical piety. What else could develop from the whole idea of the pilgrimage feast? The pilgrimage was itself a sacrament, just as the city to which one journeyed was a sacrament. Long before Origen, even long before Philo, the Tabernacle and the Temple were understood to be copies of a heavenly reality (Exod. 25:40 and Heb. 8:5). They became a means of entering into God's presence while still living on this earth. We spoke in the last chapter about how Jesus presented himself to the crowds of Jerusalem as the fulfillment of the Temple; about how his body, if destroyed, would be raised up on the third day and how this same body is the Church, not made by human hands but edified by the Holy Spirit, and now a spiritual temple. Whoever made sure that the Gospels recorded that the veil of the Temple had been rent from top to bottom not only understood the Temple typology but figured that his readers would understand it as well. Indeed he was right, for Hebrews as well as Revelation assume an elaborate typological understanding of both the Tabernacle and the Temple. In I Peter we find the same assumption. Unless one could assume that one's readers understood this typology, how could one ever expect them to understand "Come to him, to that living stone, rejected by men but in God's sight chosen and precious; and like living stones be yourselves built into a spiritual house, to be a holy priesthood, to offer spiritual sacrifices acceptable to God through Jesus Christ" (I Pet. 2:4-5)?

The Joshua-Jesus typology is implicit in the story of Christ's baptism. Already we find it intimated in the Gospel of Matthew when we are told how an angel directed that the Christ child was to be named Jesus, " 'for he will save his people from their sins' " (Matt. 1:21). In fact, John the Baptist himself probably assumed that Joshua was a type of the coming Christ. He knew well that he was dealing with well-established biblical signs when he carried out his ministry in the wilderness and baptized in the Jordan.

That Noah is a type of Christ, the ark a type of the Church, and the flood a type of the last judgment were not constructions of Origen's. As we pointed out above, Origen knew well that Jesus himself had understood this typology. "As it was in the days of Noah, so will it be in the days of the Son of Man' " (Luke 17:26).

It was the same way with the typological understanding of the Song of Solomon. Only a typological understanding that these songs are the hymnody of the divine wisdom, that Israel is the bride and God himself the bridegroom, could explain why already in New Testament times the Song of Solomon was considered Scripture. The roots of this typology go way back into Scripture. Isaiah, Jeremiah, and Hosea all spoke of Israel as the bride. Had Jesus not himself told the parable of the wedding feast of the king's son? For the Gospel of John this typology is clearly assumed both in the story of the wedding at Cana, where Christ reveals himself as the true bridegroom, and in the story of Christ's resurrection appearance to Mary in the garden. In the Revelation of John the wedding feast of the lamb who was slain and lives evermore makes this typology even clearer (Rev. 19:9).

This whole tradition of understanding Scripture in terms of types, Origen had learned from reading the Scriptures, for it is deeply imbedded in both the Old and New Testament. Perhaps even more importantly, Origen had learned this approach to Scripture from living oral tradition in the church of Alexandria. This living tradition, it must be remembered, was unique. It inherited the traditions of Alexandrian Judaism which had tried so hard to establish itself in the Hellenistic world and make itself understandable to its cultural environment. It inherited the Alexandrian exegesis which Philo had worked out with such genius and imagination.

Origen was not altogether an innovator. He stood in a long tradition. In this tradition there had already been an attempt to make Scripture understandable in terms of Greek philosophy, and this tradition Origen was eager to continue.[188] The Alexandrian school of exegesis had approached the task of interpreting Scripture from the Platonic doctrine of forms. It saw the stories of the Old Testament as manifestations of eternal principles. No matter how perverted some of these stories might be, speaking of the bigamy of Jacob or the incest of the daughters of Lot, for instance, they were really speaking of higher realities. The obvious perversion in such stories was a divinely given hint that one was not to take them literally but to seek in them a higher reality. The theory was that the Greek myths were allegories.[189] They were not really told because they gave the histories of the loves and wars of the gods and heroes of antiquity; they were told to speak of eternal realities. This was the way the Greek philosophers had tried to salvage Greek mythology for the enlightened, and this was the way Jewish and Christian exegetes of Alexandria would explain the Hebrew Scriptures to their congregations. It all made sense in terms of Platonic philosophy.

The biggest problem with the Alexandrian exegesis is that it confused Greek allegory and Hebrew typology. This was the case with Philo in a

---

185. Origen, *Sermons on Luke* 31.2.

186. There is an extensive literature on Origen's approach to the interpretation of Scripture. Among the most important works are the following: Henri Crouzel, *Origène et*

rather flat and outright way, but it was also true of Origen, although Origen took steps to protect the uniqueness of Scripture and never disposed of its literal sense. The biblical history was to be understood quite objectively as history. The patriarchs and the prophets were to be understood as historical figures in the usual sense. It was quite different with the stories of the Greek gods and the way they were interpreted by the enlightened pagan with inclinations toward Platonic philosophy. Now it is true there is a certain similarity between Hebrew typology and Greek allegory, but there is also a great difference. The types of the Old Testament were understood as events which really did happen. Origen was not willing to dismiss them as mere myth. He always insisted on the historical integrity of Scripture.

In the types of the Old Testament God's people really did experience the grace of God. This grace may not have been in full strength or in its purest form, but this experience began to give God's people an elementary apprehension of the ways of God. By experiencing the types of Christ they were prepared to receive the Christ. But that these experiences were real and not just literary constructs was an important distinction. Origen did not always guard the historicity of Scripture sufficiently. He was a bit too willing to suggest that God set up the situation to be an allegory for generations to come. To suggest, for example, that God set up the whole matter of Sarah and Abimelech so that future generations could be instructed on the relation of worldly wisdom and sacred wisdom does not really do justice to the integrity of the biblical authors.[190]

Another problem with allegorical exegesis is that it has a way of being the handmaid of asceticism. Allegorical exegesis as it was developed by Origen and his followers became the Trojan horse of a type of Christian spirituality which was markedly ascetic.[191] For the ascetic the material expression of these eternal realities was of very little importance. Origen was careful not to follow asceticism to its gnostic extremes. He always affirmed the incarnation of Christ and the resurrection of the body. Yet the understanding of the Christian life he gleaned from the Scriptures was far more ascetic than what Jesus or the apostles taught. Whoever reads the

la connaissance mystique (Paris: Desclée de Brouwer, 1961); Daniélou, *Origène;* Gögler, *Zur Theologie des biblischen Wortes bei Origen;* Hanson, *Allegory and Event.*

187. Cf. Gögler, *Zur Theologie des biblischen Wortes bei Origen,* pp. 75ff.

188. On the allegorical interpretation of the Hellenistic Jews, see Gögler, *Zur Theologie des biblischen Wortes bei Origen,* pp. 93ff.

Song of Solomon and hears nothing about the spiritual joy of marriage has missed something of the Word of God.

There is still another problem. Origen's doctrine of the inspiration of Scripture seems at times a bit Pythian. He gives the impression that Scripture was inspired in the same way that the oracles of Pythian Apollo were produced at the sanctuary of Delphi — filled with intentional ambiguities; the words of the gods, not of man. That the Word of God is to be found in the words of men was something Origen did not fully appreciate. The humanity of the biblical authors did not play a sufficient role in Origen's understanding of Scripture. There was a sort of ecstasy involved in the giving of oracles. It was the same way with the allegories of Greek mythology, which were imagined to have been given in poetic ecstasy. Once one had the sacred text, all sorts of things could be deduced from it. Because it was not the product of a rational mind or the usual processes of thought, it was no longer bound by the usual methods of making sense in human language. Origen seems sometimes to assume much the same thing for the Christian Scriptures. Perhaps the earliest Hebrew prophets understood their utterances this way, but the canonical prophets seem to have left this idea behind them, and this is not the way the apostles understood what they wrote. If Origen sometimes misunderstood the biblical typology and treated it as Greek allegory, it may have been to a large extent because of what we might call his "Pythian" doctrine of inspiration.

The greatest difference between Hebrew typology and Greek allegory is that Hebrew typology is an integral part of the way Scripture is understood. It is part of the dynamic of promise and fulfillment that is of the essence of the covenant relationship. The identifying and interpreting of the types was* part of the prophetic ministry. Not all the things that happened to ancient Israel were types of God's future redemption, so it belonged to the prophetic vision of the biblical writers to recognize the hand of God in the experience of God's people. True types are divinely given signs, and as biblical signs they do more than merely signify — they participate in the reality of which they speak. They even initiate us into the reality that is prophecy. True biblical typology takes place in Scripture itself. It is integral to the process of Scripture interpreting Scripture. The fundamental biblical typologies are all there, gradually being unfolded from Genesis to Revelation. Types are not discovered by clever exegetes either in Origen's day or ours. They are canonical. They were recognized long ago by the biblical authors.

Following the traditions of Alexandria, Origen sometimes mistook biblical typology for allegory and treated it as though it were allegory. To be sure, Origen found the terminology of Greek allegory in the New Testament. He made this all quite clear in the *Peri Archon*. Above all Origen called on Galatians 4:22-24, where the apostle Paul speaks of Sarah's giving birth to Isaac.

> For it is written that Abraham had two sons, one by a slave and one by a free woman. But the son of the slave was born according to the flesh, the son of the free woman through promise. Now this is an allegory: these women are two covenants.

Paul may be using the terminology of Alexandrian exegesis even to the point of calling the story an allegory, but he is dealing with biblical typology. The story of Sarah's motherhood is preeminently a story of promise and fulfillment and is a type of God's covenant faithfulness. One could even go so far as to say that Paul was influenced by Alexandrian exegesis. Surely one could hardly deny strong Alexandrian influence in the Epistle to the Hebrews. Nevertheless for both Paul and for the author of Hebrews the essential insights of true typology are never lost. Their use of Alexandrian exegesis was a conservative use of it.

Origen often stayed within the bonds of traditional Christian typology. We find a good example of this in Sermon 3, on Abraham's circumcision.[192] The spiritual meaning had been well established for centuries. The New Testament is quite clear on circumcision being a type of baptism, although this sermon does not go into this aspect of the tradition (Col. 2:11, 12, 17). The sermon is really on the inner meaning of covenant.

But Origen could also invent spiritual meanings for stories that have no basis in Scripture. When he does this — as he does rather blatantly in Sermon 5, on Lot and his daughters[193] — he goes completely beyond biblical typology and treats the Scripture as though it were Greek allegory. Origen is offended in this sermon by the incest of the family of Lot. Why this embarrassment about the story? Is it not because Origen has mistakenly read the story as the Greek philosophers read the stories of the Homeric gods? The Scriptures do not present the patriarchs as gods or heroes whose virtues are to be emulated. But somehow Origen feels a

---

189. On the use of allegorical interpretation by Greek philosophers, see Gögler, *Zur Theologie des biblischen Wortes bei Origen*, pp. 60-75 and 120ff.

necessity to justify the story and so turns it into an allegory without a trace of suggestion that anyone else, prophet or apostle, had ever understood the story allegorically before.

That Origen had gone too far in his use of allegory has been recognized by many biblical scholars all through the centuries, and yet even today he points out to us the legitimacy of a spiritual or contemplative exegesis. Whether dealing with the Old Testament or the New Testament, there are times when we have to go beyond the literal meaning to a deeper meaning. Today, after several generations of nothing more than flat, literal interpretations, there seems once more to be a quest for discovering a legitimate *sensus spiritualis.*

E. The Liturgical Setting of Origen's Preaching

Origen's sermons give us a good look at how the reading and preaching of Scripture fit into the worship of the ancient Church. In fact, a careful reading of his sermons allows us to gather extensive information about the liturgical setting of the Scripture lessons and sermons of the Church in the second and third centuries. Werner Schütz, who most recently has combed the writings of Origen to gather information about the worship of the period, tells us that the Scripture readings were the first and even the most important part of the service of worship.[194] The sermon had as its function the exposition of the Scripture lessons and nothing more.[195] While not going quite so far, we would certainly agree that the reading and preaching of Scripture were central to Christian worship as Origen understood it. Schütz suggests that in the reading and preaching of Scripture Origen recognized a certain "Epiphanie Jesu," by which he understood what elsewhere we have called the kerygmatic presence of Christ in worship.[196] When the Scriptures are read and preached in worship, then Christ is present and feeds the congregation with spiritual bread and wine.[197]

Pierre Nautin has given considerable attention to the liturgical setting

190. Origen, *Sermons on Genesis* 6.3.

191. On the spirituality of Origen and its influence on Christian piety, see Gustave Bardy, "La spiritualité d'Origène," *La Vie spirituelle* 31 (1932): 80-106; Louis Bouyer, *The Spirituality of the New Testament and the Fathers* (New York: Seabury Press, 1982), pp. 277-302; Daniélou, *Origène;* Quasten, *Patrology,* 2:94-101.

of Origen's preaching.[198] He explains the evidence he has assembled from the sermons of Origen by the following schedule. As he sees it, the church of Caesarea, typical for the second and third centuries, had three types of worship services.

1. There was the weekly service on the Lord's Day which included three readings from Scripture — one from the Old Testament; one from the apostles, that is, from one of the New Testament epistles or Acts; and finally one from one of the four Gospels — each of which was followed by a short sermon. The ministry of the Word was then followed by prayers and the Eucharist. Nautin figures that by the time of Origen the reading of a lesson from the Law followed by a lesson from the prophets had already been consolidated into a single lesson.

2. The second type of service was the midweek eucharistic service held on Wednesday and Friday afternoons. These services concluded the weekly fast days observed by Christians at that period. At these services, according to Nautin, there was a reading from the Gospels and perhaps one from the apostles, but probably not from the Old Testament.

3. Finally there was a third type of service, the daily morning prayer service at which there was a reading from the Old Testament and, following it, an hour-long sermon, but no New Testament reading.[199] Only these services were open to catechumens, according to Nautin.

Nautin has figured out the average length of the text for each of the sermons which has come down to us, and on the basis of that how long it would take to preach through the Old Testament and the Gospels, respectively. The whole Old Testament could be preached through in three years, Nautin estimates, as could the four Gospels. Nautin figures there was a third cycle, the apostles, which could also be preached through in three years.

Surely Nautin is on solid ground in regard to the daily morning services. Much evidence in Origen's sermons on Old Testament books indicates that they were preached at the daily service of morning prayer. It is from these series of sermons on Old Testament books that most of Origen's sermons come, that is, most of those which have been preserved. Whether this is to be explained primarily because the morning service was

---

192. Origen, *Sermons on Genesis* 3.

193. Origen, *Sermons on Genesis* 5.

194. For the most recent attempt to put this material together, see Werner Schütz, *Der christliche Gottesdienst bei Origenes* (Stuttgart: Calwer Verlag, 1984), p. 73.

aimed at the catechumens and therefore had to limit itself to the Old Testament is another matter. Nautin has shown some passages in these sermons which indicate there are catechumens in Origen's congregation, but other passages indicate that he assumes his hearers are illumined, that is, that they are already baptized. That only Old Testament books were read at morning prayer is not at all clear. What is clear is that even in Origen's time there was a considerable amount of preaching from the Old Testament. The earliest Christian services of worship continued to read the Old Testament Scriptures because those were the only Scriptures they had. To imagine that it was only a matter of necessity that kept the Church reading the Old Testament would be a mistake, however. Even less was it simply the force of habit. Origen, in opposition to Marcion, is very clear that the Old Testament is divinely inspired just as the New Testament is. As such we read the Old Testament Scriptures as a service to God's glory. This is the fundamental reason. The Old Testament is the Word of God and therefore we read it in worship as an act of honor to God.

There are other, more practical reasons, too. The interpretation of the Old Testament continued to be an important feature of the ministry of the Word, especially in cities like Caesarea and Alexandria, cities with strong Jewish communities, because the Christian interpretation of the Old Testament had constantly to be taught. As is so very clear from Origen's sermons, his preaching the Christian interpretation of the Old Testament had an evangelistic function. It was through preaching the Christian understanding of the Scriptures that the Church sought to win the Jews to the Christian faith. Then, too, in an environment where the synagogue was very strong, Christians needed to be well grounded in the Christian understanding of the Old Testament because that understanding was constantly under attack. If Christians were to remain firm in their faith, they had to know that the Scriptures of the Old Testament were fulfilled in both Christ's works of humiliation and his works of exaltation. The path Marcion had taken would have been all too easy to follow, and yet Origen and the leaders of the Church in the second and third centuries knew that was not the way the apostles had gone. They knew the apostles had not thrown out the Old Testament but rather had carefully guarded the interpretation of the Law and the prophets Jesus had taught them. Origen's sermons on the Old Testament books are not for beginners; he is preaching to the most fervent and best instructed members of the congregation. Surely there were catechumens present, but it is not to catechumens that these sermons are directed.

It is hard to believe that only the baptized were allowed to hear the reading and preaching of the New Testament and that catechumens were excluded from both the preaching service on Sunday morning and the eucharistic service.[200] Furthermore, we find it much more likely that Origen's sermons on the Gospel of Luke were allowed the usual full hour. Like the Old Testament sermons, these sermons were no doubt preached daily, possibly at evening prayer. Nautin explains the evening service only in terms of the observance of the days of fasting on Wednesdays and Fridays, whereas there may have been vesper services every day of the week at which a full sermon could have been preached. On Wednesdays and Fridays, then, this service could have been followed by the celebration of the Lord's Supper.

It would certainly seem more than likely that in a major Christian center such as Caesarea there would be daily vesper services, and that at these vesper services there would be preaching. That is the way life goes in that part of the world. After the siesta, in the cool of the day, people get dressed up and go out for a promenade. It was the perfect time in Jerusalem to go to the Temple for the evening sacrifice (Acts 3:1). For Christians in Caesarea it was the same way — the perfect time to go to church for a sermon. The evening service is old tradition going back long before Christ and the apostles. It is hard to believe that the ancient Christian Church did not honor it.

Another place we find Nautin's reconstruction convincing is in the matter of preaching the *lectio continua*. Origen preached through one book of the Bible after another, chapter by chapter, verse by verse. This is clearly the case in his series of sermons on both the Old Testament and the Gospel of Luke. What is not as clear is that the reading of either the Old Testament books or the Gospels had become a fixed three-year cycle. It seems much more likely that Origen or any other preacher in the second or third centuries began with a Gospel and preached through it at his own speed until he reached the end. There were no hard-and-fast rules about where the lessons were supposed to begin or end — generally one began where one left off at the previous service. There was no reason, however, why one could not reread part of what had been read the day before if the

195. Schütz, *Der christliche Gottesdienst bei Origenes*, p. 82.
196. Schütz, *Der christliche Gottesdienst bei Origenes*, pp. 17ff.
197. Schütz, *Der christliche Gottesdienst bei Origenes*, pp. 76ff.
198. Nautin, *Origène, sa vie et son oeuvre*, pp. 389-412.

preacher had a few points he still wanted to make on the passage. As we have said, in most cases the length of the lesson would be left to the lector. Surely the lector and the preacher must have come to an agreement from time to time, but just as surely the lector would get a feel for how long a passage a given preacher would comment on in a typical sermon, and the two would improvise — perhaps even on the spot. When Justin tells us that the memoirs of the apostles and the writings of the prophets were read as long as time allowed, we get the impression that the length of the lesson was not predetermined. The readings were not set readings, beginning at a set place and ending at a set place.

More experienced preachers would tend to go through the books much more slowly. Anyone who has preached the *lectio continua* will understand that the more one knows about Scripture, the more one has to say. Less experienced preachers will tend to go through the book more rapidly. But then it could be the other way around. A very experienced preacher might decide to preach through a book rapidly because he knows he is dealing with a congregation which has little knowledge of Scripture and he wants to emphasize the primary message of a book. However, one of the pitfalls of the *lectio continua* generally is the tendency to slow it down to a snail's pace. Origen sometimes preached through a book rapidly and sometimes slowly. This would have upset no one. No one was particularly concerned that by the winter solstice the Gospel of Luke had to be finished or the Gospel of John begun.[201] What one was concerned to do was read through the whole of Scripture and to comprehend what was read.

The Christian Church in Origen's day did not observe anything like what today we call the Christian year. There was a Christian observance of Passover each year. The Church had settled on calling the feast πάσχα, that is, they had transliterated the word rather than attempting to translate it. It was clearly an interpretation of the Jewish feast rather than a feature of specifically Christian worship. Pentecost was regarded as a Christian feast, but it was a sort of pendant of the Christian celebration of Passover. It played out the sacred numerology by completing the seven weeks of seven days of the new creation. Not until well into the fourth century was Christmas or Epiphany celebrated.

The weekly celebration of the Lord's Day was the most important

199. To argue that there was a *disciplina arcana* which was stretched to the point

observance. That the Lord's Day was particularly the day of Christian worship is frequently mentioned in the liturgical documents of the second and third centuries. The *Didache,* Pliny's letter to Trajan, Justin's *Apology,* and Tertullian all mention the observance of the Lord's Day as a characteristic feature of Christian worship. Much more than that was looked on as innovation. Origen regarded the holding of special feast days as a Judaizing tendency.

Rather than going in the direction of a Christian year, Origen seems headed in a different direction. He freely admits that Christians observe Sundays and Fridays and that they celebrate Easter and Pentecost, but to him the celebration of worship belongs to all days.[202] In his sermon on Rebecca in the series on Genesis Origen warns his congregation:

> Unless, therefore, you come daily to the wells, unless you daily draw water not only will you not be able to give drink to others, but you yourself also will suffer "a thirst for the word of God." . . . I entreat you who are always present in this place where the word is preached, listen patiently while we admonish a little the negligent and idle. . . . Tell me, you who come to Church only on festal days, are the other days not festal days? Are they not the Lord's days? It belongs to the Jews to observe religious ceremonies on fixed and infrequent days. And for this reason God says to them: "I cannot bear your new moons and sabbaths and great days. My soul hates the fast day and festival and your feast days" (Is. 1:13-14). God hates, therefore, those who think that the festal day of the Lord is one day. . . . Christians eat the flesh of the lamb every day, that is, they consume the flesh of the word. . . .[203]

From this it is obvious that for Origen the daily preaching services are more important than any kind of festal calendar of special days. Feast days and fast days were of secondary importance. The Christian interpretation of the fourth commandment as it was apparently understood in the second century was concerned to point out that we should live a holy life every day of the week.[204] As were the Old Testament prophets and the apostle Paul, Origen is very critical of an elaborate liturgical calendar. To develop a theology of the Christian year would have been abhorrent to Origen. Both in Alexandria

of not allowing the catechumens to hear the reading and preaching of the Gospel assumes that the evangelistic function of preaching had completely disappeared.

200. Nautin bases his theory that the unbaptized were excluded from the reading and preaching of the Gospel on a passage in the *Apostolic Tradition* of Hippolytus, namely,

and in Caesarea Origen had constantly to explain why Christians did not observe the Jewish Sabbath and the Jewish festal calendar. Much of what Origen has to say on this subject reflects this controversy.

When Origen was not caught up in his polemics, however, he could have quite a bit to say about the unique character of the Lord's Day. The Lord's Day was to be observed especially by the preaching of the Word. In a sermon on the Law addressed to a Christian congregation he tells us that on Sundays we should set aside the concerns of this world and devote ourselves to spiritual things, that we should go to church and listen to the readings of the Scriptures and the sermons preached on the Scriptures. For Origen the reading and preaching of the Scriptures was spiritual worship. It was one of the spiritual sacrifices of the New Testament Church. Sunday, Origen tells us, is a day to meditate on heavenly things.[205]

Clearly Origen is trying to avoid any kind of Sabbatarian legalism. He has no intention of bringing all that into the Christian observance of the Lord's Day. There was, however, something unique about the worship of the Lord's Day, and it was by dominical institution that it was unique. On the other hand, that was not the case with fasting on Friday or the Christian celebration of Passover. Origen was a confirmed ascetic and found days of fasting a most welcome opportunity to exercise this spiritual discipline. In a somewhat similar way Origen had a strong attachment to the Christian celebration of Passover. He loved typology, and this was the primal type. To relive the Passover in Christ was fundamental to his piety.

To regard the observance of the Lord's Day as a fundamental characteristic of Christian worship was the usual way of looking at the Lord's Day in the second and third centuries. The *Didascalia*, written in northern Syria about this same time, tells us that the Lord's Day is a time for putting aside the affairs of the world and devoting oneself to the Word of God. On the Lord's Day one should go to church and listen to the Word of life and be nourished by the food which satisfies us for eternity.[206] In this document the preaching of the Word and participation in the Lord's Supper are understood together as characteristic of the worship of the Lord's Day. For Origen, as for many others in the second and third centuries, to involve oneself in these two activities was the obvious way to spend the Lord's Day.

chapter 20, which seems to say something other than what Nautin claims. See Nautin, *Origène, sa vie et son oeuvre*, p. 394 n. 95.

347

One can well imagine that the eschatological significance of the worship of the Lord's Day which is so obvious in the Church Fathers of the second and third centuries was firmly based on the teaching of Jesus and the apostles. Knowing what we do about the penchant of the ancient Church for both typology and numerology, we can well understand how the early Fathers might have elaborated it. Three biblical terms were used to speak of the day on which Christians worshiped.[207] First of all, it was called the Lord's Day. Although appearing but once in the New Testament (Rev. 1:10), "Lord's Day" became very quickly the regular term in Greek, Latin, and the languages derived from Latin. Even today the French speak of Sunday as "Dimanche." The Italians say "Domenico," and the Spanish "Domingo." Second, the day of worship was considered the first day of the week, a designation we find in the New Testament. Especially noteworthy, however, is that the Gospels make a point of telling us that the resurrection took place on the first day of the week. Origen is very specific in a sermon on Psalm 91 that the Lord's Day is the first day of the week, and that it commemorates the first day of the old creation, the day on which God said let there be light and there was light. It is also the day of the resurrection, the first day of the new creation.[208] Third, the Lord's Day is the eighth day. We find this term already in the Gospel of John (20:26). The sacred numerology of the time understood the eighth day as a figure of the world to come. Origen, as we would expect, saw the significance of this designation.[209] For Origen the Lord's Day was a day to experience the heavenly reality, which was experienced with special force in the reading and preaching of the divine Word. This experience of hearing the Word on the Lord's Day here on earth was a foretaste and an assurance of the fulfillment and consummation of our communion with God in eternity.

From Origen we can get a fairly complete picture of what was in fact the practice of the Church during the second and third centuries. The Church celebrated the Lord's Day each week. It was a day on which both Christ's presence and his imminent return were experienced with special

---

201. A century or two after Origen we begin to hear of traditions of this sort. Genesis was preached during Lent and Acts between Easter and Pentecost.

202. Origen, *Contra Celsum* 8.22.

203. Origen, *Sermons on Genesis* 10.3.

204. For a full explanation of the way the fourth commandment was understood in the second and third centuries, see Rordorf, *Sunday*, pp. 100-108.

intensity. It was very specially the day of Christian worship. While each year Christians celebrated a Christian Passover and a Christian Pentecost, there was no Christian observance of the feast of tabernacles, the Day of Atonement, Purim, or the feast of dedication. We find in the early Church a very definite polemic *against* the observance of days and a very clear commitment *to* the weekly observance of the Lord's Day. That the Church observed the Lord's Day in the place of the Sabbath was often explained and defended in the apologetic literature of the ancient Church, and clear traces of this polemic are already found in the New Testament. The observance of the Lord's Day clearly went back to New Testament times. As we noticed in regard to Melito of Sardis, one of the earliest controversies in the ancient Church was over the nature of a Christian celebration of Passover, but by Origen's time there was never any suggestion as to whether Christians should celebrate it. Little was said with regard to Pentecost, except occasional evidence to indicate that it was observed. Much the same can be said about fasting on Wednesdays and Fridays. We know that weekly fasts were observed, but there was little discussion of them. As far as we can discover from Origen, the early Christian calendar had at its center the Lord's Day, the weekly celebration of the resurrection of Christ. For Origen more important than special feast days or fast days was the daily preaching of the Word of God.

Nautin's hypothetical arrangement of Christian worship services is open to a number of serious objections. The following seems more likely. Morning prayer and probably evening prayer were observed every day of the week, and there was probably preaching at each of these services. For the reading of the Scriptures and the preaching the door was open to all, even on the Lord's Day; outsiders were welcome because in the days of Origen preaching had a distinct evangelistic intent. (It may have been a different matter for the prayers which followed, and surely the catechumens were dismissed for the Eucharist.) After all, how else was the gospel to be proclaimed to all peoples? Some preachers might be more evangelistic than others, but then each church had several preachers. One preacher would quite possibly have taken the morning service for a couple months while another preacher took the evening service. On the Lord's Day all the preachers would get their chance. The Lord's Day service might go on for several hours. In spite of the objections of some of the bishops the ministry of the Word was still thought of as being essentially collegial.

In regard to the liturgical setting of Origen's sermons, one more subject deserves our attention: the relation of Origen's sermons to the prayers of the service in which he preached. Evidently it was the custom in the churches both in the Holy Land and in Egypt to begin the reading and preaching of the Scriptures with a Prayer for Illumination. A century after Origen we find the text for such a prayer in the *Euchologion* of Serapis. One often finds remarks in the sermons of Origen that indicate the readings had been prefaced by a prayer. For instance in the second sermon in his series on Genesis we read:

> But now, since we have already previously prayed to him who alone can remove the veil from the reading of the Old Testament, let us attempt to inquire what spiritual edification also this magnificent construction of the ark contains.[210]

Again in the ninth sermon on Genesis we find this magnificent introduction:

> The further we progress in reading, the greater grows the accumulation of mysteries for us. And just as if some one should embark on the sea borne by a small boat, as long as he is near the land he has little fear. But when he has advanced little by little into the deep and has begun either to be lifted on high by the swelling waves or brought down to the depths by the same gaping waves, then truly great fear and terror permeate his mind because he has entrusted a small craft to such immense waves. So we also seem to have suffered, who small in merits and slight in ability, dare to enter so vast a sea of mysteries. But if by your prayers the Lord should see fit to give us a favorable breeze of his Holy Spirit we shall enter the port of salvation with a favorable passage of the word.[211]

One is tempted to dwell on this magnificent bit of oratory. It shows that Origen was capable of great rhetoric, but it has to be said that he does not often take the trouble to produce this sort of thing. Be that as it may, this extended metaphor does indicate how important he considers it to be that the Church approach the reading and preaching of the Word in prayer. Even more these lines indicate how he understands the Holy Spirit to enliven and illumine the preaching and hearing of the Word. We find much the same thought in the introduction to Sermon 12, the sermon on the birth of Esau and Jacob.

205. Origen, *Sermons on Numbers* 23.4.

We should pray the Father of the Word during each individual reading "when Moses is read," that he might fulfill even in us that which is written in the Psalms: "Open my eyes and I will consider the wondrous things of your Law." For unless he himself opens our eyes, how shall we be able to see these great mysteries which are fashioned in the patriarchs, which are pictured now in terms of wells, now in marriages, now in births, now even in barrenness?[212]

There are plenty of other examples in other series of sermons, but these are clear enough. Before reading and preaching the Scriptures, the Church prayed that God would grant his Spirit so that the congregation might be edified by his Word. As we find it here in the sermons of Origen, this was a dynamic and vital aspect of the liturgy.

Finally, we need to say something about Origen's liturgical theology.[213] How does Origen understand the reading and preaching of Scripture as Christian worship? The most obvious thing to be said is that Origen has a strong Wisdom doxology. His understanding of worship flows naturally from his strong logos Christology. This makes it all but inevitable that his approach to worship would draw heavily on the Wisdom tradition. If Christ is indeed the Word, then the reading of the Word, the preaching of the Word, and the hearing of the Word are going to play a central role in the way we relate to Christ. Origen's whole theology is sapiential. Preaching is at the center of worship, and preaching is obviously a teaching ministry. Origen is the perfect example of what some people superciliously call a didactic preacher. For Origen, to preach was to teach the Word of God. Yet, his preaching is both didactic and doxological. The teaching of the divine Word reveals God's wisdom. When God's wisdom is revealed God is glorified. Origen's long series of sermons on the books of the Law and the books of the prophets constantly show us that the ultimate mysteries of God's wisdom are revealed in Christ. He is the ultimate mystery to whom the patriarchs and the prophets all point. These sermons are therefore doxological. They glorify Christ just as Origen's sermons on the Gospels reveal Christ and witness to his glory. It is with the preaching of the Word, just as it is with the incarnation of the Word, "(And we beheld his glory, the glory as of the only begotten of the Father,) full of

206. *Didascalia* 13. Richard Hugh Connolly, *Didascalia Apostolorum* (Oxford: Clarendon Press, 1929), pp. 124ff.

207. For a thorough study of these three terms, see Rordorf, *Sunday,* pp. 274-93.

grace and truth" (John 1:14, KJV). Revelation of its very nature demands worship. The mysteries of God so amaze us that we can do nothing other than bow down before God in awe and wonder.

Another dimension of Origen's theology of worship is the clear connection between the doxological and the ethical. Here Origen stands solidly in the prophetic tradition of ancient Israel. We have noticed so often in the sermons of Origen that his hermeneutic issues in an exhortation to live the Christian life. This is particularly evident in the sermons on the temptation of Christ. It is because Christ has been victorious over Satan for us, *pro nobis,* that we glorify him. We are filled with awe and wonder at his love for us. That is worship, but it is only the first part of it. There is a second part like unto it. When we follow his example and resist Satan as Christ resisted Satan before us, we not only glorify him but we magnify his glory.

Bibliography

Select Bibliography for Chapter 1

Andersen, Francis I., and David Noel Freedman. *Amos: A New Translation with Introduction and Commentary.* The Anchor Bible, vol. 24A. New York, London, Toronto, Sydney, and Auckland: Doubleday, 1989.

Berg, W. *Die sogenannten Hymnenfragmente in Amosbuch.* Bern: Lang, 1974.

Begrich, J. "Das priesterliche Heilsorakel." *Zeitschrift für die alttestamentliche Wissenschaft* 52 (1923): 81ff.

——. "Die priesterliche Tora." *Beihefte zum Zeitschrift für die alttestamentliche Wissenschaft* 66 (1926): 81ff.

Beyerlin, W. *Origins and History of the Oldest Semitic Traditions.* Oxford: B. Blackwell, 1965.

Billerbeck, Paul, and Hermann L. Strack. *Kommentar zum Neuen Testament aus Talmud und Midrasch.* Munich: Beck, 1961-65.

Bright, John. *A History of Israel.* 2nd ed. Philadelphia: Westminster Press, 1976.

——. *Jeremiah: A New Translation with Introduction and Commentary.* The Anchor Bible, vol. 21. Garden City, N.Y.: Doubleday & Company, 1965.

Buber, Martin. *Moses: The Revelation and the Covenant.* New York: Harper Torch Books, 1958.

Buttrick, George A., ed. *Interpreter's Bible.* 12 vols. Nashville: Abingdon, 1952.

——. *Interpreter's Dictionary of the Bible.* 4 vols. plus supp. vol. Nashville: Abingdon, 1982.

Carney, P. "Doxologies: A Scientific Myth." *Hebrew Studies* 18 (1977): 149-59.

Carroll, Robert P. *Jeremiah.* Sheffield: JSOT Press, 1989.

Chary, T. *Les prophets et le cult à partir de l'Exil.* Paris: Desclée, 1955.

Childs, Brevard S. *The Book of Exodus: A Critical, Theological Commentary.* The Old Testament Library. Philadelphia: Westminster Press, 1974.

————. *Introduction to the Old Testament as Scripture.* Philadelphia: Fortress Press, 1979.

————. *Memory and Tradition in Israel.* London: SCM Press, 1962.

Christensen, Duane L. *Deuteronomy 1–11.* Word Biblical Commentary, vol. 6A. Dallas: Word Books, 1991.

Clements, Ronald E. *Exodus.* Cambridge Commentaries. Cambridge: Cambridge University Press, 1972.

————. *God's Chosen People, A Theological Interpretation of the Book of Deuteronomy.* Valley Forge: Judson Press, 1969.

————. *"Zākhār."* *Theological Dictionary of the Old Testament,* 4:82-87. Edited by G. Johannes Botterweck and Helmer Ringgren. Translated by David E. Green. Grand Rapids: Wm. B. Eerdmans Publishing Co., 1980.

Craigie, Peter C. *The Book of Deuteronomy.* The New International Commentary on the Old Testament. Grand Rapids: William B. Eerdmans Publishing Co., 1976.

Crenshaw, James L. *Studies in Ancient Israelite Wisdom.* New York: KTAV Publishing House, 1976.

Daniélou, Jean. *Origène.* Paris: La table ronde, 1948.

de Vaux, Roland. *Ancient Israel.* 2 vols. New York and Toronto: McGraw-Hill Book Company, 1965.

Driver, Samuel. *A Critical and Exegetical Commentary on Deuteronomy.* 3rd ed. Edinburgh: T. & T. Clark, 1901.

Durham, John I. *Exodus.* Word Biblical Commentary, vol. 3. Waco: Word Books, 1987.

Eichrodt, Walther. *Theology of the Old Testament.* Translated by J. A. Baker. 2 vols. Philadelphia: The Westminster Press, 1967.

Eising, H. *"Zākhār."* *Theological Dictionary of the Old Testament,* 4:64-82. Edited by G. Johannes Botterweck and Helmer Ringgren. Translated by David E. Green. Grand Rapids: Wm. B. Eerdmans Publishing Co., 1980.

Elbogen, Ismar. *Der jüdische Gottesdienst in seiner geschictlichen Entwicklung.* Hildesheim: Georg Olms, 1962.

Elliger, Karl. *Deuterojesaja.* Biblischer Kommentar altes Testament, vol. XI/1. Neukirchen-Vluyn: Verlag des Erziehungsvereins, 1978.

Fensham, F. Charles. *The Books of Ezra and Nehemiah.* The New International Commentary on the Old Testament. Grand Rapids: William B. Eerdmans Publishing Co., 1982.

Fohrer, G. *Die symbolischen Handlungen der Propheten.* Zurich: n.p., 1953.

Gemser, Berend. *Sprüche Solomons.* Tübingen: J. C. B. Mohr (Paul Siebeck), 1963.

Gerhardsson, Birger. *Memory and Manuscript: Oral Tradition and Written Trans-*

mission in Rabbinic Judaism and Early Christianity. Uppsala: C. W. K. Gleerup, 1961.

Gunneweg, Antonius H. J. *Nehemia.* Kommentar zum alten Testament, vol. XIX/2. Gütersloh: Gerd Mohn, 1987.

Hertzberg, H. W. "Die prophetische Kritik am Kult." *Theologische Literaturzeitung* 75 (1950): 219-26.

Horst, F. "Die Doxologien im Amosbuch." *Zeitschrift für die alttestamentliche Wissenschaft* 47 (1929): 45-54.

Idelsohn, A. Z. *Jewish Liturgy and Its Development.* New York: Schocken Books, 1975.

Kaiser, Otto. *Isaiah 1–12.* The Old Testament Library. Philadelphia: Westminster Press, 1972.

Kittel, G., et al., eds. *Theological Dictionary of the New Testament.* Translated by Geoffrey W. Bromiley. 10 vols. Grand Rapids: Wm. B. Eerdmans Publishing Co., 1964-76.

Kline, M. G. *Treaty of the Great King.* Grand Rapids: Wm. B. Eerdmans Publishing Co., 1963.

Kraus, Hans-Joachim. *Gottesdienst in Israel.* Munich: Chr. Kaiser Verlag, 1962.

———. *Psalmen.* 2 vols. Neukirchen-Vluyn: Neukirchener Verlag, 1961.

Leclercq, Jean. *The Love of Learning and the Desire for God: A Study of Monastic Culture.* Translated by Catharine Misrahi. New York: Fordham University Press, 1961.

Lohfink, Norbert, S.J. *Das Hauptgebot. Eine Untersuchung literarischer Einleitungsfragen zu Dtn 5–11.* Rome: Pontificio Instituto Biblico, 1963.

MacLean, H. B. "Josiah." *Interpreter's Dictionary of the Bible,* 2:996-99. 4 vols. plus supp. vol. Nashville: Abingdon, 1982.

McCarthy, Dennis J. *Old Testament Covenant.* Richmond: John Knox Press, 1972.

McKane, William. *Proverbs: A New Approach.* The Old Testament Library. Philadelphia: Westminster Press, 1975.

McNamara, M. "Targums." *Interpreter's Dictionary of the Bible.* Supp. vol., pp. 856-61. 4 vols. plus supp. vol. Nashville: Abingdon, 1982.

Mann, Jacob, and Isaiah Sonne. *The Bible as Read and Preached in the Old Synagogue.* 2 vols. Cincinnati: Hebrew Union College, 1966 and New York: KTAV Publishing House, 1971.

Mays, James Luther. *Amos: A Commentary.* The Old Testament Library. Philadelphia: Westminster, 1976.

———. *Micah: A Commentary.* The Old Testament Library. Philadelphia: Westminster Press, 1976.

Mendenhall, George E. "Covenant." *Interpreter's Dictionary of the Bible,* 1:714-23. 4 vols. plus supp. vol. Nashville: Abingdon, 1982.

———. *Law and Covenant in Israel and the Ancient Near East.* Pittsburgh: Biblical Colloquium, 1955.

355

The Mishnah. Translated by Herbert Danby. Oxford: Oxford University Press, 1933.

Moore, George Foot. *Judaism in the First Centuries of the Christian Era.* 2 vols. Cambridge, Mass.: Harvard University Press, 1927-30.

Mowinckel, Sigmund. *Preaching and Tradition.* Oslo: I kommisjon hos J. Dybwod, 1946.

———. *The Psalms in Israel's Worship.* Translated by D. R. Ap-Thomas. 2 vols. New York and Nashville: Abingdon, 1962.

Muilenburg, James. "The Book of Isaiah, 40–66: Introduction and Exegesis." *Interpreter's Bible,* 5:381ff. 12 vols. Nashville: Abingdon, 1952.

Myers, Jacob. *Ezra, Nehemiah.* The Anchor Bible, vol. 14. Garden City, N.Y.: Doubleday, 1965.

Napier, B. D. "Prophet." *Interpreter's Dictionary of the Bible,* 3:896-919. 4 vols. plus supp. vol. Nashville: Abingdon, 1982.

Nautin, Pierre. *Origène, sa vie et son oeuvre.* Paris: Beauchesne, 1977.

Nicholson, E. W. *Preaching to the Exiles.* Oxford: B. Blackwell, 1970.

Noth, Martin. *Exodus: A Commentary.* The Old Testament Library. Philadelphia: Westminster Press, 1962.

Odes of Solomon. Translated by James H. Charlesworth. Chico, Calif.: Scholars Press, 1977.

Old, Hughes Oliphant. "Biblical Wisdom Theology and Calvin's Understanding of the Lord's Supper." *Calvin Studies* 6 (1992): 111-36.

———. *Themes and Variations for a Christian Doxology.* Grand Rapids: Wm. B. Eerdmans Publishing Co., 1992.

Oswalt, J. N. *The Book of Isaiah 1–39.* The New International Commentary on the Old Testament. Grand Rapids: Wm. B. Eerdmans Publishing Co., 1986.

Pedersen, Johannes. *Israel: Its Life and Culture.* 4 vols. London: Geoffrey Cumberlege; Copenhagen: Banner og Korch, 1959.

Procksch, O. "λέγω." *Theological Dictionary of the New Testament,* 4:91ff. Edited by G. Kittel et al. Translated by Geoffrey Bromiley. 10 vols. Grand Rapids: Wm. B. Eerdmans Publishing Co., 1964-76.

Rankin, O. S. *Israel's Wisdom Literature.* Edinburgh: T. & T. Clark, 1936.

Rendtorff, R. "προφήτης κτλ." *Theological Dictionary of the New Testament,* 6: 796-812. 10 vols. Grand Rapids: Wm B. Eerdmans Publishing Co., 1964-76.

Rengstorf, K. H. "σημεῖον." *Theological Dictionary of the New Testament,* 7:213ff. 10 vols. Grand Rapids: Wm B. Eerdmans Publishing Co., 1964-76.

Rousseau, Olivier. *Origène, Homélies sur le Cantique des Cantiques.* Paris: Éditions du Cerf, 1966.

Rowley, H. H. *Worship in Ancient Israel: Its Forms and Meaning.* London: S.P.C.K., 1981.

Rudolph, Wilhelm. *Jeremia*. Handbuch zum alten Testament. 2nd ed. Tübingen: J. C. B. Mohr (Paul Siebeck), 1958.

Schottroff, W. *"Gedenken" im alten Orient und in Alten Testament*. Neukirchen: Neukirchener Verlag, 1967.

Scott, R. B. Y. "The Book of Isaiah, 1–39: Introduction and Exegesis." *Interpreter's Bible*, 5:151-381. 12 vols. Nashville: Abingdon, 1952.

————. *The Way of Wisdom in the Old Testament*. New York: Collier Books, 1986.

Sekine, Masao. "Das Problem der Kultpolemik bei den Propheten." *Evangelische Theologie* 28 (1968): 605-9.

Skinner, John. *The Book of the Prophet Isaiah I–XXXIX*. Cambridge Bible for Schools and Colleges. Cambridge: University Press, 1954.

————. *The Book of the Prophet Isaiah XL LXVI*. Cambridge Bible for Schools and Colleges. Cambridge: University Press, 1954.

Smith, George Adam. *The Book of Isaiah*. 2 vols. New York: Harper and Brothers, 1927.

Song Tse-Gun. *Sinai Covenant and Moab Covenant: An Exegetical Study of the Covenants in Exodus 19:1–24:11 and Deuteronomy 4:45–28:69*. Cheltenham and Gloucester: College of Higher Education, 1992.

Sonne, Isaiah. "Synagogue." *Interpreter's Dictionary of the Bible*, 4:476-91. 4 vols. plus supp. vol. Nashville: Abingdon, 1982.

Strack, Hermann L. *Introduction to the Talmud and Midrash*. New York: Harper and Row, 1965.

Stuart, Douglas. *Hosea-Jonah*. Word Biblical Commentary, vol. 31. Waco, Tex.: Word Books, 1984.

The Talmud. Edited by I. Epstein. London: The Soncino Press, 1938.

Thompson, J. A. *The Book of Jeremiah*. The New International Commentary on the Old Testament. Grand Rapids: Wm. B. Eerdmans Publishing Co., 1992.

von Rad, Gerhard. *Das fünfte Buch Mose: Deuteronomium*. Göttingen: Vandenhoeck & Ruprecht, 1968.

————. *Old Testament Theology*. Translated by David M. G. Stalker. 2 vols. Edinburgh: Oliver & Boyd, 1973.

————. *Studies in Deuteronomy*. Translated by David M. G. Stalker. Chicago: Henry Regnery, 1953.

————. *Wisdom in Israel*. Translated by James D. Morton. Nashville: Abingdon Press, 1972.

Watts, John D. W. *Isaiah 1–33*. Word Biblical Commentary, vol. 24. Waco, Tex.: Word Books, 1985.

————. *Isaiah 34–66*. Word Biblical Commentary, vol. 25. Waco, Tex.: Word Books, 1987.

————. "An Old Hymn Preserved in the Book of Amos." *Journal of Near Eastern Studies* 15 (1956): 33-39.

357

Westermann, Claus. *Isaiah 40–66: A Commentary.* The Old Testament Library. Philadelphia: Westminster Press, 1969.

Wildberger, Hans. *Jesaja.* 3 vols. 2nd ed. Biblischer Kommentar altes Testament, vols. X/1, X/2, and X/3. Neukirchen-Vluyn: Verlag des Erziehungsvereins, 1980.

Wolff, Hans Walter. *Dodekapropheton 2: Joel und Amos.* Biblischer Kommentar altes Testament, vol. XIV/2. 2nd ed. Neukirchen-Vluyn: Neukirchener Verlag, 1975.

Wright, G. Ernest. "Deuteronomy: Introduction and Exegesis." *Interpreter's Bible,* 2:329ff. 12 vols. Nashville: Abingdon, 1952.

Zunz, Leopold. *Die gottesdienstlichen Vorträge der Juden, historisch entwickelt.* Berlin: A. Asher, 1832.

Select Bibliography for Chapter 2

Adamson, James. *The Epistle of James.* The New International Commentary on the New Testament. Grand Rapids: Wm. B. Eerdmans Publishing Co., 1974.

Audet, Jean Paul. *La Didachè, instructions des Apôtres, Études Bibliques.* Paris: J. Gabalda, 1958.

Barrett, Charles Kingsley. *The First Epistle to the Corinthians.* New York: Harper & Row, 1968.

———. *The Gospel According to St. John.* New York: Macmillan, 1956.

Barth, Markus. *Ephesians.* 2 vols. The Anchor Bible, vols. 34 and 34A. New York, London, Toronto, Sydney, and Auckland: Doubleday, 1974.

Behm, J. "θύω." *Theological Dictionary of the New Testament,* 3:180-90. 10 vols. Grand Rapids: Wm. B. Eerdmans Publishing Co., 1964-76.

Betz, Hans Dieter. *Galatians.* Philadelphia: Fortress Press, 1979.

Beyer, H. W. "εὐλογέω." *Theological Dictionary of the New Testament,* 2:754ff. 10 vols. Grand Rapids: Wm. B. Eerdmans Publishing Co., 1964-76.

———. "κατηχέω." *Theological Dictionary of the New Testament,* 3:638-40. 10 vols. Grand Rapids: Wm. B. Eerdmans Publishing Co., 1964-76.

Billerbeck, Paul, and Hermann L. Strack. *Kommentar zum Neuen Testament aus Talmud und Midrasch.* 4 vols. 3rd ed. Munich: Beck, 1951-56.

Blank, S. H. "Wisdom." *Interpreter's Dictionary of the Bible,* 4:852-61. 4 vols. plus supp. vol. Nashville: Abingdon, 1982.

Bonsirven, Joseph. *Exégèse rabbinique et exégèse paulinienne.* Paris: Beauchesne, 1939.

Bornkamm, Günther. "μυστήριον." *Theological Dictionary of the New Testament,* 4:819-24. 10 vols. Grand Rapids: Wm. B. Eerdmans Publishing Co., 1964-76.

————. "Glaube und Vernunft bei Paulus." In *Studien zu Antike und Urchristentum, Gesammelte Aufsätze.* Munich: Chr. Kaiser, 1963.

————. *Paulus.* Stuttgart: W. Kohlhammer, 1969.

Bornkamm, Günther, Gerhard Barth, and Heinz Joachim Held. *Überlieferung und Auslegung im Matthäus Evangelium.* 4th ed. Neukirchen-Vluyn: Neukirchener, 1965.

Bowker, J. W. "Speeches in Acts: A Study in Proem and Yelammedenu Form." *New Testament Studies* 14 (1967-68): 96-111.

Broneer, O. "Athens, City of Idol Worship." *Biblical Archaeologist* 21 (1958).

Brown, Raymond E. *The Gospel According to John.* 2 vols. The Anchor Bible, vols. 29 and 29A. Garden City, N.Y.: Doubleday & Co., 1966.

————. *The Semitic Background of the Term "Mystery" in the New Testament.* Philadelphia: Fortress Press, 1968.

Bruce, F. F. *The Acts of the Apostles: The Greek Text with Introduction and Commentary.* 3rd rev. ed. Grand Rapids: Wm. B. Eerdmans Publishing Co., 1990.

————. *The Book of the Acts: The English Text with Introduction, Exposition, and Notes.* Rev. ed. Grand Rapids: Wm. B. Eerdmans Publishing Co., 1988.

————. *The Epistle to the Galatians.* The New International Greek Testament Commentary. Grand Rapids: Wm. B. Eerdmans Publishing Co., 1982.

Bultmann, Rudolf. "ἀναγινώσκω." *Theological Dictionary of the New Testament,* 1:343-44. 10 vols. Grand Rapids: Wm. B. Eerdmans Publishing Co., 1964-76.

————. *Das Evangelium des Johannes.* Meyers Kritisch-exegetischer Kommentar über das neue Testament. Göttingen: Vandenhoeck & Ruprecht, 1964.

Buttrick, George A., et al. *Interpreter's Dictionary of the Bible.* 4 vols. plus supp. vol. Nashville: Abingdon, 1982.

Cadbury, Henry. *The Book of Acts in Historical Perspective.* London: A. & C. Clark, 1955.

————. *The Making of Luke-Acts.* 1st ed. New York: Macmillan, 1927.

Cambier, J. "La Bénédiction d'Éphésiens 1,3-14." *Zeitschrift für die neutestamentliche Wissenschaft* 54 (1963): 58-104.

Campenhausen, Hans von. "Der urchristliche Apostelbegriff." *Studia Theologica* 1 (1947): 96-130.

Carrington, Philip. *The Primitive Christian Catechism.* Cambridge: University Press, 1940.

Cerfaux, Lucien. *Le chrétien dans la théologie paulinienne.* Paris: Les Éditions du Cerf, 1962.

————. *Le Christ dans la théologie de St. Paul.* Paris: Les Éditions du Cerf, 1954.

————. "La connaissance des secrets du royaume d'après Matt. xiii.II et par." *New Testament Studies* 2 (1956): 238-49.

————. "En faveur de l'authenticité des épîtres de la captivité. Homogénéité doctrinale entre Éphésiens et les grandes épîtres." *Litterature et Théologie pauliniennes.* Recherches bibliques, vol. 5. Bruges: Desclée de Brouwer, 1960.

Congar, Yves. *Le mystère du Temple.* 2nd ed. Paris: Les Éditions du Cerf, 1963.

Conzelmann, Hans. "The Address of Paul on the Areopagus." In *Studies in Luke-Acts.* Edited by L. E. Keck and J. L. Martin. Nashville and New York: Abingdon, 1958.

—————. *Der erste Brief an die Korinther.* Meyers Kritisch-exegetischer Kommentar über das neue Testament. Göttingen: Vandenhoeck & Ruprecht, 1969.

—————. "On the Analysis of the Confessional Formula in I Corinthians 15:3-5." *Interpretation* 20 (1966): 15-25.

—————. *The Theology of St. Luke.* Translated by Geoffrey Buswell. New York: Harper & Row, 1961.

Cross, F. L. *I Peter: A Paschal Liturgy.* London: A. R. Mowbray, 1954.

Cullmann, Oscar. *The Christology of the New Testament.* Translated by Shirley Guthrie and Charles Hall. London: SCM Press, 1963.

—————. *Early Christian Worship.* Translated by A. Stewart Todd and James B. Torrance. London: SCM Press, 1954.

—————. *Les premières confessions de foi.* Paris: Presses Universitaires de France, 1948.

Dahl, N. A. "Adresse und Proömium des Epheserbriefs." *Theologische Zeitschrift* 7 (1951): 241-64.

—————. "Cosmic Dimensions and Religious Knowledge (Ephesians 3:18)." In *Jesus and Paul.* Edited by E. E. Ellis and E. Grässer. Göttingen: Vandenhoeck & Ruprecht, 1975.

Davids, Peter H. *The First Epistle of Peter.* The New International Commentary on the New Testament. Grand Rapids: Wm. B. Eerdmans Publishing Co., 1990.

Davies, W. D. *Paul and Rabbinic Judaism.* 2nd ed. London: S.P.C.K., 1965.

—————. *The Setting of the Sermon on the Mount.* Cambridge: University Press, 1966.

Deichgräber, R. *Gotteshymnus und Christushymnus in der frühen Christenheit.* Göttingen: Vandenhoeck & Ruprecht, 1967.

Dentan, Robert C. "The Book of Malachi: Introduction and Exegesis." *Interpreter's Bible,* 6:1132ff. 12 vols. Nashville: Abingdon, 1952.

Dibelius, Martin. *Der Brief des Jakobus.* Originally 1921, enlarged and reedited by Heinrich Greeven. Meyers Kritisch-exegetischer Kommentar über das neue Testament. Göttingen: Vandenhoeck & Ruprecht, 1964.

—————. *Studies in the Acts of the Apostles.* London: S.C.M. Press, 1956.

Dietrich, E. L. "Rabbiner." *Die Religion in Geschichte und Gegenwart,* 5:759. 3rd ed. 6 vols. Tübingen: J. C. B. Mohr (Paul Siebeck), 1957-65.

Dodd, C. H. *The Apostolic Preaching and Its Development*. London: Hodder & Stoughton, 1936.

————. *The Interpretation of the Fourth Gospel*. Cambridge: University Press, 1958.

————. "Jesus as Teacher and Prophet." *Mysterium Christi* (1930): 53-66.

————. *The Parables of the Kingdom*. London: Nisbet, 1935; New York: Scribner's, 1936.

Doeve, J. W. *Jewish Hermeneutics in the Synoptic Gospels and Acts*. Assen: Van Gorcum, 1954.

Dupont, Jacques. *Gnosis: La connaissance religieuse dans les Épîtres de Saint Paul.* Paris: J. Gabalda, 1949.

Eichholz, Georg. *Auslegung der Bergpredigt*. 2nd ed. Neukirchen-Vluyn: Neukirchener, 1970.

Ellis, E. Earle. *Pauline Theology: Ministry and Society*. Grand Rapids: Wm. B. Eerdmans Publishing Co., 1989.

————. *Paul's Use of the Old Testament*. Edinburgh: Oliver & Boyd, 1957.

Fee, Gordon D. *The First Epistle to the Corinthians*. The New International Commentary on the New Testament. Grand Rapids: Wm. B. Eerdmans Publishing Co., 1993.

Feuillet, André. *Le Christ, Sagesse de Dieu*. Paris: J. Gabalda, 1966.

————. "Les 'sacrifices spirituelles' du sacerdoce royal des baptises (I Pierre 2:5) et leur préparation dans l'Ancient Testament." *Nouvelle Revue Theologique* 96 (1974): 704-28.

Filson, Floyd V. "The Christian Teacher in the First Century." *Journal of Biblical Literature* 60 (1941): 317-28.

————. *Jesus Christ, the Risen Lord*. New York and Nashville: Abingdon, 1956.

Finegan, J. "Areopagus." *Interpreter's Dictionary of the Bible*, 1:216ff. 4 vols. plus supp. vol. Nashville: Abingdon, 1982.

Fitzmyer, Joseph A. *The Gospel According to Luke*. 2 vols. The Anchor Bible, vols. 28 and 28A. Garden City, N.Y.: Doubleday & Company, 1981 and 1985.

Friedrich, G. "εὐαγγελίζομαι." *Theological Dictionary of the New Testament*, 2:707-37. 10 vols. Grand Rapids: Wm. B. Eerdmans Publishing Co., 1964-76.

————. "κῆρυξ." *Theological Dictionary of the New Testament*, 3:697-717. 10 vols. Grand Rapids: Wm. B. Eerdmans Publishing Co., 1964-76.

————. "προφήτης κτλ." *Theological Dictionary of the New Testament*, 6:848-56. 10 vols. Grand Rapids: Wm. B. Eerdmans Publishing Co., 1964-76.

Foakes-Jackson, Frederick J., and Kirsopp Lake, eds. *The Beginnings of Christianity.* 5 vols. London: Macmillan, 1920-33.

Fuchs, Ernst. "Die Auferstehung Jesu Christi und der Anfang der Kirche." In *Glaube und Erfahrung*. Tübingen: J. C. B. Mohr (Paul Siebeck), 1965.

Fung, Ronald Y. K. *Galatians.* The New International Commentary on the New Testament. Grand Rapids: Wm. B. Eerdmans Publishing Co., 1988.

Gärtner, Bertil. *The Areopagus Speech and Natural Revelation.* Lund: C. W. K. Gleerup, 1955.

————. *John 6 and the Jewish Passover.* Lund: C. W. K. Gleerup, 1959.

————. *The Temple and the Community in Qumran and the New Testament.* Cambridge: University Press, 1965.

Geldenhuys, Norval. *The Gospel of Luke.* The New International Commentary on the New Testament. Grand Rapids: Wm. B. Eerdmans Publishing Co., 1951.

George, Augustin. *Études sur L'oeuvre de Luc.* Paris: J. Gabalda, 1978.

Gerhardsson, Birger. "If We Do Not Cut the Parables Out of Their Frames." *New Testament Studies* 37 (1991): 321-35.

————. *Memory and Manuscript.* Lund: C. W. K. Gleerup and Copenhagen: Ejnar Monksgaard, 1961.

————. "The Seven Parables in Matthew XIII." *New Testament Studies* 19 (1972-73): 16-37.

Goldammer, K. "Der Kerygma begriff in der ältesten christlichen Literatur." *Zeitschrift für die neutestamentliche Wissenschaft* 48 (1957): 77-101.

Goppelt, Leonhard. *Der erste Petrusbrief.* Meyers Kritisch-exegetischer Kommentar über das neue Testament. Göttingen: Vandenhoeck & Ruprecht, 1978. English translation: *A Commentary on I Peter.* Edited by Ferdinand Hahn. Translated by John E. Alsup. Grand Rapids: Wm. B. Eerdmans Publishing Co., 1993.

Greeven, Heinrich. "Propheten, Lehrer, Vorsteher bei Paulus." *Zeitschrift für die neutestamentliche Wissenschaft* 44 (1952/53): 3-15.

Grudem, W. A. *The Gift of Prophecy in I Corinthians.* Lanham, Md., New York, and London: University Press of America, 1982.

Guelich, Robert A. *Mark.* 2 vols. Word Biblical Commentary. Dallas: Word Books, 1989.

Haenchen, Ernst. *Die Apostelgeschichte.* 5th edition. Meyers Kritisch-exegetischer Kommentar über das neue Testament. Göttingen: Vandenhoeck & Ruprecht, 1965.

Hagner, Donald A. *Matthew.* 2 vols. Word Biblical Commentary. Dallas: Word Books, 1993.

Hendry, George. "Revelation." In *Theological Word Book of the Bible.* Edited by A. Richardson. New York: Macmillan Company, 1951.

Hengel, M. *The Charismatic Leader and His Followers.* Translated by J. Greig. New York: Crossroads, 1981.

Hodge, Charles. *A Commentary on Romans.* London: Banner of Truth Trust, 1972.

Jeremias, Joachim. "παῖς θεοῦ C, D." *Theological Dictionary of the New Testament,*

5:677-717. 10 vols. Grand Rapids: Wm. B. Eerdmans Publishing Co., 1964-76.

————. *Die Briefe an Timotheus und Titus.* 6th ed. Göttingen: Vandenhoeck & Ruprecht, 1957.

————. "Paarweise Sendung im Neuen Testament." In *Abba. Studien zur neutestamentlichen Theologie und Zeitgeschichte*, pp. 132-39. Göttingen: Vandenhoeck & Ruprecht, 1966.

————. *The Parables of Jesus.* Translated by S. H. Hooke. London: SCM; Philadelphia: Westminster, 1972.

Johnson, G. "Letter to the Ephesians." *Interpreter's Dictionary of the Bible*, 2:108-14. 4 vols. plus supp. vol. Nashville: Abingdon, 1982.

Käsemann, Ernst. "Epheserbrief." *Die Religion in Geschichte und Gegenwart.* Edited by Kurt Galling. 6 vols. Tübingen: J. C. B. Mohr (Paul Siebeck), 1957-65.

————. "Das Interpretationsproblem des Epheserbriefes." In *Exegetische Versuche und Besinnungen*, 2:253-61. 2 vols. 2nd ed. Göttingen: Vandenhoeck & Ruprecht, 1965.

————. "Paulus und der Frühkatholizismus." In *Exegetische Versuche und Besinnungen*, 2:239-52. 2 vols. 2nd ed. Göttingen: Vandenhoeck & Ruprecht, 1965.

Kelly, J. N. D. *A Commentary on the Epistles of Peter and Jude.* London: Adam and Charles Black, 1969.

————. *The Pastoral Epistles.* London: Adam and Charles Black, 1963.

Kingsbury, J. D. "Form and Message of Matthew." *Interpretation* 29 (1975): 13-23.

Kittel, Gerhard. "λέγω D." *Theological Dictionary of the New Testament*, 4:127-36. 10 vols. Grand Rapids: Wm. B. Eerdmans Publishing Co., 1964-76.

Kittel, Gerhard, et al. *Theological Dictionary of the New Testament.* Translated by Geoffrey W. Bromiley. 10 vols. Grand Rapids: Wm. B. Eerdmans Publishing Co., 1964-76.

Kleinknecht, H. "λέγω B." *Theological Dictionary of the New Testament*, 4:77-91. 10 vols. Grand Rapids: Wm. B. Eerdmans Publishing Co., 1964-76.

Kloppenborg, J. "An Analysis of the Pre-Pauline Formula in I Cor. 15:3b-5 in Light of Some Recent Literature." *Catholic Biblical Quarterly* 40 (1978): 351-67.

Kraus, Hans-Joachim. *Psalmen.* 2 vols. Neukirchen: Neukirchener Verlag, 1961.

Lane, William. *The Gospel of Mark.* New International Commentary on the New Testament. Grand Rapids: Wm. B. Eerdmans Publishing Co., 1970.

la Verdière, E. A. "A Grammatical Ambiguity in 1 Peter 1:23." *Catholic Biblical Quarterly* 36 (1974): 89-94.

Lietzmann, Hans. *An die Korinther I/II.* 4th ed. Tübingen: J. C. B. Mohr, 1949.

Lincoln, Andrew T. *Ephesians.* Word Biblical Commentary. Dallas: Word Books, 1990.

Lohmeyer, Ernst. *Das Evangelium des Markus.* Meyers Kritisch-exegetischer Kommentar über das neue Testament. Göttingen: Vandenhoeck & Ruprecht, 1963.

————. *Lord of the Temple: A Study of the Relation between Cult and Gospel.* Translated by Stewart Todd. Richmond: John Knox Press, 1962.

————. "Das Proömium des Epheserbriefs." *Theologische Blätter* 5 (1926): 120-25.

Lohse, E. "Paränese und Kerygma im I Petrusbrief." *Zeitschrift für die neutestamentliche Wissenschaft* 45 (1954): 68-89.

Longenecker, Richard. *Galatians.* Word Biblical Commentary. Waco, Tex.: Word, 1990.

Mackay, John Alexander. *God's Order: The Ephesian Letter and This Present Time.* New York: Macmillan, 1956.

M'Neile, Alan Hugh. *The Gospel According to Matthew.* London: Macmillan & Co., 1955.

Mann, C. S. *Mark.* The Anchor Bible, vol. 27. Garden City, N.Y.: Doubleday, 1986.

Mann, Jacob, and Isaiah Sonne. *The Bible as Read and Preached in the Old Synagogue.* 2 vols. Cincinnati: Hebrew Union College, 1966; New York: KTAV Publishing House, 1971.

Manson, Thomas W. *The Church's Ministry.* Philadelphia: Westminster Press, 1948.

Manson, William. *The Epistle to the Hebrews.* London: Hodder & Stoughton, 1951.

Marxsen, Willi. *Mark the Evangelist: Studies on the Redaction History of the Gospel.* Translated by Roy A. Harrisville et al. Nashville: Abingdon, 1969.

Maurer, C. "Der hymnus von Epheser 1 als Schlüssel zum ganzen Brief." *Evangelische Theologie* 11 (1951-52): 151-72.

Mauser, Ulrich. *Christ in the Wilderness.* Naperville, Ill.: A. R. Allenson, 1963.

Menoud, Philippe-H. *L'Église et les ministères selon le Nouveau Testament.* Neuchâtel and Paris: Delachaux & Niestlé, 1949.

————. "Preaching." *Interpreter's Dictionary of the Bible,* 3:868-69. 4 vols. plus supp. vol. Nashville: Abingdon Press, 1982.

————. "Revelation and Tradition: The Influence of Paul's Conversion on His Theology." *Interpretation* 7 (1953): 131-41.

Metzger, Bruce M. "Literary Forgeries and Canonical Pseudepigrapha." *Journal of Biblical Literature* 91 (1972): 3-24.

————. "A Reconsideration of Certain Arguments against the Pauline Authorship of the Pastoral Epistles." *Expository Times* 70 (1958).

————. "A Suggestion Concerning the Meaning of I Cor. XV,4b." *Journal of Theological Studies* 8 (1957): 118-23.

Meye, Robert P. *Jesus and the Twelve: Discipleship and Revelation in Mark's Gospel.* Grand Rapids: Wm. B. Eerdmans Publishing Co., 1968.

Michaels, J. Ramsey. *1 Peter.* Word Biblical Commentary. Waco, Tex.: Word Books, 1988.

Michel, Otto. *Der Brief an die Römer.* Meyers Kritisch-exegetischer Kommentar über das neue Testament. Göttingen: Vandenhoeck & Ruprecht, 1966.

————. *Paulus und seine Bibel.* Gütersloh: Bertelsmann, 1929.

Moore, George Foote. *Judaism.* 2 vols. New York: Schocken Books, 1971.

Morris, Leon. *The Gospel According to John.* The New International Commentary on the New Testament. Grand Rapids: Wm. B. Eerdmans Publishing Co., 1971.

Mosbech, H. "Apostolos in the New Testament." *Studia Theologica* 2 (1948): 166-200.

Moule, C. F. D. *Worship in the New Testament.* Richmond: John Knox Press, 1967.

Mounce, Robert. *The Essential Nature of New Testament Preaching.* Grand Rapids: Wm. B. Eerdmans Publishing Co., 1960.

Murray, John. *The Epistle to the Romans.* Two vols. reprinted in one. Grand Rapids: Wm. B. Eerdmans Publishing Co., 1993.

Niederwimmer, Kurt. *Die Didache.* Kommentar zu den Apostolischen Vätern. Göttingen: Vandenhoeck & Ruprecht, 1989.

Nolland, John. *Luke.* 3 vols. Word Biblical Commentary. Dallas: Word Books, 1989-93.

Oepke, A. "ἀποκαλύπτω." *Theological Dictionary of the New Testament,* 3:580-91. 10 vols. Grand Rapids: Wm. B. Eerdmans Publishing Co., 1964-76.

Parker, P. "Rabbi." *Interpreter's Dictionary of the Bible,* 4:3. 4 vols. plus supp. vol. Nashville: Abingdon, 1982.

————. "Teacher." *Interpreter's Dictionary of the Bible,* 4:522-23. 4 vols. plus supp. vol. Nashville: Abingdon, 1982.

Peterson, David. *Engaging with God: A Biblical Theology of Worship.* Grand Rapids: Wm. B. Eerdmans Publishing Co., 1993.

Plank, K. A. "Resurrection Theology: The Corinthian Controversy Reexamined." *Perspectives in Religious Studies* 8 (1981): 41-54.

Plummer, Alfred. *The Gospel According to Luke.* 5th ed. Edinburgh: T. & T. Clark, 1922.

Procksch, O. "λέγω C." *Theological Dictionary of the New Testament,* 4:91-100. 10 vols. Grand Rapids: Wm. B. Eerdmans Publishing Co., 1964-76.

Ramsey, W. M. *St. Paul the Traveller.* 14th ed. London: n.p., 1920.

Rengstorf, K. H. "ἀπόστολος." *Theological Dictionary of the New Testament,* 1:420-50. 10 vols. Grand Rapids: Wm. B. Eerdmans Publishing Co., 1964-76.

————. "διδάσκω." *Theological Dictionary of the New Testament,* 2:135-65. 10 vols. Grand Rapids: Wm. B. Eerdmans Publishing Co., 1964-76.

————. "διδάσκαλος." *Theological Dictionary of the New Testament,* 2:161-63. 10 vols. Grand Rapids: Wm. B. Eerdmans Publishing Co., 1964-76.

————. "διδασκαλία." *Theological Dictionary of the New Testament,* 2:160ff. and 2:163ff. 10 vols. Grand Rapids: Wm. B. Eerdmans Publishing Co., 1964-76.

————. "The Classical Form of the Apostolate in the Person of Paul." *Theological Dictionary of the New Testament,* 1:437-43. 10 vols. Grand Rapids: Wm. B. Eerdmans Publishing Co., 1964-76.

Ridderbos, H. "The Earliest Confession of the Atonement in Paul." In *Reconciliation and Hope,* pp. 78-89. Edited by Robert Banks. Grand Rapids: Wm. B. Eerdmans Publishing Co., 1974.

Robbins, Vernon K. *Jesus the Teacher: A Socio-Rhetorical Interpretation of Mark.* Philadelphia: Fortress Press, 1984.

Robertson, Archibald, and Alfred Plummer. *A Critical and Exegetical Commentary on the First Epistle of St. Paul to the Corinthians.* 2nd ed. International Critical Commentary. Edinburgh: T. & T. Clark, 1914.

Robinson, W. C., Jr. "Acts of the Apostles." *Interpreter's Dictionary of the Bible.* Supp. vol., pp. 7-9. 4 vols. plus supp. vol. Nashville: Abingdon, 1982.

————. "Gospel of Luke." *Interpreter's Dictionary of the Bible.* Supp. vol., pp. 558-60. 4 vols. plus supp. vol. Nashville: Abingdon, 1982.

Ropes, James H. *A Critical and Exegetical Commentary on the Epistle of James.* International Critical Commentary. Edinburgh: T. & T. Clark, 1911.

Rordorf, Willy. "Un chapître d'éthique judéo-chrétienne: les Deux Voies." In *Liturgie, foi et vie des premiers Chrétiens, études patristiques,* pp. 155-74. Paris: Beauchesne, 1986.

Sanders, J. T. "Hymnic Elements in Ephesians 1–3." *Zeitschrift für die neutestamentliche Wissenschaft* 56 (1965): 214-32.

Schille, G. "Das Evangelium des Matthäus als Katechismus." *New Testament Studies* (1958): 101-14.

————. "Katechese und Taufliturgie." *Zeitschrift für die neutestamentliche Wissenschaft* (1960): 112-31.

Schillebeeckx, Edward. *Le Christ, Sacrament de la rencontre de Dieu.* Paris: Éditions du Cerf, 1960.

Schlatter, Adolf. *The Church in the New Testament Period.* London: S.P.C.K., 1955.

————. *Der Evangelist Matthäus, seine Sprache, sein Ziel, seine Selbständigkeit.* 6th ed. Stuttgart: Calwer Verlag, 1963.

Schlier, Heinrich. *Der Brief an die Epheser.* 2nd ed. Düsseldorf: Patmos Verlag, 1958.

————. *Der Brief an die Galater.* Meyers Kritisch-exegetischer Kommentar über das neue Testament. Göttingen: Vandenhoeck & Ruprecht, 1971.

————. "Kerygma und Sophia." *Die Zeit der Kirche* (1956): 206-32.

Schmithals, Walter. *Paulus und die Gnostiker Untersuchungen zu den kleinen Paulusbriefen.* Hamburg-Bergstedt: Reich, 1965.

Schmitz, O. "παρακαλέω, παράκλησις F." *Theological Dictionary of the New Testament,* 5:793-99. 10 vols. Grand Rapids: Wm. B. Eerdmans Publishing Co., 1964-76.

Schweizer, Eduard. *The Good News According to Matthew.* Atlanta: John Knox Press, 1975.

Scott, Charles A. Anderson. *Christianity According to St. Paul.* Cambridge: University Press, 1927.

Selwyn, Edward Gordon. *The First Epistle of St. Peter.* 2nd ed. London: Macmillan & Co., 1955.

Shubert, P. "The Structure and Significance of Luke 24." Neutestamentliche Studien für Rudolf Bultmann. *Beihefte zur Zeitschrift für die neutestamentliche Wissenschaft* 21 (1954): 165-86.

Sider, R. J. "St. Paul's Understanding of the Nature and Significance of the Resurrection in I Corinthians XV,1-19." *Novum Testamentum* 19 (1977): 124-41.

Spicq, C. *Saint Paul: les Épîtres pastorales.* Paris: J. Gabalda, 1947.

Spörlein, B. *Die Leugnung der Auferstehung. Eine historisch-kritische Untersuchung zu I Kor 15.* Regensburg: F. Pustet, 1971.

Stendahl, Krister. *The School of Matthew.* 2nd ed. Philadelphia: Fortress Press, 1968.

Stewart, James Stuart. *The Life and Teaching of Jesus Christ.* Nashville: Abingdon Press, n.d.

————. *A Man in Christ: The Vital Elements of Paul's Religion.* New York and London: Harper & Brothers, 1955.

Stonehouse, Ned B. *Paul before the Areopagus and Other New Testament Studies.* Grand Rapids: Wm. B. Eerdmans Publishing Co., 1957.

————. *The Witness of Luke to Christ.* Grand Rapids and London: Wm. B. Eerdmans Publishing Co., 1951.

Strathmann, H. "μάρτυς κτλ." *Theological Dictionary of the New Testament,* 4:499-504. 10 vols. Grand Rapids: Wm. B. Eerdmans Publishing Co., 1964-76.

Taylor, Vincent. *The Gospel According to St. Mark.* London: Macmillan, 1955.

Turck, André. *Évangélisation et catéchèse aux deux premiers siècles.* Paris: Les Éditions du Cerf, 1962.

Vanderpool, E. "Areopagus." *Interpreter's Dictionary of the Bible.* Supp. vol., p. 52. 4 vols. plus supp. vol. Nashville: Abingdon, 1982.

Wedderburn, A. J. M. "The Problem of the Denial of the Resurrection in I Corinthians XV," *Novum Testamentum* 23 (1981): 229-41.

Werner, Eric. *The Sacred Bridge: Liturgical Parallels in Synagogue and Early Church.* New York: Schocken Books, 1970.

Westcott, Brooke Foss. *The Gospel according to St. John.* Photolithographic edition. Grand Rapids: Wm. B. Eerdmans Publishing Co., 1954.

————. *Paul's Epistle to the Ephesians.* Grand Rapids: Wm. B. Eerdmans Publishing Co., 1952.

Wilckens, Ulrich. "σοφία κτλ.," *Theological Dictionary of the New Testament,* 7:514-26. 10 vols. Grand Rapids: Wm. B. Eerdmans Publishing Co., 1964-76.

Wilson, J. H. "The Corinthians Who Say There Is No Resurrection of the Dead." *Zeitschrift für die neutestamentliche Wissenschaft* 59 (1968): 90-107.

Select Bibliography for Chapter 3

The Apostolic Fathers. Edited and translated by Kirsopp Lake. 2 vols. Loeb Classical Library. London: William Heinemann Ltd. and Cambridge, Mass.: Harvard University Press, 1965.

Audet, Jean Paul. *La Didachè, Instructions des apôtres.* Paris: J. Gabalda, 1958.

Baasland, Ernst. "Der 2. Klemensbrief, und frühchristliche Rhetorik: 'Die erste christliche Predigt im Licht der neueren Forschung.'" In *Aufstieg und niedergang der Römischen Welt.* Edited by W. Haase and H. Temporini. Berlin: Walter de Gruyter, 1993.

Bardy, Gustave. "Aux origines de l'école d'Alexandrie," *Recherches de Science Religieuse* (1933): 430-50.

————. "Un prédicateur populaire au IIIe siècle." *Revue practique d'apologétique* 45 (1927): 513-26 and 679-98.

————. "La spiritualité d'Origène." *La Vie spirituelle* 31 (1932): 80-106.

Barnes, Timothy D. *Tertullian: A Historical and Literary Study.* Oxford: Clarendon Press, 1971.

Bigg, Charles. *The Christian Platonists of Alexandria.* Oxford: Clarendon Press, 1886.

Bonner, Campbell, ed. *The Homily on the Passion.* Philadelphia: University of Pennsylvania Press, 1940.

————. "A Supplementary Note on the Opening of Melito's Homily." *Harvard Theological Review* 36 (1943): 317-19.

Botte, Dom Bernard, ed. *La tradition apostolique de saint Hippolyte, essai de reconstruction.* Münster in Westphalia: Aschendorf, 1963.

Bouyer, Louis. *The Spirituality of the New Testament and the Fathers.* New York: Seabury Press, 1982.

Capelle, Bernard. "Hippolyte de Rome." Originally in *Recherches de Théologie ancienne et Médiévale* 17 (1950): 145-74. Reprinted in the collected works of Capelle. *Travaux liturgiques.* 3 vols. Louvain: Centre liturgique, 1962.

Castagno, Adele Monaci. *Origene, predicatore e il suo pubblico.* Turin: Aranco Angeli, 1987.

Chadwick, Henry. *Christianity and the Classical Tradition.* Oxford: Clarendon Press, 1966.

Champonier, J. "Naissance de l'humanisme chrétien." *Bulletin de l'Association G. Budé* 3 (1947): 58-96.

Clement of Alexandria. *Exhortation to the Greeks, the Rich Man's Salvation and a Fragment of an Address Entitled "To the Newly Baptized."* Greek text with English translation by George William Butterworth. Loeb Classical Library. London: William Heinemann, 1919.

———. *A Homily of Clement of Alexandria Entitled "Who Is the Rich Man That Is Being Saved?"* Translated by P. M. Barnard. London and New York: S.P.C.K., 1901.

———. *Who Is the Rich Man That Is Being Saved?* English translation by W. Wilson. In *The Ante-Nicene Fathers,* 2:591-604. Grand Rapids: Wm. B. Eerdmans Publishing Co., 1969.

Clement of Rome. *Second Clement.* In *The Apostolic Fathers.* Edited and translated by Kirsopp Lake. 2 vols. Loeb Classical Library. London: William Heinemann Ltd. and Cambridge, Mass.: Harvard University Press, 1965.

Connolly, Richard Hugh. *Didascalia Apostolorum.* Oxford: Clarendon Press, 1929.

———. "The Eucharistic Prayer of Hippolytus." *Journal of Theological Studies* 31:350-69.

———. *The So-called Egyptian Church Order.* Cambridge: University Press, 1916.

Crouzel, Henri. *Origène et la connaissance mystique.* Paris: Desclée de Brouwer, 1961.

Daniélou, Jean. *Origène.* Paris: La table ronde, 1948.

Dekkers, Eligius. *Tertullianus en der Geschiedenis der Liturgie.* Brussels: De Kinkhoren, 1947.

Didache. In *The Apostolic Fathers.* Edited and translated by Kirsopp Lake. 2 vols. Loeb Classical Library. Cambridge, Mass.: Harvard University Press, 1965.

Didache. Edited by Willy Rordorf and A. Tuilier. Paris: Éditions du Cerf, 1978.

Dix, Gregory. *The Treatise on the Apostolic Tradition of St. Hippolytus of Rome.* London: Alban Press, 1937.

Elfers, Heinrich. *Die Kirchenordnung Hippolyts von Rom.* Paderborn: Bonifacius Druckerei, 1938.

Gögler, Rolf. *Zur theologie des biblischen Wortes bei Origen.* Düsseldorf: Patmos Verlag, 1963.

Hanson, R. P. C. *Allegory and Event: A Study of the Sources and Significance of Origen's Interpretation of Scripture.* Richmond: John Knox Press, 1959.

Hanssens, Jean Michel. *La Liturgie d'Hippolyte: Ses documents, son titulaire, ses origines et son caractère.* Rome: Pontifical Institute for Oriental Studies, 1959.

Harris, Carl Vernon. *Origen of Alexandria's Interpretation of the Teacher's Function in the Early Christian Hierarchy and Community.* New York: The American Press, 1966.

Hippolytus. *La tradition apostolique de saint Hippolyte, essai de reconstruction.* Edited by Dom Bernard Botte. Münster in Westphalia: Aschendorf, 1963.

Huber, Wolfgang. *Passa und Ostern: Untersuchungen zur Osterfeier der alten Kirche.* Berlin: Verlag Alfred Töpelmann, 1969.

Jeremias, Joachim. "πάσχα." *Theological Dictionary of the New Testament,* 5:896-904. 10 vols. Grand Rapids: Wm. B. Eerdmans Publishing Co., 1964-76.

Jungmann, Josef Andreas. *Missarum sollemnia.* 2 vols. 5th ed. Wien, Freiburg, and Basel: Herder, 1962.

Justin Martyr. *Apology.* English translation. In *The Ante-Nicene Fathers,* vol. 1. Grand Rapids: Wm. B. Eerdmans Publishing Co., 1969.

Justin Martyr. *Apology.* Original Greek text edited by Anton Hängi and Irmgard Pahl. *Prex eucharistica, textus e variis liturgiis, antiquioribus selecti.* Fribourg: Éditions universitaires, 1968.

Kraus, Hans-Joachim. "Zur Geschichte des Passah-Massot-Festes im Alten Testament." *Evangelische Theologie* 18 (1958): 47-67.

Lietzmann, Hans. *A History of the Early Church.* 4 vols. Cleveland and New York: Meridian Books, 1963.

Lohse, Bernhard. *Das Passafest der Quartadecimaner.* Gütersloh: C. Bertelsmann, 1953.

Martimort, A. G. *L'Église en Prière. Introduction à la Liturgie.* Paris, Tournai, Rome, and New York: Desclée, 1961.

McGuire, M. R. P. "St. Hippolytus of Rome." *New Catholic Encyclopedia,* 6:1139-41. 17 vols. Washington, D.C.: The Catholic University of America, 1967.

Melito of Sardis. *The Homily on the Passion.* Edited by Campbell Bonner. Philadelphia: University of Pennsylvania Press, 1940.

————. *Méliton de Sardes, Sur la pâques et Fragments.* Introduction, critical text, translation, and notes by Othmar Perler. Source chrétiennes. Paris: Éditions du Cerf, 1966.

Mondésert, C. *Clément d'Alexandrie.* Paris: Aubier, Éditions Montaigne, 1944.

Nautin, Pierre. *Hippolyte et Josipe: Contribution à l'histoire de la litterature chrétienne au IIIe siècle.* Paris: Éditions du Cerf, 1947.

————. *Lettres et écrivains au IIe et IIIe siècles.* Paris: Éditions du Cerf, 1961.

————. *Origène, sa vie et son oeuvre.* Paris: Beauchesne, 1977.

————. *Trois homélies dans la tradition d'Origène.* Paris: Éditions du Cerf, 1953.

Niederwimmer, Kurt. *Die Didache.* Kommentar zu den Apostolischen Vätern. Göttingen: Vandenhoeck & Ruprecht, 1989.

Origen. *First Principles: Book IV.* Translation by Rowan Greer. The Classics of Western Spirituality. New York, Ramsey, Toronto: Paulist Press, 1979.

———. *Homélies sur Jérémie.* Edited by P. Husson and P. Nautin. 2 vols. Paris: Éditions du Cerf, 1976 and 1977.

———. *Homélies sur la Genèse.* Edited by H. de Lubac and L. Doutreleau. Sources chrétiennes, vol. 7. Paris: Éditions du Cerf, 1972.

———. *Homélies sur S. Luc, text Latin et fragments Grec.* Edited and translated by Henri Crouzel, François Fournier, and Pierre Périchon. 2 vols. Sources chrétiennes, vols. 45 and 52. Paris: Éditions du Cerf, 1962.

———. *Homilies on Genesis and Exodus.* Translated by Ronald E. Heine. Washington, D.C.: Catholic University of America Press, 1982.

———. *On First Principles, Being Koetschau's Text of the De Principiis.* Translated into English together with an introduction and notes by G. W. Butterworth. London: S.P.C.K., 1936. American edition, Gloucester, Mass.: Peter Smith, 1973.

———. *On First Principles.* Translated by F. Crombie. In *The Ante-Nicene Fathers*, 4:237-382. Grand Rapids: Wm. B. Eerdmans Publishing Co., 1969.

———. *Origenes, Homilien zum Lukasevangelium.* German translation by Herman Josef Sieben. 2 vols. Freiburg: Herder, 1991-92.

Osborn, Eric Francis. *The Philosophy of Clement of Alexandria.* Cambridge: University Press, 1957.

Patrick, John. *Clement of Alexandria.* Edinburgh: Wm. Blackwood, 1914.

Pelikan, Jaroslav. *The Christian Tradition: A History of the Development of Doctrine.* 5 vols. Chicago: University of Chicago Press, 1971-89.

Perler, Othmar. "Logos und Eucharistie nach Justinus I Apol. c. 66." *Divus Thomas* 18 (Freiburg, 1940): 296-316.

Prat, F. "Projet littéraires de Clément d'Alexandrie." *Recherches de Science Religieuse* 15 (1925): 234-57.

Quasten, Johannes, et al. *Patrology.* 4 vols. Utrecht and Antwerp: Spectrum Publishers; Westminster, Md.: The Newman Press and Christian Classics, 1966-94.

Richardson, C. C. "The Date and Setting of the Apostolic Tradition of Hippolytus." *Anglican Theological Review* 30 (1948): 38-44.

Rordorf, Willy. "Un chapître d'éthique judéo-chrétienne: les Deux Voies." *Recherches de Science Religieuse* 60 (1972): 109-28.

———. *Geschichte der Ruhe- und Gottesdiensttages im ältesten Christentum.* Zurich: Zwingli Verlag, 1962. English translation: *Sunday: The History of the Day of Rest and Worship in the Earliest Centuries of the Christian Church.* Translated by A. A. K. Graham. Philadelphia: Westminster Press, 1968.

———. *Liturgie, foi et vie des premiers chrétiens.* Études patristiques. Paris: Beauchesne, 1986.

———. "Origine et signification de la célébration du dimanche dans le Christianisme primitif. Etat actuel de la recherche." *La Maison-Dieu* 148 (Paris, 1981): 103-22.

371

————. "Le problème de la transmission textuelle de *Didachè* 1,3b–2,1." *Über-lieferungsgeschichtliche Untersuchungen.* Texte und Untersuchungen 125:499-513. Berlin: Akademie Verlag, 1981.

————. "Zur Ursprung des Osterfestes am Sonntag." *Theologische Zeitschrift* 18 (1962): 167-89.

Rordorf, Willy, and A. Tuilier. *La Doctrine des douze apôtres (Didachè), Introduction, Texte, Traduction, Notes.* Paris: Éditions du Cerf, 1978.

Rylaarsdam, J. C. "Passover." *Interpreter's Dictionary of the Bible,* 3:663-68. 4 vols. plus supp. vol. Nashville: Abingdon, 1982.

Schütz, Werner. *Der christliche Gottesdienst bei Origenes.* Stuttgart: Calwer Verlag, 1984.

Sider, Robert D. *Ancient Rhetoric and the Art of Tertullian.* London: Oxford University Press, 1971.

Spanneut, M. *Le Stoïcisme des Pères de l'Église.* Paris: Éditions du Seuil, 1957.

Tertullian. *Tertullien, Apologétique, texte établi et traduit.* Latin text edited by Jean-Pierre Waltzing. 10th ed. Paris: "Les Belles Lettres," 1961.

————. *Q. Septimi Florentis Tertulliani, De corona.* Edited by Jacques Fontaine. Paris: Presses universitaires de France, 1966.

Thompson, Bard. *Liturgies of the Western Church.* Cleveland and New York: The World Publishing Company, 1961.

Tollington, R. B. *Clement of Alexandria, A Study in Christian Liberalism.* London: n.p., 1914.

Torjesen, Karen Jo. *Hermeneutical Procedure and Theological Method in Origen's Exegesis.* Berlin and New York: Walter de Gruyter, 1986.

Vagaggini, Cipriano. *Maria nelle opere di Origene.* Rome: Pontifical Institute for Oriental Studies, 1942.

Völker, W. *Der wahre Gnostiker nach Clemens Alexandrinus.* Texte und Untersuchungen 57. Berlin: Akademie Verlag, 1952.

Wright, David, ed. *Chosen by God: Mary in Evangelical Perspective.* London: Marshall Pickering, 1989.

Zuntz, G. "On the Opening Sentence of Melito's Paschal Homily." *Harvard Theological Review* 36 (1943): 299-315.

Index

Printed in the United States
33349LVS00006B/64-135